Olivia de Havilland and the Golden Age of Hollywood

Olivia de Havilland

and the
Golden Age of Hollywood

Ellis Amburn

Guilford, Connecticut

An imprint of The Rowman & Littlefield Publishing Group, Inc.
4501 Forbes Blvd., Ste. 200
Lanham, MD 20706
www.rowman.com

Distributed by NATIONAL BOOK NETWORK

Copyright © 2018 Ellis Amburn

British Library Cataloguing in Publication Information available

Library of Congress Cataloging-in-Publication Data available

ISBN 978-1-4930-3409-3 (hardcover)
ISBN 978-1-4930-3410-9 (e-book)

♾™ The paper used in this publication meets the minimum requirements of American National Standard for Information Sciences—Permanence of Paper for Printed Library Materials, ANSI/ NISO Z39.48-1992.

Printed in the United States of America

To

Dame Olivia de Havilland

Ad majorem Dei gloriam—*to the greater glory of God.*

"*Be bold, and mighty forces will come to your aid.*"

—Goethe

Contents

Prologue

I was a New York book editor in 1973 when I had lunch with Olivia de Havilland, hoping to persuade her to write her autobiography. I'd loved her as Melanie Wilkes in *Gone With the Wind*, the one movie seen by almost everyone on the planet, and as Catherine Sloper in *The Heiress*, the film that brought her the second of her two best-actress Academy Awards.

To me she was the consummate star of Hollywood's Golden Age, the era of big-studio dominance that flourished from the 1920s to roughly 1960. We met in Paris, where she'd lived since the mid-1950s, when she left Hollywood in the middle of a staggeringly successful career. She was not at all the diva I'd expected, and seemed reluctant to discuss her enormous achievements as an actress, but appeared to relax and enjoy herself when the focus shifted from her work to her personal life. When I asked, "Who was the love of your life?" she readily answered, "Errol Flynn!" She also spoke of her young son Benjamin Goodrich, proudly stating he was exceptionally gifted at math. I didn't learn until later that she was tirelessly devoting her life to helping him survive a deadly disease. He was planning to go for an advanced degree in America. "I suspect he has made up his mind what sort of career he wants, but he doesn't find it necessary to tell his mother," Olivia observed in 1973 to AP correspondent Vivian Brown. "However, French children do not usually treat their parents casually."[1]

Helping others seemed to be her main interest. She spoke of saving an ailing relative from the clutches of an officious and overbearing nurse. Altogether she appeared to be a woman wholly alive in the present moment with no interest in the past. She'd once remarked, "I don't want yesterday. I want today. And, even more, I want tomorrow. Tomorrow means promise, and that's what I live for."[2]

That is, of course, the ideal way to live, but it is the polar opposite of the stereotypical view of the aging movie queen as personified by Gloria Swanson as the delusional Norma Desmond in *Sunset Boulevard* and Bette Davis as the temperamental Margo Channing in *All About Eve*. Olivia does not fit into this or any other category. Her complex and many-splendored life includes a surprising triumph when she dared to sue Warner Brothers, resulting in the "De Havilland Decision," which protects performers to this day.

I would never have attempted this portrait of her life and art without having known David O. Selznick, producer of *GWTW*; director George Cukor, who guided her through the early stages of *GWTW*; Jimmy Stewart, who fell in love with her; Mickey Rooney, one of her costars in *A Midsummer Night's Dream*; Leonida Karpik, publicist for Olivia's sister Joan Fontaine; editor Lois Dwight Cole, who discovered *GWTW*; Kay Brown, who bought the film rights for Selznick; Annie Laurie Williams, author Margaret Mitchell's film agent; and Sheilah Graham, domestic partner of F. Scott Fitzgerald at the time he worked on the *GWTW* script.

In writing this, the first full-length biography of Olivia de Havilland, I discovered the many dimensions of this remarkable human being. On one level she is the insecure survivor of a broken home who found meaning and purpose in life during her struggle to become a serious dramatic actress. At the same time, she was striving to attain the normal human fulfillments, principally marriage and motherhood. Some of the most famous and gifted men of her time were drawn to her: Future U.S. Presidents John F. Kennedy and Ronald Reagan, Jimmy Stewart, Howard Hughes, Burgess Meredith, John Huston, British Prime Minister Edward Heath—and of course Errol Flynn.

Another aspect of Olivia's nature is her compassion, selflessness, and valor as the mother of a brilliant son who struggled with cancer. She gave up everything to stay by the side of this handsome, headstrong, and lovable young man, driving him to complete his education and realize his wildest professional dreams before his death at forty-two. Her lovely daughter, Gisele, truly a credit to her mother's parenting skills, excels at both journalism and the law.

Bold is the word that best describes Dame Olivia—boldness made her a star while still in her teens, empowered her to take a major movie studio to court and win, and enabled her to keep searching for love despite heartbreak, and to eventually attain a spiritual life of service to others. In the latter capacity, she at last became the person she was originally intended to be.

PART ONE

DAWN

Land of the Rising Sun

Olivia Mary de Havilland and Joan de Beauvoir de Havilland (later Joan Fontaine), both destined for Hollywood stardom, were born in Tokyo, Japan—Olivia on July 1, 1916, and Joan the following year.

Their parents were British. Walter de Havilland, a patent attorney, was a cousin of aviation pioneer Sir Geoffrey de Havilland,[1] and Lilian Augusta Ruse was an actress, possibly the reason she named her firstborn after the wealthy and comely heroine of *Twelfth Night*. Shakespeare's Olivia is pursued by many men, one of whom says, "If music be the food of love, play on. Give me excess of it, that surfeiting, the appetite may sicken, and so die."

Trained in 1912 at Sir Herbert Beerbohm Tree's Academy, which would shortly be licensed as the Royal Academy of Dramatic Art (RADA), Lilian starred in a 1918 Tokyo production of *Kismet*, giving a command performance for the Duke of Cornwall, brother of the King of England.[2] An officer at the British Embassy wrote her about the Duke of Cornwall's admiration for her performance.[3] Olivia didn't learn about the letter until many years later, because Lilian concealed her work on the professional stage; such behavior was deemed shady for women at the time. Her occasional appearances in amateur productions, however, were considered socially acceptable. Decades later, Lilian would appear in such films as *The Lost Weekend* and *Ivy*, but for the most part she gave up acting once she became a wife and mother, except for teaching her daughters such basics of the art as voice modulation and elocution.[4] Around 7 p.m. she'd sit her daughters at the dining room table and have them recite Shakespeare, and according to Joan, "We got our knuckles rapped if we didn't do it well."[5] Acting was in Olivia's blood, and at five she discovered a secret stash of rouge, eye shadow, and lipstick, and it was like coming upon hidden treasure. She was unable to resist applying her mother's stage makeup. Unfortunately, she failed to remove some of the rouge and Lilian was not pleased when she saw it.

"Never do this again!" she yelled, and admonished Olivia not to tell Joan. Lilian gave Olivia a serious spanking, according to *Vanity Fair* writer William Stadiem, who interviewed Olivia for an article published in the magazine in May 2016.[6]

Walter de Havilland had grown up on the island of Guernsey between Britain and France, becoming a first-rate tennis player, crack shot, and member of the Cambridge rowing team. "On Guernsey," Joan would later write, "his ancestors, the de Havillands, the de Beauvoirs, the Saumarezes, and the de Carteres, had intermarried for centuries."[7] During Joan's first trip to England in 1949, she met her cousins Geoffrey and Hereward de Havilland, scions of the de Havilland Aircraft Co., which was celebrated in aviation history for manufacturing the Moth, a revolutionary 1920 biplane, the wooden fighter Hornet, and finally the Comet, the first commercial jet airliner. In 1949, the de Havilland family flew Joan in one of its DH Doves for her first visit to the ancestral home, Havilland Hall, on Guernsey.[8] One of Britain's most successful postwar designs, the de Havilland Dove was a short-haul twin-engine feeder airliner accommodating eight to eleven passengers. Young Geoffrey de Havilland, according to Joan, was "goggle-eyed" over meeting her, as he'd also been upon meeting Olivia earlier.[9]

When Olivia was two and a half years old, her parents parted, apparently over a misunderstanding about Walter's fidelity, though, as the prudish son of a vicar, Walter seemed an unlikely candidate for extramarital affairs; he'd been a virgin until he was thirty-six.[10] A British intelligence officer had prevailed on Walter to put his mistress up for a while during a crisis that placed her in danger, possibly triggering the break with Lilian.[11] In 1919, Lilian moved with her baby daughters to the United States, and Walter eventually married his housekeeper.[12]

Settling in Saratoga, California, a town of 800 in the foothills of the Santa Cruz Mountains, twenty miles from San Francisco, Lilian raised her daughters as Christians, though she was not a churchgoer herself. When Olivia was baptized, it was not Lilian's doing but Olivia's, who must have sensed that mighty forces were available to her for the asking. "Miss de Havilland is a woman of genuine faith," the Right Reverend Pierre Whalon, Bishop in Charge of the Congregation of Episcopal Churches in Europe, said years later. "Her British mother raised her as an Episcopalian, though she did have a stint as a girl in a Roman Catholic convent school, which gave her a lasting admiration for women religious."[13]

Lilian found work in a milliner's store in Saratoga, and the family lived at Lundblad's Lodge on Oak Street."[14] In the attic Olivia and Joan found a steamer trunk full of flowery hats and whalebone ball gowns with stoles and ruffles, dressed themselves in finery, pretended they were adults, and paraded up and down the hallway, flourishing their fans and whirling their petticoats.[15] Later they moved into two houses joined by a latticed turnstile, and in 1924 Lilian built a two-story Tudorish house at 21 La Paloma Avenue. "No longer nomads, we would have a permanent home," Joan later wrote. "'Befitting our station,' Mother said."[16]

In April 1925, at a ceremony in Santa Barbara, Lilian married her second husband, George Milan Fontaine,[17] part-owner and general manager of a department store in San Jose."[18] Olivia and Joan started out as devoted siblings. "I loved her so much as a child," Olivia said, according to Stadiem.[19] At bedtime Joan would "put her little head on my shoulder" and Olivia would spin fairy tales and imitate rabbits, turkeys, donkeys, and dogs. "[Joan] was so darling, with those adorable freckles on her nose and a ducktail of blond hair, cute as a button."[20] According to journalist Erskine Johnson, "They called themselves 'The Prune Belt Sisters' since many of the nation's dried prunes came from their area of Northern California.[21]

Joan blamed their mother for the rivalry that, for her, spoiled her relationship with Olivia. Following her mother's death, Joan wrote an extraordinary letter to her mother that appears at the conclusion of her scathing memoir, *No Bed of Roses*. Joan stated, "I never knew why you didn't try to make us kinder, more understanding, more forgiving of one another—or did you prefer us at each other's throat?"[22] For many years, Olivia declined to comment on Joan,[23] but after Joan's death she referred to her as "Dragon Lady," a term that denotes such powerful Asian women as Madame Chiang Kai-shek, and told the Associated Press, "I cannot think of a single instance wherein I initiated hostile behavior. But I can think of many occasions where my reaction to deliberately inconsiderate behavior was defensive. On my part, it was always loving, but sometimes estranged and, in the later years, severed."[24]

The girls had to share the same room whether they liked it or not, and neither seemed comfortable with the arrangement. Joan was sickly as a child, required much of Lilian's attention, and possibly resented her sister's robust health.[25] The two girls were polar opposites—Olivia "the quiet, introspective type and Joan vivacious and extroverted," according to one reporter;[26] Olivia "serious and intense," Joan "always tak[ing] a wry view of things," according to columnist Bob Thomas.[27] "All [Lilian's] efforts were on Olivia's behalf," Joan wrote.[28] That was hardly the case when the sisters contracted chicken pox; a great fuss was made over Joan, but Olivia was told only to stay still and avoid scratching.[29]

Joan developed a nasty habit of slapping Olivia's face, and Olivia tolerated it for a while.[30] When she was six and Joan five, Joan grasped Olivia's foot and attempted to yank her into a swimming pool. Joan chipped her collarbone and ended up in a cast.[31] "I'm sure it wasn't entirely intentional,"

Joan allowed.[32] Lilian blamed the media for overstating the sisters' rivalry. "The girls' differences have never been as bad as they appear to be in print," she'd tell Associated Press correspondent Bob Thomas in 1953."[33]

With her growing interest in acting, Olivia was fortunate to live in Saratoga with its active little theatre community. At thirteen she performed in local productions, and she once traveled to San Jose with other girls to see Eva Le Gallienne in *Hedda Gabler*. After the performance Olivia and her friends went backstage and secured the star's autograph. Le Gallienne in turn asked for Olivia's autograph.[34] Olivia briefly attended Notre Dame Convent Catholic Girls' School in Belmont, California. She later told journalist J. Maurice Ruddy that she didn't like the discipline and once had to write 100 times that in the future she'd be modest and never again display her bloomers while playing basketball.[35] Later, at Los Gatos High School, she began to develop her aptitude for theatre and drama. A movie fan, at twelve she sent a letter to actor Ronald Colman asking for a picture, and he sent her one, which she still had almost ten years later.[36] Upon graduation at thirteen, she acted in *Alice in Wonderland* and later toured in towns all the way to San Francisco, where, when she was sixteen, critic George C. Warren of the *San Francisco Chronicle* gave her a rave review.[37]

Her mother had once told her she'd be no good under pressure, but she proved her mother wrong. Though reputedly "painfully shy,"[38] she went before large audiences with poise, grace, and no visible signs of stage fright. Joan, in Olivia's estimation, had uncanny intuitive gifts as well as plenty of brains, but in emergencies always acted entirely on intuition and was always right. Olivia tended to analyze a crisis and then follow her plan, but emergencies, she knew, seldom allow for plans. She was once intuitive enough, however, to avoid a nasty spill from a runaway horse headed straight for a cliff by giving him his head and letting him tire out in the nick of time. At that speed, and on that rocky hill, a leap off the animal would likely have killed her or left her severely impaired.

Her circle of friends included five other stagestruck classmates, who were so close they decided to have a reunion in ten years' time, and even specified the park where they'd meet, as well as the date and the hour. In school-girl fashion, they swore a solemn oath to come back from wherever they were, no matter how far. Olivia knew in her heart she'd keep this promise, whatever the future held.[39]

Joan took drama lessons but soon dropped them, convinced that she was smarter than her teachers. "'Liv' and I used to do readings for guests, and 18th-century playlets in our backyard theater," she said.[40]

Romantic love engulfed Olivia at sixteen when she reportedly fell for a boy she'd known since the first grade, identified only as Peter. A class ahead of her at Los Gatos High, he was a future Yalie, sensitive, good-looking, and intelligent. His kisses allegedly electrified her, and she'd later reportedly tell interviewers she'd loved kissing ever since Peter's busses in her sixteenth year.[41] The story goes that they got engaged, but her love of theatre came between them. Peter wanted her all to himself and became possessive and demanding when she went to rehearsals, which Olivia found unreasonable.[42] Acting seems to have been both an artistic and psychological necessity. "I have a fear of being unloved," she said, "or of believing I'm loved and finding out I'm not."[43] Elsewhere she was quoted as saying, "I really like people, but panic always stays between me and them."[44] Later she added that "by representing someone else I was relieved of my own personality."[45] To another interviewer she confided, "I'm like a snake—I like to put on a new skin with every role."[46]

In 1938 she'd reflect, "I don't believe in early marriage. It nearly always flops! . . . The first boy I was mad about I met at school when I was about 16—maybe younger. We were terribly attracted, but we seemed to arouse each other's worst sides. We brought out frightful tempers in one another, but we weren't happy unless we could be together. Then he went to college and we were separated for nine months. I thought I'd die without him, but somehow I didn't. When he came home we had both had time to grow up. I saw at once that he wasn't at all the boy I dreamed about, and almost immediately I got over being in love—or thinking I was in love."[47]

After high school she wanted to continue her education and won a scholarship to Mills College for Women in Oakland, California, where she hoped that in four years of being sequestered from life she'd realize her true calling.[48] Meanwhile she followed her current passion: the theatre. When her stepfather George Fontaine learned she'd taken a role in a play without his permission, he confronted her.[49] In one of Joan's only kind comments about Olivia, she wrote, "Unable to let the school or her classmates down, she left forever."[50] Olivia appealed to her real father, Walter, who granted her a $50-per-month allowance.[51] Leaving home was a courageous act indeed for a high schooler, and it would be richly rewarded. Goethe once wrote, "Be bold, and mighty forces will come to your aid." They came rushing at Olivia in the guise of a gifted and benevolent woman who would hand her the key to stardom.

2

Max Reinhardt, Dick Powell, Mickey Rooney, and James Cagney

D orothea Johnston, a clever producer and pillar of the little theatre in Saratoga, asked Olivia, who was seventeen, to appear in *A Midsummer Night's Dream*, playing the role of Puck. In Olivia's description, Johnston somewhat resembled the native American Indian chief depicted on the five-cent coin. Her performances as an Indian on the London stage had made her the toast of the town, and she was presented to the Queen of England as a celebrated artist.[1]

Johnston persuaded her friend Katherine Sibley, who worked for the renowned European director Max Reinhardt, to attend the Saratoga performance of *Dream* at the same time that Reinhardt was preparing a far more spectacular production of *Dream* for the Hollywood Bowl. Olivia had wondered if she might watch the great Reinhardt conduct rehearsals for the Bowl production, and Sibley not only arranged it, she persuaded Felix Weissberger, Reinhardt's associate, to rehearse Olivia as Puck. Johnston drove Olivia thirty-five miles up the valley to Weissberger's hotel in San Francisco. Olivia donned her athlete's bloomers and sneakers and sprang into Puckish action, jumping over furniture and delivering a high-spirited presentation.

Impressed, Weissberger told her, "If you come down to Hollywood in four weeks' time, you may understudy the role of Hermia." It was a watershed moment for Olivia, who'd recall seventy-three years later, "Well, can you imagine what that meant? Incredible news! I was now going to be an official member of the Reinhardt company."[2] Upon arriving in Hollywood, she discovered that Jean Rouverol, a Paramount starlet, was actually understudying Gloria Stuart as Hermia, and Olivia was only Rouverol's understudy.[3] Then, fortuitously, Rouverol dropped out to make a film with W.C. Fields, and Stuart's agent, Jesse Wadsworth, appeared at a morning rehearsal to announce that Stuart's current film was still in production. "We're very sorry," Wadsworth said, "but Miss Stuart will not be able to go on opening night."[4] Reinhardt turned and looked at Olivia.

"You will play the part," he said.[5]

Working with Reinhardt was a cinch; he acted out all the parts, making it easy for the actors, but Olivia would have preferred her own interpretation. An attack of stage fright hit her on opening night, September 17, 1934, and she had to be pushed onstage by an assistant director, who said, "You're on!"[6]

"I opened my mouth and these perfectly strange words came out . . . and nobody looked surprised . . . or horrified."[7] Then, as if in a trance, at her next cue, she opened her mouth and again words came out, and finally, at the end of the scene, "there was this great round of applause . . . I couldn't wait to get back onstage."[8] A born trouper, she finished the performance without a trace of stage fright and received an ovation from an audience of 30,000.[9] "I owe my whole career to that lady," Olivia said, referring to Stuart, who some six decades later would be nominated for a supporting-actress Oscar for her performance as Old Rose in James Cameron's *Titanic*.[10]

Olivia, now eighteen years old, had wowed an audience that included Joan Crawford, Gary Cooper, Clark Gable, Norma Shearer, and studio chiefs Louis B. Mayer of MGM and Jack L. Warner of Warner Brothers. "She had a fresh young beauty that would soon stir a lot of tired old muscles around film town," Warner said. "She had a voice that was music to the ears, like a cello, low and vibrant, and the Hollywood wolves would be milling around in the woods, hoping she could be had."[11]

Reinhardt considered her the most beautiful Hermia he'd directed in America or Europe. After the Bowl, the show went on tour, playing the San Francisco Opera House, the University of California at Berkeley, and as far as Milwaukee, and Reinhardt decided to film it at Warner Brothers, keeping two stars from the stage production—Olivia as Hermia and Mickey Rooney as Puck. She was summoned back to Hollywood from Milwaukee to be screen-tested. "I played Hermia, thanks to Reinhardt," she said.[12] Lilian told a reporter she handled Olivia's first contract and managed her career.[13] Actually, Olivia took her three-year Warner contract to agent Ivan Kahn at the suggestion of a fellow cast member, the exquisite Danish ballerina Nina Theilade, and had it cosigned by Lilian in December 1934.[14]

With decidedly mixed feelings[15] about going to work at eighteen, even as a movie star, instead of matriculating at Mills College as planned, Olivia later said she regretted her decision to go to Hollywood instead of attending college. Four years of higher education would have afforded an opportunity to discover her true calling. There might have been a profession more suited to her. She was, after all, a person of many aptitudes, including teaching.[16]

Dream went into production at Warner on December 17, 1934, and cameraman Hal Mohr realized at once that Olivia instinctively grasped the basics of movie acting—how to move for the camera and show her best angles and know precisely where the light was. "She seemed so demure and restrained," producer Henry Blanke said, "but all the time, behind that innocent gaze, I could see her watching, watching, she observed everything; when she wasn't required for a scene she would come and look at the other actresses. You felt that she could have taken over any part in the film that she chose."[17]

Hal B. Wallis, Warner production chief, seemed less enamored of Olivia, warning William Dieterle, Reinhardt's co-director, that he must closely monitor Olivia's strenuous breathing and huffing between lines of dialogue because it was "annoying," as well as her lowering her head toward her shoulder while continuing to talk, which made her voice less audible.[18] Two weeks into filming he cautioned that he'd been viewing the *Dream* dailies with growing concern that the scene in which Olivia and Ross Alexander race to the forefront of the screen while Olivia is speaking and breathing hard might require titles—Wallis complained that he couldn't make out "what the hell" she was saying, nor would the audience.[19]

Alexander, the film's well-built, boyish-eyed, six-foot-one romantic lead, was on his way to stardom when a panicky Warner front office decided it was too chancy to develop him as a potential matinee idol and conceal his homosexuality at the same time. After his demotion to insignificant movies, he committed suicide at twenty-nine.[20]

Remembering thirteen-year-old Mickey Rooney years later, Olivia would say, "You hand me your work copy of *A Midsummer Night's Dream*, climb onto the banquette beside me, place your head on my lap, and ask me to awake you nine lines before your cue."[21]

Olivia, who'd long nursed a schoolgirl crush on Dick Powell, was so upset when a columnist reported she and Powell were engaged that she cried and apologized to Powell, who laughed it off, patted her shoulder, and said, "Listen, Livey [sic], you're just a baby in this business. It doesn't matter at all—so forget it!"[22] She found that easier said than done and continued to worry. When the next Powell–de Havilland engagement rumor hit the press, this time she blew it off, realizing she "might as well forget about a private life" if she wanted to remain a movie actress.[23]

For all the loving effort expended on *Dream*, the public found it arty, and it failed at the box office. Studios shunned Max Reinhardt after word got around that he'd been unable to control the large, complex film unit and restricted himself to coaching the actors, leaving the camera, lighting, set designs, and costumes up to Dieterle.[24] After MGM's *Romeo and Juliet* bombed the following year, Hollywood abandoned Shakespeare for over a decade.

A year after her debut at the Bowl, she made a sentimental journey back to the scene of her initial triumph and found the same gateman, stage manager, and dancers. The young thespians formed an adoring circle around her and begged her to perform with them that night in the role of an angel in *Everyman*. All they could pay her was seventy-five cents. She must have rehearsed with them a bit, because she went onstage that night, no doubt surprising an audience that had not expected to see a bona fide movie star.[25]

"My career began in the middle of the Golden Age of Hollywood," Olivia recalled. "It was an illustrious beginning."[26]

Joan Fontaine attended the opening night of *Dream* in the San Francisco Opera House, but she'd changed so much that Olivia "didn't even recognize her," Olivia recalled. "She had bleached her hair. She was smoking. She was no longer my younger sister."[27] When Olivia urged her to finish high school, Joan refused.

"I don't want to," she said. "I want to do what you're doing!"[28]

"Change your name and you can come to Hollywood and live with me and Mummy," Olivia urged, but Joan refused. "She wanted to do it exactly as I was doing it, all by herself."[29]

Having been the first to establish herself with the de Havilland name, Olivia "drew the line at sharing her name in Hollywood," William Stadiem wrote. Olivia said, "I gave her examples of younger sisters who changed their names and had the best careers. Loretta Young and Sally Blane, for instance."[30]

Growing up, Joan had been kicked around from Saratoga to Tokyo and back. Her stepfather George abandoned her while she was still an adolescent living in California. In 1933 she went to Japan to her biological father, but he found her so attractive in her bathing suit during a walk on the beach that he tried to move his bed into her room.[31] She returned to the United States in 1934 on the USS *President Hoover*.[32] By then she'd matured into an alluring teenage siren, and during the voyage she went from one handsome beau to another, including Fred Maytag, heir to the washing-machine fortune.

She arrived in San Francisco with twenty-two dollars, and a kindly uncle sheltered her while she waited for her mother to call. When Lilian finally appeared, their reunion was anything but warm.[33] "This pale, blond, fully grown stranger had no place in Mother's life as she now lived it," Joan wrote.[34] Devoted exclusively to making a home for George Fontaine, Lilian seemed reluctant to "assume a mother role again,"[35] and let Joan remain with her uncle. Eventually Joan would be dependent on Olivia, as would their mother.

Olivia was by now the darling of the press, striking reporters as a likable, level-headed maiden, which was refreshing in a town of ostentation and loose morals. A well-known publicist named Spide Rathbun helped her learn the publicity ropes, taking her to the Kellogg Ranch in Pomona for some promotional stills.[36] "She's a real home girl, the kind any father would be proud to have as a daughter," reporter Linda Lane wrote after meeting her in 1936. "She has captivated Hollywood."[37]

"Outside of my work at the studio," Olivia told Lane, "my life isn't much different than it would be if I was still living in Saratoga."[38]

Deciding to make good on the oath she'd sworn with five high school chums to meet ten years after graduation, she went home to Saratoga, arrived at the appointed reunion place on time, but found nothing but "the ghosts of her girlhood to keep her company . . . Friends of Miss de Havilland say this story is most typical of her."[39] Success had not spoiled the goodness, loyalty, and romanticism at the core of her nature. She was the only one of the six girls who'd achieved stardom, yet she'd remembered and honored her promise.

Stardom at Warner Brothers would prove disappointing. Bette Davis was set on being queen of the lot, and the studio typecast Olivia as a featherweight ingénue suitable for romantic comedies, rushing her into several films in 1935. Audiences first saw her in *Alibi Ike*, released while *Dream* was still in post-production. Joe E. Brown, who'd played Flute in *Dream*, was a former professional baseball player with a muscular build and a trademark smile that never failed to charm. Since he easily carried his successful comic films at Warner by himself, the studio, in casting his leading ladies, used his movies as a rotating showcase for its stable of aspiring starlets. *New York Times* reviewer Frank S. Nugent found Olivia appealing in *Alibi Ike* and welcomed her warmly as "a charming newcomer."[40] The studio continued to cast her as the love interest in trite fare, and whatever excitement she may have felt over her precocious breakthrough quickly subsided.[41] Henry Blanke tried to persuade Jack Warner to assign her better material, but Warner said her weekly salary required her to appear regularly on screen if she expected to remain a star.

"Film work is much too hard for an 18-year-old," Olivia observed.[42] "You would work until 6 to 6:30 at night, but six days a week."[43] On Saturdays the cameras were still whirring at midnight to feed the world's voracious appetite for movies in the industry's Golden Age. Olivia resorted to putting dark circles under her eyes and suggesting to a cameraman "that he photograph me very badly." When Jack Warner viewed the rushes, he asked what was going on with Olivia. The cameraman replied that she was quite tired after a week of exhausting work. The grind took its toll on her "nerves and physical strength," she confided to a reporter. "It does great injury to one emotionally."[44] In 1937, Warner released three de Havilland films. Ross Claiborne, who published books by Joan Blondell and Mary Astor, two other survivors of the dark side of Hollywood's prime years, said, "Joan told me Warner had her working on four films at the same time."

In *The Irish in Us*, released in August 1935, just one month after *Alibi Ike*, Olivia played Lucille Jackson, a police captain's daughter, wooed by the O'Hara brothers: Danny, a rascal who promotes prize fights, played by James Cagney, and serious, sober Pat, a policeman, played by Pat O'Brien. When Danny's fighter Car-Barn Hammerschlog (Allen Jenkins) gets too drunk to make it to the ring, Danny steps up and wins the fight—and Lucille. "[Olivia de Havilland] gives every indication of a gal who can be steered into lights," *Variety's* reviewer wrote. "Class looking, she also has a warm personality and seems to know what it's all about, even in the midst of boxing gloves and ad-lib slapstick."[45]

The nation's press began to follow Olivia closely and fondly, partially as a result of her savvy courtship of reporters, who flocked to her for feature articles. The *Pittsburgh Press's* Dan Thomas found "Livvy"—as Joan addressed her sister—relaxing with her family at home. Having just arrived from Warner Bros. for a short break, she was still made up for the camera but had slipped into a blue lounging suit, though she had to return to the Burbank lot shortly.[46] Lilian joined them, bringing tea, and Joan followed with finger sandwiches. Thomas thought it noteworthy that at eighteen Olivia planned to remain single for approximately a decade.[47] "Romance doesn't seem to mix with a career and pictures," she said. The hours of filming were so unpredictable that she ended up having to reschedule dates. "Boys don't like that. So I'm not even going to think about romance until I'm finished in pictures."[48]

Lilian blossomed in Hollywood, vicariously basking in the refracted glow of her daughter's success and resurrecting her old acting ambitions. After taking her one-woman monologue readings on the road, she realized she'd become "pretty hammy," and studied acting with Maria Ouspenskaya, a Stanislavsky-trained performer of the Moscow Art Theatre who emerged as one of the best character actresses of Hollywood's Golden

Age in *Dodsworth, Love Affair, The Rains Came, Waterloo Bridge*, and *Kings Row*. Lilian appeared in plays at the Pasadena Playhouse, which brought her "back down to earth."[49]

After looking for a permanent home in Hollywood, Olivia settled on the Chateau des Fleurs on Franklin Avenue, a short hop—by Los Angeles standards—from the studio. With its kitschy sunken court and wishing well, the faux chateau was pretentious, drafty, and damp, but at least it boasted spacious, airy rooms, high ceilings, and tall French windows with handles. Flush with her Warner salary, she offered to put Joan through Katharine Bronson, a Bay Area prep school for girls in search of affluent husbands, but Joan turned her down again, repeating what she'd said before: "I want to do what you're doing."[50] Olivia welcomed her, according to Joan, at her Chateau des Fleurs apartment."[51]

She also welcomed their mother, Rosalind Shaffer wrote in the *Chicago Tribune* on March 14, 1937. She enjoyed providing a home for her family, and though she'd been quite content to be alone and curl up with a book and the radio,[52] she valued the camaraderie of Lilian and Joan. "'What a household we have!' bubbled Olivia, all smiles as we sat down to lunch together," the *Chicago Tribune* reporter wrote. "'Three females of us, all moved into a new house, all dressing before one mirror . . . Mother is wonderful.'"[53]

Joan was later quoted by the *Los Angeles Times* saying she paid her share of the rent, but in *No Bed of Roses* she wrote, "Olivia was now the head of the household, to be nurtured, curried, obeyed. A surrogate G.M. [George Fontaine], Olivia now ruled with total autonomy. Joan made a passable cook, housekeeper, chauffeur for the rented Ford, a go-for. After all, Olivia was paying the rent."[54] Joan added that she felt like "the no-talent, no-future little sister." Her life at home, she concluded, "was untenable."[55]

The sisters' differing accounts at least agree on one salient and resounding point—that upon striking it rich as a teenager, the first thing

Olivia did was not to run out and buy a Cadillac and a house in Beverly Hills, but to take care of her family. Unable to see Olivia as the good sister she was, Joan wrote, "From birth, we were not encouraged by our parents or nurses to be anything but rivals."[56]

3

Errol Flynn

Olivia and Errol Flynn first met when producer Hal B. Wallis ordered a joint screen test for *Captain Blood* in 1935. She was nineteen and Flynn was twenty-six, but she'd already made her breakthrough in movies while Flynn was getting nowhere playing bit parts.

He'd begun his career at the Royal Theatre in Northampton, England, appearing in twenty-two productions between December 1933 and June 1934, playing, among other small roles, the first senator in *Othello* and the second bystander in Shaw's *Pygmalion*. Jack L. Warner claimed he saw Flynn in one of his London studios and hired him for $150 a week. "He showered an audience with sparks when he laughed, when he fought, or when he loved," Warner said.[1] Flynn had Jack Warner in his pocket from day one. No sooner had Flynn arrived in Los Angeles and checked into the Garden of Allah, home to F. Scott Fitzgerald, Dorothy Parker, and Robert Benchley, than Warner ordered Wallis to give him a small part in *The Case of the Curious Bride* in 1935. Flynn played a corpse, a role the randy actor called "perfect typecasting. No one's been under more sheets than I."[2]

It took Jack Warner a while to realize he had a first-rate action hero on his hands, a perfect candidate for the popular costume melodramas of the day. When the swashbuckling epic *Captain Blood* came along, Flynn seemed the natural choice for the lead. For the role opposite him, Arabella Bishop, Warner wanted Marion Davies, but at thirty-eight she was a bit long in the tooth to be playing ingénues, and she wisely declined.[3] Contract actresses at Warner were clamoring for the role. Anita Louise and Jean Muir were considered, and director Michael Curtiz tested Bette Davis.[4] Actors up for the title role, apart from Flynn, included Fredric March, Leslie Howard, Clark Gable, Ronald Coleman, George Brent, Brian Aherne, Ian Hunter, and Robert Donat. The latter won the role but backed out while the picture was still in pre-production, possibly due to health or contractual issues.[5]

Warner and Wallis studied individual dailies of Olivia and Flynn for six months without making a decision on either until, according to Flynn, "it was decided, by Mervyn LeRoy and Harry Joe Brown, I think, to test an unknown . . . I tested with a young woman of extraordinary charm, Olivia de Havilland. She was only 19 then, with warm brown eyes, a soft manner."[6] "I was called for a test," Olivia remembered, "to see how the two of us in costume would look together . . . They said, 'Would you please stand next to Mr. Flynn?' . . . Oh my! Oh my! Struck dumb. I knew it was what the French call a *coup de foudre* [love at first sight] . . . He is the handsomest, most charming, most virile young man in the entire world!"[7] Jack Warner agreed when he saw the test. "He was all the heroes in one magnificent sexy package," the boss said.[8] Equally impressed, Hal Wallis said the actor "leapt from the screen . . . with the impact of [a] bullet."[9] Flynn won the role, and later recalled, "Jack Warner . . . had the . . . guts to take a complete unknown and put me in the lead of a big production."[10]

During lunch break one day, Flynn and Olivia walked to the commissary, and he stood ahead of her in the cafeteria line. By the time she was served, he'd already taken a table, and she chose a different one, reluctant to appear bold, but they returned to the sound stage together and chatted on a loading ramp to a huge open door.[11]

"What do you want out of life?" she asked. "I would like respect for difficult work well done . . . Well, what do you want out of life?"[12]

"I want success."[13]

She thought, "What he meant by that was fame and riches . . . I thought, 'But that's not enough.'"[14]

Sixty-one years later, in 1977, she told TCM's Robert Osborne, "We both got what we wanted. Though our motives couldn't have been more different, it was his honesty that charmed and disarmed me."[15] She was intrigued by "his offstage look of inner torment. I can still see him biting and pulling his fingernails right down to the cuticle. Errol was a very unhappy man."[16] Both beautiful, they seemed like a matched set, with Flynn at six foot two as agile as a panther and Olivia at 5'3", a delicate and beguiling contrast. Olivia as the uppity Arabella and Flynn as a dashing doctor-turned-pirate possessed exactly what their roles called for: cultivated upper-class elocution, chiseled looks, and an air of aristocracy—but their teeth were less than perfect. "It looks bad when she smiles," Wallis told producer Henry Blanke. "There is no reason she shouldn't do it at her own expense so have her do it."[17]

The film told the story of Peter Blood, who has been convicted of treason and sold into slavery for having treated a wounded rebel. Exiled in chains to Jamaica, he falls in love with Arabella, who buys him in the slave market. He manages to escape and slashes his way through the Caribbean as a pirate, eventually winning both Arabella and the governorship of Jamaica. Olivia and Flynn ignited romantic sparks the moment they exchanged saucy banter at the auction block.

"You could learn a lesson in gratitude," Arabella tells him.

"Your very humble slave, Mrs. Bishop."

His cockiness and her spunk assured their future as a popular movie team.

During countless hours together on the lot, she listened raptly as the silver-tongued rake regaled her with tales of a misspent youth raising hell Down Under. After they'd worked on the film a few weeks, the studio brass was not entirely pleased, and both of them came under fire from Wallis and director Michael Curtiz. The latter, a hot-headed

Hungarian—as well as a formidable filmmaker, with *Casablanca* and *Mildred Pierce* in his future—derided Flynn as a rank amateur and resented Jack Warner's infatuation with him. Warner didn't care whether Flynn could act; he sensed that Flynn's virile visage and strong body, along with the most skillful swordsmanship and gymnastic stunts seen since the heyday of Douglas Fairbanks Sr., would sell tickets in the millions, bringing profit and honor to his studio. "He made people feel young and alive," Warner said.

Wallis tried to protect Flynn from Curtiz, telling the director to practice patience, give Flynn gentler direction, instill some confidence in him, and stop scaring him with shouted orders and displays of angry exasperation, and he assured him that Flynn would be twice as effective.[18]

"I worked as hard as I knew how," Flynn recalled.[19]

"We would sit very quietly in our canvas chairs, saying very little to each other," Olivia said.[20] "He has so much humor and charm and vitality."[21] Touched by his drive to succeed, she felt a deep compassion when the director viewed their first *Captain Blood* dailies in a screening room and Flynn had to endure Curtiz's stinging rebukes. "I could feel the hurt for him on the other side of the room," she recalled.[22] Flynn in turn empathized with Olivia when her performance was criticized. Wallis told Curtiz that "the little girl," Olivia de Havilland, was less effective in *Captain Blood* than she'd been in such previous Warner outings as *Alibi Ike* and *The Irish in Us,* that her gifts of spontaneity, glowing demeanor, and sunny disposition were no longer in evidence.[23]

Her breasts disturbed film-industry censors. "Olivia's cleavage would cause U.K. newspapers to harp about Nell Gwyn again," Frederick Herron said. "If Warner Brothers are inclined to do things in that manner I think the studio ought to be watched."[24] Olivia rejoined, "You mustn't think . . . that I have one of those over-exuberant superstructures that really needs lashing to the decks to keep it from going overboard. No, no, not at all. It is, rather, the sort you might call appropriate, quite becoming, so it's been said. Neat but not gaudy."[25]

During location filming in Laguna Beach, a seaside town near Los Angeles, she was perched on a rock about ten feet from shore when a mountainous wave sent her like a rocket into the roiling surf. Flynn plunged in and rescued her.[26] "He really is all of those things that a hero is supposed to be," she realized. "He can ride and swim and play tennis and sail, and . . . fence and fight."[27]

The grueling shoot paid off, and upon the film's release, both critics and public swooned over it, paying $8.5 million at the box office (adjusted for inflation: $150,000,000). The production had cost Warner only $800,000, or $14,300,000 in today's economy.[28] Flynn became an overnight star—it was his picture, replete with his unique blend of elegance and derring-do. "With a spirited and criminally good-looking Australian named Errol Flynn playing the genteel buccaneer to the hilt, the photoplay recaptures the air of high romantic adventure which is so essential to the tale," wrote *New York Times* reviewer Andre Sennwald, who found Olivia "effective . . . a lady of rapturous loveliness and well worth fighting for."[29] One reporter objected to her name, grumbling, "Personally I think Olivia de Havilland would get farther with half as many syllables . . . I always get a callous on the typing finger when I have to spell it out."[30]

With instant stardom Flynn knew he was worth more than $500 per week when actors Guy Kibbee, Ross Alexander, and Robert Barrett received $9,000, $5,000, and $3,000 per week, respectively.[31] After the movie became a success, Flynn was raised to $800 per week with a bonus of $750, but that was still less than the salaries of the third lead in some of his films. He refused to show up for work, notifying the studio he'd rather not make films than do them for pocket lint. Jack Warner suffered a heart attack but from the hospital raised Flynn to $125,000 per year, today's equivalent of $2.2 million—still a bargain for the studio.[32]

These staggering amounts were possible because movies, apart from radio, were virtually the only form of affordable entertainment during the Great Depression of the 1930s, a time when hundreds of thousands were homeless, living in shantytowns, hitchhiking or riding the rails from town to town in search of work, sometimes only to find 1,000 people applying for the same job. According to the Bureau of Labor Statistics, the average income for those fortunate enough to find work dipped to as low as fifteen to twenty dollars per week. The economic turnaround would not begin until World War II.

Olivia and Flynn costarred in a total of eight movies. Screen teams were in vogue, having been a big draw ever since Francis X. Bushman and Beverly Bayne appeared together in 1915's *Pennington's Choice*, the first of their twenty-four films. Fred Astaire and Ginger Rogers made ten films together, William Powell and Myrna Loy nine, Spencer Tracy and Katharine Hepburn nine, Jeannette McDonald and Nelson Eddy eight, Joan Crawford and Franchot Tone seven, Barbara Stanwyck and Joel McCrea five, Mickey Rooney and Judy Garland five, and Ray Milland and Paulette Goddard four.[33]

"During the making of *Captain Blood*, I had grown very fond of Olivia de Havilland," Flynn recalled.[34] Theirs was a star-crossed love, because Flynn was married, and they were unwilling to admit, to themselves or to each other, their mutual passion.[35]

4

Anthony Adverse, The Charge of the Light Brigade, and *Call It a Day*

Olivia's 1936 film *Anthony Adverse* failed to capture the mystical component in Hervey Allen's historical novel. Without the spiritual redemption at the end of Anthony's picaresque, kaleidoscopic journey through an action-packed life in Europe, Cuba, and Africa, the film amounts to little more than a routine romantic costume drama. The *New York Times* critic Frank S. Nugent found it "bulky, rambling, and indecisive," but he liked Olivia, writing, "Olivia de Havilland, always an attractive addition to any cast, is a winsome Angela."

Slated to support Fredric March, who played Anthony, Flynn was reassigned to *The Charge of the Light Brigade* when the studio decided the entire cast should be British in this story of two Army brothers in love with the same girl during the Crimean War. For the feminine lead, screenwriter Rowland Leigh urged Wallis not to cast Anita Louise in the role of the British heroine because English audiences would never accept her American accent. Jack Warner wired Wallis to "definitely" give the role to Olivia because he could then exploit the popularity of Flynn and Olivia as the new screen team.[1] Flynn was delighted, later writing, "By the time we made *Brigade* I was sure I was in love with her. So that acting in that hard-to-make picture became bearable. It took a long time to produce this vehicle, and all through it I fear I bothered

Miss de Havilland in very teasing ways—I was really trying to display my affection."[2]

Though pleased to be working again with Flynn, Olivia had little respect for the picture. "Those Flynn films didn't have much prestige on the lot . . . We were second-class citizens out there."[3] She was asked to participate in the screen tests of a number of young actors auditioning for the role of Flynn's friend, Captain Randall, who appears with Flynn in *Brigade*'s best scene, a solemn and moving vignette in which Randall, facing the possibility of imminent death, hands Flynn's character, Geoffrey Vickers, a pocket watch and says, "You wouldn't mind giving this to my family, just in case."

One of the young men whom director Michael Curtiz tested with Olivia was the still-unknown David Niven, who'd already found his way into Hollywood's elite British colony—consisting, among others, of Donald Crisp, Christopher Isherwood, Aldous Huxley, Ronald Colman, Sir Cedric Hardwicke, Herbert Marshall, Maureen O'Sullivan, John Farrow, Sir C. Aubrey Smith, Merle Oberon, Walter Pidgeon, Claude Rains, Ray Milland, Cary Grant, Boris Karloff, Madeleine Carroll, Ida Lupino, and Basil Rathbone.[4]

"By the time the scene had been played a dozen times and six actors curtly dismissed by Curtiz," Niven recalled, "everything I had hoped to do had already been done. My mind was a blank when Curtiz, with heavy accent, called out, 'Next man.' I was led out of the shadows by an assistant and introduced to Miss de Havilland and Curtiz. She smiled a tired resigned smile and shook hands." The test went well and Curtiz announced, "This man gets the part."[5] Niven evidently fell in love with Olivia, if syndicated columnist Sheilah Graham was correct in reporting, "Olivia de Havilland has said 'No' to the proposal of David Niven, whom many unmarried stars would like for a husband."[6]

On March 30, 1936, Olivia and Flynn began dangerous location work at Lone Pine, 3,700 feet above sea level, and later moved on to Lake

Sherwood, where they toiled in neck-deep water while Curtiz drove them mercilessly. According to film historian David Thomson, "Curtiz was . . . infamous for . . . his arrogance."[7]

"[Errol] never guessed I had a crush on him," Olivia said, "and . . . [later] he wrote that he was in love with me when we made *Brigade*." The information stunned her, because she'd never been sure of his love, despite the countless hours they'd spent together on film sets at Warner.[8] In a clumsy bid for her affection, he began to annoy her with impish pranks, and on May 12, 1936, he placed a dead snake in her pantalets. "Out slithered a long, dead snake, four feet long," Olivia recalled.[9] She shrieked, and as she dashed to a nearby lake and jumped in, she heard Flynn's laughter. Discussing the prank later, Flynn explained he was unhappily married, and "Olivia was lovely—and distant . . . It slowly penetrated my obtuse mind that such juvenile pranks weren't the way to any girl's heart."[10]

"He was sure it was love," Olivia said, "and I didn't think it was anything of the kind . . . He thought, somehow, that this message would get across to me. And you know—it didn't."[11] Much as she adored him, she was concerned for his wife, Lili Damita, an exotic Franco-American spitfire and Curtiz's ex-spouse. Flynn and Damita had nothing in common but sex, and they fought over his womanizing and her possessiveness. "Bottles crashed against the wall," he recalled. "When Lili raged she . . . threw them one by one from their shelves and their tables and they came in rocket succession. Tears came. Torrents. Then hysteria."[12]

Flynn stayed with Damita because he was addicted to "Tiger Lil's" innovative, athletic tricks in bed, but he tired of them after a while and longed for someone with whom he could discuss literature and ideas. Olivia would have been perfect, but he wasn't cut out for marriage because fidelity went against his very nature. "I had an insatiable desire to run through the world and not be hemmed in by anybody," he wrote.[13] Their thwarted love eventually led to a kind of cold war, during which he continued to harass her with asinine pranks, making sure the restroom she used had no toilet paper, swatting a nonexistent insect on her derrière, and sprinkling her ice cream with salt and pepper. After such hazing, she was not inclined to forgive him when he accidentally knocked her out of a boat, striking her head with a sword. "Olivia! Look at me!" he cried. "Are you hurt?' She replied, "No, but I'm disgusted."[14]

On release, *Brigade* was a hit, Flynn's career took a quantum leap, and Olivia's held steady. "He moves beautifully," Burt Reynolds, an action star of the next generation, said. "You can't take your eyes off him."[15] *New York Times* reviewer Frank S. Nugent called Olivia "attractive, but thematically unnecessary."[16] Nonetheless, entertainment reporter Linda Lane wrote, "With extraordinary acting performances to her credit . . . Olivia has made a place for herself high above all the other leading women of the movies."[17]

After the rigors of *Brigade*, she needed a break. "I talked the matter over with my mother, whose advice has always been invaluable to me," she said. Lilian convinced Warner to grant Olivia brief vacations after each film, beginning with *Brigade*. Mother and daughter returned to Saratoga and then went to Carmel, where Olivia "could be a normal girl of 19, and not a Hollywood actress to be pointed at."[18] In Carmel-by-the-Sea, arguably the most beautiful town in America, with giant eucalyptus trees, a salubrious clime, a Spanish mission, magical mists, sea otters, surfers, and close proximity to the Big Sur redwood wilderness, Olivia enjoyed a 12-mile walk by the ocean and felt a thrill more intense than any she'd experienced in Hollywood.[19]

Flynn did not appear in her next four films, *Call It a Day, The Great Garrick, It's Love I'm After*, and *Gold Is Where You Find It*, none of which matched the popularity of *Captain Blood*. In 1937's *Call It a Day*, a fluffy comedy about twenty-four hours in the life of a family reacting to the first romantic stirrings of spring, Olivia played an ingénue who goes after a married artist. Joan Fontaine had starred in a regional Los Angeles production without garnering any movie offers.[20] One day Flynn showed up on the set when Olivia was working with director Archibald L. "Archie" Mayo and trying to finish an emotional scene requiring tears.

"I have come to see Miss de Havilland act," Flynn said, taking a seat next to the camera and smirking. He begged her to flood the room with her emotions and said he could watch her all day because she was a great inspiration. She called him "big shot" and he called her "beautiful." Later she told reporter George Shaffer she thought Flynn was handsome, humorous, and gentlemanly but not particularly solicitous of her, not even when she was anxious about a shot. "He'll never do anything to put me at ease," she said.[21]

Archie Mayo, who'd guided Mae West to fame in *Night After Night*, proved to be volatile and erratic, but he changed his tune when he discovered Olivia could cry on cue. "Fine, fine," he murmured when she turned on the tears during a take. "Cut," he said. "Olivia, that was great. Now you knock off for a while until you feel better." As she headed for her dressing room, Mayo looked admiringly after her and said, "There [goes] the best and most natural crier in the movies. And what a godsend to a director who needs an especially good weeping sequence!" She couldn't always turn off the tears after an emotional scene. "I found myself crying so hard I couldn't stop. . . . We had to quit work for half an hour until I could . . . get back into the rhythm of the rest of the picture."[22]

Tony Thomas, author of *The Films of Olivia de Havilland*, wrote off *Call It a Day* as "paper thin . . . frou-frou."[23] According to *The Brooklyn Daily Eagle*'s Winston Burdett, "Olivia de Havilland, whom one would have imagined to be just the girl for the part of the older daughter, keys her performance, from the start, in much too feverish a pitch."[24]

In *The Great Garrick*, produced by Mervyn LeRoy and directed by James Whale, Olivia portrayed Germaine Dupont, Countess de la Corbe, who falls in love with Garrick, England's renowned eighteenth-century actor-manager, played by Brian Aherne. *Variety* wrote, "Romantic passages between Aherne and de Havilland are quite charming, but much too long."[25] Though their onscreen chemistry was lacking, off screen they clicked. Aherne repeatedly urged her to play opposite him on Broadway, "but she still says 'No,'" columnist Virginia Dale wrote in December 1937.[26] In May of that year Walter Winchell had written, "Olivia de Havilland prefers boyfriends who aren't actors."[27] That was the month, elsewhere in the world, that the Hindenberg dirigible crashed and killed thirty-six, a civil war raged in Spain, and the Golden Gate Bridge opened.

In the de Havilland household, Olivia and Joan experimented with a way to get along by establishing a "temperament schedule" to forestall their being difficult on the same days. The timetable was so effective that they began to spend Sunday afternoons in Griffith Park, riding on the merry-go-round and visiting the zoo.[28] Olivia seemed to tolerate Joan's insensitive remarks to the press. One columnist wrote, "Joan Fontaine pretends to be very much annoyed with me because I have continued to identify her as Olivia de Havilland's sister," and another advised, "Act like you don't know who [Joan] really is or she won't like it . . . It's her ambition to be a star in her own right, not as Olivia de Havilland's 'kid sister.'"[29]

"[Errol Flynn] never guessed I had a crush on him," Olivia recalled. "And then he got one, too." She later told journalist Emily Andrews, "Chemistry was there." And she told writer John Lichfield, "I said that nothing could happen while he was still with Lili . . . He was in deep thrall to her in some way." Biographer Judith M. Kass quoted Olivia: "He proposed . . . but he was not divorced from Lili." Lichfield reported that she said, "So nothing did ever happen between us."[30]

Evelyn Keyes saw Flynn and Damita at a Malibu beach party and later wrote, "God, were they good-looking. She had an extraordinary figure that fairly undulated across the sand and to the sea. And Errol Flynn. He was so beautiful it stopped my breath. I was just the right age for the Flynn taste. He made it clear too, with eyes for me and nobody else, in spite of Lily's [sic] presence. I went all flurry."[31]

"Stay away from Errol, Evelyn, he's bad news for dames," Van Heflin, who was also at the party, told her.[32]

Flynn proved to be such a cruel and unfeeling husband that he told his wife to live elsewhere while he shared a bachelor pad with Niven. "I was determined not to shack up with Lily [*sic*]," Flynn wrote, as if she were a girlfriend instead of his wife. "See her, have her, yes; but have my own life at the same time."[33] His problem, Niven thought, "was a deep inferiority complex."[34] Flynn's emotional issues were the legacy of a brutal mother who, when he was seven, beat him and locked him in a room for two days.[35] When she discovered he'd had sex with the girl next door, she gave him "a hell of a shellacking," Flynn wrote. "My young, beautiful, impatient mother, with the itch to live—perhaps too much like my own—was a tempest about my ears, as I was about hers . . . I wanted to get away from her, get away from home."[36] He succeeded but would spend the rest of his life trying to find a woman like her, "and I have never found her," he wrote.[37] Olivia felt the irresolvable obstacles in their relationship were not his wife's but his mother's fault. "Most men who have perhaps been ridiculed by their mothers," she said, "are never quite sure of themselves with women."[38]

"The relationship was not consummated," Olivia recalled at ninety-two. She declined his offer of marriage, later explaining, "It was just as well that I said no. He would have ruined my life."[39] But a warm collegial relationship continued to develop and deepen, and it would enrich both them and the studio.

They had in common a burning desire for more creative work. "She was sick to death of playing 'the girl' and badly wanted a few good roles," Flynn said.[40] Olivia saw beneath his defensive veneer and liked what was there: "a thoughtful, Irish-tweed-and-books-and-tea-by-the-fireside . . . a poetic, gentle creature, behind all the braggadocio and wildness . . . It was inevitable to fall in love with him."[41] She "felt great tenderness" for him, she said, "but he still had no idea how to woo me."[42]

He had time to devise new strategies, for they had six more pictures to make together.

——

Movie audiences in the 1930s demanded clever variations of the same tried-and-true plots, and a star was expected to establish an image and rigidly stick to it. Fed up with grinding out Warner's assembly-line fodder, down to ninety-eight pounds, and anorexic,[43] Olivia was shaken by the pressure of making back-to-back films, but studio manager Terry Wright told Jack Warner, "I suggest this matter be turned over to the Actors' Guild to have them police Miss de Havilland."[44] Warner passed the buck to Max Arnow in casting, ordering him to tell Olivia "that when she has a noon call, we have the right and privilege to work her for eight hours."[45] Studio doctor W.R. Meals warned Wallis that her health was in jeopardy and the studio shouldn't overwork her, especially at night.[46] Her agent had a word with Jack Warner and the studio briefly acquiesced.[47]

She lived a healthy life, enjoying hobbies like fencing, sketching, and bird-watching. "I'll not only watch them but I'll make sketches," she said.[48] She liked reading biographies and wrote enough poetry to fill a book.[49] After visiting a trailer-house display she chose a deluxe model with a kitchenette and shower, and on a vacation she visited old friends in Northern California and noticed "they seem to be having a great deal more fun than I have. They hadn't a worry in the world. They weren't afraid of the future because they didn't even think about it. They seemed to be living from day to day—just as I used to when I was in school."[50]

A reporter noted that she didn't have a boyfriend,[51] but "I'm looking for the right man," she said. "Certainly I like men—but I haven't found one yet who really appeals to me. He should be intelligent, well-read, and interesting. Not arty—I don't like arty men or men who pose . . . He must have a sense of humor and a nice smile. He doesn't have to be handsome, but he must have charm. He needn't be a six footer, but he should be lean and hard and dark. I don't like blond men."[52]

She posed for a cheesecake photo in a swimsuit and heels and in another as a scantily clad, pistol-packing lady pirate. Other photos showed her in the activities that kept her slim and shapely. Her regimen was up at 6 a.m. for breakfast on workdays, breakfast at noon on days off, a morning dip in the Pacific, fishing, hiking, tennis, ping pong, and bicycling—"an excellent way to keep the legs in form."[53] Every time she made a film, she lost five to eight pounds and, to regain them for her health, she devised a homemade breakfast made up of blanched almonds ground up with seedless raisins and topped with two tablespoons of cream and sugar, guaranteed to put on two pounds a week.[54] Her daily luncheon was vegetarian.[55]

She was perhaps unwittingly spearheading a movement that would change Hollywood and reinvent the concept of beauty, transforming it from the heavily painted vampish mask of Theda Bara in the silent era and the brazen hussy look of Clara (The It Girl) Bow and Zelda Fitzgerald in the Roaring Twenties into a more natural and recognizably human countenance in the 1930s. Studios at first balked at the new casual look and sent down edicts warning actresses to avoid informal clothes, and always to appear in public in full makeup and glamorous dresses because the paparazzi were so rampant on the streets and at parties, theatres, football games, and race tracks that celebrities were sure to be photographed.[56] In Hollywood the order was interpreted to mean that slacks were taboo except at home. "Stars who fell under the ban," a reporter wrote, "are Kay Francis, Bette Davis, Ruby Keeler, Joan Blondell, Olivia de Havilland, and many others who are in the habit of wearing slacks almost exclusively during leisure hours."[57] Fortunately, the reporter added, "There is no way the order can be positively enforced."[58]

Olivia pointed out that in ancient Egypt men had worn skirts shorter than the sixteen-inchers predicted for next autumn's women's wear, that jewelry had begun as a masculine adornment, handbags originated as a male accoutrement suspended from the waist, and high heels for men were all the rage in sixteenth-century France.[59] So much for male chauvinist critics of women in slacks.

Still-photographer Elmer Fry cited Olivia's shoulders as among the few that matched those of Billie Dove, who'd possessed "the most beautiful shoulders ever seen in Hollywood." They were "so smoothly rounded, so youthful, that [Olivia] is peculiarly suited to play in costume pictures in which off-the-shoulder necklines' predominate," journalist Hubbard Keavy wrote.[60]

Her understated haute couture was regularly tracked by such journalists as the North American Newspaper Alliance's syndicated columnist Sheilah Graham, who wrote, "The problem of what to wear on warm Indian summer evenings has been solved by Olivia de Havilland, who manages to look sweet and fresh in a gown of black chiffon, its somberness relieved by a double sash of salmon and powder-blue taffeta ribbons."[61] Posing with all the flair of a professional model, Olivia decorated the nation's fashion pages, especially when she wore such Orry-Kelly creations as his flowing white crepe gown with a tailored top, corselet waistline, full bodice, and a gilded alligator belt with a gold fastener. Along with Virginia Bruce, Miriam Hopkins, Myrna Loy, Dolores Del Rio, and Sonja Henie, she was considered to be one of the best-dressed women in Hollywood. Graham particularly liked Olivia's "white crepe with oriental trim down the front. Shirred matching jacket, white sandals, high white turban."[62]

As documented in the press in early 1937, her busy leisure hours seemed to include everything but male companionship, and in the spring she thought of going back to college to study anthropology, but no such courses were offered that semester, so she started reading books on the subject, beginning with Clark Wissler's study of American Indians.[63]

5

It's Love I'm After

Ascrewball romance, *It's Love I'm After* proved a difficult shoot in May 1937 under the direction of the moody and unpredictable Archie Mayo. Olivia was playing another of her rich girls, and Leslie Howard was cast as Basil Underwood, a matinee idol she had a crush on, though Bette Davis was his fiancée. "Bette used to be my ideal when we were both at Warners," Olivia told Louella O. Parsons in 1960. "I studied her, the way she acted and how she became any character that she played."[1] In a 1965 interview she recalled that she'd "worked with Bette on two pictures in the 1930s, and she ignored me just as any reigning queen would ignore a teen-ager."[2]

After Olivia and Leslie Howard did ten takes on an eight-minute scene, Mayo put them through an eleventh and Olivia muffed a line. She blushed and glanced at Mayo. "Olivia!" he shouted, and told a prop man, "Go get me a gun!" She looked repentant, and both smiled, but Mayo yelled after the prop man, "Be sure it's loaded!" Then he saw the tears in Olivia's eyes and said, "I'm going home and shoot my wife."[3]

His mood had improved later in the month when the cast convened at 11 a.m. to rehearse a scene that would take up three minutes on screen. Howard was to arrive at Olivia's Pasadena mansion with his valet, played by Eric Blore. The script called for them to be stopped at the entrance by Olivia's father, played by George Barbier, and for Olivia to run down a curving staircase. Mayo circulated among his actors revving them up for the camera. "All right, you lovely people," he said, "we're going to make a picture."[4] Jack Sullivan, the assistant director, alerted the actors involved in the scene, telling them to take their places on the set.

Howard and Blore stationed themselves at the foot of the stairs, near the camera, and Olivia stood in the upper hallway, looking down. "All right, you loves," Mayo said. "Let's rehearse it." The action began, but Olivia, positioned out of camera range, spotted a reporter, Clarke Wales, who'd come to interview her, and waved to him. She watched the other actors rush to the stairs, where Howard was ordered out of the house by her father. Howard tried to explain that he'd been invited and that he was calling on Marcia West, Olivia's character.[5]

Barbier yelled. "Marcia!" It was Olivia's cue to emerge from upstairs and say she'd hurry down.[6]

And hurry she did—faster and nimbler than any actor Clarke Wales had ever seen.[7] Running to the head of the stairs, she came into camera range, smiling with delight when she saw Leslie Howard. Darting downstairs—recklessly but expertly—she exchanged a few lines of dialogue, then charged back upstairs. That completed the scene. Clarke Wales later wrote that the way she took the stairs could easily have resulted in broken bones or death. Mayo called for rehearsal after rehearsal, and Olivia gave it her all as the reporter watched her take the stairs at a dead run with growing anxiety. Just seeing her do it made him so tired he had to ask for a chair.

Mayo finally announced that he was ready to shoot the last take— "for posterity."[8]

The assistant director called for quiet.[9]

The cinematographer pushed a buzzer, and the sound technicians pushed another. Mayo yelled *action*. The actors dashed up the stairs. As Spring Byington delivered her eight lines of dialogue, Bonita Granville was startled by a sudden, unscripted noise and craned her neck to see what had caused it. A curler had dropped from another actress's hair and landed on the floor below the stair landing. Granville apologized, saying she knew she'd goofed and should have stayed in character.

It was now 2:30 p.m., and the actors continued to blow takes for another hour. Summoning his patience, Mayo indicated he was ready to shoot take 47. He was joking, but Clarke Wales later wrote that the figure sounded accurate to him.[10]

At 3:30 p.m. an acceptable take was at last in the can. Olivia told Wales that she was sorry for all the delays and explained that a take was often difficult when so many actors were involved. The interview got underway at last, and she discussed her home life, mentioning how thrilled she was to run her house while Lilian was out of town. The crew finished setting up, and the assistant director assembled the actors who would be in the shot—Olivia, Barbier, Howard, and Blore. The 47th take hadn't been the final one after all; more were required. Powdering her nose, Olivia ran upstairs and continued to dash up and down for another hour. Clarke Wales later wrote it was a myth that stand-ins slave on a hot sound stage while stars luxuriate in lavish dressing rooms. Olivia's stand-in relaxed in the director's chair, wandered around the set, and chatted with Leslie Howard's stand-in.[11]

Olivia rejoined the reporter at 4:30 p.m. and talked about how she'd scolded the telephone company for making a mistake. The reporter scribbled down every word because when you're a movie star, no matter how trivial or inconsequential the subject, every word is copy. Then it was back to work for more takes on the same scene. Olivia went up on one of her lines, and everyone looked at Mayo, waiting for him to explode. Olivia, penitent, could "look more apologetic than anybody else in pictures," Wales wrote. Archie Mayo told his company to behold their leading lady—an absolute angel—and threatened to personally slay anyone who dared to criticize her. At 5:30, as the crew shifted the cameras and lights, Olivia grabbed another five minutes to talk with Wales. The assistant director approached her and said that she could sleep late tomorrow because they didn't need her until 9:30 a.m. [12]

"Did you hear what he said?" she asked Wales. "Isn't that nice of him?"[13]

"You'll think it's nicer tomorrow morning," the reporter commented.[14]

For the 9:30 call, she would have to rise at 6:30 a.m.[15]

She did three or four more takes before Mayo called it a night and dismissed cast and crew. Olivia snatched her makeup kit and ran for the door, tripping and falling as her makeup gear scattered. "Down she went," Wales wrote, "ending the day flat on her face."[16]

Time liked *It's Love I'm After*, calling it "refreshing, impudent fun: a buoyant cinema making faces at its precise old aunt, the theater."[17]

— ᴥ —

Working at Warner, Olivia could've used a guard to ward off the wolves in the Green Room. In September 1937, in spite of her snubs, a prominent actor kept pursuing her, even showing up on the set one afternoon and skulking around until she started blowing her lines and had to insist he be expelled. He hurriedly beat it out of the sound stage.[18] A more welcome admirer was Brian Aherne, who was still in her life, according to a UP dispatch dated July 8, 1937. "A romance for Brian Aherne and Olivia de Havilland is reported from the Warner lot," the article stated.[19]

"I have yet to meet the man I could love," she said.[20] There were few opportunities, according to a newspaper article that stated, "Olivia eschews parties. She maintains that late nights are no good for work the next day, and her career is the most important thing to her at present."[21] She must have made an exception the night a fashion reporter saw her at the Cocoanut Grove in the midst of a star-studded crowd that included Joan Bennett, Mary Brian, Jeanette MacDonald, Walter Winchell, Eddie Cantor, Al Jolson, and Ruby Keeler—not to mention Lum and Abner. "Who's that pretty girl with the big brown eyes?" someone inquired, and a reporter on the scene later wrote, "I looked up just in time to see Olivia de Havilland wave as she danced by in the arms of John Arlidge."[22] The journalist added that Olivia wore "a full skirted gown of white chiffon, Grecian style, the high waistline girdled with bands of narrow black velvet ribbon."[23]

A minor grievance for Olivia on the Warner lot was presented by *Dead End* kid Leo Gorcey, who bumped into her car twice though it was parked in her assigned space. Taken from the streets of New York to appear in the Broadway hit *Dead End*, the boys later had been kicked out of the Goldwyn Studio for crashing a truck into a sound stage, and at Warner they would make six films, including *Angels with Dirty Faces*, before their antics cost them their contract. They resurfaced at other studios under such monikers as the Bowery Boys and the East Side Kids.[24]

Olivia continued to solidify her excellent relations with the press, establishing cordial relations with Louella O. Parsons, the most powerful woman in Hollywood. Syndicated in four hundred newspapers worldwide, her news of the movie capital and its personalities was avidly consumed by twenty million readers. She earned $250,000 per year—approximately $4 million by today's standards—and became a fixture on the American scene with seven newspaper columns a week and a popular radio anthology show, *Hollywood Hotel*. Spies inside the studios, hairdressers, and workers in doctors' and lawyers' offices kept her so well-informed that she sometimes knew of a pregnancy before the expectant star did. A devout Catholic, she had a ten-foot statue of the Virgin Mary in her garden.

Parsons's drunken husband, urologist Harry Martin, whom Parsons called Docky, was known as "Hollywood's clap doctor" because of his adeptness at curing venereal diseases. At an industry party one night, someone told Parsons that Docky had passed out under the piano. "Let Docky sleep," she said. "He has surgery at seven tomorrow morning."[25]

Olivia also had Hedda Hopper on her side, a columnist who was so vicious to Spencer Tracy that he kicked her in the rear. Broadcaster

Jimmie Fidler, more feared and brazen than Parsons and Hopper, was won over by Olivia's upright character. "Completely disregarding stellar practice, Olivia is always on the dot for her appointments," Fidler wrote in his snappy syndicated column, which featured such items as "One-word description of Hedy Lamarr: 'Sextraordinary.'"[26] On his radio show he punctuated his scoops on stars' tantrums and foibles with a Morse-code-like beeping and signed off every week with the crisp valediction, "Good night to you, and I do mean you."

In Hollywood's Golden Age, gossip columnists were the modern-day equivalent of the Greek chorus in classical tragedy, providing a running commentary on the lives of the stars and creating an intimate connection between celebrities and their audience. In Aeschylus's *Prometheus Bound*, members of the chorus are called Oceanids, or sea nymphs, and in Sophocles's *Oedipus Rex,* they're the fifteen Theban elders. In the latter, the chorus advises Oedipus to stop speaking in anger, saying, "That's not what we need. Instead, we should be looking into this: How can we best carry out god's decree?" Likewise, Hollywood gossips measured stars' behavior against the standards of morality in contemporary society. Jimmie Fidler admonished Martha Raye to stay out of nightclubs and scolded George Brent for stringing along Ann Sheridan.[27] Hedda Hopper chastised Charlie Chaplin for getting a girl pregnant and thereafter was so feared around Hollywood that she could cut short an extramarital affair by merely wagging her finger,[28] but she found a more formidable adversary when she messed with Joan Fontaine. When Hopper told her, "The trouble with you, Joan, is that you've no humility," Joan said, "Fuck you, Hedda," and later recalled, "She didn't give me much trouble after that."[29]

Columnists usually get a bad rap and are disdained by their colleagues in the press as the toe-cheese of journalism. Sometimes they get things wrong, but on balance they make valuable contributions to history and deserve more credit, as is generally true of the much-maligned media.

6

Joan Falls in Love,
Olivia Makes a Western

Joan's career took much more time to launch than Olivia's had. She'd come to Olivia in necessitous circumstances, lacking food and shelter, and Olivia had taken her in. Now, ensconced in her sister's apartment, she had ample opportunity to begin edging her way into show business, and yet she'd always insist she received no encouragement or help from her family. "I am proud that I have carved my path on earth almost entirely by my own efforts," Joan asserted.[1] Her attitude had its roots in childhood. Having been deprived of the three things every child needs—consistent love, guidance, and a stable home—she understandably became in adulthood a hotbed of resentments, writing, "Weekdays at dawn, I drove Olivia up Highland and over the pass to her studio in Burbank, returned to the apartment to do her personal laundry, tidy the two-and-a-half rooms, pack her lunch, and have it ready in her dressing room when she broke from her set at noon. The trip was repeated in the evening, when the Ford and I would wait outside in the dark until my sister was good and ready to depart from her cronies in the makeup department. I did all the errands, most of the cooking . . . As for Olivia's and my relationship, she was the star and I was the servitor on probation . . . I was ruled by Mother and Olivia with an iron hand.[2] Apparently it never occurred to Joan that all but the very rich have to work for their keep.

43

There is something poignant in her anger and bitterness, both of which are the completely natural result of her having been robbed of a normal childhood, with all its cozy comforts and carefree days. The episode that changed her life occurred in her sixth year when her stepfather was bathing her one night. "The washcloth would tarry too long in intimate places . . . Something was odd." Many women never recover from such abuse, and Joan's hard, supercilious exterior suggests that she was one of them.[3] She further charged that George Fontaine threatened to bury her alive, knocked her through a glass door, and subjected her to "blinding rages."[4] Her mother also could be unduly harsh. Lilian went berserk when she caught Joan holding hands with a boy. "I saw you," she said. "You're nothing but a whore!"[5]

I was fortunate enough to see another, softer side of Joan when I caught her performance in *Tea and Sympathy* at the Ethel Barrymore Theatre on Broadway in 1954, after she replaced Deborah Kerr in the role of a prep-school headmaster's wife who helps a youth navigate his way through the humiliation of having been ridiculed because he appeared to be homosexual. Her total identification with this shattered young soul, played by Anthony Perkins, was a marvel of empathy, compassion, and love. She helped him recover his youth and self-esteem as no one had ever helped Joan recover hers, and she would remain angry forever.

In the 1930s, her career at last began to flourish the moment she met the crusty old character actress May Robson, much loved for her sharp-tongued portrayal of Aunt Polly in *The Adventures of Tom Sawyer*. In her mid-seventies, Robson was preparing a stage production of Edward Chodorov's *Kind Lady*, and she invited Joan to join the cast. Olivia introduced Joan to her agent Ivan Kahn, but Joan complained, "My agent didn't catapult me over the studio walls. I beat against studio gates to no avail."[6] The chauffeuring she hated performing for Olivia at least got her through security at the Warner entrance and on to the lot, where she was noticed by producer Mervyn Le Roy, who spotted her waiting for Olivia in their Ford. He offered her a contract with his independent production unit.

"Mother agreed with Olivia that I simply could not accept this opportunity," Joan wrote. "Warner's was Olivia's studio, her domain. What's more, I must change my name—'De Havilland' was Olivia's, she was the firstborn, and I was not to disgrace her name. Mother's bet was on her firstborn, her proven breadwinner with a long-term contract . . . I did resent having to change my name. Terribly. I still do. Joan Fontaine. I don't know who she is."[7]

The name Fontaine was not her first choice; she tried de Beauvoir,[8] Burfield, and St. John before settling for stepfather George's surname, but she'd still be grousing about sacrificing her real name Joan de Havilland four decades later when she came to William Morrow and Company with her autobiography. "I'm Joan de Havilland," she insisted.[9] Joan Fontaine was just some distant weirdo she looked after. She felt robbed of her sense of self.

When she broke into films at the age of twenty, she began to compete with Olivia "for the same roles—and then the same men."[10] Producer Jesse L. Lasky had seen her onstage at Duffy's Theatre on Hollywood Boulevard and signed her to RKO Radio Pictures at three hundred dollars per week. "Little Sister found herself a run-of-the-mill player at RKO," Joan recalled. In 1937 she filmed the screwball comedy *You Can't Beat Love* but received little praise in the *New York Times*, whose reviewer mentioned her only as "the Mayor's attractive daughter."[11] She failed at RKO, she claimed, because she refused to sleep with "producers [who] were looking for sex kittens . . . who would be available, both night and day, to entertain their out-of-town business associates."[12] A virgin at twenty, she started dating one-time star Conrad Nagel, now somewhat faded and living with a daughter two years younger than Joan. Nagel occasionally visited her at RKO, and one day a member of the crew saw him at the gates and, to Joan's embarrassment, yelled, "'Wheel him in!'"[13]

Nagel had the experience and sensitivity to recognize the peculiar nature of Joan's desperate needs as a woman. "And always Mother's 'You're nothing but a whore' rang in my ears whenever the bedroom door closed behind us," she wrote in *No Bed of Roses*.[14] She got nowhere with director George Stevens, with whom she became infatuated after he hired her to replace Ginger Rogers as Fred Astaire's dancing partner in the 1937 George Gershwin–P.G. Woodhouse musical *A Damsel in Distress*. One day Stevens asked Joan her real name, and when she told him, he laughed and said when Olivia's agent had suggested Olivia for a role in one of his films, he'd automatically declined because "any actress who'd assume as theatrical a name as Olivia de Havilland I can do without."[15]

"I was in love with George Stevens for many years, as were many other of his leading ladies," Joan recalled. "But I learned little or nothing from him as a director. His direction to me was simply, 'I don't know what's wrong. Let's shoot it again.'"[16]

When *Damsel* was released, Joan's reviews were dismal, the *New York Times* sniping, "What more can one ask of a Fred Astaire show? Ginger Rogers?" The *New York Daily News* agreed that "an Astaire picture isn't itself without Ginger."[17] Joan borrowed one of Olivia's boyfriends for the premiere at the Pantages Theatre on Hollywood Boulevard, and when her dancing scene with Astaire came on screen it was greeted with groans of derision.[18]

Good or bad, Joan was here to stay. "Contrast in sisters," Jimmie Fidler wrote in April 1937. "Demure Olivia de Havilland, and emotional, Jeanne Eagles–type Joan Fontaine."[19]

No wonder Olivia disdained so many of her early Warner films. Four were released in 1938, all of them except *The Adventures of Robin Hood* formulaic drivel. *Gold Is Where You Find It*, little more than a routine Western—even Gabby Hayes shows up in the cast—is about the 1877

Sacramento gold-rush war between wheat farmers and hydraulic-mining workers polluting the land and water supply.

In October 1937, Olivia made her way over a perilous one-way mountain road full of sharp curves and occasional oncoming vehicles to the ramshackle town of Weaverville to begin her work on *Gold*. Her abode on the remote location site was one of a dozen tents, which at least had hastily laid redwood floors. In the following days she was assailed alternately by rain, fog, chilly nights, and unendurable daytime heat. Though she looked beautiful in Technicolor, especially her soft brown hair, coiffed by Tillie Starlett, there could have been little joy in playing such a one-dimensional character, the homespun daughter of the leader of the farmers, played by Claude Rains.

A crisis erupted when Wallis viewed the rushes and charged that Olivia's "school girlish" acting was turning the movie into "a high-school play," and her makeup by Perc Westmore was a disaster, "lips are much too red, lower lip is much too heavy . . . We have to make retakes because the stuff is so bad."[20] He recalled her to the studio for new makeup tests. Such production details were not the real problem with *Gold*; the picture simply wasn't good enough, lacking substance and depth.[21] "Of Miss de Havilland it can be said that Technicolor suits her better than her role," the *New York Herald Tribune* wrote. "Even when she scrubs around in the dirt or rides a harrow, shouting 'Giddap' and 'Whoa!' she remains decorative. Never for a minute is she convincing."[22]

Her costars Claude Rains and George Brent looked uncomfortable in their cowboy getups, and Rains would never be cast in another Western. In the only sequence in the film of any interest, a dam is dynamited, destroying all the mining camps in seemingly realistic shots. Special effects artist Byron Haskins devised the models and later went on to science-fiction projects.[23] For its prophetic awareness of ecology and the environment, the film deserves some credit.

Screenland magazine reported that her *Gold* costar George Brent loved yachts, planes, fancy cars, and romancing "Greta Garbo, Bette Davis, Loretta Young, Merle Oberon, and Olivia de Havilland."[24] Gallant and gentlemanly, Brent personified the then-popular strong silent type, but in a bland way. He was Davis's leading man in numerous films, including *Dark Victory* and *Jezebel*, and her lover, briefly.[25] Donald Crisp, an especial friend of Olivia's, ribbed her about "her publicized romance with George Brent" during a November 1938 luncheon she and Crisp had with Hollywood columnist Paul Harrison, during which the two friends "spent time trading outrageous insults . . . He calls her hag." According to Harrison, Olivia acknowledged Brent possessed "a certain small boy charm," but she found his thinking somewhat juvenile.[26]

Brent's marriage to Ann Sheridan, the red-haired Oomph Girl from Denton, Texas, ended in divorce after a year. She didn't like his "Black Irish" moods, wildly at variance with her famous conviviality, so warm and jolly that within minutes of her entrance into the Green Room at Warner Brothers, she had everyone laughing. Lowly gaffers and movie moguls crowded around to crack their latest jokes, to which her customary response was, "Brother that's a honey."[27]

7

The Adventures of Robin Hood

Shortly to appear in the most expensive film ever made by Warner Brothers, *The Adventures of Robin Hood*, Olivia and Flynn enjoyed their first public date at the Coronation Ball for King George VI at the Ambassador Hotel in May 1937. She was tricked into the rendezvous by David Niven, who asked her to be his date for the ball, which was to start at 12:01 a.m., following dinner at Flynn's house on North Linden Drive in Beverly Hills. Flynn's companion was Mrs. Lewis Milestone, wife of the director of *All Quiet on the Western Front,* and not until they arrived at the Ambassador did Olivia realize she'd been deceived.

"Suddenly," she recalled, "[Errol] takes my arm and David Niven takes somebody else's arm, and I . . . get the picture." After the ball Olivia and Flynn retired to the Cocoanut Grove downstairs, and "one photographer got that picture."[1] They danced to "Sweet Leilani," the Harry Owens song from the film *Cocoanut Grove* that could scarcely have expressed their feelings for each other more precisely or poignantly.[2] Romance, trade winds, and freedom from Lili Damita were exactly what they needed. Though at the height of her happiness, Olivia's strong moral sense required her to risk losing Flynn by leveling with him. "We really mustn't see each other again until you've straightened out your situation with Lili," she said.[3]

Years later she'd ruefully reflect, "I suppose I regret that now. I was inclined to—maybe if it were today I might, but you kept those things very much to yourself then. But I was deeply affected by him. It was impossible for me not to be."[4] Their first public date would also be their last. Ironically, *The Adventures of Robin Hood* would represent the epitome of their achievement as a screen couple. James Cagney, set to play Robin, had walked out of the studio over a contractual dispute, and he did not return for two years.[5] Wallis successfully lobbied for Flynn, and though Jack Warner instructed Wallis to cast Anita Louise as Maid Marian, saying, "We won't have de Havilland in every other picture," Warner later recanted upon reflecting that the teaming of Flynn and Anita Louise had come a cropper in *Green Light* but the Flynn–de Havilland combination had turned *Captain Blood* into a blockbuster. Wallis voiced reservations about Olivia, pointing out that she was less impressive than he'd originally thought and was now just one more ingénue in their stable of starlets, but Jack Warner insisted on Olivia.[6]

Construction of Nottingham Castle began on Warner Sound Stage No. 2, an elephantine facility the set filled to capacity.[7] For several weeks Flynn and twenty-four male members of the cast rehearsed broadsword and quarterstave duels, and all the while Flynn continued his late-night binges, causing production manager T.C. Wright to advise Jack Warner that he should tell the actor to stop "dissipating around . . . with bags under his eyes."[8]

Olivia arrived at the Sherwood Forest location site in Chico, California, aboard the Southern Pacific and avoided a mob at the station by debarking hundreds of yards down the track, where location manager Al Alleborn, two publicists, and fellow cast member Patric Knowles, in costume as Will Scarlet, greeted her and rushed her to the Hotel Oaks. With no break she was driven to the base camp, a town of tents on the edge of the woods, known as Warner City, where two hundred thirty box lunches were laid out for cast and crew. She and Flynn sat at a banquet table in the forest and talked. They hadn't seen each other since the Coronation Ball.

"It was very hard," Olivia recalled, "because Lili was there on the set on location."[9] Whenever Olivia performed with Flynn, Damita sat in a director's chair, scrutinizing every scene for telltale signs of infidelity. "I thought, well I'm going to torture Errol Flynn," Olivia recounted. "And so we had one kissing scene, which I looked forward to with great delight. I remember I blew every take, at least six in a row, maybe seven, maybe eight, and we had to kiss all over again. And Errol Flynn got really rather uncomfortable, and he had, if I may say so, a little trouble with his tights. The love scenes were marvelous! I couldn't wait to get to them, especially when I had to kiss Errol."[10]

"Am I having fun," Olivia asked on the set one day, flashing a smile at journalist Alice Pardoe West and Una O'Connor, who was cast as Maid Marian's nurse Bess. "I'm free—not even chaperoned . . . There are lots and lots of swell people in it. I even like Errol Flynn."[11] The reporter noticed that "she dropped her eyes demurely . . . Miss de Havilland says she is not in love, although she admits that she has been twice."[12]

Later, another journalist, syndicated newspaper columnist George Shaffer, got fresh with her, asking if she liked men. She engaged him in bold, playful, but edgy repartee while taking off her shoes and stockings.

"I've been in Sherwood lake all morning," she explained, "and Errol Flynn's been rescuing me."[13]

"Then you do like men?"[14]

"Certainly . . . I like them poetic and practical! And sensitive, but I like them to do the talking . . . You do the talking," she ordered Shaffer. He asked if she'd ever been married, and she replied, "No. I was only 16. He went away. . . . He came back, but he was wearing a bow tie and had a funny haircut."[15]

Someone poetic, practical, sensitive, and willing to do all the talking appeared to be right around the corner, according to Louella O. Parsons, who revealed on January 13, 1938, that "Willie Wyler [the director] isn't making any secret of his admiration for Olivia de Havilland."[16]

After *Robin Hood* was completed, Olivia rushed to her dressing room, shed her cumbersome costume for the last time, shouted a loud "Goodbye" to everyone, and disappeared for what she hoped would be a long vacation, but after four arduous months as Lady Marian, she was slammed into *Four's a Crowd* with only a few days' break.

She had become a popular member of Hollywood's exclusive British colony,[17] and, according to journalist Milton Harker, Mr. and Mrs. Basil Rathbone were Olivia's "closest friends in town."[18] Olivia was planning for the three of them to go on a hunting trip in the mountains with her friend Howard Hill, world's champion archer, who'd given her a personally constructed English yew bow and a quiver of arrows after serving as Flynn's stand-in bowman and executing *Robin Hood*'s famous split-arrow shot, in which he sliced apart a target-embedded arrow with his own, a feat which was probably accomplished with a blade-headed arrow, according to some skeptical expert archers.[19] All she managed to squeeze in was a two-week Palm Springs vacation.

She and Flynn were paired again by the Lux Radio Theatre in a January 31, 1938, broadcast of Lutheran minister-turned-author Lloyd C. Douglas's pious but popular *Green Light*. She assumed the role that Margaret Lindsay had played in the film, which had starred Flynn and Anita Louise and was only a moderate success, convincing Jack Warner that he should have cast Olivia. He was right. In the broadcast, the sexual voltage between the stars sparked an otherwise soppy and improbable story of a noble young surgeon who takes the rap for a colleague's malpractice in the operating room and later volunteers as a guinea pig for a dangerous medical experiment. Olivia plays the good doctor's loyal gal Friday with a sassy zest that blends nicely with Flynn's solemnity.

In Cecil B. DeMille's chat with the stars at the end of the broadcast, Flynn said he was taking his ketch *Sirocco* to the Caribbean through the West Indies. Olivia plugged *Gold Is Where You Find It*, saying she'd attend the premiere in Weaverville.[20]

When the critical and financial returns came in for *The Adventures of Robin Hood*, they were extraordinary, the critics raving and the box office jingling to the tune of a four million dollar profit for the studio—today's equivalent of $68,000,000—an immense figure considering the depression-era admission price of twenty-five cents.[21] When the film opened at the Radio City Music Hall in May, Frank S. Nugent wrote, "A richly produced, bravely bedecked, romantic and colorful show, it leaps boldly to the forefront of this year's best . . . Maid Marian has the grace to suit Olivia de Havilland."[22] *Variety* wrote, "It is cinematic pageantry at its best."[23]

In a 2003 reassessment, Roger Ebert called *Robin Hood* "a masterpiece . . . a triumph of the studio system . . . Olivia de Havilland was a great beauty . . . The shift in her feelings about Sir Robin is measured out scene by scene . . . a textbook on how to get it right."[24]

The American Film Institute included *Robin Hood* in its top 100 movies and rated Flynn's Robin number 18 among the all-time greatest screen characters, between Clint Eastwood's *Dirty Harry* and Sidney Poitier's Virgil Tibbs of *In the Heat of the Night*, and composer Erich Wolfgang Korngold's music number 11 among the best screen scores, between Dimitri Tomkins's *High Noon* and Bernard Herrmann's *Vertigo*.[25]

8

Brian Aherne

According to press reports in early 1938, Olivia, now twenty-one, held the studio record at Warner for receiving the most marriage proposals, with buxom blond comedienne Marie (*My Friend Irma*) Wilson coming in at second place.[1] By the time Olivia headed for England in the spring for some much-needed rest, rumors were rife that she would wed Herman Alfred Stern, second Baron Michelhom, of Hellingly, Sussex, thirty-eight, scion of a rich mining and railroad family. "Friends here [in Hollywood] nodded significantly. They hinted a formal engagement would be announced soon," the Associated Press stated, adding that Olivia would meet with the baron in London. Olivia and her mother, going undercover as Mrs. Halliday and her daughter Lavinia, embarked on the French liner *Normandie*, which Olivia termed "the most beautiful ship in the world."[2] The interior was a masterpiece of Art Deco and Streamline Moderne elegance, and she was the fastest ship afloat. Sheilah Graham wrote on April 18 that Olivia had cabled her to dismiss all claims that she'd have a romantic tryst with the baron "who is old enough to be her father," Graham wrote. That would have been possible only if his lordship had sired her at the tender age of seventeen.

Brian Aherne, whose vitality was hard to resist, was also on board. Like Olivia, Aherne had ambivalent feelings about Hollywood, evinced by his having turned down an offer from the crown prince of MGM, Irving Thalberg, who promised to make him a major star at Metro. Having been the leading man of the first lady of the American stage, Katharine Cornell, Aherne felt he could progress more rapidly on the stage and in films if he remained free to choose good roles.

A cultivated English gentleman, Aherne's conversational style was refreshingly urbane and wide-ranging for Hollywood, a company town that was in many respects quite provincial. A former habitué of London's Clubland, he knew Galsworthy and Somerset Maugham and could spin anecdotes about Rudyard Kipling, who told him that "If" had been written about George Washington. "Livvie is seen around town with Aherne," wrote biographer Robert Matzen,[3] and Aherne would state in his memoir, "Costarred with me in *The Great Garrick* was the young and entrancing Olivia de Havilland, to whom I gave a [birthday] cake at a party on the set."[4] He had been deeply attached to the British actress Clare Eames, who left her husband, Sidney Howard, Pulitzer Prize–winning author of *The Silver Cord*, to live openly and scandalously with him virtually from the day they met. When Aherne and Howard bumped into each other at a party, the playwright wittily apologized for always getting in his way. In 1930, Clare underwent an operation for intestinal stoppage and never recovered. "And so, holding my hand and looking desperately into my eyes . . . she passed away . . . I went on blindly running, for the next 20 years."[5] Sheilah Graham would later write, "I've known Olivia through several romances that included John Huston, Brian Aherne, and Jimmy Stewart."[6]

Olivia and Lilian returned on the *Queen Mary* on May 17, 1938, along with Claudette Colbert, Metropolitan Opera soprano Lily Pons, and heiress Doris Duke. The United Press reported that Olivia "branded as 'out of whole cloth'" the rumor that she'd gone to England to wed a "baron and found him already married."[7] On her way to Los Angeles Olivia made two stops to publicize *Robin Hood* and sign autographs, arriving on May 19 in Philadelphia to lunch at the Warwick with a *Philadelphia Inquirer* reporter, who later wrote that she feasted on fried chicken, creamed shrimp, and a chocolate éclair, explaining she needed to add six pounds to her 106. Afterward they ambled along Chestnut Street, where no one recognized her, and she mentioned she'd be twenty-two on July 1. "I'm not crazy about the movies," she said, making the reporter wonder about "the noses that will go up when she gets back."[8] She added that she liked getting older "because that means my contract will be up sooner."[9]

"She looks tired," the reporter later wrote, "even though she's just had a vacation."[10]

In Pittsburgh the next day, when asked about her romance with Baron Michelhom, she said the same rumors had circulated regarding "Kay Francis and a title and I guess they thought it would be a good thing to say about me."[11] Back in Hollywood the following day she laughed at the incognito "Mrs. Halliday and her daughter Lavinia," which had fooled everyone, save only a child who recognized her in a small town.[12] Evidently the trip hadn't achieved its purpose of providing rest and relaxation. The Associated Press reported on August 1, 1938, that shortly before a brief respite in Saratoga she'd possibly been fatigued due to a punishing work load at Warner. In Saratoga, friends had helped by regarding her as just another neighbor rather than a celebrity, "which was exactly the medicine she needed." Twelve days of getting out of bed at a normal hour and enjoying picnics and an occasional swim had enabled her to put on ten pounds and restore her usual weight.[13] The United Press reported on September 1 that her European jaunt had in fact been good for her health, and that a doctor had prescribed vitamins and lots of food, "including a five-course breakfast and roast beef for lunch and dinners which start with soup and end with nuts."[14]

Jimmie Fidler was convinced she was "getting an inferiority complex" because her boyfriends were falling in love with her sister.[15] Conrad Nagel had been good for Joan, who wrote, "Conrad instructed me carefully and thoroughly. He was a kind, sophisticated lover."[16] The breakthrough occurred when Nagel "put the twin beds together, laid the mattresses crosswise on the frames, and began to teach me the intricacies of the game . . . I saw distinct possibilities in this newfound indoor sport."[17]

In September 1938 columnist Read Kendall reported in the *Los Angeles Times* that Joan and Nagel, amid rumors of a breakup, were seen with Olivia at the Brown Derby.[18] By November Joan wasn't along when Olivia attended the premiere of *Soliloquy* "with Sister Joan Fontaine's boyfriend, Conrad Nagel," King Features Syndicate columnist Harrison Carroll wrote.[19] In November Ed Sullivan reported that Olivia was seen with Phil Kellog,[20] and added in the same column, "Ann Sheridan [was] on Ronald Reagan's arm."[21]

The British Service Club's Fourth Annual Armistice Ball on November 11, 1938, brought out Hollywood's British colony in force, including Olivia and Joan, Ronald Colman, Leslie Howard, Sir C. Aubrey Smith, Basil Rathbone, Madeleine Carroll, Boris Karloff, Ella Logan, W.S. Van Dyke, and Nigel Bruce. At this patriotic event, guests likely would have been acutely conscious of warlike disasters in Europe, where on November 9, known as Kristallnacht, Nazi thugs arrested 20,000 Jews and destroyed their shops and synagogues throughout Germany and Austria. In the following days, 3,500 members of the motion picture industry, including John Garfield, Joan Crawford, and Frank Capra, petitioned President Roosevelt to confront Hitler's persecution of the Jews. Nobel Prize–winner Thomas Mann also signed the petition.

The British colony went in for a lot of ribbing when the blokes got together for a jolly all-male gabfest. Though Olivia, according to the *Chicago Tribune*, was the colony's "darling child,"[22] she came in for her share of teasing. As *Dawn Patrol* was being filmed on the Warner lot, the antics of director Edmund Goulding, Basil Rathbone, Errol Flynn, David Niven, Donald Crisp, and the Earl of Warwick, all Englishmen, "dissipated for all time the legend that the Britishers are lacking in a sense of humor," Ed Sullivan wrote. Olivia, at her prettiest, walked onto the set one day in the middle of a ribald and profane bull session.

"Hello, hag," Donald Crisp, one of her most devoted friends, said with a straight face.

"Gad, you are getting fat," Flynn observed.

"In the wrong place," Niven added.

"I don't think you are getting plump," Rathbone said. "It is just that you are untidy."

Sullivan wrote, "Olivia fled and never returned."[23]

"Joan Fontaine and Conrad Nagel have iced," Ed Sullivan wrote, and included in the same December 6, 1938, column that Olivia was reportedly seeing George Brent, and they were "more serious than you think."[24] Joan had ended her affair with Nagel, refusing "to share my man's life with a daughter almost my age."[25]

Olivia was earning enough money to take Joan and Lilian with her when she rented a three-bedroom, gray stucco, ivy-covered North Hollywood house at 2337 Nella Vista Street. Basil Rathbone lived nearby on Los Feliz Boulevard in a very grand house. Using her RKO salary, Joan acquired a secondhand Mercury convertible. "I continued to be housekeeper," she recalled. "If Olivia had special guests to dinner, I was served a tray upstairs in my bedroom."[26] Metro gave her a small part in *The Women*, starring Norma Shearer, that resulted in Joan's first good reviews. Soon she turned the handsome head of Brian Aherne, who'd invited Olivia, Joan, and Lilian to a cocktail party at his colonial abode on Rodeo Drive in Beverly Hills. Joan began to flirt with Aherne after another guest, a fortune-teller, said Joan was going to marry him. Aherne asked if he could have a date on Wednesday or Friday evening.[27]

"I said I'd take both," Joan later wrote in her memoir.[28]

9

Howard Hughes

When Louella O. Parsons reported that Olivia was engaged to Howard Hughes, it was news to Olivia, but shortly she received a telephone call from the billionaire industrialist. "This is Howard Hughes speaking," he said. "Now that we're engaged, don't you think we ought to meet?" She told Lilian, "One of the world's most renowned wolves has just asked me to go out. . . . He doesn't sound very dangerous to me."[1]

On their first date, Hughes took her to the Victor Hugo cafe, where they sat in a corner banquette and drank champagne. A dark, lanky but ruggedly built Texan,[2] Hughes had just made aviation history and been feted with a ticker-tape parade in New York for breaking Wiley Post's record by flying around the world in a twin-engine Lockheed Electra in three days and nineteen hours. "He was a great hero, and that impressed me . . . and his rather shy manner," Olivia recalled.[3] Also a boy-wonder filmmaker, he'd directed *Hell's Angels* in 1930, when he was twenty-five.

Though Hughes was ten years her senior, *Time* magazine celebrated him as "the young man who looked like Gary Cooper and flew like Lindbergh."[4] A major power in films, he'd eventually own RKO. He took Olivia bowling and to Santa Barbara in his plane for hamburgers.[5] Aviation was their great bond; she loved flying and soon got her pilot's license. Christopher Andersen of *People* magazine wrote, "Silent-screen beauty Billie Dove, Jean Harlow, and Ginger Rogers were just a few of his conquests, which would grow to include Bette Davis, Lana Turner, Olivia de Havilland, Rita Hayworth, Jane Russell, Ava Gardner, Susan Hayward, Gene Tierney, and Marilyn Monroe."[6]

Hughes asked Olivia to marry him but stipulated a bizarre condition—they'd have to wait seventeen years.[7] That Hughes was engaged to Ginger Rogers never got in the way of his proposing to any girl who struck his fancy. He gave Ginger a five-carat square-cut emerald engagement ring, but she returned it to him, saying, "I have inadvertently found out you have been dividing your time between me and someone else."[8] In tears, he told Noah Dietrich, his right-hand man, "It's Ginger. She left me!"[9] Ginger knew she was right—she didn't want to be dominated, possessed, or made a prisoner in her own home. "That's what happened to [his wife] Jean Peters," Ginger would later write.[10]

His attraction as a lover was perseverance, according to Terry Moore, an Oscar-nominated actress for *Come Back, Little Sheba*, who showed up in my Delacorte Press office in the 1970s offering her memoir and told me, "I was secretly married to Howard Hughes." She'd met him when she was still in her teens and Hughes in his mid-thirties. "Let me take care of you," he begged. On their wedding night in 1949, "a series of explosions detonated inside me," she wrote.[11] "Each time I thought him spent, he wanted more."[12] In 1951 she married West Point football hero Glenn Davis but returned to Hughes after two months.[13] After Hughes's death in 1976, Moore was legally recognized as his widow and received a settlement not to exceed eight figures.

It's tempting to ponder why Hughes imposed such a strange—and, to Olivia, impossible—stipulation when he proposed to her. Was it so he could continue to see such other girlfriends as Katharine Hepburn, Loretta Young, Veronica Lake, Ingrid Bergman, Gloria Vanderbilt, and Constance Bennett, not to mention Cary Grant, Randolph Scott, and cinematographer/actor David Bacon?[14] Did he want to remain free to make future conquests until he was too old, seventeen years later, to cut the mustard? According to Evelyn Keyes, who knew Hughes, he "was famous for keeping several girls stashed away at the same time, calling each of them every so often, promising to come around to see them within the hour, calling again later that hour, saying he was delayed, but would be along, et cetera, et cetera."[15]

Kathryn Grayson, another paramour, called him "the loneliest man in the world."[16] When he tried that line on Ingrid Bergman, she said, "I'm having a good time; you're not lonely tonight, are you?"[17]

Sheilah Graham finally got fed up when Hughes proposed to Yvonne De Carlo, who confided to Sheilah, "He wants to wait awhile. He wants us to be sure."[18] When Sheilah scolded Hughes in print for leading so many girls down the primrose path, the great man himself summoned Sheilah to a meeting in his office on the Goldwyn lot. "We sat almost knee to knee and his mournful brown eyes bored penetratingly into mine."[19]

"Why don't you like me . . . Why are you attacking me all the time?"[20]

They made a deal. If she'd go easy on him, he'd feed her scoops. Keeping his promise, he let her be the first to know that Cary Grant and Betsy Drake had eloped, calling her from Arizona, where he'd been best man, and enabling her to beat the wire services by three or four hours.

"Honest [and] fair" was the way Olivia would remember Hughes in an interview with Peter Mikelbank of *People*. "I never ceased to admire him."[21] When *Evening Standard* reporter Hermoine Eyre asked her if their relationship was love or friendship, she replied, "Hmm—mixed."[22]

Working with Flynn again in *Dodge City* marked, in Olivia's estimation, the rock bottom of her career. "I was in such a depressed state that I could hardly remember the lines[23] . . . I wanted to do complex roles, more developed human beings, and Jack Warner [put me in] roles that really had no character or quality in them."[24] During one interview, she broke down and "just started to cry. I didn't know why, but I couldn't stop."[25] The reporter gave her a lift home, where she took to her bed for days, "simply crying. I went to bed and I wasn't going to get out of it."[26] With the help of a neurologist, she gradually recovered.[27]

Dodge City, viewed today, has aged like a good wine. Flynn turns in a performance of manly poise and steely conviction. He didn't use a stunt man when he was required, in one scene, to grab a would-be assassin and toss him headfirst through a barbershop window; he couldn't have done it better, more effortlessly or gracefully, if choreographed by Jerome Robbins or Michael Kidd. There is no swagger in his performance, just subtly conveyed courage and dignity. Compared with some of the undistinguished celluloid nonsense Warner had imposed on Olivia—*Wings of the Navy, Gold Is Where You Find It*, and *The Great Garrick*—*Dodge City* is solid entertainment.

Good-time-gal Ann Sheridan played the Western's mandatory barroom charmer, and as she sat under a hair dryer in the makeup department at Warner one day, Olivia came in, following a practice gallop on one of the film's many rented horses. Sheridan was being interviewed. "You wear things that cut in at the waist. And very low cut here," she told the journalist, indicating her ample bosom. "Lots of sex, honey. And diamond things here and here."

"Wouldn't you like to have my opinion of Miss Sheridan?" Olivia asked.

"Get out of here, Livia!"

"I just want to say that she's a lov-ely girl. I think she's swell!"

"You're a . . . liar!"

Sheridan whooped and made an ugly face in the mirror. After Olivia left, she said, "You know, that girl could do a perfectly marvelous job in a low-down part if they'd ever let her."

"I'm so tired of being called a 'sweet girl' I could scream," Olivia told an interviewer. "I've never had a chance to do the kind of parts I'd like.[28] . . . Too many people . . . associate 'sweet young ladies' with dumbness."[29]

Shortly before *Dodge City* wrapped, Olivia fell ill with bronchitis. A good trouper, she reported for work, but unit manager Frank Mattison told Hal Wallis "she is really sick . . . she has no color whatever."[30] While in this condition, she received an invitation to a New Year's Eve party on December 31, 1938, from Jimmy Stewart. Still coping with bronchitis, she had to decline. Howard Hughes, who'd also been invited to the party, wouldn't take no for answer when he called her at 10:30 p.m., and upon their arrival at the party, "Jimmy came up a little put out and took the other arm," she recalled. "We sat down at the bar and Errol Flynn started serving me drinks. I was 22, with three of the most attractive men in the world around me. I don't know how my reputation survived."[31] In another interview she added, "I danced for six hours and went home without a temperature."[32]

Later, when an interviewer asked her about Flynn, the reporter noted "the elated sparkle in her eyes," thought she saw Olivia blush, and assumed she and Flynn were romantically involved. Olivia quickly recovered her composure and tried to disabuse her interviewer of any such illusion. "Errol is a big, overgrown boy, who hasn't yet learned how to keep out of trouble," she said. "I have a great deal of admiration for the big, grinning Irishman and like his complete disregard for conventions . . . and believe me, I mean disregard."[33]

Still uncertain about the exact nature of their relationship, the reporter decided to interview Flynn. "Olivia has a complex nature," he said. In their four years together he'd tried to figure her out, but each time he thought he understood her, he would see another aspect of her character. "She is definitely shy in the company of men," he said, but when they'd begun filming *The Adventures of Robin Hood*, he "began hearing rumors of romance concerning her. I believed them until months later." They were doing some location work approximately 350 miles from Los Angeles, and Olivia was at last unchaperoned. She dashed Flynn's suspicions of romance when she was given a day's break and, instead of going on a date, went to the local park, located the playground, "slid down the shoots with kids, and ruined a perfectly good dress. What a girl!"[34]

Coping with a dead-end job at Warner, Olivia learned to ferret out better material instead of waiting for assignments. At the studio, scripts went first to the makeup department for Perc Westmore's perusal. Slipping into his office, she discovered *The Strawberry Blonde*, a screenplay slated for James Cagney that had a juicy role, Cagney's gutsy wife Amy Lind. The producer told her she wasn't right for the part, which called for a small-town girl. "I was brought up in Saratoga, California, a village!" she said, and got the role.[35] Such chutzpah paid off handsomely, the *New York Times* critic extolling her as "sweet and sympathetic as the girl [Cagney] marries . . . [in this] nostalgic delight."[36]

Cagney taught her an important lesson. "Jimmy, what is acting?" she asked.[37]

"I don't know. All I can tell you is whatever you say, mean it."[38] Later she reflected, "That was marvelous counsel. It is key. Wonderful."[39]

PART TWO

GONE WITH THE WIND

David O. Selznick

In 1938 Olivia finally met the man, producer David O. Selznick, who'd give her the opportunity to become a major dramatic star, tapping all the talent that had lain dormant during her Warner years. *Gone With the Wind*, often considered the best movie ever made, was based on the 1,037-page Pulitzer Prize–winning novel by Margaret Mitchell, who'd been discovered by a Macmillan assistant editor named Lois Dwight Cole, later my beloved mentor and boss at Putnam, where she was a senior editor. Over lunch at the Italian Pavilion in Manhattan, Lois told me that Peggy Marsh, as she referred to Mitchell, had introduced Lois to her future husband Allan Taylor, who, like Mitchell, was a local reporter. Mitchell had been working on a novel for ten years, from 1926 to 1936. "I loved the way Peggy talked and knew if she could write half as well we'd have a best seller," Lois said. In the spring of 1935, Lois and Harold Latham, fiction editor at Macmillan, read the manuscript, loved it, consulted Professor Charles Everitt of Columbia, and then signed it up.[1] Lois became Mitchell's confidante and protector, a role she relished and maintained throughout the author's life.

The title had originally been *Tomorrow Is Another Day*, but the author finally chose a phrase she found in Ernest Dawson's poem "'Non Sum Qualis Bonae Sub Regno Cynarae" (I Am Not as I Was Under the Reign of Good Cynara): "I am desolate and sick of an old passion . . . gone with the wind." The theme of the poem, and of Mitchell's novel and the movie based on it, is lost love and the pursuit of an old flame. The film's narrative titles mourning the loss of the Old South, "of knights and their ladies fair, of masters and slaves," were written by Selznick and scenarist Ben Hecht, and they seem absurdly naïve and sentimental today, as does the positive depiction of the Ku Klux Klan. In this respect, the movie has not aged well and is only saved by epic storytelling, heroic acting, and overpowering production values.

David O. Selznick acquired the movie rights through Kay Brown, his New York representative, who secured a copy of the book prior to publication. On June 30, 1936, it hit the stores and began to accrue an astounding world sales record of twenty million copies.

I came to know David Selznick in the 1960s as we discussed a possible book he could write for me at the Putnam subsidiary Coward-McCann. Though often maligned as a tyrant who interfered with the work of his artists, David was a genuine auteur, a term that would not come into common usage until the advent of the French New Wave in 1960. It denotes a filmmaker who involves himself in every detail of production to such an extent that each frame bears his indelible stamp. All one has to do is look at David's films, especially *David Copperfield, A Tale of Two Cities, Gone With the Wind, Since You Went Away,* and *Duel in the Sun,* to see the distinctive Selznick touch, just as *The Shining* and *Barry Lyndon* are unmistakably the work of Stanley Kubrick.

Olivia landed the role of Melanie Hamilton Wilkes in *GWTW* because David liked her in *Robin Hood,*[2] but Joan Fontaine claimed she told director George Cukor to give the role to Olivia.[3] David, however, was hopelessly in love with Joan, and though he didn't think much of her acting, he tested her throughout the fall of 1938 and the spring of 1939, looking for any chance to be with her. As someone who'd flopped at RKO, Joan was up against more successful actresses, including Olivia. "My agent advised me to forget it," she recalled.[4] Finally, David sent her to Cukor for a test, and when she flunked it for being too chic for plain Melanie, Joan said, "What about my sister?"

"Who's she?" Cukor asked.[5]

Having already rejected Jane Wyman, Marsha Hunt, Fay Wray, Gloria Stuart, Anne Shirley, Dorothy Jordan, Frances Fuller, and Jean Kent as potential Melanies, Cukor rang Olivia and asked her to come in for a test, warning her to keep it secret since her home studio could sue him for poaching.[6] David loved the test and told her the role was hers.[7] Now all that stood between her and a starring role in *GWTW* was Jack Warner.

"Olivia, you don't want to be in the picture at all," Warner said. "It's going to be the biggest bust in town."[8]

"I don't care if it *is* the biggest bust in town, I want to be in the picture. Can't you lend me?"[9]

"You'll go out there and you'll come back and you'll be difficult."[10]

Cukor continued testing other actresses, including Geraldine Fitzgerald, Priscilla Lane, Jane Bryan, Janet Gaynor, Ann Dvorak, Frances Dee, Elizabeth Allan, Julie Hayden, and Dorothy Jordan, but no one understood Melanie as well as Olivia did. "[Melanie] knew her man," she said. "She must have known that Scarlett had a big crush on Ashley. But she knew that Ashley, no matter how much Scarlett might tempt him, in the long run might get very close to the edge but he would not leap over the edge. And also he knew he had the perfect wife . . . She probably didn't take Scarlett's feelings too seriously."[11] David wanted her and told his general manager, Daniel T. O'Shea, "Warners have so far definitely refused to consider letting us have [Olivia] but I think they might be persuaded, especially if we offered [Paulette] Goddard in trade, since I understand Jack Warner thinks well of Goddard. This would mean giving a star-making role to a Warner player, but it looks as though we may be stuck, in which case we may want to break our necks to get de Havilland."[12]

Margaret Mitchell told David that Olivia was "made for the part,"[13] and Howard Hughes assured him there was "no other Melanie in the world."[14] Hughes also urged David's financial backer Jock Whitney to plump for Olivia.[15] When Warner remained intransigent, she girded herself for perhaps the boldest act of her life, devising a scheme that involved going behind her boss's back and risking her entire career, for a wrathful Jack Warner could have her banned from every studio in Hollywood. The clever Lili Damita had manipulated Warner's wife into using her power over her husband to get Flynn into *Captain Blood*.[16] Perhaps the same strategy would work again.

"I did something, age twenty-two, that really was not correct, but I did it," Olivia recalled.[17] She rang Mrs. Jack L. Warner, a former bit actress, a woman Olivia admired as a person, explained that she needed to meet with her, and invited her to tea at the Brown Derby. Mrs. Warner accepted the invitation, and arrangements were made. It was raining on the day they met, and over tea Olivia told her how extremely important it was to her to play Melanie Hamilton Wilkes in *GWTW*.

Ann Warner, described by Jean-Pierre Aumont as "a dark, oriental-looking beauty,"[18] was once married to Don Alvarado, a Valentino imitator. She made important friends in "Marlene's Sewing Circle," Dietrich's clique of such closeted lesbian and bisexual women as Claudette Colbert, Dolores del Rio, Lili Damita, and cross-dresser "Joe" Carstairs, the fastest female speedboat racer, who inherited a Standard Oil fortune and enraptured both Greta Garbo and Dietrich.[19] Jack Warner left his wife Irma Solomons for Ann in 1935 after years of looking for a stylish, witty woman who'd give him the class he sorely lacked. His vulgarity served him well in making Warner Brothers the number 1 purveyor of low-life gangster films, but it hadn't helped him socially. Ann possessed the wit and sangfroid to make him look good at Beverly Hills parties and official industry functions, or so he thought. His biographer David Thomson called him a "scumbag."

Over tea with Olivia, Ann sympathized with her plight, possibly out of gratitude to her for having delivered four years of box-office hits that helped finance such luxuries as her portrait by Salvador Dali. She said she understood Olivia and would help her get the part.[20]

Within hours David rang Olivia and said, "I think we have you."[21]

Olivia later recalled, "It was through her that Jack eventually agreed. It was Ann who did it."[22]

She sent Mitchell a telegram saying how honored she was to portray Melanie,[23] and Mitchell replied that she was delighted and that Olivia's victory "met with general approval." *Captain Blood*, she explained, was SRO at theatres all over Atlanta.[24]

Jack Warner agreed to lend Olivia to David from January 12, 1939, to May 4, 1939, and in return David gave him James Stewart for one film and Ingrid Bergman for *Casablanca*.[25] On January 17, Louella O. Parsons announced her approval, writing, "*GWTW* couldn't have a prettier Melanie," adding that the star was off to Washington, D.C. to help President and Mrs. Roosevelt celebrate his birthday.[26] Ed Sullivan wrote that Olivia exuded "a quality of young beauty and helplessness."[27]

For the part of Ashley Wilkes, Irene Selznick suggested Ray Milland, but David rarely agreed with his wife.[28] Melvyn Douglas, Vincent Price, Joel McRae, Franchot Tone, and Humphrey Bogart were also considered, but Margaret Mitchell told both David and Leslie Howard that her readers favored Howard.[29] David offered the actor the role, but he was forty-five and Ashley was in his twenties. "I hate that damn part," Howard said. "I'm not nearly beautiful or young enough for Ashley, and it makes me sick being fixed up to look attractive."[30] He complained that Ashley's Confederate uniform made him "look like a fairy doorman at the Beverly Wilshire—a fine thought at my age."[31] Money changed his mind when David offered him what would be $1.2 million in today's dollars.[32] Margaret Mitchell told Leslie Howard that the Southland heaved a "sigh of relief" when word got out that he would be *GWTW*'s Ashley Wilkes.[33]

Gary Cooper was offered Rhett, but Samuel Goldwyn had him under contract and refused a loan-out. Errol Flynn was next in line, but Warner would release him only if Bette Davis played Scarlett and David granted Warner distribution rights. The public was clamoring for Clark Gable, but he was MGM's hottest star and the studio refused to let him go. Only by giving Metro half of *GWTW*'s profits as well as releasing rights to Loew's, MGM's parent company, did David finally, on August 24, 1938, acquire Gable, who, although thirty-eight, fit the role of world-weary young Rhett like a glove. He was paid the equivalent of $1.8 million in today's dollars.[34]

Lillian Gish turned down the role of Ellen O'Hara, Scarlett's mother, and Cornelia Otis Skinner was up for the part when David decided on Barbara O'Neil, though she was only twenty-nine, and would be playing the mother of sixteen-year-old Scarlett.[35] Billie Burke, the Good Witch in *The Wizard of Oz*, was considered for Aunt Pittypat Hamilton but was deemed by David to be, at fifty-four, too young for the part, which then went to Laura Hope Crews, who, born in 1879, had been a leading stage actress in the early years of the twentieth century. In films like Garbo's *Camille*, Crews's harried voice and fluttery mannerisms made her an instant scene stealer.[36] Mitchell thought her "too cute to be true," and felt Crews would be a hoot to know.[37]

After David rejected Tallulah Bankhead as Scarlett, he offered her Belle Watling, the lovable brothel keeper, and when Bankhead ignored him, the offer went to Joan Blondell, Loretta Young, and Gladys Cooper. David wanted earthy, wisecracking Ann Sheridan, but she was under contract to Warner, where casting director Steve Trilling held out for star billing.[38] David finally cast an older actress, thirty-five-year-old Ona Munson, who'd excelled on Broadway, introducing "You're the Cream in My Coffee" in the Bert Lahr musical *Hold Everything*. Munson had bisexual affairs with Dorothy Arzner, the first woman film director, and playwright Mercedes de Acosta.[39] Apart from *GWTW*, Munson's only significant movie was *The Shanghai Gesture*. She committed suicide at fifty-one, leaving a note saying she was freeing herself but hoped no one would "follow me."[40]

For the role of Suellen O'Hara, David called Evelyn Keyes into his office and chased her around his mahogany desk "in a rather obligatory fashion," Keyes recalled.[41] For Scarlett's other sister Carreen, David had in mind Judy Garland, but she was still filming *The Wizard of Oz*.[42] Although L.B. Mayer didn't want his up-and-coming starlet Ann Rutherford to play Carreen, claiming "it's a nothing part," he relented when she started sobbing in his office.[43]

Eleanor Roosevelt's White House maid Elizabeth McDuffie, Louise Beavers of *Imitation of Life*, Etta McDaniel, Ruby Dandridge, and Hattie Noel were up for the role of Mammy before Hattie McDaniel, in full Mammy costume, visited David and beat out front runner Beavers.[44] Prissy, one of the most delightful parts in *GWTW*, went to Thelma "Butterfly" McQueen from Tampa, Florida, after a Selznick representative saw her in a play in Philadelphia.[45] In *GWTW* she'd effortlessly steal scenes, and David subsequently cast her as Lillian Gish's maid Vashti in his postwar epic *Duel in the Sun*, in which she was equally outrageous, funny, and compelling. She received two hundred dollars per week for *GWTW* ($3,500 by today's standards), which she used to pay for furniture. In 1949 she'd leave Hollywood, "tired of waiting for roles," she said, and open a snack shop in New York, also working as a taxi dispatcher.[46] Lionel Barrymore was to play Dr. Meade, but he was incapacitated from arthritis. Lewis Stone, Andy Hardy's father, tested for the role, which finally went to Harry Davenport. Thomas Mitchell was signed for Scarlett's father.

The key role of Scarlett, who appears in virtually every scene in the film, had still not been cast in December 1938. David dreaded the looming prospect of commencing principal photography without the principal player.[47] Mitchell sent Katharine Hepburn the manuscript prior to publication, but RKO warned the role was heartless.[48] David knew Hepburn well, having cast her in 1932's *A Bill of Divorcement* and used her again in 1933's *Little Women*, and though her agent Leland Hayward and lover Howard Hughes negotiated a deal, David doubted she had sufficient sex appeal for Scarlett.[49] Her late 1930s flops *Mary of Scotland, A Woman Rebels,* and *Bringing Up Baby* convinced distributors she was "Box Office Poison."[50] David said Hepburn gave him "a swift pain . . . The more I see her, the colder I get on her."[51] The deal fell through, according to Hughes, who told Dan O'Shea that Hepburn sensed David's lack of enthusiasm.[52]

Bette Davis in essence tested for the role by making an entire film, *Jezebel,* released in March 1938, with Davis cast as a Scarlett knockoff, a role that won her an Academy Award but did not get her into *GWTW*. "It could have been written for me," Davis said. "I was as perfect for Scarlett as Clark Gable was for Rhett . . . It was insanity that I was not given Scarlett."[53]

On December 10, 1938, *GWTW* began filming—*sans* Scarlett—with the burning of Atlanta on David's back lot in Culver City, known as Forty Acres. The *King Kong* set, erected earlier in the decade, was burned down as the Los Angeles Fire Department stood by. Suddenly, like a phoenix rising from the flames, Vivien Leigh arrived on the scene with David's brother, Myron Selznick, whom she'd persuaded to agent her as a way of getting to David. "I took one look," David recalled, "and knew she was right."[54] But David insisted Cukor test her, and she'd be considered among other such Scarlett finalists as Paulette Goddard, Jean Arthur, and Joan Bennett.[55] Cukor gave Leigh a scene to read, the one at Twelve Oaks when Scarlett slaps Ashley. Feeling self-conscious, Leigh began reading in a saccharine, clipped manner, and Cukor told her she sounded "like someone's got their finger up your ass."[56] Leigh screamed with laughter and then fell quiet and started shivering.

"What is it?" Cukor inquired.

"I love you!" she said, quoting from the scene they were about to read.

Cukor immediately sensed the tension and excitement in her stage presence, and responded with Ashley's line, "Isn't it enough that you've collected every other man's heart here today?"

She landed the role, and immediately wired Mitchell that if she could only feel the author's complete support she'd bring Scarlett to the same vibrant life the character possessed in the book.[57] In her reply, Mitchell frostily sent "sincere good wishes" and little else, pointing out that she had "nothing to do with the film," but at least she conceded Leigh was "charming."[58] Mitchell bitterly resented having been drawn into the long, much publicized quest for an actress to play Scarlett, and when David's publicity department made the mistake of announcing Mitchell approved of Leigh, the disgruntled author informed David she'd "neither approved nor disapproved," and unless he controlled his publicists she'd tell the press she'd been misrepresented.[59] Even after the movie was released, and rumors persisted she'd preferred Katharine Hepburn, Mitchell said, "Nobody was my choice."[60] After years of unrelenting hoopla over the book and the movie, she was burnt out on fame.

Olivia, Leigh, and Leslie Howard all signed their contracts in David's office on Friday the 13th, January, 1939.[61] Dressed in black and wearing a large-brimmed hat with a long cream silk scarf wrapped around the crown, Leigh signed a standard seven-year contract. Fearful that her extramarital affair with Laurence Olivier would ignite a scandal and damage *GWTW*, David slapped a press ban on her.

Some of the earliest footage involved Olivia and Leigh, and they were so powerful together that Gable feared they'd steal the movie from him. After *GWTW*'s opening scene—Scarlett and the Tarlton twins on the steps of Tara, which had been constructed on the back lot—Cukor guided Olivia and Leigh through the Atlanta hospital sequence and the childbirth crisis at Aunt Pittypat's. Melanie was shown in the throes of labor, and to prepare for the scene Olivia visited a maternity hospital. When the sequence was shot Cukor pinched her to induce pain.[62] He also directed the bloody Tara episode when Scarlett kills the Yankee and Melanie helps lug out the corpse. He then filmed Gable giving Scarlett a Paris bonnet, and finally Olivia, Leigh, and Gable at the Atlanta bazaar. In the latter scene as originally filmed, it was dominated by Scarlett and Melanie, with Rhett of secondary importance. "Melanie had an extraordinary speech, quite remarkable," Olivia recalled. "[Gable] may have thought . . . '[Cukor] may turn this into a woman's picture' . . . We went back and reshot the scene and that long speech of Melanie's was out."[63] Rhett dominates the scene in the final cut.

Olivia and Leigh emerged in the rushes as two of the best actresses of their generation. John Lichfield, who interviewed Olivia, wrote, "She and Vivien Leigh threatened to dominate the movie so much that Clark protested."[64]

George Cukor, F. Scott Fitzgerald, Victor Fleming

The onerous task of carving a shooting script out of the novel had fallen to Sidney Howard, who was paid $34,000 per week (adjusted for inflation).[1] The film would run 168 hours if he used every scene in the book, as readers were demanding. When Howard finished writing the screenplay, David insisted he reduce it to two and one-half or three hours, but Howard couldn't do it. His wife had just given birth to their baby, and he wanted to be with her. Unable to pare the gigantic document down to useable proportions, he returned to his farm in Massachusetts.[2]

"What the hell is Howard doing?" David asked Kay Brown.

"How would I know what Howard's doing?" she snapped. "I'm not sitting there."[3]

David hired F. Scott Fitzgerald to work on the script, stating in a memo that he was a Fitzgerald fan.[4] When Margaret Mitchell heard the news, she said if she'd dared even to dream F. Scott Fitzgerald would be adapting her book she'd have come down with "hardening of the arteries or something."[5] A flapper at heart, she venerated Fitzgerald's novel *This Side of Paradise* as the "crystallization" of the Jazz Age, and she remembered giving Fitzgerald a ride into town in 1918 when he was a lieutenant in the 45th Infantry at Camp Gordon outside Atlanta.[6]

Bringing his talent as arguably America's best writer to bear on *GWTW*, Fitzgerald felt the easiest way to cut the movie's unwieldy length would be to remove much of the dialogue, and explained, "It's dull and false for one character to describe another."[7] It was Fitzgerald who wrote Ashley's memorable line, "Some of our men are barefooted now, and the snow is deep in Virginia."[8] The novelist considered images and expressions on actors' faces far more cinematically effective than dialogue and explained to David that the scene in which Scarlett watches newlyweds Melanie and Ashley retire to their bedroom was too wordy. "It seems to me stronger in silence," he said.[9]

It's not true, as often claimed, that Fitzgerald looked down on *GWTW*. After studying the book more closely, he said Mitchell's dialogue was sharper than any scenarist could make it and should be left intact wherever possible. "I felt no contempt for it, but only a certain pity for those who consider it the supreme achievement of the human mind," he said.[10]

With or without a finished script, shooting had to continue on schedule, and in desperation Cukor and his cast began to improvise. David testily reminded George that the director was contractually bound to adhere to all script changes approved by the producer before shooting. There were reports, unsubstantiated, that David felt George was throwing *GWTW* to Scarlett.[11] During a script conference with Fitzgerald, David warned the novelist that Scarlett would upstage Rhett unless Fitzgerald kept Cukor from favoring Leigh in every shot. "You and I have got to watch out for Clark," David said.[12] Cukor begged for reinstatement of the original Howard screenplay.[13]

At this impasse Louis B. Mayer offered to loan out a director who was a good friend of Gable's, Victor Fleming, even though Fleming was still shooting *The Wizard of Oz* at Metro. According to Daniel Selznick, David and Irene's son, Fleming summarily informed David, "You haven't got a fucking script," and he strongly advised him to do exactly what Cukor had recommended—go back to the original Howard version, except that he still needed to find a script doctor who could cut it down to manageable length.[14]

According to Gavin Lambert, who spoke with Lee Garmes and Ray Klune, *GWTW*'s cinematographer and production manager, respectively, Gable's unhappiness with George Cukor, who had an undeserved reputation as exclusively "a women's director," made Gable increasingly tense and nervous.[15] He reportedly referred to George as "that fag."[16] George's biographer Patrick McGilligan offered what he called "a precise contemporary account" of the clash between the actor and his director. When Gable was younger, he'd had drunken sex with director William Haines,[17] and he was furious when he heard that actor Anderson Lawler quipped at a Hollywood party, "George is directing one of Billy's old tricks."[18] Gable threatened to beat Haines up the next time they met, and on the *GWTW* set, after a strained moment with George, Gable said, "I can't do this . . . I can't do this scene."[19]

"What's the matter with you today," someone had the nerve to inquire, and Gable lashed out, saying, "I can't go on with this picture! I won't be directed by a fairy! I have to work with a *real man!*"[20]

Scott Fitzgerald had been unable, or unwilling, to switch the focus of the film from Leigh and Olivia to Gable, and he was fired after three weeks at $1,250 per week (adjusted for inflation: $21,500 weekly for a grand total of $64,000),[21] reportedly for failing to supply enough laughs for Aunt Pittypat.[22] Fitzgerald relapsed into alcoholism, and on the day he died in 1940, only months following the release of *GWTW*, he was with Sheilah Graham in her Hollywood apartment. A quarter of a century later, I worked with Sheilah as her editor at Coward-McCann for *The Rest of the Story*, her 1964 memoir about the aftermath of her love affair with Fitzgerald. "It was about three in the afternoon," she recalled.

"We were in the living room . . . He was eating a chocolate bar; he always craved candy when he was on the wagon, and he was jotting down football plays in the *Princeton Alumni Weekly*. And then something pulled him up from the green armchair, he clutched the mantelpiece and fell to the floor and died."[23] It had been just eighteen months since his firing from *GWTW*. He was forty-four.

The relationship between Cukor and Gable deteriorated to the point that the director walked off the set, and the actor didn't show up for work the following day.[24] Gable's biographer Charles Samuels spoke with a friend of Gable's who said the actor told him, "I don't want Cukor. I'm going to have him changed."[25] The decisive moment occurred when Cukor defied David during an altercation over the scene in which Ashley descends the stairs to meet Scarlett. "I don't think Ashley, at that moment, would be scared to meet her," David said. "I disagree wholeheartedly," George replied, and threatened to quit.[26] "O.K get out!" David said.[27]

Cukor was already scheduled to dine with the Selznicks, and "it was awful," Irene recalled. "David and I sat upstairs waiting in loud silence. When I heard the bell, then a voice in the downstairs hall, I flew down to greet him . . . As George came around the bend halfway up the staircase, he guessed from the look on my face . . . that the verdict was in. I ran down and flung myself on him, weeping."[28]

Having known David, George, Irene, Sheilah Graham, and Irene's sister Edie Goetz, I believe one of the reasons David canned George was because George took Irene's side when the Selznick marriage began to unravel due to David's promiscuity. George loved both David and Irene, but he loved nothing more than being Irene's confidante and swapping gossip with her, a dangerous game when you work for the husband. She could probably have saved George's job, but it is likely that she was well aware of David's disdain for her opinions.

"My God, imagine picking up a project like that at this stage," Victor Fleming said on the set of his current picture, *The Wizard of Oz*, upon hearing he was being reassigned by Metro to *GWTW*. It was February 13, 1939, and *GWTW* had been in production three weeks.[29] "George would have done just as good a job as I. He'd probably have done a lot better on the intimate scenes . . . It's bullshit that he's just a woman's director. He's not. He can direct anybody."[30]

When Olivia and Leigh heard that George was no longer on the picture, they confronted David. "In our garb of deep mourning, Vivien and I stormed his office," Olivia recalled. "For three solid hours, we beseeched him not to let George go."[31] Risking everything, Leigh said she'd drop out of the picture unless he reinstated George. Calling her bluff, David threatened she'd never work in Hollywood again.[32] He later said both actresses were "sore" enough to appeal to his brother Myron, inquiring "if Fleming [was] a good man." Myron sarcastically replied, "David's going all over town looking for a bad director."[33] Later Leigh consulted Laurence Olivier, who warned her of inevitable litigation should she violate her contract.

"Leigh hated Fleming," David told the *New York Times*. She dismissed the director as "a mere workaday hack."[34] When Leigh asked Fleming for more explicit direction, he replied, "Ham it up! Ham it, baby, just ham it!"[35] Marcella Rabin, who'd been in charge of organizing Selznick International Pictures (SIP) in 1935, called Fleming "a bastard . . . obnoxious . . . a very, very strong macho man,"[36] but Charles Samuels, who quizzed David about Fleming, wrote that David said, "I don't think he was sadistic. He was another of that extremely masculine breed. The most attractive man, in my opinion, who ever came to Hollywood. Physically and in personality. He had a kind of Indian quality. American Indian, that is. Women were crazy about him, and understandably so."[37] Gable molded his screen persona on Fleming, according to director Henry Hathaway, a protégé of Fleming's, who said, "Clark Gable on the screen is Fleming.

He dressed like him, talked like him, stood like him, his attitude was the same toward women . . . Every man who worked for him patterned himself after him. Clark Gable, Spencer Tracy, all of them . . . forceful and masculine."[38]

Born in 1889, the son of migrant Missourians who'd come to California during the land boom and found work in the citrus fields around Los Angeles, Fleming lost his father when he was four, and a kindly uncle took him in, which explains why, as he admitted, he expressed little sentiment and betrayed no softness. After quitting school in the seventh grade, when he was fourteen, and working as an auto mechanic and taxi driver, he begged Paramount for a job, saying he'd work for no salary, and gradually progressed from repairing cameras to being a director of Douglas Fairbanks's silent action films.

Fleming's trademark flair for stories of epic sweep and power, mightily displayed in *GWTW*, had its origin in his work with the pioneering film genius D.W. Griffith, for whom Fleming served as one of *Intolerance*'s many assistant directors, managing thousands of extras in massive battle scenes, mingling with them, in full costume, while another assistant director, positioned above the action on a high parapet, shouted Griffith's instructions through a bullhorn. As Fleming matured he acquired other gifts essential to a director, whose job it is to supply emotional and intellectual meaning while actors lend their looks and charisma. One of the players in 1938's *The Crowd Roars*, Gene Reynolds, later a TV director, recalled that Fleming taught him how to react when the character he was playing learns of his mother's death. "The emotion in [Fleming's] voice made me get it," Reynolds said. "His emotion overtook me, so I did it and he got it in one or two takes."[39]

Standing at six feet, two-and-a-half inches, and sporting a tough-guy broken nose, Fleming was invariably the handsomest and sexiest man on his sets at Metro-Goldwyn-Mayer, recalled publicist Emily Torchia.[40] All this was completely lost on Leigh, but not on Olivia, who recalled, "Vic was attractive because he was intelligent, talented, handsomely built, and virile in a nonaggressive way. He was also sensitive. A potent combination."[41] Henry Hathaway claimed that "every dame he ever worked with fell on her ass for him. Norma Shearer. Clara Bow. Ingrid Bergman."[42]

While Leigh would remain oblivious to Fleming's influence on a conscious level, the anger he ignited in her provided the edge and venom the role of Scarlett calls for. He brought out Leigh's fighting spirit, which is largely responsible for the film's feeling of valor and grandeur, while Olivia supplied nobility and emotional wallop. Leigh resorted to asking George Cukor for direction on weekends at his house, where she ran into Olivia, who'd come there for the same purpose. "[Olivia] felt really guilty about going behind Vivien's back," Cukor said, "until she found out that Vivien was doing exactly the same thing, too."[43]

Olivia would prove to be as open as Leigh was closed to Fleming's nonverbal but highly effective direction, which was done not with words but by osmosis. Some actors got it and others didn't, depending on their intuitive acuity. At first Olivia was apprehensive. "My fear was that with a change of directors, I would lose my grasp of Melanie's character."[44] Out on a date with Howard Hughes the day Cukor was fired, Olivia was reassured when Hughes said, "With George and Victor, it's the same talent, only Victor's is strained through a coarser sieve."[45] She later reflected, "It was the most extraordinary thing. You would never think that a man like that would have quite that degree of sensitivity and insight, but . . . he gave me one of the nicest gifts that any human being has ever given me by the reassurance that he offered that night . . . Therefore I was able to start work with Victor Fleming with a positive and receptive viewpoint."[46]

There was something primal in Olivia's affinity with Fleming. "It's almost sexual, really, between the woman and the director," she said. "It's the most intimate kind of collaboration. It's exquisite and it's sexual without being physiological, and it's a unique experience."[47] He helped her make Melanie's sincerity convincing. At the Twelve Oaks barbecue, it seemed unbelievable that Melanie could remain polite in the face of Scarlett's acerbic condescension until, as Olivia later explained, "Victor . . . drew me aside and said just this: 'Whatever Melanie says, she means.' Thus he gave me not only the key to playing the scene but also the key to Melanie's whole character."[48]

As her relationship with Fleming developed, she related to his dark side. "He gravely told me . . . he had driven to the top of a cliff and contemplated leaping from its edge . . . He was a deeply suffering man . . . [and] may have sensed a kinship of some sort."[49] They were indeed kindred souls, and their synergy produced one of *GWTW*'s most moving scenes. Sunny Alexander, an employee of Myron Selznick's, who'd been engaged to live with Leigh as her secretary/companion at 520 North Camden Drive, said that Melanie's death in Atlanta "was so real and everybody so emotional and so tired from working so hard that when [Fleming] said 'Cut,' everyone on that set was crying—the crew, the electricians, the third and fourth assistant—everybody was weeping as if we'd been to a memorial service or something. That's how real it all seemed. Vic knew he had a good shot when he saw tears in everybody's eyes—including his own."[50]

Sidney Howard agreed at David's urging to return to the studio for two weeks to review the rough cut, but he found it "dull and cold . . . Gable simply terrible as Rhett, awkward, hick, unconvincing. Melanie virtually cut out of the picture along with any scenes of heart interest . . . Fleming takes four shots of something a day to keep him going and another shot or so to fix him so he can sleep after the day's stimulation. Selznick is bent double with permanent, and, I should think, chronic indigestion. Half the staff look, talk, and behave as though they were on the verge of breakdowns."[51]

Relieved to have *GWTW* behind him, Howard retreated to his farm in Tyringham, Massachusetts, where he found peace working his 700 acres and driving his 2.5-ton tractor. One day he went into the garage to crank the tractor, but someone had left it in gear, and it pinned him against the garage wall and crushed him to death. He was only forty-eight. *New York Times* drama critic Brooks Atkinson wrote, "His death was a Broadway calamity. [The theatre lost] one of its most admirable people . . . in the midst of an active career and full of ideas for more plays."[52]

David turned to his old friend Ben Hecht, on whom he'd often depended to bail him out of impossible script predicaments, using him on the Janet Gaynor version of *A Star Is Born* and on *Viva Villa!* Hecht would later patch together *Spellbound, Duel in the Sun, The Paradine Case,* and David's television special *Light's Diamond Jubilee.*

"Other screenwriters aspired to be Ben," Irene said. "He tore through things, and he tore through life."[53] Though a serious writer whose autobiography *A Child of the Century* was praised by Saul Bellow as "independent, forthright, and original,"[54] Hecht understood the movie business better perhaps than any other writer. He'd been involved in the new art of motion pictures from its inception in the silent era, when "movies were seldom written," he recalled. "They were yelled into existence in conferences that kept going in saloons, brothels, and all-night poker games. Movie sets roared with arguments and organ music."[55]

Though uncredited, Hecht played a crucial role in getting *GWTW* in the can. He was paid $15,000 (today's equivalent to $257,000) for his first week, during which he knocked out the first half of the screenplay. Hecht said he worked two weeks at $10,000 per week for a total of $20,000 ($343,000).[56] Whatever the cost, Hecht was worth it, as the trim and burnished shooting script of *GWTW* amply demonstrates.

The atmosphere on the *GWTW* set did not improve when Fleming finally cracked up under pressure and told Vivien Leigh, "You can stick this script up your royal British ass."[57] He left the picture on doctor's orders on February 17, 1939, and withdrew to his Balboa beach house, where he was confined to his bedroom for two weeks, and no one was allowed in except his doctor and Slocum, his butler. When he was well enough to see visitors, David, Leigh, and Gable drove out to visit, and David tried to give him a share of *GWTW*'s profits. "What do you take me for, a chump?" Fleming growled, losing a fortune.[58]

Sam Wood took over the direction, and though he helmed such classics as *Goodbye, Mr. Chips, Kings Row,* and *For Whom the Bell Tolls,* he was at a loss to explain how Ashley, the most nonviolent of men, participates in a killing during a Ku Klux Klan raid of a squatters camp following an African-American's assault on Scarlett. Since Olivia dominates the scene, she appealed to George Cukor for help, "going to see George at his house on a Sunday afternoon, to ask him his views about this scene and how he thought Melanie would react to it." When the scene was shot, Olivia played it brilliantly, focusing solely on Melanie's determination to save her husband's life when federal soldiers come to arrest him.

Both Olivia and Leigh were deeply involved in romantic relationships. Howard Hughes was continuing to court Olivia, and Leigh's romance with Olivier was as frenetic as it was obsessive. "We fucked and we fucked and we fucked the whole weekend," she said.[59] Years later, when Olivia was asked if she and Leigh had become friends, she replied, "Well, as much as you can when you're working very hard."[60] Leigh and the future Lord Olivier both looked down their noses at Hollywood and the movies in general; their mutual dream was to become the first couple of the legitimate theatre, specializing in Shakespearean roles. Despite their arch attitude, they never failed to take Hollywood's money, which they needed to support their aristocratic way of life, including the purchase and restoration of the gothic Notley Abby in Buckinghamshire.

Though Gable and Leigh were projecting plenty of on-screen chemistry in the rushes, Leigh privately complained about his dentures and their awful smell.[61] She customarily lunched alone in the bungalow in which she and Gable had separate quarters on the lot, while he ate with the gang in the studio café. On the set she sat behind the cinematographer with Leslie Howard or Olivia. Reporter Paul Harrison noticed that Olivia was "Scarlett's most articulate and enthusiastic champion."[62] In conversation with her colleagues on the set, Leigh related no anecdotes and told no jokes, though she roared at those told by others. She evinced a youthful curiosity in everything but stood up rather inhospitably to check out everyone who entered the set. In lighter moments, she'd play catch with fruit and show off by juggling three oranges.[63]

In time Leigh and Gable drew closer, huddling together between scenes and playing a board game called Battleship. "Occasionally they would invite me to join them," Olivia said. When the assistant director called, "Ten minutes," Olivia would repair to her dressing room, where she'd look at herself in the mirror in her nineteenth-century costume to get back into character. Leigh was different. According to Olivia, the minute the assistant director alerted Leigh, she'd stop playing Battleship with Gable, go instantly before the camera, and knock the scene out of the ball park.[64]

Leslie Howard seemed distracted and aloof during the one time Olivia was with him off the *GWTW* set. Well-known as a ladies' man who'd romanced Tallulah Bankhead, Merle Oberon, Norma Shearer, and Myrna Loy, he was living with his beautiful secretary Violette Cunningham when his matronly wife Ruth arrived from England with their daughter during *GWTW* filming, creating a tense situation for everyone. Later, in September 1939, when World War II broke out in Europe, Howard became a British Intelligence operative, and in 1943 was dispatched by Prime Minister Winston Churchill to carry a message to Spanish dictator Francisco Franco, urging him not to join Axis powers. According to Howard's Spanish mistress, Conchita Montenegro, Germans discovered the mission and ordered Howard's assassination. Others theorized that since the Enigma Code, Germany's means of encrypting secret messages, had been cracked by British mathematician Alan Turing, both Churchill and Howard were aware the Germans would attempt to gun down Howard's plane when he flew back to England, but let the flight go ahead as scheduled so the Germans wouldn't learn the Enigma Code had been compromised.

Carrying Howard to Bristol, U.K., from Lisbon, Portugal, KLM Royal Dutch Airline/BOAC Flight 777 was attacked by Luftwaffe Junkers and crashed in the Bay of Biscay, killing all seventeen on board. Howard's son Ronald believed his father had been murdered because Germans considered him to be a dangerous purveyor of British propaganda. According to another theory, Germans believed Churchill was aboard the flight. In his autobiography Churchill wrote that a mistake about his whereabouts may have cost Howard his life. Former CIA agent Joseph B. Smith recalled in a 1957 meeting with the National Security Agency that Howard himself was aware that he was to be sacrificed to keep the Enigma Code secret. In any case, as Olivia put it, "He died a hero's death."[65] In his will Howard left his Beverly Hills home to Violette Cunningham, but she never moved in, dying of cerebral meningitis in 1942.[66]

Reminiscing about the making of *GWTW*, Butterfly McQueen said, "Olivia made us laugh and laugh. There she'd be lying in her bed in labor, screaming 'Scarlett! Scarlett!' and as soon as the scene was over, she'd jump up and start telling us all jokes."[67] McQueen complained some of her lines were cut; in the scene at Tara when she says, "We don't need no cows, Miss Scarlett. I'se scared of cows," she was originally supposed to add, "Cows ain't no good iffen they're not milked. Their bags swells up and busts."[68] When a young Malcolm X saw *GWTW* in Macon, Georgia, he was the sole African-American in the audience, and he later wrote in his autobiography, "When Butterfly McQueen went into her act, I felt like crawling under the rug."[69]

Victor Fleming returned to the set on March 2, 1939, and resumed his duties as director. When he filmed Yakima Canutt on the bridge in the woods outside Atlanta where he saves Scarlett from a rapist, Canutt found Fleming to be irritable and erratic. "[He] seemed to have aged years," Canutt said.[70] Nonetheless Fleming proceeded to direct some of *GWTW*'s best scenes, beginning with the stark sequence in the wrecked garden of Tara on the first night of Scarlett's return from Atlanta, ravaged by hunger and digging up a radish. Olivia came to Leigh's aid when she refused to make Scarlett's vomiting noises, which Leigh thought unlady-like, but Olivia promised to loop the retching sounds. Fleming worked all night, putting Leigh through five takes as they filmed in Lasky Mesa, not far from Agoura. They couldn't finish until the first rays of sun appeared, signaling a new day for the shattered South. The scene became one of the film's signature moments, with Scarlett raising her fist as dawn breaks over Tara in another of *GWTW*'s incomparable crane pullback shots, accompanied by Max Steiner's swelling Tara theme.[71]

Olivia worked for 59 days for $388,000, calculated in today's dollars; Leslie Howard worked 32 days for $1.2 million; Leigh, 125 days for $472,000; Gable, 71 days for $1.8 million; and Hattie McDaniel, $99,000.[72] McDaniel didn't mind impersonating a stereotypical black because, she said, "It was better to earn $1,250 a week playing the part of a maid than $12.50 being a maid."[73] Evelyn Keyes didn't remember how many days she worked as Suellen, but there was one she'd never forget, later explaining, "[Vivien Leigh] whacked me, Suellen, because I complained. And she didn't pull her punches. My cheek wore the imprint of Vivien's fingers for the rest of the afternoon."[74] Apparently Leigh also slapped McQueen too hard during Olivia's birthing scene, and McQueen yelled, "I can't do it! She's hurting me!"[75]

"All of Hollywood was convinced that *Gone With the Wind* would be a colossal disaster and rather hoped it would be," Olivia recalled. "But not me. I believed in it. I knew that it would be a very successful movie because it had a real story to tell about real people."[76] At the conclusion of her work, the aspect of her performance of which she was proudest was the scene in which she comforts Gable as he weeps after Scarlett's miscarriage. "He was embarrassed . . . at the naked suffering of Rhett Butler," she said. "Embarrassed as a man, as an actor, and as Clark Gable. Victor tried to reassure him, and I shyly tried to do the same."[77]

"Olivia, I can't do it," Gable said. "I'm just going to have to quit."[78] When Olivia told him tears signify strength of character instead of weakness, "the tears came, and the humble grief and remorse and despair."[79] According to Rand Brooks, who played Scarlett's first husband, Fleming "got Gable drunk to get that crying scene. He would call him every name in the book, say you can't act worth shit, every name under the sun, go in and do it right or I'll go off and leave you."[80] After the ordeal was over, "Gable crept to his bungalow via the back porch of the sound stage," reporter Gladys Hall wrote, "slithering across the yard as though afraid that someone would see him, would speak to him. He wasn't himself for the rest of the day."[81]

When the movie finally wrapped on June 27, 1939, Olivia, David, Fleming, Leigh, Gable, and Leslie Howard hosted a wrap party on stage 5. The only way David had gotten through it was with seventy-two-hour Benzedrine-fueled work binges. The party invitation listed him as Jonas Wilkerson, Tara's evil overseer, and Fleming as the benign slave Big Sam. Leigh gave Fleming a pair of budgerigars, small green-and-yellow talking parakeets. He thanked her with a lingering, evidently passionate kiss.[82] Irene Selznick was burned out. "It was like being under siege," she said. "[David's] burden was formidable. He had to lay it off on someone."[83] According to David Thomson, "David's feeling for Joan Fontaine lingered—for *Rebecca* was its consummation—and amid all the upheaval, David had had twenty minutes to spare in Vivien Leigh's bungalow if Sunny Alexander had been willing."[84]

Evelyn Keyes, who'd already finished filming her bit part in Cecil B. DeMille's *Union Pacific* and flown to Omaha, Nebraska, for the premiere, received a wire from Selznick ordering her to return at once for an added scene, and in early November he summoned her again, this time to shoot the segment in which she says, "Scarlett's had three husbands, and I'm going . . . to . . . be . . . an old maid!"[85]

Scheduling conflicts developed for Olivia when *GWTW* went into over-time, and Warner insisted she start *The Private Lives of Elizabeth and Essex*, starring Errol Flynn and Bette Davis. Olivia wrote Jack Warner that she wanted to do a good job on both pictures, but found it impossible to por-tray "two decided and different characters at the same time."[86] Warner should not have cast her in *Essex* in the first place, because she was a star and the role of Lady Penelope Gray was a supporting part with under-the-title billing, a minor role that could easily have been filled by one of War-ner's young supporting players, such as Margaret Lindsay or Anita Louise, or freelance actresses Virginia Bruce, Gail Patrick, Gale Sondergaard, or Margot Grahame, all of whom were considered, but Warner seemed determined to demote Olivia to supporting status to keep her from getting a swelled head—and asking for a raise—after starring in *GWTW*.[87]

Hal Wallis warned it wouldn't look good in the industry for Warner to consign a proven star to an inferior role, but Warner remained ada-mant and insisted she start learning her lines for *Essex*. On May 5, 1939, she reported to the studio, and it was "torture for me," she said, "leaving this wonderful atmosphere at Selznick for a very different atmosphere at Warner Brothers."[88] According to Ed Sikov's biography of Bette Davis, Olivia "threw a fit on the set."[89] Olivia admitted, "I lost my cool, which was not like me, and which is unforgivable."[90]

The trouble had started when Olivia and Nanette Fabray were still rehearsing a scene at 5:15 p.m., and Olivia said she had to leave at 6:00.

Director Michael Curtiz threatened her, saying if she left he'd drop the scene—which had been inserted at Olivia's request—from the picture. The star and director exchanged strong words in front of the company, according to unit manager Frank Mattison, who shut down the set at 6:15 and later informed studio production manager T.C. Wright, "I had [a] . . . display of temperament late SATURDAY afternoon [June 10, 1939] from Miss DeHAVILLAND."[91]

Mattison advised the production manager to take Curtiz's side in the dispute, cut the scene out, and "this will put Miss DeHAVILLAND in a proper frame of mind so that she will take direction and instruction thereafter."[92]

Olivia gave her version of the fracas to Jack Warner, explaining she'd arrived at the studio at 6:45 a.m. and worked until 5:30 p.m. Around 6:00, tired and disheveled, she said the scene could be shot another day, but Curtiz tried to rush her, uttering such a tactless remark that she found herself shaking and on the verge of tears. Curtiz apologized and told everybody to go home, exactly as he'd done after reducing Davis to tears a few days before.[93]

In the aftermath of the on-set fireworks, Olivia was given the silent treatment at Warner. "I would come out and nobody would say good morning to me, nobody said good evening, nobody said anything beyond what they had to say . . . I thought, 'Well, I'm going to survive this.'"[94] Davis and Flynn were also at each other's throats. While Davis experienced no difficulty in handling playwright Maxwell Anderson's blank verse, Flynn found it impossible. "I can't remember lines like that," he complained.[95] Screenwriters Aeneas MacKenzie and Norman Reilly Raine rewrote his dialogue in prose. Davis called Flynn unprofessional, but nothing could have prepared him for what happened when the script called for her to slap his face. Ordinarily actors fake it, but Davis turned her slap into a felony. "My jaw went out," Flynn recalled. "I felt a click behind my ear and I saw all these comets, shooting stars, all in one flash.

She had given me that little dainty hand, laden with about a pound of costume jewelry, right across the ear. I felt as if I were deaf."[96]

"All right, boys and girls, we do it again," Curtiz said, calling for another rehearsal.[97] Flynn tried to reason with Davis but she said, "If I have to pull punches, I can't do this. That's the kind of actress I am—and I stress actress! Let's drop the subject."[98]

After he went to his dressing room and threw up, his anger mounted to the bursting point and he sought her out again, hinting he'd clobber her if she assaulted him. On the next take she delivered a perfect fake slap, not even touching his face. Later Curtiz instructed him to do something funny and outrageous to Davis during Elizabeth and Essex's reconciliation scene, and he walloped the actress "on her Academy Award behind. She went about two feet off the ground. She looked up at me livid with fury, and I said . . . 'I don't know how to do it any other way.'"[99] She never spoke to him again. Decades later, Olivia and Davis decided to watch *Elizabeth and Essex* together. Admitting she'd been unduly harsh on Flynn, Davis said, "Damn, he's good! I was wrong about him."[100]

Olivia at last finished *Essex* and spent much of July and August 1939 handling callbacks for *GWTW* retakes and going out with Howard Hughes. *Essex* arrived in the theatres to critical acclaim. Though Flynn had got the better of Davis in their off-screen fights, she wasted him in the reviews, garnering the critics' kudos while he got their sneers. "Bette Davis's Elizabeth is a strong, resolute, glamour-skimping characterization against which Mr. Flynn's Essex has about as much chance as a bean shooter against a tank," the reviewer for the *New York Times* wrote. Despite big-name stars and the lavish Technicolor production, *Elizabeth and Essex* was not a bona-fide hit.[101]

Nanette Fabray complained in 1962 that the studio fired her after *Elizabeth and Essex.* "Bette told me I was fired because I got better notices than de Havilland," she said.[102] Neither actress was mentioned in the *New*

York Times review on December 2, 1939, after the film opened at the Strand.[103]

———

Joan decided to marry Brian Aherne, somehow having convinced herself that he "had never asked [Olivia] for a date. . . . Despite later reports of columnists, there was no particular attraction between Olivia and Brian," Joan wrote. At the same time, Joan started flirting with Howard Hughes, Olivia's boyfriend. Lilian gave a tea party and Hughes was there "to pass inspection before being allowed to take out my older sister," Joan wrote.[104] Though uninvited, Joan decided to crash the party, and Hughes was immediately attracted to her.

Not long afterward, Olivia told Joan a surprise party was being given in Joan's honor at the Trocadero, an upscale nightclub on the Sunset Strip frequented by Fred Astaire, Judy Garland, Cary Grant, and Lucille Ball. "Olivia said I was to come unescorted," Joan recalled.[105] Arriving at the Troc, she was surprised to see Hughes among the guests, consented when he asked her to dance, and was shocked when he informed her she was going to marry him. Fully aware that Olivia's "feelings for him were intense, that the relative tranquility at [home] rested upon the frequency of his telephone calls," Joan did not hesitate to take the note with his telephone number that he slipped to her as she and Olivia exited the club, nor did she turn a deaf ear when he whispered she was to call him immediately.[106]

Though Joan later claimed she thought, "No one two-timed my sister, whatever our domestic quarrels might be," she went behind Olivia's back and called Hughes early the following day and made a date to meet him at a Polynesian restaurant in Hollywood, where he repeated his marriage proposal. According to Joan, she ignored his proposal, but continued dating him. She never fell in love with him, explaining, "I was afraid of him . . . He had no humor, no gaiety, no sense of joy, no vivacity . . . Everything seemed to be a 'deal,' a business arrangement, regardless of the picture he had tried to paint of our future together."[107]

Her account of the Hughes debacle stretches credibility to the breaking point. One of her future husbands, movie executive William Dozier, said, "Joan has always tried to give the impression that Hughes chased her, but this is completely wrong. Joan was in competition with Olivia once again. She remembered how his affair with Olivia had worked out and now she wanted him to marry her and give her all his millions. I never saw anything like the determination with which she chased her objective."[108]

On the eve of Joan's marriage to Brian Aherne, the wary bridegroom got cold feet, but Joan insisted they go through with the ceremony for appearances' sake. Olivia accompanied Joan and Aherne to St. John's Chapel in Del Monte, California, on August 19, 1939, for their wedding, at which Olivia was her sister's attendant.[109] On Joan's forlorn nuptial night, Aherne turned a cold shoulder, and Joan sat by the window till morning, consoled only by the thought she'd at least beat Olivia to the altar.

"Joan at once began ribbing Olivia about her spinsterhood," reporter Lucie Neville wrote."[110] One day, referring to a Bette Davis movie, Lilian asked Joan, "Have you seen *The Old Maid*?" and Joan replied, "No, not for several days. How is Olivia?"[111] Joan occupied herself with making over Aherne's bachelor's quarters without his encouragement, and in December 1940, she planned their spring garden down to the last tomato and salmon-colored rose. She wouldn't be caught dead in his living room, she informed him, and engaged expensive decorators to redo it in a week so she could throw a party. Aherne longed to be a bachelor again and restore his furnishings to his own taste.

Though Joan loved being humored by her patient husband when she came home irritable from sitting around on movie sets waiting for a take, she soon tired of Aherne. He enjoyed reminiscing about Sir George Arthur, a friend of Queen Mary's. Arthur had introduced him to H.G.

Wells, General Haig, Marshal Foch, Churchill, and Arnold Bennett, but Joan said testily, "I don't want to hear any more about your dear old friend Sir George Arthur!"[112] The marriage was doomed. "Not even lovers, we were scarcely friends," she wrote. "I got tired of seeing that 'please do not disturb' sign on his door."[113] In his memoir *A Proper Job*, Aherne wrote, "[With] the strain of coping with the problems of my young wife, now rocketed into orbit as a movie star, I longed for peace and quiet. I found it on my desert ranch."[114] One day Joan drove out to the ranch and asked him how long they'd been married. "Nearly four years," he answered. "What?" she cried. "My God! I never meant to stay married to you that long!" Striding off, she stole his new pale green convertible Buick and left him her old Packard. "Two days later," he recalled, "I read in Louella Parsons's column that she had decided to divorce me. She would keep the Beverly Hills house, she said, and I would keep the ranch."[115]

The Atlanta and New York Premieres of
Gone With the Wind

A dvance word on *GWTW* was not good, owing to its contentious shoot. Many regarded the production's statistics as a case of budgetary overkill and fiduciary irresponsibility—4,400 persons worked 1 million man hours; Walter Plunkett and a battalion of seamstresses ran up 377 costumes; props numbered 1.5 million, including a full-size sawmill; makeup artist Monty Westmore employed 34 assistants to apply lipstick and rouge in one scene alone. The 220-minute picture cost $4,085,790 (adjusted for inflation: $71,000,000), over budget by $1.242 million ($39,000,000).[1]

On November 13, 1939, a month before the premiere, United Press named Olivia the most beautiful woman in Hollywood, based on Sam Wood's poll of industry old-timers, who selected runners-up Billie Dove because of her figure, Gloria Swanson for her exotic demeanor, Claudette Colbert for her chic, Dietrich for her legs, and Madeleine Carroll for her dignity. "Miss de Havilland was credited with no less than 'general perfection,'" the UP wrote, adding that Olivia felt people didn't take pretty girls seriously and sometimes wished she were less attractive.[2]

In mid-December 1939, with the Atlanta premiere of *GWTW* approaching, David told Leigh she couldn't bring Olivier and risk scandal. "Then I won't be going either," she said. David relented, and told Kay

Brown, who was helping him orchestrate everything, "She's not going to be exactly Pollyanna about what we put her through."[3] Claudette Colbert's insistence on going to Atlanta puzzled David—she'd had nothing to do with *GWTW*—and he told Kay, "Poor deluded Claudette is coming under the notion that she is going to have a good time. It's okay with me, as she really is a terribly sweet girl and we will have no trouble with her of any kind."[4] Colbert was probably angling for a starring role in one of David's forthcoming super-productions and, if so, her strategy worked; in 1944 she'd receive top billing in the all-star cast of *Since You Went Away*.

Olivia's escort was John Hay "Jock" Whitney, whom Irene described as "big in size, spirit, and energy . . . He was catnip for ladies (or was it vice versa?) . . . an athlete, a sport . . . a gentleman . . . and a man of letters . . . He led a lusty, strenuous, swashbuckling life."[5] Joseph L. Mankiewicz, later the director of *All About Eve*, once observed, "David just wanted to be Jock Whitney—his money, his style, his entrée."[6] Jock was married to Liz Whitney, and theirs was anything but a conventional arrangement. He had an affair with Nina Vidal while Nina's husband Eugene was having an affair with Liz.[7] "Olivia's romances have always been very tense," Sheilah Graham wrote. "For a while she was madly enamored of millionaire Jock Whitney."[8]

Ann Rutherford, Scarlett's little sister Carreen, was the first of the Hollywood contingent to arrive in Atlanta, detraining at 10 a.m. at Terminal Station on Wednesday, December 13. Familiar to moviegoers as Polly Benedict in MGM's *Andy Hardy* series, she was transported by car to the Georgian Terrace hotel on Peachtree and Ponce de Leon and then to the Confederate Soldier's Home, where six surviving Civil War veterans gave her a rose corsage tied with the red, white, and blue colors of the Confederacy.

At 3 p.m. an Eastern Airlines airplane deposited Olivia, Leigh, Olivier, David, and Irene at the Atlanta Municipal Airport, where they boarded a sporty convertible in a long motorcade. In Mayor William Hartsfield's home movie, Gable and Carole Lombard arrived later, and they joined the cavalcade as it snaked through a cheering Atlanta, the automobiles bedecked with garlands and flying Confederate flags from their front fenders, crowds ten deep on either side and following solidly behind as far as the eye could see. The stars were engulfed in a sea of adoration, their expressions clearly indicating they were stunned and had never seen anything like this. They waved enthusiastically from their backseat perches as darkness fell on Atlanta and klieg lights went into action, strafing the gathering. The roaring reached a crescendo as the procession arrived at the Georgian Terrace, where Governor Eurith Dickinson Rivers declared a three-day holiday and asked Georgians to wear period clothing. People were packed shoulder to shoulder in the throng standing in front of David, who doffed his felt hat and spoke briefly into the microphone. He looked as if everything he'd been through in the past few years had been worth it, but Irene remained stoic and expressionless. Olivia linked arms with Leigh, who told Olivier, "Reminds you of the Coronation."[9] Somewhere in the crowd was future U.S. President Jimmy Carter, who later termed the world premiere "the biggest event to happen in the South" in his lifetime.[10]

"If I don't like the picture," Margaret Mitchell told David, "I am going to say so, and very strongly."[11] Recalling her threat in 1954, David admitted, "We were terrified at the first premiere in Atlanta. The press was there from all over the country."[12] Thursday night's attraction was the *GWTW* ball, where guests included Captain Eddie Rickenbacker, William S. Paley of CBS, and Laura Hope Crews, a favorite of the Georgia crowd. Kay Kyser and his College of Musical Knowledge played for what appeared to be a debutante cotillion, but Mayor Hartsfield described it as a Junior League ball with Atlanta debutantes re-enacting an Old South pageant. A young Martin Luther King Jr. sang in the boys choir from his father's Ebenezer Baptist Church.[13]

"Folks, you should see my costume for the Thursday night ball," Atlanta newspaperman Henry McLemore wrote. "I am going to look exactly like a slightly fat member of Nathan Bedford Forrest's cavalry unit. This costume belonged to my Great-Uncle Ben."[14] A sportswriter, he was taking bets on how Olivia would eat her hoe-cake, a cross between a pancake and cornbread, strong enough to work as a shovel for whatever is on the plate. According to legend, slaves had cooked hoe-cakes on field hoes. "Will she take the good crisp end, that has . . . butter sunk into it, or will she cut herself a mealy piece out of the middle? Is she a lady or ain't she?"[15]

Seats in the gallery at the ball were 25 cents (inflation adjusted: $4.50) and the first three rows ringside, $1.00 ($17.00). Neither McDaniel nor McQueen, the most outstanding actresses in *GWTW*'s large supporting cast, was deemed worthy of invitations in white-supremacist Atlanta. On Friday Mayor Hartsfield hosted a luncheon for Gable and Lombard and later took them on a tour of historic homes in a blade-silver Lincoln Continental convertible with white sidewalls. Major Clark Powell, publisher of the *Atlanta Constitution*, met the party as it inspected the site of the Battle of Peachtree Creek. Next, all the stars visited the city's principal tourist attraction, the Battle of Atlanta Cyclorama, a 400-foot assemblage. Gable joked with Hartsfield and Atlanta Parks director George Simmons, saying, "The only thing missing was a likeness of Rhett Butler," an oversight that was quickly remedied by a plaster-of-Paris Rhett. The shy Margaret Mitchell, uncomfortable with notoriety, appeared at an afternoon press conference with Gable, David, and Olivia.

The world premiere occurred Friday night, December 15, at the opulent Loew's Grand theatre, an old opera house built in 1893 at Peachtree and Pryor Streets, its marquee surrounded by faux Greek Revival columns. Confederate veterans received a rousing ovation in a brief ceremony during which Mitchell was also applauded. Hartsfield said the Hollywood stars had captured the heart of Atlanta, and the crowd of 300,000 southerners acclaimed the arrival of the performers and executives, each given a turn at the mike. In newsreel footage, Olivia made no effort to seek the spotlight during her modest entrance, nor did Leigh, who avoided the mike, threw a hasty wave in the direction of the crowd, and buried herself in the group on the platform. Laura Hope Crews seemed flustered, but that was completely in character and what people expected.

Introduced as "Atlanta's own," Evelyn Keyes displayed the glamour expected of a celebrity, her silken red hair shimmering in the lights as she seized the moment, saying a few words, generously giving the crowd what it had come for—an opportunity to see and hear a Hollywood star up close and spend a few moments with her. Ann Rutherford, Gable, Lombard, and Olivier were also appropriately in the spirit of the occasion, giving the assembled fans a gander at mythic stars in person, willing to relax and tarry with them a while.

A kid jumped on the platform to get in a shot with Gable and was allowed to stand and beam at the crowd before nimbly ducking away. Other luminaries were introduced—Atlanta-born Bobby Jones, world's number-one amateur golfer; Democratic U.S. Senator Walter George of Georgia, who'd be remembered principally for missing 551 of 4,485 roll-call votes between 1922 and 1956; Jock Whitney; Colbert; Mitchell; David and Irene; and Ona Munson. Conspicuous by his absence was Victor Fleming, who would never forgive David for saying he'd "supervised" all the directors of *GWTW*. David begged Fleming to believe that the Metro-Goldwyn-Mayer publicity department was to blame, and Gable urged Fleming to make the trip to Atlanta, all to no avail.

At the conclusion of the film, the ecstatic audience screamed for the author, and Mitchell was escorted to the stage by Carole Lombard. The author expressed her gratitude on behalf of "me and my poor Scarlett."[16] Emerging from the auditorium, Mitchell, much to David's relief, called the film "a great emotional experience . . . It was heartbreaking, and I know I'm not the only person who's got a drippin' wet handkerchief!"[17]

She commended David for his courage and obstinacy in assembling "the perfect cast,"[18] and, at long last, deigned to acknowledge Leigh, saying, "She is my Scarlett."[19] Leigh privately complained that the film was "hard on one's ass,"[20] but commented that her favorite scene was Scarlett's drunken tryst with Rhett in Aunt Pittypat's home when she accepts his marriage proposal with tipsy aplomb.[21] The following day Mitchell gave a luncheon at the Riding Club for Selznick and his stars, and that night the film people boarded a plane with *Gone With the Wind* painted on the side, bound for New York.

On opening night in Manhattan, Jimmy Stewart was Olivia's date. Two venues had been selected, the intimate Astor and colossal Capitol theatres in Times Square. Though Olivia's biographer Robert Matzen wrote that she'd been dating Stewart since 1938, another Stewart biographer, Marc Eliot, claimed that MGM may have arranged the date to keep Jimmy's name in the press. According to a third biographer, Jhan Robbins, author of *Everybody's Man*, Olivia allegedly said, "Irene Selznick arranged for Jimmy to be my escort. At the time, I didn't even know him, just about him."[22] Eliot referred to the premiere as "a lavish, publicity-soaked affair that helped intensify the planted rumors of a Stewart/de Havilland romance."[23] Matzen added, "Rosalind Russell had suggested to Livvy way back during production of *Four's a Crowd* that she might like Stewart, so they had been dating for quite a while by the time of the New York premiere; dating so ardently that rumors are already swirling that Stewart and de Havilland are about to wed."[24]

However the date came about, Olivia confirmed that "Jimmy met me at LaGuardia airport, even had the limousine drive out to the airfield—we were both quite shy and ventured one word at a time in our conversation."[25] Though a quiet and unassuming person who never boasted, Stewart had a reputation as the best lover in Hollywood, dating

Margaret Sullavan, Barbara Stanwyck, Ginger Rogers, Loretta Young, and, most recently, Marlene Dietrich, his costar in the saucy Western spoof, *Destry Rides Again*, which had just opened at the Rivoli Theatre in Manhattan. The *New York Times* critic found it difficult to accept Dietrich as a barroom floozy in the Old West but hailed Jimmy's performance as the local sheriff.

Stewart was one of the men who dated both Olivia and Joan. The latter preferred a more cosmopolitan type—Joan was bored when he took her to church, and thought it amusing that his idea of a good time was going to a soda fountain. "He was very appealing, a charming man," she said, "but he was a country boy on a date as well."[26]

Thousands packed Times Square shoulder-to-shoulder as if it were New Year's Eve. Barbara O'Neil was there with Josh Logan, who called it "the exciting New York opening" in his memoir.[27] Watching the mob from a balloon directly overhead, journalist Alice Hughes later described the chaos down below as beyond anything ever seen at a movie premiere. "Broadway [resembled] a condensed field maneuver of the Army. Flood-lights blinded thousands—police struggled vainly with hundreds of autograph fiends as Vivien Leigh and Olivia de Havilland and Ona Munson . . . fought their way into the Astor." Surging around them were familiar faces from the worlds of society, politics, and art.[28]

Louella O. Parsons wrote, "Instead of the usual microphone at the entrance of the theatre, television was used in the foyer and what a thrill I got out of my first appearance on it." Television had been introduced to the American public earlier in 1939 by Robert Sarnoff in RCA's vacuum-tube-shaped pavilion at the New York World's Fair in Flushing Meadows.

The woman in the balloon hovering over Broadway may have been mistaken when she thought she spotted Olivia and Jimmy heading toward the Astor. The *Daily News* reporter recognized them in front of the Capitol, in a crowd that included Joan Bennett and Woolie Donahue, Alice Faye and Tony Martin, Fredric March and Florence Eldridge, Doris

Duke Cromwell, David Sarnoff, Hope Hampton, Bob Ritchie, Myron Selznick, Sir Cedric Hardwicke, Faye Marbe, Adrienne Ames, Walter Damrosch, Robert E. Sherwood, Will Hays, Laura Hope Crews, Barbara O'Neil, Ann Rutherford, Brenda Frazier, Esme O'Brien and Herbert Klotz, Cornelius "Sonny" Whitney, 20 police sergeants, and 205 patrolmen, some on horses. Very possibly Olivia and Jimmy put in appearances at both theatres.

The entire block between 50th and 51st Streets was blocked to pedestrians, and only persons holding admission tickets were allowed through police barricades. Entering the Astor were Mr. and Mrs. Bernard Gimbel, Ilka Chase, Burgess Meredith and ex-wife Margaret Perry, Jack Haley, Mr. and Mrs. John Jacob Astor, Charles Ruggles, John Hertz Jr., and Lee Shubert.[29]

Louella O. Parsons finally tore herself away from her televised image, entered the auditorium, and came out four hours later, singing *GWTW*'s praises to high heaven, calling it the best movie since *Birth of a Nation* and a classic that would live forever.

Jock Whitney's mother opened her Fifth Avenue mansion for the *après*-theatre party. When Jimmy and Olivia arrived, the guests applauded until she was forced to acknowledge them so the party could proceed. Irene's sister Edie Goetz arrived with her husband Bill, a founder of 20th Century Fox, followed by Claudette Colbert and Selznick, who was overwhelmed with congratulations. He joined Jock and Joan Whitney Payson to receive the guests, including Condé Nast, publisher of *Vogue* and *Vanity Fair*; Herbert Swope, the Algonquin Round Table sage at whose Sands Point, New York, mansion Land's End David and Jock had hammered out the funding for *GWTW*; Harold Ross, editor of the *New Yorker*; Countess Dorothy Di Frasso, the Hollywood hostess who counted Gary Cooper and mobster Bugsy Siegel among her lovers; Nicholas Schenck, head of the entertainment empire that included MGM; Irving Berlin; Joan Bennett; Fredric March; Florence Eldridge; Myron Selznick; Eddie Duchin;

Richard Rodgers; Cole Porter; Ona Munson; grand opera mezzo soprano Gladys Swarthout, singing star of five Paramount pictures; playwright Moss Hart, riding high on the success of his play at the Music Box, *The Man Who Came to Dinner*; Alfred Vanderbilt, who owned Pimlico Racetrack and arranged the 1938 match race between Seabiscuit and War Admiral; and Tallulah Bankhead, who, Parsons wrote, "vivacious as ever, flitted here and there."[30] Vivien Leigh was nowhere in evidence, having shunned the premiere.[31]

The *New York Times*'s Frank S. Nugent called *GWTW* "the greatest motion mural we have seen and the most ambitious filmmaking venture in Hollywood's spectacular history . . . Olivia de Havilland's Melanie is a gracious, dignified, tender gem of characterization."[32] Kate Cameron wrote in the *New York Daily News*, "There has never been a picture like David O. Selznick's production of *Gone With the Wind* . . . Olivia de Havilland comes close to matching Vivien Leigh in the perfection of her characterization. Here is a muted performance that never once misses the true note."[33] Even high-brow critics would bow to the film's majesty in the decades to come, the *Village Voice*'s Andrew Sarris rating it "the single most beloved entertainment ever produced."[34] In 1973 Judith Crist would call it "undoubtedly still the best and most durable piece of popular entertainment . . . from . . . Hollywood."[35]

Alice Hughes had descended from her balloon in time to see the film and later wrote that Olivia was "so fine" as Melanie that nothing in her Warner films had given the slightest hint of the range and depth of her talent.[36] Years later, novelist Robert Ruark, a journalist at the *Washington Daily News* in 1939, would recall, "[Olivia's] quiet Melanie in *Gone With the Wind* was even more impressive than the much-publicized Miss Leigh's Scarlett."[37]

The film broke every record, from the longest movie ever made to the most successful—$3.400 billion, a status it has held to this day, followed by *Avatar* at $3.020 billion, *Star Wars* at $2.825 billion, *Titanic* at $2.516

billion, *The Sound of Music* at $2.366 billion, and *E.T.* at 2.310 billion (inflation adjusted).[38] Harris Interactive polled the American public in 2014 and found *GWTW*, 75 years after its release, still the most popular film in history.

13

Jimmy Stewart

At the premiere, Jimmy and Olivia clicked at once; she liked her men tall, handsome, and slender, and although Jimmy liked his women flashy and trashy, when it came to marriage, he preferred a nice girl like Olivia. He was thirty-one and his playboy timeclock was running out. Decades later, in 1986, I'd spend time with Jimmy and find him to be exactly as he appeared on screen, a reticent but warm man of admirable modesty. We talked in the den of his Beverly Hills home, a comfortable, bright room with a big slip-covered sofa and a vintage convex mirror over the fireplace. The room opened onto a flagstone terrace where his wife Gloria was gardening and occasionally looking in on us. Jimmy and I spoke of such mutual friends as Kim Novak, and I showed him a recent photo of Kim and me at Gull House, once her home in Big Sur, California. Kim was standing atop a steep rocky embankment leading to the house, looking smilingly down at me as I scrambled up to join her. Jimmy pointed to my Adidas and said, "Good thing you wore the right shoes that day." He grew misty-eyed as we talked about *Vertigo*, remembering how active and agile Kim was. Gloria stuck her head in from the terrace and said, somewhat tartly, "Why don't you tell Ellis about how I got you to go on safari in Africa? How's that for 'active'?"

Her cordial but edgy vibe was very different from his mellow nature, which no one, not even his wife, could ruffle. He was the kind of guy who would never start a fight, nor lose one if drawn into it. During a pause in our conversation, he picked up a Volvo promotional pamphlet from the coffee table and said, "I've driven one of these for years and never had to take it to the garage." I got up to look at the framed pictures by the fireplace and became intrigued by one of him and John Ford on location. He joined me, standing close, and said, "I was very pleased with a scene we'd shot one day, but John just shook his head and said, 'Too many words.'" Their films together included *Two Rode Together*, *The Man Who Shot Liberty Valance*, and *Cheyenne Autumn*.[1]

Despite studio pressure on Jimmy and Olivia in the early 1940s to costar in a film, they never made a movie together. The press predicted they'd marry, syndicated columnist Ken Morgan writing, "Lt. Jimmie [*sic*] Stewart popped the question to Olivia de Havilland."[2] Warner Brothers suggested costarring them, but they refused, according to a reporter, who wrote, "They would be embarrassed to make love—in public."[3]

In the days following *GWTW*'s premiere, Jimmy continued to squire Olivia around Manhattan, taking her to the theatre and dinner at the "21" Club. He was just emerging from a torrid affair with Marlene Dietrich that had begun when they filmed *Destry Rides Again*. She was thirty-eight and he was thirty-one, but during their first kiss, Jimmy's arousal was so obvious to everyone on the set that director George Marshall wagged his forefinger accusatorially at the actor and said, '*Jimmy*,'" Dietrich later told Peter Bogdanovich.[4] Her jealous lover, novelist Erich Maria Remarque, was on the set and saw it happen, later writing, "She'd slept with him from day one. It was a dream: It had been magical. For him, too."[5] Years later, Jimmy recalled, "We dated quite a few times, which was fairly romantic . . . I was taken off guard by her adult concept of life."[6] That concept included affairs with members of both genders, such as Greta Garbo, Frank Sinatra, Yul Brynner, Mercedes de Acosta, John Wayne, Errol Flynn, JFK, and George Bernard Shaw.[7]

Olivia remembered that one of the plays she and Jimmy saw after the *GWTW* premiere was John Osborne's *Mornings at Seven*, directed by

Josh Logan. After the show Jimmy took Olivia backstage and introduced her to Josh, who'd later direct two of the greatest hits of the post-WWII years, *Mister Roberts* and *South Pacific.* Jimmy and Henry Fonda had been Josh's roommates when they were aspiring young hopefuls, first in New York, where they lived on the West Side near Central Park, and later, as they attempted to break into movies, on Carmelina Street in Brentwood.[8] Eventually I would know all three, especially Josh, who over the years gave me two memoirs to publish at Delacorte, *Josh* and *Movie Stars, Real People, and Me.*

Both Olivia and Jimmy were aficionados of flying, and one day impulsively decided to fly to Coronado, Mexico, for "a gay lunch at the beach."[9] Later that afternoon they were back in LA, but newspapers reported they'd crossed the border to wed. "It took weeks for that one to die down!" she recalled, but the rumors would pop up again, as would the romance.[10]

In the wake of Olivia's breakthrough as a major dramatic actress in *GWTW*, it is difficult to comprehend the senseless reaction of her home studio. Logically Warner would have stepped up the quality of her roles, but no such thing happened. "News that Warners has suspended Olivia de Havilland, right on the heels of her triumph in *Gone With the Wind*, is this morning's big surprise from Hollywood," Louella O. Parsons wrote. "The trouble is over Olivia's refusal to return to the Coast immediately to play the femme lead in *Married, Pretty, and Poor* with John Garfield. Her side of the story is that . . . she is very tired . . . and she is going to take a rest—suspension or no suspension."[11]

❦

When Dietrich read reports that Jimmy was romancing Olivia, she hired private detectives to stalk them and give her regular reports on their activities so she could determine how serious they were about each other.[12] "[Marlene] had become pregnant by him the first time that they slept together," Remarque wrote in his diary.[13] She constructed a makeshift shrine to Jimmy in her apartment, surrounded by flowers and decorated with photos of him. She was obsessed, and Jimmy began to feel uncomfortable in the relationship.[14]

As *GWTW* became a national sensation, and soon an international icon, President Franklin Delano Roosevelt invited Olivia to lunch at the White House, an honor that left her awestruck. "I began to realize he took initiatives during the Depression that saved the country—and probably saved it from Communism," she recalled in 2006. Roosevelt's New Deal brought about the Social Security Act and put millions of the unemployed to work building the Hoover and Grand Coulee Dams, the Lincoln Tunnel, the Blue Ridge Parkway, La Guardia Airport, the Great Smoky Mountain National Park, and the Tennessee Valley Authority. Olivia would campaign for FDR's reelection in 1944.[15]

Though many in the film capital regarded Olivia after *GWTW* with a new respect, Jack Warner, who'd put her on suspension on December 12, 1939, demanded she return to the studio at once to make a flimsy movie called *Flight Angels*. The studio owned plenty of properties for which Olivia would've been perfect, including *Kings Row*, but Hal Wallis told director Sam Wood, "I think it most important to get Ida Lupino for 'Cassie' if possible. When I was talking to Miss de Havilland today, I kept thinking how much older and more matured she was than Cassie should be and in addition Lupino has a natural something that Cassie should have."[16] In the end, the part went to Betty Field, wife of playwright Elmer Rice, in whose play *Dream Girl* she would appear on Broadway. Field turned in a haunting, mysterious, and unforgettable performance in *Kings Row*.

"Perhaps I should not be surprised at all by your behavior because your present attitude is my anticipated reward for permitting you to play in outside pictures," Jack Warner wrote Olivia. "Am certainly amazed at your neglect and apparent refusal to answer the telephone calls of Mr. Wallis and myself. Please remember you are under contract to this company and accordingly I believe it would be good taste for you to answer our phone calls. Please telephone me immediately at the studio in order that I may personally hear your assurances that you are reporting to the studio tomorrow for work."[17]

Another Warner executive who stubbornly refused to acknowledge her new status in the industry was the legal department's R.J. Obringer, who took a swipe at Olivia, mentioning "difficulties . . . every time someone pats an artist on the back after a successful picture."[18]

Her studio might not appreciate her, but Jimmy Stewart emphatically did, taking her on double-dates with his sometime roommate John Swope and Elsie West Duvall, an MGM starlet who later recalled, "It was a great picnic. Olivia brought a delicious catered lunch with matching paper plates and napkins. After, Jimmy played the piano at his home and sang silly ditties before we went to the MGM studio for a private movie showing."[19]

In 1940 Jimmy proposed to Olivia. "For Jim, Olivia looked like being the real thing," recalled Burgess Meredith. "I am sure they were in love, although both like to pretend that they were only playing the game . . . He did once ask her to marry him, but again he didn't seem too sincere about it, and they both laughed at the idea . . . The biggest thing that prevented him from giving all his love to one woman . . . was Margaret Sullavan. He would never admit it, but he still loved her, even though he knew he would never have her."[20] Hank Fonda warned him that Sullavan was a ball breaker.[21]

"Come out right now and we'll have dinner," Jimmy told Meredith one evening. "Olivia is here and I'd like you to meet her. We're going to the theatre after dinner, if you'd like to join us."[22] Meredith was late and they left without him, but he dispatched his valet Malcolm to take roses to Olivia during intermission. Meredith arrived at the theatre in time to see her open a box of roses, with a card Malcolm had taken the liberty of writing: "Dearest Olivia, again I am late—and again, forgive me. Much love, Buzz." Later he reflected, "The touch too much! Olivia and Jimmy were 'an item' for a while . . . Malcolm played Cyrano to my Christian."[23] Later, during Jimmy's absence in World War II, Meredith would resume his pursuit of Olivia.

In speaking of Jimmy in 2016, Olivia sounded as if she'd never been very serious about Stewart either. "In retrospect, I think Jimmy was a very complex man and revealed himself to very few people."[24] According to Marc Eliot, Stewart's biographer, "Even as the gossip columnists continued to cluck about the possibility of his upcoming marriage to Olivia de Havilland, Jimmy was busy diving into the deep deep waters of Dietrich's ocean of sexual delights."[25] Dietrich's long-suffering lover Erich Remarque wrote in his diary that Jimmy and Marlene's romance "had all been poetic and romantic, hour by hour. That had held her bound to him, making her happy and unhappy. She never knew from one week to the next. He had never talked about love, but told her he was not in love, couldn't afford it. It hadn't bothered him not to be responsible for anybody."[26] When Jimmy finally did propose to Olivia, she was skeptical. "I think his offer of marriage was just a frivolous thing on his part," she said. "Jimmy wasn't ready for a wife. I guess he still had a few more wild oats to sow."[27]

Bette Davis's biographer Ed Sikov wrote that on the evening of February 8, 1940, "Jack Warner saw Litvak and Olivia de Havilland coming out of the studio café together at 2:15 a.m."[28] Director Anatole Litvak was working on the Warner lot,[29] trying to control Bette Davis in *All This and Heaven, Too*, but their screaming fights could be heard "all the way to Santa Monica," according to Basil Rathbone.[30] Jack Warner said, "I told [Litvak] it would be very funny if [Edmund] Goulding had to finish his picture [with Bette Davis]."[31] Louella O. Parsons wrote about "Anatole Litvak hosting a small dinner at his beach house for Olivia de Havilland."[32] Born in Kiev, Russia, in 1902 and trained in the Russian theatre, Litvak came to Hollywood, and in 1942 would direct Joan Fontaine and Tyrone Power in *This Above All* for 20th Century Fox. He struck

St. Louis Post-Dispatch correspondent Harry Niemeyer as "one of Hollywood's quietest director-producers."[33] Years later he'd direct Olivia in *The Snake Pit*.

Her dance card could scarcely have been fuller than it was in the early 1940s. "Olivia de Havilland spurned Glenn Ford's middidge proposal . . . Said he was too juvenile," Walter Winchell wrote.[34] "Olivia de Havilland is among the missing," Hedda Hopper reported. "Her studio doesn't know whether she's hiding in Santa Barbara, the Canadian Rockies, or en route to the Big Town."[35] From New York, Dorothy Kilgallen added, "Olivia de Havilland's latest lad is George Gregson."[36] NEA's Erskine Johnson wired, "Olivia de Havilland is the G.I.'s No. 1 favorite,"[37] and Kilgallen reported, "There is a rumor that Olivia de Havilland is trying to get a commission in the WAC's."[38] At twenty-four she was a wonderful person having a wonderful life, and her prime was yet before her.

She also found time to go house-hunting, according to Hopper, who wrote, "Olivia de Havilland is looking for a small house with a swimming pool. Hey, Livvy! I'm looking for a quiet neighbor, and you can use my pool. I'm through with it by 8 a.m." Louella O. Parsons confided, "Olivia de Havilland, paged by Warners, was located at the home of Geraldine Fitzgerald, where she is spending a month until her own home is finished."[39] The auburn-haired Fitzgerald, one of the natural beauties of the Golden Age, was notable for her superb supporting work during Bette Davis's death scene in *Dark Victory* and her Oscar-nominated performance in *Wuthering Heights*. Her husband, Sir Edward Lindsay-Hogg, was the fourth baronet of Rotherfield Hall, and her son, Sir Michael Lindsay-Hogg, would one day co-direct the celebrated TV series *Brideshead Revisited*. Fitzgerald had an affair with Orson Welles, whose first child, Chris Welles Feder, wrote, "My memory is that nobody knows for sure whether Orson was Michael's father. My mother told me that even Geraldine Fitzgerald didn't know."[40] Sir Michael initiated a DNA test, but it proved inconclusive.[41] According to Gloria Vanderbilt, Fitzgerald told her that Welles was Sir Michael's father, but Welles biographer Patrick McGilligan sought to put the matter to rest by stating Fitzgerald was in Ireland when she got pregnant, and Welles was in the U.S.[42]

Like Olivia, Fitzgerald fought Warner for better roles, and Warner took its vengeance by limiting her to second-rate parts. Twentieth Century Fox employed her to more advantage—Darryl F. Zanuck gave her a starring role as the President's wife in his epic production, *Wilson*, in 1944. She also won starring roles on the New York stage, playing Mary Tyrone in Eugene O'Neill's *Long Day's Journey Into Night* and appearing with Jason Robards Jr. in *A Touch of the Poet*.

In May 1940 *Motion Picture* magazine ran a cover story headlined WHAT KIND OF HUSBAND WILL JIMMY STEWART BE, claiming Olivia and Jimmy were madly in love and had told their families they were getting married.[43] In fact, Jimmy was having a torrid affair with Loretta Young, who'd gone on a sexual binge after divorcing actor Grant Withers, going from Clark Gable to Spencer Tracy, George Brent, Gilbert Roland, Ricardo Cortez, Wayne Morris, Joe Mankiewicz, Robert Riskin, Jock Whitney, Tyrone Power, Cesar Romero, and David Niven.[44] Young and Gable had a daughter, Judy Lewis, conceived when they filmed *Call of the Wild* in 1935. The best-kept secret of Hollywood's Golden Age, the truth wasn't made public for fifty-nine years, when Lewis published her book *Uncommon Knowledge* in 1994.[45]

Dietrich was now history in Jimmy's life. According to Remarque, "She didn't want to abort [their] child, in order to continue sleeping with him, but she gave in to his wishes,"[46] but that is not what she told Peter Bogdanovich when they sat next to each other during an airplane flight years later. "[She] had the baby surreptitiously without telling Stewart," Bogdanovich wrote.[47]

At Oscar time 1940, both Olivia and Jimmy were among the nominees, he in the best-actor category for *Mr. Smith Goes to Washington*, Olivia a best-supporting actress nominee for *GWTW*. Understandably, Olivia was disappointed she wasn't nominated in the best-actress category, since she shared equal above-the-title billing with Leigh, Gable, and Leslie Howard. Like Olivia, Hattie McDaniel was also nominated as best-supporting actress, and the other performers in that category—Geraldine Fitzgerald in *Wuthering Heights*, Edna May Oliver in *Drums Along the Mohawk*, and Maria Ouspenskaya in *Love Affair*—made it clear by their brief on-screen time and secondary billing that an outrageous, fraudulent, and probably actionable error had been committed in placing Olivia among them. Both the Academy and David were to blame; he wanted Leigh to win in the more prestigious best-actress category and wouldn't hear of placing her in direct competition with Olivia and splitting the vote, costing them both the Oscar.[48]

"I never said a word when that happened," Olivia recalled, "but of course it was a crushing blow."[49] Prior to the presentation ceremony at the Ambassador Hotel, David and Irene hosted a cocktail party at their home for the picture's thirteen nominees, a record for a single film. Jock Whitney and *New Yorker* wit Robert Benchley were also present. The *Los Angeles Times* somehow knew the winners and telephoned David with the scoop.

"David picked it up, and he intoned a list of names," Olivia recalled. "'Victor, Hattie. Er, yes. Vivien.' My heart sank. David rushed Jock, Vivien, and Larry into a waiting limo, and left right away. Nobody said a word to me. It was up to Irene to take the loser—me—and Robert Benchley to the Cocoanut Grove . . . I was crestfallen."[50] So was Irene; David left her "with nary a look behind. I'd been forgotten. I was dumbfounded."[51]

Olivia sat next to David at one of the tables in the MGM section reserved for *GWTW*. David was flanked by his two leading ladies, Leigh and Olivia, and Laurence Olivier was placed next to Leigh,[52] but Jimmy

Stewart's biographer Marc Eliot stated that at one point Olivia was "wrapped around Leigh's husband, Laurence Olivier . . . Dietrich, accompanied by [*Destry Rides Again* producer] Joe Pasternak, sat several sections away from Stewart, in the Universal section, and avoided his eyes, as he did hers."[53] Leigh had arrived on David's arm. Irene recalled, "I went in but I wouldn't sit down next to him because I wasn't sure I was going to stay. It would have been unspeakable!"[54] Jock Whitney came over to her twice, pleading David's case, but she sent him away, saying, "Don't you come back. You're making it worse."[55] The Selznick marriage in effect ended that night. "I never got over it," Irene recalled fifty-two years later, "and he never got over it."[56]

GWTW made movie history that night, taking home a record ten Oscars as well as the Irving G. Thalberg Memorial Award to David for overall career achievement. He also won the Oscar for best picture, Vivien Leigh won best actress, and Victor Fleming won for direction. Other awards included best screenplay, cinematography, film editing, art direction, color innovation, and technical achievement. When Fay Bainter rose to announce the best supporting actress, she said, "It is a tribute to a country where people are free to honor noteworthy achievements regardless of creed, race, or color." Hattie McDaniel yelled "Hallelujah!" from the back of the room, where she'd been consigned to a table near the kitchen. Columnist Jimmie Fidler later wrote, "Hattie, with one of the greatest dramatic performances of all time, steals that picture . . . An actress comparable with the immortal Marie Dressler has flashed like a dark meteor across the screen—and now must disappear because Hollywood can't give her adequate parts."[57]

"Luckily I had British upbringing," Olivia recalled. "Not a flicker crossed my face. I held on to my equanimity, which was purely a mask, right through dinner and the presentations." After the ceremony was over, Irene saw a tear on Olivia's face and spirited her to the hotel kitchen. "There was a huge cauldron of soup—bouillon—and I wept copiously, I'm afraid, into the cauldron, and my tears were just as hot."[58] When asked in 2004 if it was heartbreaking to lose, Olivia replied, "Yes, it was. For two weeks."[59] The original billing for the program for the Atlanta premiere had listed Gable, Howard, and herself as the stars of the film, followed by the line, "and presenting Vivien Leigh as Scarlett O'Hara." No one knew before the premiere whether the South, Margaret Mitchell, the people of Atlanta, and other Georgians would approve of a British actress playing a Southern belle. After the opening, Leigh shot to stardom, and David hastily rearranged the billing, keeping Gable on top, but placing Leigh before Howard and Olivia. Many Oscar voters liked Olivia better than Leigh, but Selznick thought a Leigh win would ensure the film's box-office appeal. "The night of the awards, oh, there was no God!" Olivia said. "He didn't exist. I ceased to believe in him."[60]

Later she'd come to understand "the system. I didn't feel horrible at all. There was a God, after all," and acknowledged, "It was wonderful that [Hattie] should win."[61]

It was fortunate that she recovered her faith. She would need it in the difficult years to come.

PART THREE

AFFAIRS OF THE HEART

14

Vying with Vivien Leigh and
Joan Fontaine for *Rebecca*

With *GWTW* now behind them, Olivia and Leigh found themselves competing for the title role in *Rebecca*, which David had
in pre-production while making *GWTW*. Joan, too, was up for the lead,
admitting, "We both went after the same parts."[1] Despite David's crush
on Joan, Olivia had the inside track. David told Daniel O'Shea, "I want
to be sure we have exhausted every possible means of getting Olivia de
Havilland. Miss de Havilland's unwillingness to be considered because
her sister, Joan Fontaine, being up for it, [is] foolish . . . since it might very
well wind up that she would make the sacrifice for her sister only to have
someone else play it, perhaps Vivien Leigh."[2]

In a memo to Jock Whitney, David wrote, "Olivia de Havilland,
despite our conviction that she might be superb in the role, and her own
anxiety to play it, we have had to rule out."[3] His reason: Jack Warner had
loaned her to Samuel Goldwyn for a remake of the mundane romantic
comedy *Raffles*, and David was no longer willing to haggle with Warner
for her services. Nor was he interested in dickering with Goldwyn.[4]

With Olivia out of the running, David was torn between Joan,
Loretta Young, Leigh, Bette Davis, Margaret Sullavan, Anne Baxter,
Virginia Mayo, Susan Hayward, Lana Turner, and Geraldine Fitzgerald.
Leigh was eliminated, David said, because "she doesn't seem at all right

as to sincerity or age or innocence."[5] Despite David's shabby treatment of George Cukor, he asked the director to view Leigh's screen test and later told Jock Whitney that George had laughed out loud at Leigh's struggle to appear earnest and helpless.[6] Bette Davis would be no better than Vivien, David added in his memo to Jock, but at least Davis the diva could sometimes shed her worldly façade, as in the final scenes of *Dark Victory*, in which she's tender and vulnerable.[7] The staff at SIP favored Sullavan until they viewed Baxter's test, but David found Baxter vastly less photogenic than Fontaine, and he couldn't as easily envisage Max de Winter falling in love with her as he could with Fontaine.[8]

David's crush on Joan had continued unabatedly from mid-1938, and she could still be found in his office virtually every day. He even wrote love poems to her, and the longer she kept him panting, the more passionate and heartsick he became.[9] In his more objective moments he voiced serious doubts about her acting ability, perhaps mindful that RKO had given her a shot at stardom and she'd blown it. He was aware that numerous industry insiders deemed her so devoid of talent that they referred to her as "the wooden woman." No one at his studio took her seriously as an actress.[10]

Though he feared Hollywood would laugh at him if he cast someone to whom he was emotionally enslaved,[11] he tested Joan many times in 1938 and 1939, first with John Cromwell directing and later with Alfred Hitchcock. David called and asked her to test one more time. "I declined," Joan later wrote.[12]

She still struck David as the single performer they'd considered who truly understood Rebecca, he told Jock Whitney, who responded with a threat to withdraw all his backing, pointing out that "the last test of Joan Fontaine was so bad that I cannot see her playing the role otherwise than a dithering idiot."[13] Joan succeeded in bewitching Irene, who told David, "Please tell Miss Fontaine for me to take pity on you and would she please give you an evening. Besides I think she's a dream."[14]

George Cukor was asked to choose between Baxter, favored by Whitney, and Joan, and George told David to go with Joan. When David finally gave up all hope of getting Jack Warner to release Olivia on another one-picture loan-out, he asked Olivia, "Would you mind if I took your sister?"[15]

"She's perfect," Olivia replied,[16] later reflecting, "I was losing a brilliant part, but O.K. She was really better for it than I was. She was blond; Larry was brunette."[17]

Joan did not enjoy working with the great director, Hitchcock, or starring opposite the world's best actor, Laurence Olivier. The cast snubbed her, and Hitchcock did nothing about it, knowing that if Joan felt like an outsider, her hurt feelings and anxiety would enhance her performance as the unwanted and resented new mistress of Manderley.[18]

When Olivier learned she was married to Brian Aherne, he insulted her, saying, "Can't you do better than that?" Instead of flying to Aherne's defense, she took it as a kind of compliment.[19] "Larry had rudely awakened me from my pillow dream," she wrote.[20]

She missed the premiere due to surgery for removal of an ovarian cyst and prevailed upon Aherne to escort her mother to the theatre and the party afterward. Listening to the radio from her bed, Joan heard Louella O. Parsons tell Lilian, "Now, not only one daughter but another is to be found in the firmament of stars!" Lilian replied, "Joan may be phony in real life, but she's almost believable on screen."[21] Critics were kinder than her own mother. Kate Cameron wrote in the *New York Daily News*, "The loveliest star born this year is Joan Fontaine."[22]

The Academy of Motion Picture Arts and Sciences included Joan among such veteran stars nominated for the 1940 Oscar in the best-actress category as Bette Davis, Katharine Hepburn, and Ginger Rogers. Ginger, who'd known she'd win the Oscar from the moment she read *Kitty Foyle*, wrote, "I saw it that vividly. Sorry, Olivia, you didn't get this one! Olivia de Havilland landed some very good roles."[23]

On the night of the presentations at the Biltmore Hotel, February 27, 1941, Ginger was resplendent at the RKO table in black lace and gray peau-de-soie by the designer Irene. When Lynn Fontanne, the first lady of the American theatre, handed her the Oscar, Ginger said, "This is the greatest moment of my life."[24] As she returned to her seat, Jimmy Stewart was announced as the best-actor winner for the *Philadelphia Story*, and Ginger "jumped with joy to think my sweet friend Jimmy and I were in the same bivouac together."[25]

Joan did not admit disappointment over losing, convinced that if she'd won, Hitchcock would have got all the credit. Everyone, she assumed, would think he'd played Svengali and mesmerized her.[26] Perhaps he had. Where other such great directors as George Cukor and George Stevens had failed—in *The Women* and *Gunga Din*, respectively—Hitchcock succeeded in eliciting her star quality—an appealing fragility and vulnerability. Constitutionally incapable of gratitude, she'd later write in her memoir, "I have carved my path on earth almost entirely on my own."[27] Even toward the end of her life, when she spoke of her lavish Manhattan condo, she'd say, "I did it all myself. Not one person helped me."[28]

Jimmy Stewart began his training in the Army Air Corps in March 1941 but soon returned on leave, went fishing, and told Olivia he'd caught a big fish and would like to bring it over and give it to her. She said she'd cook it and invite a few friends to dinner, including Maureen O'Hara, a red-haired beauty who'd been discovered by Charles Laughton. O'Hara later recalled that everyone enjoyed the fish and were having such a good time they decided, as a joke, to tell Jimmy it made them quite ill. "But he didn't pay the slightest bit of attention," she said. "He knew."[29]

The western railroad saga *Santa Fe Trail* again teamed Olivia and Flynn, but by now she'd grown tired of his tricks, though she would always care deeply for him, saying, "There are no words to describe my feelings for Errol Flynn."[30] Jeb Stuart, played by Flynn, and George Armstrong Custer, played by Ronald Reagan, vie for the hand of Kit Carson Halliday, played by Olivia with spirited tongue-in-cheek élan. Olivia had been one of the stars Reagan wanted to meet when he was discovered by Warner in 1937 while traveling with the Chicago Cubs baseball team in California as its sportscaster. He was soon known around the Warner lot as Dutch, a nickname his father, a salesman, gave him because of his "fat little Dutch-boy" appearance. Growing up in Illinois Reagan had been on the football and swim teams at Dixon High School and worked as a lifeguard from 1926 to 1933, reportedly saving seventy-seven lives. At Eureka College he served on the school newspaper and yearbook and developed an interest in acting.

Warner put him to work in the B-film unit, and prior to his big break in *Santa Fe Trail* he'd appeared in nineteen pictures, including *Knute Rockne, All American*, in which he played George (The Gipper) Gipp. One day, he was in the makeup department bare-chested and being worked on by makeup man Clay Campbell when Olivia came in and, ignoring Reagan, started talking with Campbell. Reagan was a fan of hers and sat there gaping until she finished removing her eyelashes and left. Reagan told Campbell he was dying to meet her, and Campbell went to the door and yelled, "Liver!" She reappeared, her face covered in cold cream, her hair under a towel, and wearing a kimono.

"Olivia, a new Warner Brothers player wants to meet you," Campbell said. "This is Miss de Havilland, Mr. Reagan."[31]

"Oh, dear, such a way to meet a stranger," Olivia said, hastening from the room.[32]

Later Olivia and Reagan began a long friendship when they shared a meal in the studio commissary. She was "something special" to Reagan, he recalled.[33] Errol Flynn witnessed their quiet private conversations and felt a surge of envy and anger.[34] Flynn found her, at twenty-four, more beautiful and intelligent than ever, and so did Jimmy Stewart.[35] "I think that [Errol] was annoyed because Jimmy Stewart was making another film on the same lot and kept coming over to see me," Olivia recalled. "I was seeing a lot of Jimmy in 1940. We were together for several months in that year and I suppose Errol was jealous."[36]

The breaking point came during night shooting at Calabasas when Flynn, still smarting over Olivia and Reagan's friendship, edged Reagan out of camera range. Reagan got even by finding ways to upstage Flynn, who complained that Reagan "was conscious every minute of scenes favoring other actors and their position on the screen in relation to himself."[37] At 3:15 a.m. Flynn stormed off the set with Olivia hard on his heels.

"Errol, can't you finish this one setup so we won't have to come out again tomorrow night?"[38]

"Why must you approach me on a personal basis?" he said, possibly assuming Reagan had put her up to it.[39]

"If by personal you mean this involves my comfort and convenience as well as that of a lot of other people, you're right. Otherwise, I don't know what you're talking about."[40]

Hal Wallis told Jack Warner about Flynn's walkout, and Warner scolded production manager Tenny Wright, who in turn demanded a full report on Flynn from associate producer Robert Fellows. "His behavior . . . has been one of continual complaint . . . that of a typical star," Fellows responded.[41] When Flynn failed to show up for shots with Olivia, supporting actor Henry O'Neill had to read Flynn's lines off-stage. Wallis saw the rushes and asked Fellows, "How can you expect to get any feeling into the scene? The girl is supposed to be playing a scene with a man that she's in love with."[42]

Nor was she pleased when Flynn deliberately upstaged her. In one scene he was supposed to come in and sit down beside her, but when the cameras rolled, he moved his chair so that "you could only see my back," Olivia said, "That was very unfair."[43]

Upon finishing the picture, Olivia informed Flynn that she was "bored to death" with him and wanted to end their screen partnership, It wasn't a personal matter, she said, and the feeling was probably mutual that they should terminate their costarring efforts, since their differences would inevitably be noticed by audiences. In view of his greater clout with the studio, perhaps he should take the issue up with Jack Warner.[44]

"Glad to," Flynn said. "And may I add that I agree with you?"[45]

Wallis required retakes, telling Michael Curtiz to extract from Olivia "some sincerity, some feeling, some warmth, and some charm into the reading and playing of her lines."[46] For the premiere in Santa Fe, New Mexico, on December 13, 1940, the stars rode on a special train, making many stops to promote the movie. Olivia was ill, and Flynn began to sweat when the sound system failed during their first whistle stop, Barstow, California. They had to ad-lib, which seemed to rattle the usually cool and confident Flynn.

"Is this you, or is this the other one?" Olivia asked.[47]

"Which other one?"[48]

"The one who wouldn't finish one more scene at three in the morning?"[49]

Flynn confessed he'd resented seeing her with Reagan and asked her to forgive his rude behavior. They settled down for an intimate talk, holding hands and alternately laughing and then drawing near and gazing into each other's eyes. A photographer from *Screen Guide* got some extraordinary shots that capture the closeness and warmth of their rapport.[50] "They really are very intense stills that for all the world suggest some kind of off-screen relationship," film historian John McElwee wrote.[51]

When the train pulled into Santa Fe, both Olivia and May Robson, Joan's early mentor, had to be taken to the ER. Diagnosed with appendicitis, Olivia was flown on a TWA charter back to Burbank, where Joan and Brian Aherne met her. Olivia underwent surgery in Hollywood, according to NEA correspondent Erskine Johnson,[52] and Rita Hayworth replaced Olivia on the train for the remainder of the tour.

The movie-going public embraced *Santa Fe Trail*, and the film became one of the top grossers of 1940, earning $1.48 million—$26,381,422 in today's dollars.

In August 1940, when America was still neutral in World War II, Jimmy Stewart organized a benefit to support war-torn England, where 75 continuous nights of Luftwaffe bombing had destroyed 1 million London homes, and, across Britain, killed 40,000. Invited to participate in the Houston, Texas, show, Olivia readily accepted, sparking gossip that "the real reason de Havilland attended" was that she and Stewart were shortly to become affianced.[53] At the benefit, Jimmy performed magic tricks recalled from younger days. Henry Fonda was part of his act, and Tyrone Power and Mischa Auer also appeared. "De Havilland increasingly felt that Stewart's marriage proposal was pro forma, that he didn't really want to settle down," Stewart's biographer Gary Fishgall wrote. "Still, they continued to date for nearly another year."[54]

15

With Ingrid Bergman, Burgess Meredith, John Huston, Bette Davis, and George Brent

Burgess Meredith, the future raspy-voiced boxing trainer Mickey Goldmill in Sylvester Stallone's *Rocky* franchise, became one of Olivia's close friends in Hollywood. He was at the peak of his career, costarring with Ingrid Bergman in a Broadway revival of *Liliom*, the Ferencz Molnar play that would shortly become the basis for the Rodgers and Hammerstein musical *Carousel*. Producer Vinton Freedly, columnist Radie Harris's lover, was responsible for casting Bergman. Molnar took one look at Meredith, who was much shorter than Ingrid, and asked, "He's playing Liliom?" Turning to Ingrid, Molnar said, "Why don't you play Liliom?"[1] *New York Times* critic Brooks Atkinson praised Meredith, writing, "His swagger is genuine; it arises from real strength." Ingrid, he wrote, kept the part of Julie "wholly alive and lightens it from within with luminous beauty."[2]

In June 1941, Meredith invited Olivia and Ingrid to his home in Rockland County, New York, 35 miles north of Manhattan, a bucolic area of winding country roads, farms, apple orchards, the foothills of the Ramapo Mountains, and the mighty Hudson River below. It was here that George Washington's soldiers are said to have bivouacked on Camp

131

Hill Road during the Revolution. In the first half of the twentieth century, the tiny tranquil Village of Pomona, still untouched by development, attracted such celebrities as Charlie Chaplin, Sophie Tucker, Alan Jay Lerner, Paulette Goddard, and Burgess Meredith, who were seeking a refuge from the limelight.

I was a guest in Meredith's house in 1978, when it was occupied by Robert Masters and Jean Houston, leading figures in the human potential movement. It is a spacious, airy dwelling, with mellow light coming from banks of big windows and lending a soft, comfortable feeling to the sprawling wooden floors and walls and high ceilings—a place that seems to be an organic part of its woodsy surroundings. Somehow I wasn't aware of the living room having any corners; whether it was round or not, it felt round, and it was quiet and peaceful on the day Masters put me through a series of exercises that extended my physical abilities beyond anything I'd ever thought possible, and yet were not strenuous but slow and easy. At the end of an hour on a floor mat, I experienced a sense of colossal calm. Such was the enchanted house where Ingrid Bergman and Olivia de Havilland became friends.

They'd met at Selznick International in Culver City during the filming of *GWTW*, and their lives would intersect in the early 1940s at the crucial moment of Ingrid's career. She was under contract to Selznick and unavailable to Warner on loan-out for *Casablanca* until Selznick decided to swap her for Olivia, whom he'd acquired from Warner for two pictures, an exchange that would lead to *Time* magazine's 2012 claim that *Casablanca* is "the best movie of all time."[3]

Ingrid brought along her husband Petter Lindstrom, a dentist and later brain surgeon, and their three-year-old daughter Pia, who'd grow up to be a television journalist. The Lindstrom marriage was headed for trouble, and when, years later, I attempted to write a book with Petter, I understood why Ingrid left him. At some point while collaborating on his memoir, I realized it was going to be a vengeful attack on Ingrid, which placed me in a difficult position because I knew and liked Ingrid, to whom I'd been introduced by Radie Harris. A woman of quiet dignity and warmth, Ingrid had a disarming way of gazing directly into one's eyes as if eager to know you better. Ingrid was also close to an author I edited at Putnam, Ann Todd, star of *The Seventh Veil*, who loved Ingrid and had come to her aid in Rome after Ingrid sparked a scandal by leaving Petter and Pia to live with her lover, Italian director Roberto Rossellini.

Petter told me Ingrid had affairs with all her leading men[4] and came home drunk one night, falling and cutting her face. Using his surgical equipment, he closed the wound and stitched up her face, sparing her scandal and scars. His fury over her desertion had never abated. I ultimately found his anger and domineering personality as suffocating as Ingrid had, and dropped out of the project. Ross Claiborne, who published Ingrid's autobiography, *Ingrid Bergman, My Story*, at the Delacorte Press in 1980, recalled, "Ingrid said that she was so stunned at the anger and rage still boiling in Petter after all these years that she almost abandoned the book."[5]

At Burgess Meredith's home that morning in 1941, Olivia saw Petter and Ingrid sitting in canvas chairs outside the guesthouse, Ingrid reading scripts and Petter absorbed in a book. "He adored her and she knew it," Olivia recalled, "but I think every man adored her."[6] Olivia and Ingrid chatted while Petter continued reading. At lunchtime, Ingrid went to the main house and raided the refrigerator, enlisting Olivia to help prepare a wholesome, simple meal. Ingrid supervised the operation like a chef giving orders to the staff.[7] In the years to come the two actresses would compete for the same roles, but Ingrid would always speak of Olivia with the greatest respect.[8]

In the early 1940s Olivia and Meredith were seen in each other's company, laughing and holding hands at an Oscar ceremony.[9] He belonged to the most elite and desirable young show-business circle in Hollywood, the Rat Pack of its day, composed of Meredith, Franchot Tone, Henry

Fonda, Jimmy Stewart, director Joshua Logan, and actor Myron McCormick. Olivia dated at least three of them, Stewart, Meredith, and Tone,[10] and later appeared in a Broadway play with Fonda. The group had originated in New York as the Thursday Night Beer Club when Jimmy, Hank, Josh, and Myron were eking out a living and sharing a $35-per-month apartment in a building full of prostitutes.[11] Once they moved on to Hollywood, Meredith, Fonda, and talent scout Bill Brady bunked in Jimmy's house, which later would be sublet by Meredith.[12]

Before marrying Paulette Goddard in 1944, and making three films with her, Meredith also dated tennis star Gussy Moran, Carole Landis, Norma Shearer, Hedy Lamarr, Peggy Ashcroft, Lauren Bacall, and Tallulah Bankhead.[13] He provided the seed money to form the Village of Pomona, and was repaid from the proceeds of a horse show after the Village was incorporated. One of Pomona's major attractions today is Burgess Meredith Park, twenty-one acres of paths along Minisceongo Creek, a playground, a running track with exercise stations, a basketball court, and a ballfield. Meredith attended the dedication and said he was honored to have a park named after him.

The first director since George Cukor to perceive Olivia's unplumbed depths as a dramatic actress was Mitchell Leisen, who directed her in 1941's *Hold Back the Dawn*. "He was Paramount's answer to George Cukor," Victoria Wilson, Barbara Stanwyck's biographer, wrote. "If Leisen snapped his fingers, he got what he wanted."[14] He'd begun as a costume designer and art director for Cecil B. DeMille, creating the distinctive look of such DeMille classics as *The Sign of the Cross*. Actors loved him. "Mitch left the acting to the actors," Claudette Colbert said.[15]

Costarring Charles Boyer, *Hold Back the Dawn* tells the story of a duplicitous gigolo who marries a gullible American schoolteacher—a spinster chaperoning her students in Mexico—in order to gain entry to the United States. Although she uncovers his treachery, as do the border police, she keeps him from being deported by lying to the authorities, claiming he'd not tricked her at all, for it was she, not he, who'd proposed marriage. Deeply moved by her kindness and compassion, the gigolo undergoes an abrupt transformation of character, falls in love with her, and at fadeout they're embarking on a happy life together.

The movie was a critical and commercial success, and Olivia thought it "a beautiful film."[16] *New York Times* critic Bosley Crowther wrote, "You will enjoy it as a straight-away romance, crowded with most engaging characters and smoking with Mr. Boyer's charm . . . Olivia de Havilland plays the schoolteacher with romantic fancies whose honesty and pride are her own and the film's chief support. Incidentally, she is excellent."[17]

The Academy of Motion Picture Arts and Sciences gave Olivia her first crack at the best-actress Oscar, also nominating the film for four other Academy Awards, including best picture, musical score, screenplay, and cinematography. Charles Brackett, who co-wrote the script with Billy Wilder, became a lifelong friend of Olivia's. According to film historian Anthony Slide, who edited Brackett's diaries, she was Brackett's favorite leading lady,[18] a formidable compliment coming from the director of Garbo, Marilyn Monroe, Katharine Hepburn, Barbara Stanwyck, Jane Wyman, Gloria Swanson, Jean Arthur, and Marlene Dietrich.

At once an action-packed adventure and the story of the marriage of George Armstrong Custer and his wife Elizabeth, *They Died with Their Boots On*, Olivia and Flynn's eighth and last film together, is one of the best examples of their dynamism as an acting team.

During casting, Flynn insisted on Olivia because he was uncomfortable with other leading ladies and she understood him, he could be at ease with her, and the tender feelings she brought out in him would make his depiction of a devoted husband ring true. Warner felt sure she'd rather go on suspension than film another picture with him. Joan Fontaine was approached, but Selznick thought the property not good enough after her triumph in *Rebecca*. Joan Leslie, Nancy Coleman, and Priscilla Lane all vied for the part, but Flynn sought out Jack Warner and went to bat for Olivia, who subsequently told Warner, "You know how Flynn and I feel about playing together."[19]

"Maybe you feel that way but Flynn doesn't," Warner said.[20]

"What do you mean, Flynn doesn't?"[21]

"He asked for you in this picture."[22]

Touched that Flynn had cared enough to go to the front office for her, she accepted.[23] It was a wise decision. They were never better together than in the scene in which Elizabeth, experiencing grave premonitions, bids goodbye to her husband before he rides to certain death. "Errol was quite sensitive," she recalled.[24] "I think he knew it would be the last time we worked together." She sensed it, too, later recalling "this tremendous feeling of grief while we were shooting it . . . I realized that it was a real farewell, because we never worked together again."[25]

What Olivia said to John Lichfield in 2009 sounded like undying love. "I didn't reject him . . . I said he had to resolve things with Lili first . . . He did not leave her then and he never approached me in that way again. So nothing did ever happen between us."[26] Lichfield wrote that she then made a "touching admission," saying, "What I felt for Errol was not a trivial matter at all. I felt terribly attracted to him. And do you know, I still feel it. I still feel very close to him to this day."[27]

Just before the United States entered World War II, Olivia's citizenship papers came through, on November 28, 1941. "I wasn't American at all," she said. "I was naturalized right before Pearl Harbor. Nine days later, I would have been classified as an enemy alien. I might have been sent to a camp."[28] Despite movie stardom and the wealth and fame it entailed, she could say, after taking the oath of allegiance to the United States, "This is the most wonderful moment of my entire life[29] . . . You may talk about your grand and glorious feelings, but there is nothing in the whole wide world to compare with the privilege of actually being a real citizen of the United States of America."[30] According to the United Press, "The actress, only 23 years old, was accompanied to court by George Schaeffer, studio representative."[31] The naturalization process would take some time to complete.

Gene Markey, producer of Shirley Temple's *Wee Willie Winkle,* whose wives included Joan Bennett, Hedy Lamarr, and Myrna Loy, fell in love with Olivia in 1941.[32] Walter Winchell wrote that Markey "sure Has It Bad . . . over Olivia de Havilland."[33] Such was his charm that, according to Loy, "He could make a scrubwoman feel she was a queen, and he could make a queen think she was the queen of queens."[34] On February 9, 1941, columnist John Truesdell wrote that Markey found "Olivia exciting, sophisticated, and smart. . . . He even leaves his job at a studio . . . and drives through the mountain pass to . . . where Warner Bros. is located— just to have a luncheon with Olivia."[35] Truesdell wrote on November 2 that Olivia was having "cupid confabs" with Markey, though she and Bob Arden had "pitched their tent in Mocambo."[36] The *Des Moines Register* reported on November 9 that Olivia was "still bouncing around" with Arden, and on the same day Harrison Carroll wrote he'd seen Olivia at the Rhum Boogie on the arm of bandleader Roger Pryor, whose date of the previous week, Lana Turner, was seated only a few tables away.[37]

By November 16, the *St. Louis Courier-Journal* Hollywood bureau considered Olivia and Pryor "an inseparable two-some" at Ciro's.[38] On November 20, columnist Ken Morgan reported that Pryor was still "doing all right,"[39] but Jimmie Fidler, on December 7, 1941, the day Japan bombed Pearl Harbor and plunged the nation into World War II, wrote that although Olivia was "supposed to be waiting for Jimmy (Army Man) Stewart or Gene (Navy Man) Markey," she was "tête-à-têting almost nightly" with John Huston at the Lakeside Golf Club.[40] Truesdell disclosed on December 16 that Olivia's "handsome new date is a lad for the cameras named James Lamore."[41] An AP wirephoto shows Olivia having a sweater arranged on her by a soldier who'd knitted it while on active duty at Camp Haan in Riverside, California.[42]

George Brent was also in pursuit; after their *In This Our Life* kissing scene, he'd gasped, 'Whoo-ee! You certainly have grown up."[43] On February 4, 1942, columnist Steffi Roberts wrote that, with Markey away in Panama, Olivia became the bachelor girl of choice and was dating Lew Ayres, "her new heart interest."[44] On February 13, Dorothy Kilgallen wrote from New York that Garson Kanin was showing Manhattan's "midnight life" to Olivia."[45]

"Every time I poked my head out of the house with a man, it was in print," Olivia told interviewer Dee Lowrance. "I even find myself opening the papers with great glee to find out who my next husband-to-be is."[46] Among her alleged future spouses were Tim Durant, who'd later appear in John Huston's *Red Badge of Courage*, Jock Whitney, and someone named Billy Batewell.[47] "I'd make a poor wife, I'm afraid," she said. "I'm not at all domestic, can't cook, and don't have much of a house feeling."[48]

Usually a staunch supporter of Olivia, Jimmie Fidler wasn't sure he approved of what he called her "demureealizing."[49] "I have never witnessed a more amazing change in personality than the transition of Olivia de Havilland from a very prim and demure 'young thing' to an ultrasophisticated Hollywood play-gal—all within a period of two years."[50] Since the town was full of glamour girls, the columnist predicted "she might be lost in the crowd," though, he admitted, "she's become more popular socially."[51]

Despite many dates, Olivia's strenuous work ethic remained as strong as ever in 1941. In one of her most demanding years as a Warner star, she completed *They Died with Their Boots On*, worked on *The Male Animal* and *In This Our Life*,[52] and underwent two days of extensive screen tests for *Saratoga Trunk*, which Hal Wallis liked so much he telephoned Jack Warner to give her, instead of Ann Sheridan, the role,[53] but in the end the spicy part went to Ingrid Bergman. Ingrid was still under contract to David O. Selznick, who received $253,802.08 from Warner for her services, but paid Ingrid only $69,562.30. As part of the deal, David got Olivia from Warner for one film for $30,000 but immediately sold her to RKO for $130,000.[54] RKO then wasted her in a harebrained Sonny Tufts romp called *Government Girl,* "a muddled . . . attempt to make . . . sport out of wartime crowded conditions . . . in Washington," Bosley Crowther wrote, dismissing it as "hopelessly dull." The only thing in its favor, Olivia told an interviewer, was box-office success.[55]

In *The Male Animal,* the Warner version of James Thurber and Elliott Nugent's Broadway satire of rah-rah college life, Olivia worked again with Hattie McDaniel, who kept ruining takes by calling Olivia "Miss Mellie." Though three years had passed since their collaboration in *GWTW,* McDaniel said, "It just don't seem natural to call that girl anything else."[56] Even in a dumb movie like *The Male Animal,* Olivia gave her all, crying so hard in a scene that called for tears that she was too upset to drive herself home and had to be chauffeured in a company automobile. The following morning, she hadn't fully recovered, slipped on a rug, and fell. To make matters worse, she'd already injured her shins while taking spills required by the script.[57]

The Male Animal has not aged well, but the *New York Times* critic, Bosley Crowther, loved Olivia, writing that she "concocts a delightfully pleasant and saucy character."[58] One reporter called Olivia "an authority on kissing," explaining that her smooch with Henry Fonda was "her 100th kiss since entering the movies."[59]

⁓

Playing the field in the early 1940s, Olivia was strongly drawn to lean, mean John Huston, who'd be instrumental, in the 1942 Warner film in which he directed Olivia, *In This Our Life,* in completing her transformation, begun in *GWTW*, from stereotypical love interest to first-rank dramatic actress. Huston's future wife Evelyn Keyes, though she rated him borderline ugly, was drawn to his brown eyes, sorrowful-looking pouches, long hunched back, sensuous mouth, and broken nose. "He had a way of talking, leaning in, wrapping his melted caramel voice around you, and appealing pied-piper fashion."[60]

I met John in the 1970s and admired his quiet, rather ironic take on life, gracious manners, and easy-going ways. He was about seventy at the time, owlish and polite when he came to visit me and Ross Claiborne at Dell/Delacorte to discuss a hardcover/paperback deal for his proposed autobiography. I quizzed him about his marriage to Evelyn Keyes, but he said, "Mr. Amburn, I do not believe the American public would be interested in my romantic life." John and his agent Irving (Swifty) Lazar had to take his proposal elsewhere.

Novelist Ellen Glasgow's melodrama *In This Our Life* brought John and Olivia together at a decisive moment in her life. Inferior roles at Warner were impeding her career, and John reversed her fortunes when he directed her as the gutsy girl who decides at the end of the film to send her own sister to prison. Olivia emerged as a better actress than Bette Davis, who played the bad sister. "I've been a movie namby-pamby long enough," Olivia told columnist May Mann on April 25, 1942. "In my new picture . . . I don't let my sweetness interfere with having my sister all but hanged."[61]

So devoted to Olivia was Huston that he neglected Davis and focused all his directorial attention on Olivia, seeing her potential as a serious artist. He was also falling in love with her. "Huston is a most attractive man," Jack Warner said, "and during the filming of his Davis-de Havilland epic anyone could see that it was cold outside but Valentine's Day on the set. When I saw the first rushes I said to myself: 'Oh-oh, Bette has the lines, but Livvy is getting the best camera shots.'"[62] Davis said, "He fawned on her like a lap dog," and Huston called Davis, years later, "a hell-raising bitch. I know she's never liked me and all I can say is fuck her!"[63]

Davis's biographer Ed Sikov wrote that "Huston and de Havilland weren't just having [an] . . . affair. They were openly living together at the time."[64] Jack Warner felt it necessary to remind John, "Bette Davis gets top billing in this picture, but you're writing her out of the big scenes and giving them to de Havilland. Let's get back on the track . . . He told me to go you know where."[65] Davis later denounced *In This Our Life* as "one of the worst films made in the history of all the world."[66] Author Ellen Glasgow in turn denounced Davis, saying, "If I had chosen acting over writing, I wouldn't be the overacting ham you are!" Though Davis posed no problem for Olivia on their first two pictures together, she now sized Olivia up as a rival, as she did most actresses, and set out to destroy her.[67] "Although Davis, after Greta Garbo, was the female star Olivia admired most, Davis did anything but return the esteem," William Stadiem wrote in *Vanity Fair*. "Davis's first take on Olivia's acting was the insulting 'what is she doing?'"[68]

On the set of *In This Our Life*, Olivia was filming a scene one day when Davis did something no actress should ever do.[69] She pulled her chair directly under the camera and fired up a cigarette, trying to distract Olivia and ruin the scene. Though others withered in the queen bee's presence, Olivia stood her ground. She said nothing to Davis and just did her scene.[70] The following day Olivia appeared on the set while Davis was shooting a sequence. Davis expected Olivia to get even with her and do something disruptive, but Olivia just looked at her, and Davis got the message: Olivia could not be provoked into a fight, nor would she accept any challenge. Try as she might, Davis could not push her buttons. During their scenes together, the more hysterical Davis got, the more unshakably Olivia maintained her equanimity.[71] It was impossible to steal a scene from Olivia as Davis routinely had done with Leslie Howard, Joan Crawford, Glenn Ford, Anne Baxter, and just about everyone except Claude

Raines. Rattled by Olivia's inner strength, Davis delivered a ragged, shrill, unhinged performance, her worst ever. After *In This Our Life,* Olivia had no more trouble with Davis.[72] She'd won her respect, and by Christmas 1941, when *In This Our Life* was in its final days of filming, Davis rose from a sick bed and reported to work at Warner so that Olivia wouldn't have to cancel her plans for the holidays.[73]

"I have utter admiration for the career of Olivia de Havilland," Davis later wrote. "She had a big hurdle in the beginning, which I did not have ... She was beautiful and therefore [Warner] cast her ... as a leading lady opposite male stars as their love interest."[74]

16

Olivia and Joan Compete for the Best-Actress Oscar

O n February 26, 1942, Olivia, nominated for the best-actress Oscar for *Hold Back the Dawn*, attended the annual awards presentation ceremony at the Biltmore Hotel on Burgess Meredith's arm, while Joan Fontaine, nominated in the same category for *Suspicion*, appeared with Brian Aherne.[1] "The girls, each looking like a page out of *Harper's Bazaar*, were the guests of David O. Selznick," according to Louella O. Parsons.[2] World War II had started just three months previously and was on everyone's mind, with Lieutenant Colonel Darryl F. Zanuck pointing out that the film industry was the only business contributing to the War Department without any profit. Seated next to Joan Bennett, Wendell Willkie, the Republican nominee who'd lost to Franklin D. Roosevelt in his bid for the U.S. Presidency, and who was now a member of the board of directors of 20th Century Fox, referred in his keynote talk to Nazi air raids he'd witnessed in England.[3] During the Battle of Britain in 1940, Willkie had fought for greater American involvement in the war. The *Los Angeles Times* later referred to the "many salvos of applause punctuating the high points in his [Oscar] address."[4] Sporting a Willkie campaign button, emcee Bob Hope joked, "Politics is very funny. Roosevelt wins and winds up with Madam Perkins [U.S. Secretary of Labor]. Willkie lost and winds up with Joan Bennett."[5] Referring to Willkie's warning about air raids,

Hope said, "There were no planes. That was John Barrymore on his way home from W.C. Fields's house."[6]

The dark cloud of war hovered over the entire ceremony, which usually featured *après*-banquet dancing, but it was ruled inappropriate under the nation's emergency circumstances. Men eschewed formal attire, and women chose less colorful gowns—both Olivia and Joan wore black—and many women sported hats, a rarity in Oscar history.[7]

There was an was awkward moment for Olivia and Meredith when the latter's roommate and bosom buddy Army Air Corps 2nd Lt. Jimmy Stewart, in full dress uniform at the specific request of Academy president Walter Wanger, stopped to talk with them. Meredith was being inducted into the army the following morning, and Jimmy grinned and offered congratulations. "Only then," according to Stewart biographer Marc Eliot, "did he turn once, wordlessly, to de Havilland."[8] Columnist Jimmie Fidler wondered if Stewart was still lavishing bouquets of yellow roses on Olivia despite his much lower Army pay.[9]

In a photograph of Olivia and Meredith at their table, they are holding hands and looking very happy.[10] In another, Joan is leaning down over Olivia's shoulder and holding her hand as both smile warmly.[11] Their evident familial affection was in marked contrast to newspaper headlines across the nation warning of an imminent battle royal over the Oscar. As the star of Alfred Hitchcock's *Suspicion*, Joan was competing with Olivia for the best-actress trophy. With Olivia already considered a favorite for *Hold Back the Dawn*, Joan had unexpectedly joined the race when *Suspicion* opened at the last possible moment to qualify for the contest.

They faced tough opposition from Bette Davis in *The Little Foxes*, Greer Garson in *Blossoms in the Dusk*, and Barbara Stanwyck in *Ball of Fire*. Convinced the Academy would again snub her, Joan decided to skip the ceremony, but Olivia appeared on the set of her film at RKO carrying an evening gown and persuaded her to attend. At the Biltmore, many of the guests, estimated at 1,425 by the *Los Angeles Times*, kept their eyes glued on Olivia and Joan. Associated Press correspondent Rosalind Shaffer saw Joan "sticking out her tongue at Olivia" and later wrote, "Stretched nerves resulted in funny didoes."[12]

Ginger Rogers, the previous year's winner, stood up and announced that the best actress of the year was Joan Fontaine, the youngest actress, at twenty-four, to win the top acting prize at that time. "Olivia . . . became tearful," according to the AP,[13] but Parsons wrote, "If Olivia was disappointed, no one in that crowded room suspected the inner turmoil. One big gasp, then she leaned over and kissed Joan and congratulated her."[14]

"We've got it!" Olivia said.[15]

The AP reported that Joan was in a "semi-swooning condition" when she finally went to receive the award, and she "dissolved in tears and stole the show," according to Oscar historians Kinn and Piazza.[16] Columnist Sidney Skolsky wrote, "Burgess Meredith, who was Olivia de Havilland's escort, pressed her hand tightly."[17] "I won from my sister," Joan recalled. "There was no joy in that."[18] But she later gloated, "Olivia always said I was first at everything—I got married first, got an Academy Award first."[19]

For Whom the Bell Tolls, one of the major films of the Golden Era, was getting underway at Paramount in the spring of 1942 with a search for an actress to play Maria, who is raped by Nazis during the Spanish Civil War but survives to find love with Robert Jordan, played by Gary Cooper. Jimmie Fidler reported, "Paramount is taking a loan of Olivia de Havilland from Warners for Maria in *For Whom the Bell Tolls* (their best idea yet!)."[20] Vera Zorina, Larraine Day, and Olivia were in the final running[21] when Ernest Hemingway, author of the novel, took Ingrid Bergman and Petter to dinner in San Francisco and assured Ingrid, "You'll get the part, don't worry."[22] Olivia went back to fighting off insignificant roles in *The Gay Sisters* and *The Adventures of Mark Twain* at Warner and getting suspended for declining the inane *Princess O'Rourke*, into which the studio finally forced her. She succeeded in avoiding *The Gay Sisters* but at the cost of a "technical suspension," Louella O. Parsons wrote. "She felt she'd made too many pictures. Her bosses said 'maybe so'—and it was mutually agreed that she take time out. After Olivia has a rest . . . she'll return to Burbank . . . Nancy Coleman, a Warner newcomer, gets her role in *The Gay Sisters*." A technical suspension, the Warner suits explained to Parsons, is "where everybody is speaking and no hard feelings on either side."[23]

Grauman's Chinese Theatre summoned Joan on May 6, 1942, to leave her handprints in its Forecourt of the Stars in front of the box office at 6925 Hollywood Boulevard, among those of such Golden Age icons as Jean Harlow and John Barrymore. The ceremony, during which honorees press their hands and feet, and sometimes, as in the case of WWII pinup girl Betty Grable, their legs, into wet cement. The honor, according to the theatre's secret selection committee, is reserved for performers "who have made a lasting impact on cinema."[24] As many as 8,000 fans have been known to show up for the zany ritual, which, like motion-picture premieres, was an innovation of Sidney Patrick "Sid" Grauman, builder of both the Chinese and Egyptian Theatres.[25]

World War II motivated movie stars to sell millions of war bonds and establish a nightclub called the Hollywood Canteen, where soldiers could meet such G.I. favorites as Olivia, Betty Grable, Rita Hayworth, Ingrid Bergman, Jennifer Jones, Errol Flynn, Vivien Leigh, Frank Sinatra, and Mae West. The celebrities worked the chow line, entertained, washed dishes, and danced with the soldiers.[26] Olivia was "one of the most conscientious in attendance," the *Los Angeles Times* reported. "Three hours of standing on her feet after a long day at the studio is no easy stint."[27] Journalist May Mann saw Olivia emerging from the kitchen one night "without a bit of movie makeup," carrying a tray of cake.[28]

The brainchild of Bette Davis and John Garfield, the Canteen, a converted barn, had opened at 1451 Cahuenga Boulevard on October 3, 1943, hosting 2,000 to 4,000 servicemen and women nightly. Davis dated a corporal she met at the Canteen until he was shipped overseas,[29] and Dietrich was photographed passionately smooching with a master sergeant in the kitchen.[30] One night, Olivia was photographed on the dance floor of the Mocambo, looking ecstatic in the arms of a blond young officer named Woodward Melone.[31]

Olivia's cousin Lt. Geoffrey de Havilland, RAF, who'd shortly be knighted, was in the midst of a business trip to the United States for de Havilland Aircraft Co. when he visited her on the set of *Devotion*, a grossly inaccurate story of the Bronte sisters, in which she played Charlotte. She went to lunch with Geoffrey in full ruffled taffeta costume and stage makeup.[32] A daring test pilot, he fell alternately in love with Olivia and Joan, "depending," Joan wrote, "on which of us was in the Aherne bar at the time and from which bottle he was drinking."[33] Nursing a hangover the morning after, Geoffrey buzzed the Aherne residence in his airplane, alarming Beverly Hills neighbors but, according to Joan, he was nonetheless "clear-eyed and intrepid."[34]

The de Havilland Aircraft Co. was contributing significantly to Allied victories, manufacturing the WWII light bomber Mosquito and other combat planes. Tragically, Geoffrey's daredevil brother John, testing the Mosquito Mark VI, perished in a midair collision with another Mark VI in 1943.[35]

⎯⎯

"She was not an easy pick-up," said Howard Koch, who wrote the screenplay for *In This Our Life*, "and with John [Huston], it was partly the game: here was a beautiful woman, could he win her?"[36] Possibly, but he was hardly the only man in Olivia's life. In late February 1942, she attended the opening of the USO canteen in the Beverly Hills Hotel. "I am having a good time," she said, "but I am especially happy there are no boys from my home town here, you see I was born in Tokyo."[37] On April 9, columnist May Mann saw her with Clifford Odets at the Brown Derby, "all wrapped up" in a long, intense conversation.[38] In July, Huston began to show up with Olivia in public despite his marriage to Lesley Black, who'd helped him control his drinking and encouraged him to make a new start in Hollywood. "I had no more business marrying Lesley than I had marrying my first wife," he admitted.[39]

John and Lesley separated, and, amid rumors of a Reno divorce, he took Olivia to lunch at the Brown Derby.[40] In August he and Olivia were seen at Chasen's, the Players, and Mocambo, Hedda Hopper revealed in the *Los Angeles Times*, foreseeing a likely "march to the altar."[41] Warner producer Henry Blanke said in October 1942 that Huston "had been seen quite a bit with Olivia de Havilland and was believed by most observers to be very much in love with her."[42]

Born in Weatherford, Texas, in 1906, John Huston was only three when his father, Walter, future Oscar winner for *The Treasure of the Sierra Madre*, drifted out of his life. John's mother Rhea was neglectful, leaving her son with a nursemaid. "That led to my introduction to sex," he wrote, and he recalled being in bed with the maid, fondling her bare behind, and resting his cheek on it. His mother discharged the maid, to his acute disappointment.[43] Rhea's self-centeredness, remarriage, and parental negligence during his formative years contributed to his adult problems with women.

Olivia was aware that John had brought chaos and despair into the lives of Lesley Black and other women.[44] On September 25, 1933, John was driving on Sunset Boulevard when Brazilian dancer Tosca Roulein suddenly emerged from between parked cars. He hit her, throwing her onto the hood and into the windshield before flinging her thirty feet. Her head had been crushed, and he very nearly ran over her dead body.[45] Evidently he hadn't been drinking, but his past arrest record included a DUI, arrest, and jailing.[46]

According to one of Huston's writing partners, Ben Maddow, "He would indulge himself in any possible way, whose consequences on other people's lives he observed with great interest, but no compassion. He needs new people to feed on all the time. The desert is littered with their bones."[47] John's loves included Mary Astor, Suzanne Flon, Ava Gardner, Evelyn Keyes, and Marietta Tree.[48] He directed Astor in *The Maltese Falcon*, Flon in *Moulin Rouge*, and Gardner in *The Night of the Iguana*.

Despite his faults, he proved to be irresistible. "John was a very great love of mine," Olivia said. "He's capable of tremendous love of a very intense order . . . He was a man I wanted to marry, and knowing him was a powerful experience, one I thought I would never get over . . . Somebody walks into your life, and before you know it, you are in love with him . . . And it's blind."[49] Movie critic James Agee thought John believed "he has the right, even the obligation, to write and to fuck as much as he can in ways he prefers to, even if doing so shortens his life or kills him on the spot."[50]

Home movies in 1943 show Olivia and John on the patio beside her swimming pool.[51] He would suddenly jump up and come at her like a charging bull and she'd ward him off with an imaginary cape. When he felt like being alone, lounging on the patio in his bathing suit, smoking cigarettes, drinking, and whiling away an afternoon reading newspapers, she was perceptive and independent enough to leave him alone. At such times they seemed a compatible couple, each content to give the other space and freedom. She became so comfortable having him around she shunned movie-star makeup and sometimes wore a sundress and no shoes, her bliss very much in evidence. In the pool, she'd hop on his shoulders and place her hands on his head.[52]

Eloise Hardt, an American half-breed daughter of a Cherokee mother and German father, was a Powers model who appeared in two Huston films, *The Asphalt Jungle* and *The Night of the Iguana*. She believed "the more you love him, the less respect he had for you."[53]

"You've got to help me make up with John," Olivia allegedly told Hardt.[54]

"What do you find so interesting and attractive about him?" Hardt asked, and later said, "Olivia was always a very outgoing and aggressive and positive person, an 'I want' kind of dame . . . [but] John was everybody's lover because he let you fulfill your fantasy."[55]

He felt free to play around but was jealous when Olivia showed the slightest interest in anyone else. Anatole Litvak was still in Olivia's life, according to Louella O. Parsons, who wrote in July 1942 that Litvak hosted an intimate dinner at his beach house for Olivia.[56] John couldn't abide any kind of rejection without desperately skulking off to seek comfort in the arms of yet another female conquest.[57] At the heart of his conflict was his mother. Though Rhea Huston died in 1938, her memory pursued him like a demon bent on his destruction.[58] Slightly horse-faced, a competitive and aggressive roving reporter when she interviewed John's father in 1904 and married him the same year, Rhea was willful, critical, smoked, and rode horses, but played the helpless female to get ahead. The marriage ended in 1909. "I was closer to her than my father," John said. She doted on her precocious son, but she was a mass of contradictions, alternately coddling and neglecting him. Ultimately John found her "suffocating . . . dominating, demeaning, hysterical, overbearing, proud, protective." He both admired her and couldn't stand her. He would bring to his adult relationships the same ambivalence, resulting in five marriages, none of which lasted.[59]

In World War II, Huston enlisted in the Army, beginning as a lieutenant assigned to filming military documentaries for the Signal Corps film unit run by Lt. Col. George Stevens. When John returned from the Aleutians, he began an affair with Boston Brahmin Marietta Tree, who was rich, tall, blond, athletic, and intelligent.[60] "Olivia wanted to get married," John said, "but it was just impossible for me to get married at that time."[61]

"I must say I felt hatred for John for a long time," she recalled. "Maybe he was the great love of my life. Yes, he probably was."[62]

17

The de Havilland Rule

O livia finally decided to take Warner Brothers to court when the studio continued to consign her to inferior roles even after she'd consistently demonstrated she could handle substantive work in *GWTW*, *Hold Back the Dawn*, and *In This Our Life*. In August 1943 Jack Warner wrote in a memo, "We brought her from obscurity to prominence and can show that we made a profit on every picture she has ever been in and made it possible for her to get $125,000 [inflation adjusted: $1,750,000] for each picture which she is now getting."[1] She was making three or four pictures a year, but being stuck at Warner meant little or no artistic growth. "I realized that at Warners I was never going to have the work that I so much wanted to have. I thought, I have to refuse, I must do it, and I did, and of course I was put on suspension."[2] With each suspension, extra time was added to her seven-year contract, and by May 1943, she found herself with six months of suspension time. In effect, this could go on until Warner owned her forever, like a slave. The dark side of the Golden Age of Hollywood was the tyrannical studio system.

In August 1943 she engaged a lawyer named Martin Gang, who assured her that the little-known anti-peonage law, which curtailed an employer from enforcing a contract against an employee for more than seven years, would give her a fair chance of winning her case against Warner. After studying the law, she told Gang, "Let's go ahead with it, and we're not going to get discouraged along the way. We will go [all the way] to the Supreme Court [if necessary]."[3] As the case worked its way through the legal system, she busied herself with volunteer war work, flying to the Aleutian Islands, which had been occupied by the Japanese before they retreated to more strategic battle zones. During a visit to a military hospital in March 1944, she received a cable from Martin Gang advising her that she'd won in Superior Court.

Warner immediately appealed and blacklisted her throughout the industry. Olivia fired back, filing an injunction against the studio. "Everyone in Hollywood knew that I would lose but I knew that I would win," she said. "I had read the law. I knew what the studios were doing was wrong."[4] She began to refer to Jack L. Warner as "Jack the Warden"[5] and the studio as "a model prison"[6]—but once more, mighty forces rewarded her courage. Martin Gang informed her in December 1944 that she'd won a unanimous decision in the Appellate Court of the State of California. Warner again appealed but lost. Her victory over the studio and in effect the entire industry was now complete.

"I freed the slaves," she said. "I did. They said that, that I had freed the slaves."[7]

"Did anyone thank you in Hollywood?" Sheilah Graham asked her.[8]

"No one, but this was very touching—Maria Montez, whom I didn't know, sent me a bouquet of flowers."[9]

Montez was Universal's Queen of Technicolor, star of such early 1940s exotic costume adventures as *Sudan* and *Cobra Woman*, and one of the most beautiful women of the movies' Golden Age. Her husband, the suave, romantic French actor Jean-Pierre Aumont, adored her, and theirs was one of Hollywood's most successful marriages.

Jack Warner, seeking revenge after Olivia asked to be released from her Warner contract, replied with an emphatic "NO" when playwright John Van Druten wanted her for the Warner version of his Broadway hit, *The Voice of the Turtle*.[10] Olivia reportedly moved in with Joan "until she finds a house of her own," Sheilah Graham wrote in January 1946,[11] and revealed on February 9 that Olivia was "living in a stable—with a horse in the next stall—until her Shoreham apartment is ready!"[12]

Though her career was stalled, her personal life blossomed with wartime romances. On January 9, 1945, columnist Inga Arvad, an attractive adventuress who'd wangled an interview with Adolf Hitler and later had a torrid affair a young John F. Kennedy, revealed that although Olivia had given "Maj. John Huston a long and beautiful kiss" on New Year's Eve, they must have had a spat because she walked out of the party without him.[13]

Three days later, Harrison Carroll wrote that Olivia and John, though they arrived separately at Sam Spiegel's house, seemed to have made up, judging from their behavior "on the stroke of midnight."[14] The *St. Louis Post-Dispatch* reported on February 18 that she had a date with Marine Lt. Philip Schwartz of Connecticut, but Joan decided Olivia might be ailing and "substituted for her as the officer's date."[15] In a photograph accompanying the item, Joan looks happy, but her tall, mustachioed Marine is frowning at another officer, with whom Joan appears to be flirting.[16]

Jimmie Fidler wrote on April 7, "If there's truth in the adage, 'Lucky at cards, unlucky at love,' I'd hate to play poker with Olivia de Havilland,"[17] and Associated Press correspondent Bob Thomas wrote April 9 that Olivia told him, "I started looking for my husband when I was six. That was 22 years ago, AND I'M STILL LOOKING."[18] The following day, Louella O. Parsons wrote that Olivia's old beau Major John Huston, who'd planned to wed her as soon as he jettisoned his wife, was now free but had his eye on model Dorris Lilly,[19] and Dorothy Kilgallen claimed Huston had already proposed to Lilly.[20] Parsons mournfully revealed on April 23 that John had tried to talk to Olivia but she'd left LA without seeing him, writing finis to the relationship. "Of course," Parsons added, "a lady can always change her mind."[21] There was small chance of that happening, according to Harrison Carroll, who wrote, also on the 23rd, that

Olivia told him she and John parted in August and had "a slight epilogue in December, but I don't expect another."[22]

Prospects were brighter on May 3, the *New York Post's* Irene Thirer reporting rumors of Olivia's "forthcoming nuptials to Maj. Joseph McKeon, war hero."[23] Olivia called him "sweet and charming and intelligent and I'm exceptionally fond of him."[24] Injured during an air raid over Germany in 1944, he returned with a limp.[25] "She's still a bachelor girl," Thirer added, "having been linked romantically over the years with Jimmy Stewart, Burgess Meredith, Lew Ayres, Captain John Huston, and now Major McKeon,"[26] but it sounded, on December 19, like Olivia's marital status might soon change, when Parsons alleged Olivia and McKeon were "making love out in front of everybody and not seeming to care."[27] Olivia was still involved with McKeon on December 28, 1945, Parsons reporting that Olivia was "very happy in her personal life right now and seemingly more interested in the very personable Major Joe McKeon than anything else."[28]

Sheilah Graham spoke with Lilian Fontaine, who was playing Paulette Goddard's mother in *Suddenly It's Spring*. "Olivia's happy now," Lilian said. "Joan was near a breakdown, but she's doing fine."[29] Graham added, "Reason for Olivia's current happiness is her beau, Major Joe McKeon. Or perhaps it's just spring."[30] Lilian appeared on stage in 1946 in *The Gentle Approach*, and Brian Aherne was present to cheer her on opening night. "Joan and Olivia de Havilland should be very proud of their parents," Hedda Hopper wrote. "[Lilian] plays a sly domestic and gets plenty of laughs."[31]

On January 21, 1946, Olivia said she and McKeon had discussed getting married before her thirtieth birthday on July 1, though they'd made no definite plans.[32] Graham revealed on July 24 that McKeon was going abroad for military duty and that this departure "would write 'end' to their romance."[33] On the contrary, on March 23, McKeon was tracked down at March Field, California, by the United Press, whose correspondent wrote that McKeon had met Olivia during her USO Pacific tour and that McKeon knew nothing about the film industry apart from whatever he'd learned from Olivia. The UP predicted "she'd drop her [No. 1 bachelor girl] title in favor of a husband."[34]

Jimmie Fidler wasn't convinced, writing on April 1 that Olivia pointed to McKeon during one of his visits to the studio and said, "Any time I marry a guy he won't be hanging around my set all day."[35]

During a "gag interview" on April 3 on the set of her psychiatric film *The Dark Mirror*, she submitted to a lie detector test, and when she denied she was getting married—not "at the moment" anyway—the detector "jimmied and jumped." When she said there'd be no important changes in her life in 1946, "The lie detector did a shimmy, a hula, and a fandango all in one."[36]

Walter Winchell saw Olivia and McKeon in New York and wrote on May 22, 1946, that Olivia was having dinner with McKeon, "who looks like John Huston, who looks like Jimmy Stewart, all former Majors and former suitors of Livvie's."[37]

━━◡━━

Achieved at an awful professional cost to Olivia, what came to be known as the de Havilland Rule helped entertainers throughout show business. "Olivia should be thanked by every actor today," Bette Davis wrote. "She won the court battle that no contract should ever have to continue more than seven years. Years ago our contracts could have been indefinite. A sort of potential contract for life."[38] Hedda Hopper added that Olivia was "being called 'the Abraham Lincoln of the acting profession.'"[39] Particularly pleased that her new law helped such old friends as Jimmy Stewart and Clark Gable, who'd gone on suspension for leaving their studios to fight at the battlefronts of WWII, Olivia said, "Jimmy Stewart was a bomber pilot, 21 raids over Germany, Clark Gable, tail gunner . . . All the time they were at war, they were on suspension. When they came back, they would have that time all over again and at the salary which had by this time become outmoded . . . They were able to rewrite their studio contracts in much more favorable terms."[40]

Davis seldom complimented anyone for anything, but she called Olivia an "artist who had the integrity [and] the will for holy battle [against] the medium which stupidly restricted its own enrichment."[41] Lucille Ball, being wasted at Metro in Abbott and Costello vehicles, asked Olivia how to take control of her career. "Watch. Ask," Olivia said. "Find out when you're supposed to be paid."[42] According to Ball's biographer Kathleen Brady, "Lucille believed that Olivia de Havilland saved her from professional limbo."[43]

John Huston returned to LA on leave and saw his Hollywood cronies, among them Errol Flynn, who'd always bitterly resented Huston's friendship with Olivia. Though John was dating others, he was still in love with Olivia, and so protective of her reputation that he clashed with Flynn for uttering something objectionable about her at a party given by Irene and David O. Selznick on April 29, 1945. "That surprised me very much," Olivia said. "I don't know what the remark was, but Errol might have tried to provoke John."[44]

John wrote, "Having just returned from working with authentic heroes, I was in no mood to put up with the screen variety. It was in this frame of mind that I encountered Errol Flynn standing in a hallway . . . Maybe he sensed my mood and picked up on it . . . [Flynn] very quickly got around to saying something wretched about someone—a woman in whom I'd been very interested and still regarded with deep affection. I was furious at his remark."[45]

"'That's a lie!'" he told Flynn. "'Even if it weren't a lie, only a sonofabitch would repeat it.' Errol asked if I'd like to make anything out of it, and I decided that I would."[46] Flynn's first punch knocked Huston to the ground, but he jumped up, and Flynn knocked him down again. "Each time I landed on my elbows," John recalled. "Beginning some months later, and continuing for a period of years, little slivers of bone came out of my right elbow."[47] They shouted imprecations that could be heard all the way to the house, drawing a crowd around them. "Motherfucker was not a term of endearment," Huston later wrote.[48] Both men fought fairly and with honor. "When I was first knocked down," Huston recalled, "I rolled, expecting Errol to come at me with his boots. He didn't. He stepped back and waited for me to get up, which I thought was rather sporting of him."[49] The fight went on for over an hour, leaving both men bloody and seriously injured, Flynn with broken ribs, Huston with a broken nose and concussions. Both were hospitalized but later laughed it off. Walter Huston suggested they sell tickets, repeat the fight, and donate all proceeds to charity.[50]

Shortly after the battle at Selznick's, Evelyn Keyes found herself seated between Huston and Flynn at a dinner party hosted by Sir Charles and Lady Elsie Mendl in their Beverly Hills home. After playing Scarlett's sister Suellen in *GWTW*, Keyes had gone on to star in the box-office smash *The Jolson Story*, which grossed $18,910,000—or $237,500,000 in today's dollars—making it the second top grosser of 1946, between Samuel Goldwyn's *The Best Years of Our Lives* at No. 1 and Selznick's *Duel in the Sun* at No. 3.[51] Keyes had heard reports of the Huston-Flynn brawl and later wrote, "Since neither of them had a scratch these few days later, it couldn't have been much of a scrap. Why Sir Charles whimsically chose to seat them so near to each other and with me in the middle, I'll never know. They behaved quite civilized that night, talking to me, ignoring each other. I had a fine time."[52] Strongly drawn to both men, she'd later become the third of Huston's five wives.

Flynn couldn't keep out of trouble. He started fooling around with minors, and his dalliances with teenagers eventually got him arrested, hauled into court, and tried for statutory rape.[53] Though acquitted on all counts, he was now a laughingstock, and "in like Flynn" entered the language as a metaphor for sexual intercourse.[54]

⌒⌒

Marcus Aurelius Goodrich first came into Olivia's life during World War II. According to Sheilah Graham, around 1941, at a dinner party given by Arthur Hornblow, producer of *The Asphalt Jungle*, Goodrich overheard Olivia say she wanted eleven children. "I want to meet that girl," Goodrich said.[55]

"Someone—it could have been I—introduced him to Olivia de Havilland, then coming to the peak of her career as a serious dramatic actress," said novelist Niven Busch, author of *Duel in the Sun* and husband of Teresa Wright.[56] Goodrich called Olivia three times, but she wasn't at home, according to Hedda Hopper, who interviewed Goodrich in 1946. "So Goodrich decided that was that and caught a train for the East," Hopper wrote."[57] Several months later Olivia and Goodrich ran into each other at Romanoff's, a Beverly Hills restaurant financed by Jack Warner and Darryl Zanuck and operated by a popular self-named prince. They exchanged polite chat, but made no plans to see each other again.[58]

"Why didn't you marry five years ago when you first met"?" Sheilah Graham asked Olivia and Goodrich in 1946. "It's all her fault," Goodrich replied. "After that first time, I called her three times, and she was out. So I decided she didn't like me." Amused, Olivia replied, "It's not true. You just didn't pursue me hard enough—that's all. Besides, I'd heard you were a devil with women."[59]

Born in San Antonio, Texas, in 1897, Goodrich had been a devotee of literature since reading Edgar Allan Poe's short stories at fourteen. "That was one of the greatest experiences of my life," he later told John K. Hutchens of the *New York Times*. "My mother was a blonde who read Elinor Glyn, but she knew what it was I wanted . . . Dostoevsky's *Crime and Punishment* made me hungry for more of that quality."[60] Dostoevsky's novel is about a man who murders a woman with an ax.

After running away to sea at eighteen, Goodrich served on a U.S Navy ship that sank in the Mediterranean, and he spent the next fourteen years writing about the experience in his novel *Delilah*.[61] In World War II, as a Navy Lieutenant Commander, he participated in amphibious operations in North Africa, Sicily, China, and Okinawa.[62] Later he attended Columbia College, though "I was drunk most of the time," he said. "Always I had wanted to write . . . a great novel . . . Yet I couldn't break the grip that alcohol had on me . . . I've been pulled out of gutters in many of the best cities in the world."[63] In 1926, he developed delirium tremens, was bound in a straitjacket, and taken to the alcoholic ward in a Paris hospital, where he detoxed.[64]

He tried his hand at advertising in 1931 but proved incapable of crafting mercantile prose, according to an article in the *New York Times*, stating that Goodrich "scorns the advertising-agency theory that the shortest and simplest word is the most effective one . . . He likes them rich, polysyllabic and freighted with meaning."[65] In December 1934 his first marriage was over in eight months when his wife realized he was a liar. An atheist, he'd promised to convert to Christianity, but reneged.[66] He went to New York, where he worked at the *Times* and the *Herald Tribune*. "I couldn't hang onto a job because I was drunk," he told *New York Times* interviewer Robert Van Gelder.[67]

Later in the 1930s Goodrich found his way to Hollywood, and although he had no movie credits, he managed, thanks to his love affair with Mary Astor, to get himself referred to in the press as a "studio executive"[68] acting "on behalf of the movie industry,"[69] and "a cane-carrying, pipe-smoking film colony *habitué*."[70] The thirty-year-old Astor, an aristocratic beauty with a Madonna-child visage, was at the peak of her career as one of the players, along with Walter Huston and Ruth Chatterton, in the film adaptation of Nobel Prize-winning novelist Sinclair

Lewis's *Dodsworth*. While the movie was in production at the Samuel Goldwyn Studio, all hell broke loose in Astor's personal life in what the press called "the worst case of dynamite in Hollywood history."[71]

Astor's "Purple Diaries," two ledger books about her trysts with priapic playwright George S. Kaufman, were leaked to the media by her irate ex-husband, Dr. Franklyn Thorpe, who'd divorced her and was now engaged in a furious court battle for custody of their four-year-old daughter Marylyn.[72] Goodrich figured significantly in the 1936 trial as well as in Astor's romantic life.[73] Sheilah Graham wrote that New York women were offering $25 for Kaufman's telephone number, and Hollywood actresses "are willing to pay much more for that of Marcus Goodrich, writer, present number one beau in Mary Astor's life."[74]

Together with MGM head of production Irving Thalberg and George S. Kaufman's lawyer Mendel Silberberg, Goodrich became a leading intermediary in the divorce case.[75] According to the *Philadelphia Inquirer*, Goodrich was instrumental in arranging the tentative agreement between Astor and Dr. Thorpe. "The move was understood to have been forced by Marcus Goodrich . . . who entered the case on behalf of the movie industry by offering to act as a mediator."[76] Goodrich told the United Press that Astor would get "full control of four-year-old Marylyn Thorpe."[77]

Under the headline HOT BOOK COMING, Winchell wrote on September 15, 1936, "Mary Astor and Marcus Goodrich are collaborating on a book that'll make Elinor Glyn's *Three Weeks* look silly."[78] Sheilah Graham stated on September 22 that when the notoriety of the trial subsided, "Mary Astor will announce her engagement to scenarist Marcus Goodrich,"[79] but their engagement aborted, as did their book.

On publication in 1941 Goodrich's novel *Delilah* sold 47,000 copies despite the terrible sense of stasis hovering over the leaden prose.[80] Goodrich told *Time*, "I have always made it clear that if Hollywood was going to do anything with [*Delilah*] that I must have complete and unquestioned control over the script, and there's never been anyone in Hollywood crazy enough to give me the authority."[81] After World War II he paid a visit to his publisher, Stanley Reinhart. "When will you be getting to work on another book?" Reinhart inquired. Goodrich replied, "I'll start writing when you find an apartment for me."[82] The following day Reinhart handed him the keys to an apartment and told him to move in and write, but the book never materialized.[83]

According to Niven Busch, it took a while for Goodrich to find Olivia. In the meantime she met future U.S. President John F. Kennedy, who was relaxing in Hollywood in 1945. With Kennedy was his long-time intimate Charles F. "Chuck" Spalding, who would later help JFK win the Wisconsin primary.[84] In 1965, Theodore Sorensen, JFK's White House Special Counsel, wrote that the President liked the companionship of Spalding "not because of [his] success in the world of business, but because [he] was amusing, easy-going."[85] Recalling his days on the campaign trail with JFK, Spalding said, "It was not a rare thing for us to drive the whole length of Wisconsin in a night, back and forth . . . Kennedy loved the fun of it . . . He [also] liked movies. His father was occupied in the movie business." Joseph P. Kennedy and a group of investors acquired R.K.O in 1926, and nine-year-old JFK enjoyed the films his father brought home for private screenings.[86]

Like his father, who had an affair with Gloria Swanson, JFK was on the lookout for pretty Hollywood actresses in 1945. Designer Oleg Cassini, who was married to Gene Tierney, was well connected socially and took JFK to Joseph Cotten's Pacific Palisades home to play tennis. The confident and handsome young Kennedy was "wearing shorts, no shoes, no stockings, and no shirt," producer Norman Lloyd recalled.[87] Eventually JFK met and fell for Joan Fontaine but "struck out,"[88] and then went after Olivia, who at the time was living in Stone Canyon in ritzy Bel-Air.[89] "He thought [Olivia] was incredible, and he was willing to make a complete fool of himself if that's what it took to win her over," Spalding said.[90] Olivia invited Kennedy and Spalding to her home for tea, and Kennedy, who was dressed in his naval uniform, was obviously enraptured. "He was quite silent," Olivia recalled. "His friend did most of the talking. He just sat there, those great big eyes staring. Then, when it was time for them to leave, we walked into the hallway and he very decisively opened the door—and it was the closet, and all my old boxes of summer hats and tennis rackets fell on his head."[91] Later he rang her.

"This is Jack. I was at your house—have dinner with me."

"I'm sorry, I can't join you for dinner. I'm studying my lines tonight."[92]

She changed her mind about staying in when Ludwig Bemelmans, who was writing *Yolanda and the Thief*, a Fred Astaire musical, called and asked her to dine at Romanoff's. Olivia later described him as "a rotund fellow with a little fringe of white hair." When they arrived at the restaurant, she saw "the lovely warrior himself," Olivia recalled, referring to JFK.[93] He did not call her again. "It was hysterical," Spalding said. "Olivia de Havilland would not go out with Kennedy but when he spotted her at a restaurant dining with her artist-writer Ludwig Bemelmans of *Madeline* fame, Jack was dumbfounded." Kennedy said, "Just look at that guy! I know he's talented, but really! Do you think it was me walking into the closet? Do you think that's what really did it?"[94]

Bemelmans is responsible for painting the murals in Manhattan's most opulent watering hole, the Bemelmans Bar in the deluxe Carlyle Hotel at 35 East 76th Street. The large-scale, whimsical murals depict frolicking animals in nearby Central Park. During the Kennedy administration the hotel became known as "the New York White House" because on trips to New York JFK always checked into his two-bedroom suite on the 34th floor.[95]

When Gene Tierney left Oleg Cassini, JFK began a love affair with her after visiting the set of her film *Dragonwyck* in 1946.[96] The star of three of the Golden Age's most popular movies, *Leave Her to Heaven*, *Laura*, and *The Razor's Edge*, Tierney was described by Darryl F. Zanuck, president of 20th Century-Fox, as " the most beautiful woman in movie history."[97] Kennedy and Tierney were together for a year before she left him after he said he couldn't marry an actress because he'd decided to go into politics.[98] When he was elected President, she sent him a letter of congratulation, and he invited her to the White House and sat next to her.[99] Oleg Cassini was First Lady Jacqueline Kennedy's favorite designer, and she appointed him as her exclusive couturier in 1961. The elegant style he created for her launched a new fashion era of timeless simplicity.[100]

Marcus Goodrich resurfaced in Olivia's life in 1946. "He came back to marry Olivia," Niven Busch wrote.[101] She'd gone to New York for the summer and later recalled, "I always have said that travel is the only way to find a husband."[102] She was soon to open in J.M. Barrie's *What Every Woman Knows* at Connecticut's Westport County Playhouse. Prophetically, it was a play about a woman who marries a man who doesn't love her but expects her to further his career.

Olivia's dialogue coach, Phyllis Laughton, the wife of director George Seaton, rang Goodrich and invited him over to meet the movie star.[103] He arrived at 10 p.m. and was still talking at 3 a.m.[104] Later, one evening as Olivia and Goodrich were driving back to New York from Easthampton, they had a flat tire, and as Goodrich fixed it, Olivia told him her life story.[105] When she finished he observed that a girl with her "nervous system" needed a businessman for a husband.[106] She wanted such a man even if she didn't know it, he said. The last thing she needed, he added, was a writer.

"Of course, I must marry a businessman," Olivia replied.[107]

"It took me three days to adjust myself to the idea of marrying a writer," she recalled.[108] Goodrich was eighteen years her senior—she was thirty, he was forty-eight—and he insisted on retaining the word "obey" in the wedding ceremony.[109] For twenty-five hours she pondered whether she wanted to obey him.[110] "After thinking it over," she later told Sheilah

Graham, "I knew that since I loved and respected him, I'd obey him anyway. So what difference did it make?"[111]

It was decided to have the wedding ceremony in the Westport home of Lawrence Langer, a Theatre Guild executive, with Laughton as matron of honor, Seaton as best man, Langer's wife Armina Marshall as bridesmaid, and Irene Mayer Selznick in attendance. Lilian was curiously absent from both of her daughters' weddings.[112]

Olivia reportedly considered canceling the ceremony.[113] To dispel her doubts, Goodrich said, "Don't think too far ahead. Just pretend this is a one-act play. Don't worry about the other two acts!"[114] She later recalled, "If Marc hadn't kept me from thinking too far ahead, I doubt if I would have gone through with it!"[115] On August 26, 1946, the AP flashed the news from Connecticut: "Requesting that the word 'obey' be retained in the wedding ceremony, screen-star Olivia de Havilland was married today to Marcus Aurelius Goodrich, scenario writer and former newspaperman."[116] Olivia later told Sheilah Graham, "Everybody thinks I insisted on having the word 'obey.' I didn't—it was Marcus."[117]

The bride wore a white print dress and a navy blue Milan hat with a blue veil. She left immediately after the ceremony to perform at the playhouse and later for a honeymoon in Bermuda.[118] In the *Philadelphia Inquirer*, a columnist wrote he received a call from Olivia "back from her honeymoon . . . 'I've got a husband who's really the boss,' she said, laughing."[119] "Marcus . . . insisted the word 'obey' be used, and I finally gave in."[120]

"For a time the marriage seemed very successful," Niven Busch wrote.[121]

Joan Fontaine said she didn't learn of her sister's marriage until Olivia's agent rang her with the news and inquired if she'd ever heard of Goodrich. "All I know about him," Joan replied, "is that he has had four wives and written one book. Too bad it's not the other way around."[122] On September 13, 1946, columnist Dorothy Kilgallen wrote, "Olivia de

Havilland became the stepmother of an eighteen-year-old son when she married Marcus Goodrich."[123] "How naïve can you get?" Walter Winchell wrote from New York, revealing that Olivia hadn't known how many times Goodrich had been married "until [she] read it in the newspapers."[124] According to the *Los Angeles Times*, "She had been led to believe . . . that there had been just one other union."[125]

Goodrich moved into Olivia's dusty-pink bachelor-girl digs, owned by Mitch Leisen, in The Shoreham. "Marcus hasn't worked since we were married," Olivia would testify six years later, "and I was the breadwinner."[126]

Associated Press correspondent Bob Thomas sent out a worrisome dispatch on November 5, 1945, stating, "She told me (in his presence) that adjustment to wedded life is not easy after her years of independence. 'You should see the apartment!' she exclaimed. 'Pipe cleaners and ashes all over the place and tired, half-smoked cigars in the most inconceivable places. And books—I personally unloaded eight cases of them. The only place where he hasn't stacked his books is the bathroom, and he's eyeing that, too. But he can't put them in the shower. My things are in there."[127]

Journalist Sidney Skolsky noticed some disquieting changes in Olivia, writing on November 9, "She used to brush her teeth seven times a day. She didn't smoke, she wrote poetry, and she always ate the same lunch— lamb chops and a baked apple. She now brushes her teeth three times a day, is a chain smoker, doesn't write poetry, and varies her lunches."[128] He added that on the third day of their marriage her husband, a Southerner, fought with her for three hours over the Civil War. "She finally surrendered," the columnist concluded.[129]

When Sheilah Graham called on the couple in December 1946, Goodrich said, "It will have to do for a while," referring to Olivia's apartment. "From the set of his jaw," Sheilah wrote, "you know he is the boss of the family. It seems that neither Marcus nor Olivia wants to pay inflated prices for a house today."[130]

"I've taken a raincheck on the 11 children," he told Graham. Olivia, wrapping herself in eiderdown and explaining she had a cold, said, "I was quite sure I wanted to be an old maid. Or rather, I'd resigned myself to that. I thought I'd like to be like Maude Adams, and spend my later years teaching drama in a university. It was a pretty picture. And I'm glad it didn't come off . . . It's so wonderful having someone to talk things over with, and it's fine to think about his work, too."[131]

Olivia noticed that Marcus had a photograph of a pretty Mexican woman on his desk. When she asked him about it, he roared with laughter and said, "I'm writing a story with a Mexican background, and it's about a Mexican woman."[132]

"I was jealous," Olivia told Graham, "and wanted him to throw it away, but he said he couldn't because she was the heroine of his new book . . . And he even said that one of the reasons he married me was because he needed a woman around, since he was writing about a woman!"[133]

"Even if Marcus weren't busy on his book," Olivia said, "we couldn't travel because wherever Marcus goes, his 11 cases of books have to go."[134]

A few months later another reporter visited their "fashionable hillside apartment, first-floor level, that looks out on a tiled patio and fountain."[135] Olivia referred to Goodrich as "head of the house," but mentioned that on two occasions they'd both lost their tempers simultaneously.[136] She looked pale to the journalist, owing, Olivia explained, to staying holed up reading scripts. She appreciated Goodrich's advice, remarking, "So many men in Hollywood are waiting to take advantage of a woman in business matters."[137] He was only one-third through with his Mexican novel, of which Olivia had read the first chapters and decided that was enough. "There's a Mexican girl in the story of whom I am terribly jealous," she said.[138]

He wrote daily from 9 a.m. to 2 p.m. on his portable typewriter on the dining-room table, concealed by two screens on which he'd appended four signs warning, "Do Not Disturb."[139] The reporter noticed "the table is strewn with business papers, chewing gum, pencils, and Marc's rack of 35 pipes. He has a pipe going nearly all day and Olivia, busy reading scenarios in the living room, loves the odor."[140]

"Writers fascinate me," Olivia said.[141] She looked nice in her pool-table green slacks, a pink blouse, gold belt, gold buttons, and gold earrings. Goodrich struck the reporter as "a tall, energetic man with dark, curly hair, who is 18½ years Olivia's senior."[142]

"A woman is psychologically 10 years older than a man, so Marc is really only eight and a half years older than I am," Olivia said.[143] His sole occupation was house husband. Years later, she was still, she said, "the family breadwinner."[144]

Leonard Lyons, a syndicated columnist, later took exception to "her having to be referred to as Mrs. Goodrich . . . The same kind of problem always arises when stars marry men whose fame doesn't equal theirs. When Miss de Havilland [later] came to Broadway in *Romeo and Juliet*, the suggestion was made that she be billed on the marquee as 'Olivia Goodrich'. . . The overruling argument was 'Goodrich is a good name if you're selling tires, but not if you're selling tickets.'"[145]

At the end of 1946, Olivia and Goodrich appeared, to Hedda Hopper at least, to be very much in love. While driving on Sunset Boulevard, Hopper reported on December 1, she saw Olivia and Goodrich walking along, holding hands. Stopping, she told Olivia she'd heard they were living in her mother's home.

"What nonsense," Goodrich said. "Of course, we're living in Olivia's. Come up to see us. I'd like to talk to you."[146] Hopper went to their apartment and later wrote, "Livvy's in love . . . She purred like a kitten . . . Goodrich is boss of the family . . . 'She has an innate goodness,' said he, 'that's what shines through every performance.'"[147]

He wanted exclusive rights to manage her career.[148] Syndicated columnist Virginia Vale reported on January 9, 1947, "Olivia de Havilland has discharged her agent, business manager, and publicity man, and turned their duties over to her new husband, Marcus Goodrich."[149] Another reporter wrote, "Suddenly, after Olivia married author Marcus Goodrich, she stopped seeing her family, answering their messages, or communicating with them in any way. Olivia discharged practically every member of her management staff."[150]

The arrangement was short-lived. Jack Lait Jr. wrote in the *Brooklyn Daily Eagle*, "Mebbe Olivia de Havilland has thought better of entrusting all her business affairs to her new hubby. I understand she has now hired herself a new agent and lawyer, to replace the ones she sacked a couple of weeks ago."[151]

The bad publicity kept coming in 1947, the UP headlining on March 16, HUSBANDS OF OSCAR-WINNING OLIVIA DE HAVILLAND AND JOAN FONTAINE JUMP INTO SISTERS' OLD FEUD. "This always happens when photographers are around," Goodrich told the UP. "Joan always comes up to have her picture taken with my wife, and Olivia doesn't like it."[152] Joan's husband, producer William Dozier, denied the allegation, saying photographers requested the joint photos.[153] Joan, he said, had no trouble attracting photographers herself.[154] That was not entirely true of either sister.[155] When a famous visiting Englishman's courteous but remote expression made it clear he didn't recognize Joan during their introduction, she said, "I am Olivia de Havilland's sister."[156] The Englishman said, "Oh, yes, of course. Stupid of me, I'm sure, but would you mind telling me who Olivia de Havilland is?"[157]

In 1947 Goodrich insisted on moving Olivia from California to "Rappahannock, Virginia, where his forebears settled," the AP reported, "She'll take classes at nearby William and Mary College."[158] Apparently the move had nothing to do with the invasion of rattlesnakes around their home in Los Angeles. After friends donated a crateful of kingsnakes, which are used to destroy rattlers, Goodrich set out to kill the rattlesnakes on their property, according to the press.[159]

On September 3, 1947, Jimmie Fidler predicted Goodrich's egomania would ultimately destroy the marriage. "If the rumor is true that Olivia de Havilland's spouse, writer Marcus Goodrich, burns whenever anyone mentions Olivia by her professional name, instead of dubbing her 'Mrs. Goodrich,' you can inscribe one more Hollywood marriage on your 'doubtful' list . . . Men who marry Hollywood stars must be content to play second fiddle."[160]

Still trying to establish himself in Hollywood, Goodrich accepted an assignment from a fan magazine. "It must be love," one reporter wrote, his pen dripping irony. "Marcus Goodrich started a fan magazine story about wifey Olivia de Havilland six months ago and hasn't finished it yet. He agreed to write the piece, providing the magazine does not change even a comma."[161]

PART FOUR

YEARS OF TRIUMPH

18

To Each His Own, the Witch Hunt, *The Snake Pit*, and the Cover of *Time*

The mid-1940s were a dicey time for Olivia's generation of actors. Jimmy Stewart had risked his life while commanding some fifty Liberator bombers that rained destruction on such German cities as Berlin, Bremen, and Brunswick, for which he received the Distinguished Flying Cross and the Croix de Guerre, only to return to an uncertain fate in Hollywood. Offers were scarce for this thirty-seven-year-old shell-shocked vet with thinning hair and a blank stare, and rumors of Jimmy's wartime breakdown were spreading.

He'd been on suspension at Metro due to military service, and as a result of time added to his contract, Metro still owned him. His shrewd agent Lew Wasserman, mindful of the de Havilland Rule that now rendered suspension penalties illegal, advised he'd be better off going freelance, which would bring him more money and artistic freedom. Many new independent companies were springing up and soon would produce half of Hollywood's output. Jimmy went to Liberty Films, co-founded by Frank Capra, who'd said of Jimmy after directing him in *You Can't Take It With You*, "I think he's probably the best actor who's ever hit the screen."[1] Although Capra now found Jimmy "older, shyer, ill at ease," he asked him to play George Bailey in *It's a Wonderful Life*, based on a short story, "The Greatest Gift," by Philip Van Doren Stern, a former editor at Pocket

Books, Simon and Schuster, and Knopf.[2] Olivia was considered for the role of George's wife Mary, as were Jean Arthur, Ginger Rogers, Martha Scott, and Ann Dvorak.[3]

"It would have meant playing opposite Jimmy Stewart, home from the wars," Olivia said. "I knew it would be awkward to work with him because of our many months together in a sort of high-school prewar romance, which came to an end."[4]

Now that Olivia was free from Warner and available for freelance assignments, she was in competition with Ingrid Bergman, who'd become the major star of the 1940s and was usually the first choice of producers and directors after her triumphs in *Casablanca, Gaslight, Spellbound,* and *For Whom the Bell Tolls. To Each His Own* was being shopped around, and David O. Selznick, who had Ingrid under contract, wanted her to play the lead, but Ingrid was sick of working for him and making him rich on loan outs. For lending her to Metro for *Gaslight,* David received $253,750, but paid her only $75,156.25. Her contract with David was near expiration, and she didn't want him tying her up for a year or more on a new project.[5]

Based on a story by Olivia's friend Charles Brackett, *To Each His Own* had been in the works at Paramount since 1943, experiencing numerous script problems. It was the emotionally charged story of an unwed girl, Jody Norris, who's in love with a gallant World War I pilot, later killed in combat and leaving her alone and pregnant. What was to befall Jody after that was yet to be decided by Brackett, the producer, and scenarists Frances Goodrich and Albert Hackett, who hadn't been able to devise a viable plot for the second half of the film.

Brackett tried to pick frequent collaborator Billy Wilder's brains to no avail and then appealed to Walter Reisch, who'd worked with Brackett and Wilder in 1939 on *Ninotchka.* Reisch suggested "a twisting-around so that the mature Jody thinks she is to have a week of being the mother of her boy on leave in England—and finds out when she goes to meet him that the last thing he wants around is his mother." Paramount's executive producer Buddy De Sylva told Brackett to describe the plot of *To Each His Own* to both Ginger Rogers and Olivia "immediately [and] to be sure to get one or the other."[6]

Over lunch with Brackett at Lucey's restaurant on December 2, 1943, director Mitchell Leisen told Brackett that *To Each His Own* should go to Claudette Colbert, but Brackett eventually followed De Sylva's advice and gave the script to Ginger, who loved it, but had second thoughts.[7] "Should she play an older woman at this time?" she wondered. "Should she play a sad picture?"[8] For Brackett, "It's the old trouble with Ginger. She hasn't a very good brain, but she insists on using it . . . I had a brief conference with Buddy re the possibility of Greta Garbo as Jody . . . I lunched with [George] Cukor at La Rue's and started to tell him *To Each His Own*, which he purported to like, but he had to hurry away to an interview with Darryl Zanuck."[9]

Ginger rejected *To Each His Own*. "I read the script and asked myself if I wanted to play the mother of a 20-year-old man who is preparing to go off to war," Ginger, who was thirty-five, wrote in her autobiography. "My answer to myself was NO!"[10] Paramount preferred Jean Arthur but Brackett said, "I don't want her."[11] Olivia was away, touring military bases abroad, but Bert Allenberg, her agent, said she might be interested and would be back in two months.[12] She first learned of the role "when I was touring the Army hospitals," she said. "I knew immediately it was a part I had to do. It was a very long part and it offered a lot of opportunities for an actress."[13]

February 27, 1945, was "a day of vast humiliations" for Brackett, who wrote, "Olivia has decided that she'd better make a comedy next."[14] On March 20 she declined to consider John Farrow as director, preferring Mitch Leisen, who read the script and liked the strong heroine's role but deplored the soppy story. "I knew it would be difficult to make a sentimental story such as this believable," Olivia said.[15] Brackett was amazed that Olivia, with no gray in her hair, was completely convincing in scenes showing Jody in middle age, a feat Olivia brought off by imitating her parent Lilian's mannerisms, "much to mother's chagrin," she said.[16] "Didn't you see yourself as Miss Norris, Mother?" Olivia asked Lilian, who replied, "I should say not. How utterly ridiculous. Olivia, you know I didn't have a line in my face at 46."[17] Lilian showed up on the Paramount lot, and after Brackett saw her, she was cast in *The Lost Weekend* as Mrs. St. James, Jane Wyman's mother.[18]

To Each His Own was a critical and popular success, *Variety* writing, "Artistry of Olivia de Havilland as the mother is superb. From the eager, young girl . . . through to the cold, brusque business woman, her performance doesn't miss a beat."[19] The buzz around the industry indicated Olivia had a good chance to win the Oscar, but, again, Goodrich made problems. ""The picture editor of *Life* . . . wanted to lunch with her and if possible work out a scheme for her to appear on the cover of *Time*," Brackett wrote on December 4, 1946. "To this Mr. Goodrich replied that Mrs. Goodrich didn't go to restaurants with newspapermen, and if there were any questions they wanted to ask, let them ask in writing and Mrs. Goodrich would answer them. The [Academy] Award chances get thinner with every such episode."[20]

Despite PR blunders on Goodrich's part, Olivia was nominated for the best-actress Oscar and Brackett invited her to a dinner party at his home prior to the 1947 Academy Awards ceremony. She wore a pale blue gown with a wide skirt decorated with a hand-painted garland of flowers. While serving the ham, Brackett accidentally spilled Madeira gravy on her dress, but fortunately the stain melded into the dress's floral design. Following the meal, they proceeded to the 6,700-seat Shrine Auditorium, where Olivia "worked the bleacher fans into a frenzy," Kinn and Piazza wrote in their history of the Academy Awards.

After Joan, as a previous Oscar winner, gave supporting actor Harold Russell his statuette for *The Best Years of Our Lives*, Olivia was announced as the winner and made her way down the aisle, though it was blocked by Louis B. Mayer and three rows of angry MGM executives staging a walkout because Jane Wyman hadn't won for the studio's highly touted *The Yearling*. Finally, gliding to the stage in her strapless light blue tulle, she took the gold-plated bronze figure, worth $96 but priceless in terms of prestige, clout in the industry, box-office draw, and future income, from the hands of Ray Milland, the previous year's winner for *The Lost Weekend*.

"In this wonderful moment," she said, "my common sense reminds me quite clearly that most of the work that went into earning this award was not done by Olivia de Havilland at all, but by a big team of other people who, if justice were really to prevail, would be standing up here beside me now . . . Then I feel humble too, as well as proud, to accept this award which I do in the name of my team as well as my own. Thank you."[21] Afterward, she and Goodrich entertained friends in their apartment, where, according to the AP, Olivia "placed the statuette on a bedroom table . . . 'But I don't know,' she said, 'whether my husband will object to having another man in my bedroom.'"[22] Louella O. Parsons wrote, "Olivia de Havilland didn't need an Academy Award to make her the most sought after actress in Hollywood, but since she carried off the Oscar, the offers have been more than she could accept in 10 years."[23]

Terrible news for the de Havilland family arrived in 1946. Olivia's cousin Geoffrey de Havilland broke his neck testing the experimental swept-wing de Havilland 108 Swallow for supersonic speed, diving from 10,000 feet and crashing into the Thames Estuary on September 27.[24] Shortly before his death, he and his friend Phillip Gordon Marshall were talking in a pub near Hatfield, England, when Geoffrey quoted some lines from Algernon Swinburne's "Laus Veneris [baleful]," a poem obsessed with death: "Ah yet would God this flesh of mine be where air might wash and long leaves cover me, where tides of grass break into foams of flowers or where the wind's feet shine along the sea." His remains were discovered in windblown marsh grass on the Isle of Sheppey, where he lay supine on the shore, washed by incoming tides.[25]

News wasn't so good for the movie industry either—1946 marked the beginning of the end of the Golden Age. Television is usually blamed, but the trend began before the advent of TV. Weekly attendance at movie houses plunged from 81 million in 1946 to 69 million in 1948. The postwar world had less interest in fantasy and spent more time going to college and paying the mortgage. The last Golden Age genre, film noir, expressed disillusion and anxiety in pictures like *Scarlet Street*, *The Third Man*, *Gentlemen's Agreement*, *Arch of Triumph*, and a picture in which Olivia would enjoy one of her biggest successes, *The Snake Pit*.

At the peak of her popularity and inundated with scripts and offers, Olivia chose to make *The Dark Mirror*, a film noir about a pair of identical twins charged with murder, both of them played by Olivia. The picture was released the same year Bette Davis portrayed identical twins in *A Stolen Life*, a better written screenplay that enabled Davis to establish separate and individual identities for each twin. According to *New York Times* critic Bosley Crowther, "Olivia de Havilland is the dual lady and for the life of us we never were sure when she was being Ruth, the good sister, or Terry, the evil one . . . Miss de Havilland does nothing in *The Dark Mirror* that will add to her stature as an actress."[26]

Fortunately, she declined the leading role in 1947's *Ivy*, the story of a woman who murders her husband and sends her lover to the gallows so she can marry a rich man. She didn't want to play a murderess after her portrayal of a ruthless character in *The Dark Mirror*. Joan, who'd wanted to play Ivy and envied Olivia when she snagged the role, promptly rang her sister. "Do you mind if I play it?" Joan asked, and Olivia said she had no objection. On the final day of filming, Joan fell down an elevator shaft, sustaining a dislocated shoulder.[27] The picture seemed hexed for both sisters.[28] "Olivia de Havilland today sued her agents, Phil Berg and Bert Allenberg, for $10,000 and asked her contract with them be voided," the UP reported in 1947. "Miss de Havilland charged she lost $175,000 from being 'unemployed' while they tried to get her to take a part in *Ivy*."[29] Allenberg, who handled Wallace Beery, Clark Gable, Jeanne Crain, Alan Ladd, Robert Mitchum, Robert Montgomery, Loretta Young, and Edward G. Robinson, said he'd lost only one major star, Olivia, in twenty-eight years. The case was settled. Syndicated Hollywood columnist Edith Gwynn questioned "the fascinating (?) privilege of obeying [Goodrich's] every word, probably alienating all her former friends."[30]

The blackest stain on Hollywood's Golden Age was the industry's shameful reaction to the Communist witch hunt during America's Cold War with the Soviet Union. The studio bosses refused to protect their artists when they were hounded as Communists or fellow travelers in the late 1940s and 1950s, after Winston Churchill kicked off the Age of Anxiety, as poet W.H. Auden called it, when he warned, "From Stetin in the Baltic to Trieste in the Adriatic an 'Iron Curtain' has descended across the continent." Careers were ruined by the infamous blacklist, and a climate of fear spread over Hollywood as actors, producers, directors, and writers informed on each other to save their jobs and escape punishment by the disgraceful House Un-American Activities Committee, which regarded Hollywood as a maker of public opinion with the power to propagandize for Russia.

Olivia joined the Hollywood Independent Citizens Committee of the Arts, Sciences, and Professions (HICCASP) in 1946 as a way of pledging her support for the legacy of President Franklin D. Roosevelt, for whom she'd vigorously campaigned when he was running for his third term and who'd died the previous year. In June she was surprised when HICCASP, intent on capitalizing on her popularity, asked her to deliver pro-Communist speeches. She not only declined but rewrote the speeches, making sure they endorsed President Harry S. Truman's anti-Communist stance. When this outraged HICCASP, she "knew they had to be Communists," she later told the *Wall Street Journal*. She decided to resign but Dore Schary, who'd shortly oust Louis B. Mayer from MGM and replace him as studio chief, persuaded her to stay. She then urged HICCASP to declare itself anti-Communist in the press. Writers and producers began to convene in her apartment above Sunset Boulevard to discuss her proposal.

At a meeting of HICCASP's membership, which numbered 3,000 and included Bette Davis, Gregory Peck, Humphrey Bogart, and Artie Shaw, Schary was seated beside Ronald Reagan and told him to come to Olivia's apartment afterward.

"You know, Olivia," Reagan later whispered to her, "I always thought you might be one of them."

"That's funny," she said, laughing. "I thought you were one of them."

She asked Reagan to write HICCASP's anti-Communist declaration for the media, and he gave it a shot, but she complained, "Ronnie, that's not strong enough. It has to be stronger than that or I won't accept it."

The *Wall Street Journal* later called her action "a galvanizing moment for the man who would be President."

HICCASP brought Olivia face to face with such openly pro-Soviet members as Artie Shaw, with whom, as a patriotic American, she inevitably clashed.

"Have you read the Russian constitution?" he asked her.

"No, I haven't," she replied. "And how recently have you read ours?"

Struggling to push through the Reagan declaration stirred up such chaos in HICCASP that she finally thought, This is it. She told the *Journal*, "I had fought long enough, as hard as I could, and I resigned." Reagan also walked out, depriving HICCASP of what he called its "last front of respectability." HICCASP collapsed soon after. More than half a century later, the *Journal* wrote that Olivia had helped Reagan find his way to the White House: "In one authoritative exclamation point for Ms. de

Havilland's side, Ronnie made the cover of the *Economist* as 'The Man Who Beat Communism.'"[31]

⌐ ⌐

On December 27, 1947, the press reported Olivia had jumped nine notches in a recent trade paper poll to become the third most popular actress in America behind Ingrid Bergman at No. 1 and Claudette Colbert at No. 2.[32] "Now that I've done paranoiac [in *The Dark Mirror*], I guess dementia praecox is next," Olivia said after reading Mary Jane Ward's *The Snake Pit*, a best-selling novel based on Ward's nervous breakdown and confinement in an insane asylum.[33] Anatole Litvak had been given galley proofs by his friend Bennett Cerf, head of Random House, in May 1945, and optioned the film rights for $75,000, immediately sending the galleys to Olivia in New York, where she was staying in a hotel. After perusing the galleys twice, she told Litvak she wanted to play the heroine, Virginia Cunningham.

Trying to raise funds to keep his option, Litvak shopped *The Snake Pit* around without success, finally offering the leading role to Ingrid Bergman, hoping she'd attract studio financing. Ingrid turned him down flat. "Then Olivia de Havilland took the part," Ingrid recalled, "and she got an Oscar for her performance which was marvelous [actually, Olivia was only nominated]. And Anatole kept saying, 'Look what you turned down!' And I'd reply, 'I know what I turned down. It all takes place in an insane asylum and I couldn't bear that. It was a very good part, but if I had played it, I wouldn't have got an Oscar for it.'"[34] Ginger Rogers also rejected the part because it was "about a women's psychiatric ward." Ginger said. "Who played the tragic woman's role? Olivia de Havilland. And she received another Oscar nomination! It seemed Olivia knew a good thing when she saw it. Perhaps Olivia should thank me for such poor judgment."[35]

Insanity was a taboo subject in 1940s America, but 20th Century Fox chief Daryl F. Zanuck courageously took on Ward's unflinching look at the barbaric asylums in which the mentally challenged were warehoused. Gene Tierney was his first choice for the lead, but she was pregnant, and when Litvak told Zanuck he'd always wanted Olivia, Zanuck hired her—two years after she'd first agreed to do the picture.[36]

Olivia's portrait of an asylum inmate was shocking in its authenticity; she used no makeup, wore a frayed sweater full of holes, schlepped around in bedroom slippers and droopy stockings, and sported a "bedlam bob" haircut. Louella O. Parsons interviewed her on the eve of her first wedding anniversary, August 26, 1947. "Marcus came with her," Parsons wrote, "and waited in another room . . . 'Still happy?' [Parsons asked]. 'Perfectly, both in my marriage and in my career . . . I can select the stories I think are right for me.'" She was through with "serious character studies," she said. "I think I should do something lighter for my next, don't you? . . . I don't want to do another *Snake Pit* . . . I might . . . lose my mind." Goodrich must have rejoined them, for Parsons wrote, "At that, Marcus, who was sitting there . . . said, 'No danger, Olivia.'" Her immediate plans were to take a rest and go on a vacation though she hated to leave their home atop Benedict Canyon, where she and Marcus enjoyed reading, playing tennis, "and having good healthy discussions."[37] On Sundays they usually invited guests and played croquet.

Her anniversary present to Goodrich was a movie projector and screen, and his gift to her was an antique bowl that she admired so much she hired decorator Tom Douglas to redo the living room in the same style.[38] Goodrich sent her white chrysanthemums with a card that read: "One year with the right woman [signed] 'Slewfoot.'"[39] That had been her pet name for him ever since they'd seen *The Yearling*, in which Old Slewfoot, a bear that won't stop attacking, symbolizes that nature is at once both thrilling and terrifying.

While filming *The Snake Pit*, she found herself "so deeply engrossed in this character that I was afraid I might suddenly do the things off screen, I did on. I was exhausted . . . I have never had any role that took so much out of me."[40] The editors of *Time*, the prestigious and powerful flagship magazine of Henry Luce's publishing empire, put Olivia on the cover of its December 20, 1948, issue. *Time*'s reporter wrote that Goodrich insisted on hovering over them and interjecting unsolicited opinions with his "quarterdeck voice and a manner to match."[41] That something was seriously awry in her marriage was immediately obvious. The *Time* reporter wrote, "Goodrich's own view of his wife (he discusses her at length and objectively, in her presence, while she listens meekly) is that she needs a firm hand."[42] When Olivia practiced screaming for her asylum scenes at home, rumors circulated "that that man Goodrich was beating his wife," the *Time* story continued. "To disprove it, Goodrich finally took to sitting in the patio in full view of the neighbors while Olivia went on screaming inside."[43] Although there is no evidence that he was physically abusing her at this time, the Associated Press would later report, "Goodrich often beat her."[44]

Samuel Goldwyn and his wife Frances hosted a dinner in Olivia's honor, but Goodrich forbade her to attend, which, socially, made no sense—socially the Goldwyns were among the A-list kingpins of Los Angeles. Goodrich allowed Olivia "to express no opinions," she'd later state.[45]

When *The Snake Pit* opened at the Rivoli in New York, Bosley Crowther wrote, "Olivia de Havilland does a brilliant, heart-rending job."[46] She won the esteemed New York Film Critics Award for best actress of the year, considered by the cognoscenti to be the ultimate acting prize. She was the unanimous choice on the first poll. Though the picture has not aged well, it's historically important because it changed the way America viewed mental illness, it improved conditions in asylums, and it triggered a breakthrough in stark realism, paving the way for such movies as *The Men, Coming Home,* and *One Flew Over the Cuckoo's Nest.*

The Academy of Motion Picture Arts and Sciences nominated Olivia for its 1948 best-actress award, but she had far graver concerns than the Oscar, which went to Jane Wyman for *Johnny Belinda.* At thirty-two, Olivia was pregnant and it wasn't going well—she was in bed through-out March and April and her physician, Dr. John McCausland, predicted she'd stay there until the baby arrived. She was so ill by April that doctors were working frantically to save the baby, expected in August.[47] Both she and the unborn child were in more danger from Goodrich than from her illness, during which he did nothing to restrain his ferocious temper. "On one occasion, while I was pregnant, we were having dinner in my room," Olivia recalled. "He got angry because he was served beef pie instead of beefsteak and kidney pie and hurled the pie across the room."[48] Though she'd been showing some improvement, now her condition worsened.[49]

Substantial movie roles were coming her way—she, Ginger Rogers, and Jean Arthur were vying for *The Life of Mary Baker Eddy,*[50] but Olivia would do nothing to jeopardize the baby's welfare, and by late April Dr. McCausland told her she now had a chance to bear the infant normally.[51] Altogether she'd been in bed for nearly seven months when Benjamin Briggs Goodrich was born on September 28, 1949. The AP announced, "Olivia de Havilland has a new name—Mama. The eight-pound young-ster was delivered by Caesarian section yesterday."[52] She was in good con-dition at Good Samaritan Hospital.[53]

"During the first five and a half weeks of the baby's life, I took care of him all by myself," Olivia said. "I wanted to take care of him all by myself and I did. During that period of time, well, the baby was four weeks old and I was caring for him in the bedroom of the house, my husband became upset over something—I cannot recall what it was—it was unim-portant—and he became extremely violent and abusive in his manner and he struck me."[54] Benjamin was in her arms and she frantically tried to protect the baby by turning and taking the blow on her body.[55] "I was afraid my son was in danger both psychologically and physically," she said, but added, "I wanted to make my marriage a success, because this was my only marriage."[56]

The Hollywood Women's Press Club was thinking of giving Olivia its annual Golden Apple for cooperation with reporters for 1948 "just for the sheer (and murderous) delight of watching Joan, who won it last year, make the presentation," a mischievous reporter wrote.[57] Louella O. Parsons was barely able to control her urge to ask Olivia, "'Isn't it wonderful Joan is going to have a baby?'. . . I did not mention Joan, and I know better when I am talking to Joan to mention Olivia."[58]

Jimmy Stewart was also careful not to mention Olivia when he worked with Joan in a forgettable 1948 film called *You Gotta Stay Happy*, produced by Joan's husband William Dozier. Jimmy's career was in a postwar slump, and he found it demeaning to settle for second billing to Joan. He feared his career was in decline. "This wasn't such a bad film," Jimmy recalled. "Joan was a nice person to work with . . . although she didn't much like her sister so we steered clear of her as a subject."[59] Though pregnant, Joan was required in one scene to leap off a hay wagon. "She shouldn't have been doing some of the stuff she had to do," Jimmy said.[60] She ended up in the hospital with "a pain in the tummy," and Jimmy was the only one to pay her a visit. "Not even the director [H.C. Potter] went to see her," Jimmy related. Fortunately, she didn't lose the baby. A few years later Jimmy's career revived, and he was back at the top, turning out *Rear Window*, *Vertigo*, and other blockbusters.

19

Working with Montgomery Clift, Ralph Richardson, and William Wyler in *The Heiress*

Artistically, 1949 would be Olivia's *annus mirabilis*. It could not have begun more providentially. *Look* magazine, with a circulation of three million, second only to *Life*, announced in early February that she and Laurence Olivier were the top movie stars of the previous year, based on their performances in *The Snake Pit* and *Hamlet*, respectively. More-over, 1949 was the year of her finest film, *The Heiress*. If producer David O. Selznick had launched her career as a transcendent dramatic actress in *GWTW*, *Heiress* director William Wyler now brought her to a magnifi-cent consummation. Wyler already had a legacy of distinguished movies almost unequaled by any other filmmaker—*The Letter, Jezebel, Wuthering Heights, The Little Foxes,* and *Mrs. Miniver,* all notable for keen psycho-logical acuity and dramatic tension.[1]

Based on Henry James's nineteenth-century classic, *Washington Square, The Heiress* focuses on the clash of wills between Olivia's character, Catherine Sloper, a plain but very rich young woman, and her domineer-ing, hateful father, Dr. Austin Sloper, when a handsome, smooth-talking fortune hunter, Morris Townsend, asks for Catherine's hand in marriage. Dr. Sloper shows him the door, rightly sizing him up as a gold digger, but Catherine loves Morris desperately, and tells him they must elope, unwisely adding that she doesn't care if it means being disinherited. Morris agrees to collect her in a carriage that night but cruelly stands her up, no longer interested in her without her money. In time she inherits her father's fortune, and when Morris returns years later, again proposing marriage, she accepts, but when he brings a carriage to take her away, she bolts the door and leaves him screaming in the street outside. Her costars were two of the best actors in the world, Montgomery Clift as Morris and Ralph Richardson as Dr. Sloper.

Perhaps no better example of theatrical intensity exists on film than the moment in *The Heiress* when Olivia, ignoring Morris's pounding on the door, snips the thread of her last needlepoint, signaling her liberation from the agonies of romantic love—and her rebirth as a mature woman of dignity, self-respect, and inner beauty.

Wyler began filming in June 1948. It was his first picture for Paramount, and though his period at the studio includes *Roman Holiday*, which brought Audrey Hepburn an Oscar, and the brilliant *Carrie*, based on Theodore Dreiser's early masterwork *Sister Carrie*, starring Jennifer Jones at her radiant best, *The Heiress* stands as Wyler's most distinguished achievement, and one of the finest movies in the American canon. When Olivia saw the play version by Ruth and Augustus Goetz in New York, she considered Wendy Hiller "a brilliant performer [but] stylized. I see another way to play Catherine. Stylization will not work on film. It'll be artificial. I knew by the end of the second act I had to do it. I thought of directors who'd have a feel for the material . . . My agent persuaded [Wyler] to get on the train and go to New York to see *The Heiress*."[2] Olivia recalled, "It was quite wonderful. Never will [I] forget the night I knew he had arrived [and] gone straight to the theatre to see the play." Wyler called and told her, "I've seen it. I like it. Let's do it."[3]

When I talked with Olivia in Paris in 1973, I asked her what she thought of twenty-seven-year-old Montgomery Clift. "Monty was wonderful," she said. "We were all excited when *Red River* opened while we were filming *The Heiress*."

It was a banner year for Clift. When his first film, *The Search*, the moving story of an American G.I. who rescues a lost and confused concentration-camp orphan in Occupied Germany, opened on March 26, 1948, critics and public alike went wild over Clift, photographer Richard Avedon remarking, "The minute Monty came on screen I cried because he was so realistic and honest . . . He seems to be creating a new kind of acting—almost documentary in approach."[4]

Red River made Clift a superstar and the herald of a new era in American movie acting, in which performers immerse themselves in the character to create believable, natural, true-to-life human beings. Marlon Brando, Julie Harris, Paul Newman, Kim Hunter, James Dean, Geraldine Page, Jane Fonda, Joanne Woodward, Al Pacino, Maureen Stapleton, Shelley Winters, and Robert De Niro would follow in Clift's footsteps as exemplars of the new super-naturalistic style, first codified by Konstantin Stanislavsky and taught by Lee Strasberg as The Method at the Actors Studio.

Olivia was possibly the first major Hollywood star to work with a Method actor; Marlon Brando would not show up in movies for another two years, in 1950's *The Men*. "Monty was painstaking and I liked that about him," she said.[5] She and Clift created magic onscreen, their scenes together bristling with life.

I asked Olivia if she remembered the haunting song Clift had sung to her. "Oh, yes. 'The Joys of Love.' Monty loved it, too. He sat down at the piano and played it for me in our scene in the parlor at Washington Square." Variously known as "Chagrin D'amore" ("The Pain of Love") and "Plaisir D'amour" ("The Joys of Love"), the song was composed by Jean Paul-Edige Martini, who lived from 1741 to 1816. Its poignant refrain, "The pleasure of love lasts only a moment, the pain of love lasts a lifetime," provides *The Heiress* with its sweetest moment but also foreshadows

Catherine's heartbreak when Morris deserts her upon discovering her father's threat to disinherit her if she marries him.

"You excel at portraying women who at first appear weak," I said to Olivia, "but in the end emerge as the strongest character in the film."

"I *certainly* do," she replied, and suddenly a strange thing happened. "The Joys of Love" came wafting over the restaurant's sound system.

"See," she said, "we were just talking about that song."

She seemed, like me, to regard coincidence as a spiritual thing, like a wink from God.

During production of *The Heiress*, problems arose early, Wyler insisting Olivia wear drab costumes, and Ralph Richardson doing his best to upstage her. Olivia's performance is breathtaking, especially in the second half of the film, when Catherine at last comes into her own, defying her father and telling him to strike her from his will at once lest he die before he has a chance to disown her. He almost expires on the spot, so withering is her hatred. In another scene, Richardson tried to deflect attention from Olivia by repeatedly flapping his gloves. He did not succeed in stealing the scene from Olivia, who was capable of holding her own with the best.[6]

Wyler did nothing about Richardson's antics and may even have encouraged them, the same way Hitchcock allowed Joan to be mistreated on the set of *Rebecca*. Great directors can be a cruel lot. When Ingrid Bergman failed to summon the distraught, frightened, hysterical look that director Victor Fleming needed for a scene in *Dr. Jekyll and Mr. Hyde*, "he took me by the shoulder with one hand," Ingrid later wrote, "spun me around, and struck me backwards and forwards across the face—hard—it hurt . . . He got performances out of me which very often I didn't think I was capable of . . . By the time the film was over I was deeply in love with Victor Fleming."[7] Directing Olivia in *The Heiress*, Wyler was inexcusably rude, excluding her from his between-take chats with Richardson, while she "sat there like Cinderella in my little chair, nobody speaking to me," Olivia recalled. "It is entirely possible Willie did that deliberately to make me feel . . . inadequate and . . . uninteresting."[8] Those were the exact characteristics Wyler needed to make Catherine both credible as a cringing wallflower and a "supreme symbol of inscrutable tragedy," as Garbo was once described. It was what Olivia had always wanted: difficult work well done.

When Wyler didn't understand a scene and couldn't figure out how to direct it, he'd tell his actors to "just get up there . . . and just show me what this scene is all about."[9]

"It was frightful," Olivia recalled. "They'd exchange ten lines and Wyler would say, 'Stop. Go back to the beginning. Keep [the] little exchanges you made . . . with the third exchange of lines. Leave everything else out. Do something different. I don't care what you do, as long as it's different, but keep just that.' So we would do that, and then he would say, 'Stop. Keep the first exchange. Then I want you to keep the sixth exchange. Drop everything else. Start again.'"[10]

She survived, as she had with Victor Fleming, by watching Wyler closely and trying to intuit his thoughts. "We were both born on the same day, July 1," she told Hedda Hopper. "I knew what he meant, regardless of his words, instantaneously . . . I always understood what he was trying to say. It was like some electrical thing between us."[11]

Clift disliked almost everyone and everything connected with the production, beginning with the script. Paramount had wanted him to play newspaperman Joe Gillis opposite Gloria Swanson's aging silent movie queen Norma Desmond in *Sunset Boulevard*, but, according to Swanson, "Mr. Clift dreaded the prospect of playing love scenes with an older woman," and he ended up in *The Heiress* by default.[12] Olivia had wanted Rex Harrison, Sheilah Graham maintained, but Harrison was already committed to *Anna and the King of Siam* with Irene Dunne and *The Ghost and Mrs. Muir* with Gene Tierney.[13]

Wyler and Olivia worked hard on the shot that shows Catherine climbing the steep staircase to her bedroom after Morris jilts her midway through the movie. She's carrying the suitcase she'll no longer need for her aborted elopement. Olivia did many takes and Wyler kept asking for more without telling her what he wanted. Finally, according to the TCM Film Archive, "the usually professional de Havilland threw the suitcase at him."[14] Lifting it, Wyler realized it was empty, and immediately knew the solution was to fill the suitcase with heavy objects, so that Olivia would have to trudge up the stairs with difficulty and at last give the director the feeling of defeat and misery he wanted.

Anyone who has seen and loved *The Heiress* knows that Wyler's technique resulted in the best performance of Olivia's career, giving it a tense, tremulous edge that keeps our eyes inexorably fixed on her. A snapshot shows Olivia and Wyler having a good time together on the set, sharing a birthday cake when the company threw a double celebration for them— he was forty-six, she, thirty-two. "I knew he was a Cancer," she said. "I recognized all the characteristics.[15] Cancers are said to be intuitive, introspective, phlegmatic, nocturnal, tenacious, indolent, domestic, refined, emphatic, clairvoyant. "Olivia de Havilland put astrology on a 'scientific' basis today," UP Hollywood correspondent Patricia Clary wrote. "The moon and planets influence people, she explained, because people are 80% water. 'You know what the moon does to the tides.'"[16]

One day during *The Heiress* shoot, word went around the Paramount lot that over on one of the big sound stages a basketball court had been set up for a few brief scenes in a movie called *Big Time Scandal*. Never one to miss an opportunity for exercise, Olivia used the court to practice some shots, as did other such Paramount contract players as Gail Russell, Veronica Lake, Hillary Brooke, and Diana Lynn. "They were all shooting some smart baskets last week," NEA reporter Howard Heffernan wrote.[17] Columnist Harrison Carroll visited the sound stage and was taken aback when he beheld Olivia's grim visage. "I do look plain, don't I?" she asked. "Well, that's the idea. I use only basic makeup so it will catch the highlights and make me look clean and scrubbed . . . It's a relief to play this type of girl . . . I don't care how I look. I can concentrate on my acting."[18]

"She works very hard," the silent screen star Pola Negri observed, "and takes her work seriously."[19]

⎯⎯ ⦁ ⎯⎯

In March 1950 Louella O. Parsons wrote, "When Olivia de Havilland and I were rehearsing our radio program, she told me she and Marcus Goodrich are going to San Antonio just as soon as the baby is old enough to travel. 'We want Ben baptized in St. Marks where Marcus was baptized and where he used to sing in the choir. The baby's paternal grandmother lives there still. Her name is Mrs. French, and we are looking forward to putting her grandson in her arms.' The radiant look in Livvy's face when she said that makes you realize what a fine person she is. It's good to see her so happy."[20] She still looked happy in May 1950 at the Club Gala, where Parsons reported she was seen with Goodrich, who was wearing a Navy uniform. "Seems he's in the reserve and is on duty," Parsons wrote. "Livvie is so pleased with his looks, she says she's going to have his picture taken with the baby."[21]

In New York *The Heiress* opened at Radio City Music Hall on October 6, 1950, and was hailed by Bosley Crowther, who said it "crackles with allusive life and fire" and credited Olivia's performance with "dignity and strength," but clearly preferred Wendy Hiller's "significant restraint" in the Broadway stage version to Olivia's "ecstasies" and "frustrations."[22] He was dead wrong about Olivia's Catherine, whose happiness when courted by Morris makes her torment when betrayed by him all the more heart-rending. Her Catherine Sloper is one of most astute performances ever caught on film, never better than when she takes her revenge on Morris at the end. Dramatically effective as it is, the scene represents a perversion of the denouement of *Washington Square*, in which Catherine treats

Morris with great courtesy, as tragic Jamesian heroines always do, like Milly Theale willing her deceitful suitor, Merton Densher, a fortune upon her death in *The Wings of the Dove*.

Having played a dull spinster and a bedraggled psychotic in rapid succession, Olivia emphatically did not want to be typecast as a plain woman. "After *The Snake Pit* and *The Heiress*, I thought it advisable to play a role in which an important part of the characterization is physical attractiveness," she told Hedda Hopper.[23]

"Oh, so you're a sexy dame?"[24]

"Yes."[25]

Hopper predicted she'd reject *Three Came Home*, Nunnally Johnson's version of Agnes Newton Keith's grim account of life in a World War II prison camp,[26] but Sheila Graham reported that Olivia was going to Japan, where General Douglas MacArthur had just given the go-ahead for making the film on location. "Though Olivia has not yet signed to star in it," Graham wrote, "this little matter will be taken care of when she returns from her 'second honeymoon' with husband Marcus Goodrich."[27] Something or someone kept her out of this movie, which could have been exactly the daring and distinguished follow-up she needed for *The Heiress*. Instead she did the bafflingly incoherent *My Cousin Rachel*, which would remind audiences she was still beautiful. Claudette Colbert snapped up *Three Came Home*, forgoing all the trappings of desirability and performing for the first time without makeup, and Bosley Crowther praised her performance as "a beautifully modulated display of moods and passions and explosions." The movie, he added, "will shock you, disturb you, tear your heart out, but it will fill you fully with a great respect for a heroic soul."[28]

Olivia's triple-threat comeback in *To Each His Own*, *The Snake Pit*, and *The Heiress* remains one of the most impressive in film history. By winning the distinguished New York Film Critics Circle award for both *The Snake Pit* and *The Heiress*, she became the first actress ever to win two

Critics Circle awards consecutively. When she received an Oscar nomination for *The Heiress* in the 1949 best-actress category, her competition was not especially impressive—Deborah Kerr in *Edward, My Son*, Loretta Young in *Come to the Stable*, Jeanne Crain in *Pinky*, and Susan Hayward in *My Foolish Heart*. In his column on March 1, 1950, Erskine Johnson predicted she'd win,[29] as did *Daily Variety* after polling four hundred Academy members—20 percent of the total membership.[30] Joan Fontaine had no intention of attending the presentation ceremony, explaining to the AP, "I thought Olivia would be happier. But I wouldn't have gone anyway, even if she hadn't been nominated."[31] Through a spokesman, Olivia said, "No comment."[32]

"I do hope Olivia wins," Jane Wyman told columnist Earl Wilson when he interviewed her minutes before the presentation ceremony at the RKO Pantages Theatre in March 1951. "She gives such good performances consistently," Wyman said.[33] As the previous year's best-actress winner for *Johnny Belinda*, Wyman would be going on stage that night to present the best-actor award. She and Ronald Reagan had recently divorced, and Wilson told her he'd seen her with Charles Sweeney, a British playboy.

"Yes," Wyman replied. "I've only seen him once but it's been in the columns every day."[34]

"Not going to get married again?" Her answer was a resounding no.[35]

"Is it easier to act well when you're single?"[36]

"No . . . except that you need a lot of time to work in this racket—of which I have plenty."[37]

The Oscar by now was America's most popular annual competition. A few years hence, in 1953, the Academy would begin televising its annual Oscar ceremony, reaching an audience that would vary in size in the decades to follow from 32 million to 55 million viewers.[38] The Oscar's origins had been modest and not particularly honorable, hatched up by Louis B. Mayer in 1927 as a way to conjoin the studios to fight labor unions. In 1929, Janet Gaynor and Emil Jannings took the top acting awards at a ceremony in the Hollywood Roosevelt Hotel's Blossom Room. The awards night for the 1950 performances was perhaps the crest and turning point of Hollywood's Golden Age. In front of the Pantages Theatre, built in 1929 by Greek theatrical impresario Alexander Pantages, who loved flamboyant lobbies, majestic staircases, and luxurious restrooms, endlessly stretched "one of the biggest traffic jams in Hollywood Boulevard history."[39]

Inside, the audience eagerly awaited what traditionally were the two most thrilling moments of the evening, the awards for best actor and actress. Host Paul Douglas introduced Wyman, and commented on her striking white lace gown, figure-hugging to her hips and flaring below in *traje de flamenco* style. She presented the best-actor award to *All the King's Men*'s Broderick Crawford, a former B movie actor. In his acceptance speech, a model of humility, he said only, "Thank all of you, and especially God."[40] Such was the power of the Academy Award that the following year he would star in one of the best pictures of 1951, *Born Yesterday*. In 1952 he would turn in a powerful performance opposite Barbara Stanwyck in Clifford Odets's *Clash by Night*, and in 1955 would be cast with Olivia in *Not as a Stranger*.

When Douglas introduced Jimmy Stewart, presenter of the best-actress Oscar, Douglas said, "During the last month of 1949, one of Hollywood's most eligible bachelors left the fold. When Jimmy Stewart was married, every bobbysoxer in America wore her socks at half-mast, and a woman in Buffalo spoke to her husband for the first time in 17 years. However, Jimmy's fans are on both sides of the screen—those who work with him, admire his talent, and enjoy his company. And to present the award to the best actress of 1949, winner Jimmy Stewart."[41]

"Please forgive me," Jimmy said, "for not stopping to acknowledge how honored I am to be here, but I can't wait to see who won it."[42]

Opening the envelope, he announced, "Olivia de Havilland."

She looked delicate and elegant in her billowing white organdy ball gown, aglow with sequin daisies, as she moved up the aisle and onto the stage. Years later, reliving the moment, she'd write, "Jimmy, Jimmy, Jimmy! How extraordinary that, almost 10 years after we first met and you escorted me to the New York premiere of *Gone With the Wind*, it should be you who presented me with the second Oscar and escorted me off the stage at the Hollywood Pantages Theatre."[43]

Accepting the statuette, Olivia said the Oscar for *To Each His Own* had served "as an incentive to move on. Thank you for this award, letting me know I have not entirely failed to do so."[44] Later she explained, "I felt solemn, very serious and . . . shocked. Yes, shocked! It's a great responsibility to win the award twice."[45]

When she came offstage, AP correspondent Bob Thomas asked her for a quote, and she said, "I would like to continue in the same serious vein that won me awards for *To Each His Own* and *The Heiress*."[46] Thomas wrote, "She accepted the award from James Stewart with the dignity becoming the fifth star in motion picture Academy history to win the grand prize twice. Other double winners are Bette Davis, Spencer Tracy, Frederick Marsh [*sic*], and Luise Rainer."[47] A *Life* magazine reporter later wrote that she "whisked off stage with an air indicating she would soon be back for more."[48] According to biographer Judith M. Kass, "Her cold acceptance speech [was] written by Goodrich."[49] Another reporter noticed that all the top winners were "jubilant . . . except for Miss de Havilland. News of her victory sent the 2,800 spectators into a thunderous ovation. But instead of running down the aisle to the stage she walked sedately and slowly. No sign of a smile flashed from her face."[50]

She went home that night and "parked her 'Oscar' on the bookcase with its twin," the UP reported, adding that her first thought was, "What do I do next? She is Mrs. Hollywood—for the next 12 months. But she hasn't made a movie for a year and a half. And she hasn't got one in mind, either. Not because nobody wants her. When Hollywood passed around its golden doorstoppers for bang-up jobs in 1949, Miss de Havilland's market value on the movie block went up one million dollars."[51]

According to the UP, she'd been in a dazed condition at the Pantages. "I was so excited when I got home from the awards I couldn't sleep," she said. "I read for a while . . . I soaked for an hour in a hot tub . . . and then I just wandered around."[52]

"That's enough of that," Goodrich, awoken from his sleep, said. "Come to bed and go to sleep!"[53]

"And you know? I did," she said.[54]

For the next few days she attempted to acknowledge the mountain of congratulatory gifts, flowers, and telegrams filling her living room. Her strict practice was to send thank-you notes in her own distinctive penmanship, so ornate it could have graced the Declaration of Independence, right under John Hancock's. Almost every studio was vying for her, but she couldn't find a suitable script, despite perusing at least three per week. According to the UP, after being homely in two tear-jerker parts, she was "ready for something glamourous and funny . . . [and] had no objections to looking her own beauteous self again." There should be some laughs, though "no comedies," she stipulated. "And no farces. I'm very serious about my acting . . . A play I would like . . . as long as it's something dramatic."[55]

In June 1950, when Olivia and her hot-tempered, unpredictable husband were driving on Sunset Boulevard toward their Bel Air home, with Goodrich at the wheel, he objected to a minor observation she expressed, and "began pounding her left arm with his closed fist," the *Los Angeles Times* would later report. "'He said he would kill me.'"[56] The Associated Press would later corroborate that he'd threatened her life.[57] She explained her reluctance to end the marriage after these physical assaults and threats, saying the idea of divorce was unbearable.[58]

PART FIVE

FATEFUL DECISIONS

20

A Streetcar Named Desire

With two Academy Awards, Olivia was at the apogee of her career and took care to protect her image as an actress of stature. "Olivia de Havilland is screaming over the reissue of her oldie, *The Dark Mirror*, with the Academy Award winner tag after her name in the billing," Erskine Johnson wrote.[1] According to Tony Thomas, author of *The Films of Olivia de Havilland*, "*The Heiress* . . . sadly marks the end of her short reign as a top-flight, greatly respected actress." Her boldness and Goethe's "mighty forces" had brought her this far, but at this perilous juncture something else seems to have taken over—Goodrich, possibly, but also such well-meaning but misguided members of the press as Erskine Johnson, who unwisely nagged her to place prettiness over substance in choosing her roles. Olivia, Johnson advised, should tie "a string on her finger to remind her to get back to glamorous roles—quick."[2]

She would shortly testify in court that her husband "said he would make the decisions for us."[3] She had gone to an agent named Kurt Frings, whose wife Kitty, later a Pulitzer Prize winner for her Broadway adaptation of Thomas Wolfe's *Look Homeward Angel*, had written the novel on which *Hold Back the Dawn* was based. Relations between the two couples, the Goodriches and the Fringses, had begun in an atmosphere of warm conviviality. When the Frings's residence burned to the ground Olivia was the first to offer help.[4] The two couples planned a European trip with the Lewis Milestones, but Kurt Frings, one of the top professionals in his field, inevitably clashed with Goodrich over the handling of Olivia's career.[5]

Robert Matzen, author of *Errol and Olivia*, characterized Goodrich as "a rigid intellectual with a hot and violent temper . . . [He] proceed[ed] to set Hollywood on its ear by his lack of civility, business acumen, and ability to play ball. As the Kafkaesque drama progress[ed], Livvy gives up liquor, cigarettes, and candy, fires her agent and staff, and makes Marcus her business manager, which further confounds the picture community since the man ha[d] no track record at much of anything, least of all at Hollywood career strategy and motion picture contracts."[6]

Two days after her Oscar victory, Kurt Frings lost her as a client, and her departure was tied to an advertisement the agency had wanted to run congratulating her on the Academy Award. "Since Kurt Frings is no longer Olivia de Havilland's agent he's not losing anything," Hedda Hopper wrote. "Her 10% went to Bert Allenberg, who had her under contract while Frings worked for her. Frings and Olivia's association ended when he wanted to buy an ad in a trade paper to congratulate her upon the [Academy] award but wouldn't let her husband write it. Marcus [Goodrich] wanted to make it sound like the acceptance speech he wrote for her, no doubt."[7] In *Inside Oscar*, Damien Bona and Mason Wiley added, "Goodrich . . . insisted on approval of the ad's copy and demanded that it refer to the actress not as 'Olivia de Havilland,' but as 'Miss' de Havilland."[8] Sheilah Graham wrote that Olivia "made the grand cycle"—when she left Frings, Goodrich became her business manager, followed by Charles Feldman, and "she is now back with Kurt Frings."[9]

In September 1950 Joan Fontaine took credit for seeing seventy-eight-year-old Walter de Havilland when he resurfaced in Canada.[10] Always an advocate of Olivia, Jimmie Fidler explained that Olivia had been "recuperating from minor surgery . . . Actually, Olivia has contributed regularly to her father's support; according to the records, she has visited him on several occasions. The difference is that Olivia dodges publicity whereas Joan seeks it . . . Miss Fontaine seldom passes up a chance to use her publicity as a weapon in the quarrel she professes to regret.'"[11]

The Hollywood Women's Press Club slapped Olivia with a "least-cooperative-actress" nomination, a designation she shared in 1950 with Lana Turner and Jane Wyman, while Joan Crawford, Loretta Young, and Marie Wilson were nominated "most cooperative."[12] The UP reported the winners on December 14, writing, "Loretta Young and Alan Ladd rated the smiles of the Hollywood Women's Press Club today, but Olivia de Havilland and Robert Mitchum got the boos . . . The winners and runners-up will be invited to a dinner Tuesday at which Miss Young and Ladd will receive solid gold apples. The 'uncooperative' stars were not expected to appear."[13]

Concerned about Olivia's career, Hedda Hopper, a longtime ally, invited her to tea in her home, where Hopper quizzed her about why she turned down *A Streetcar Named Desire*. Since Hopper was late for the appointment, Olivia made herself comfortable, ordering tea and using the telephone to check on Benjamin. She wore a teal blue satin dress with a big bow at the neck, a velvet skull cap, black shoes that Hopper's assistant admiringly noted were "nothing more than straps."[14] When she finished her phone call, she went into the den, where Hopper awaited her.

"Benjy is ill with tonsillitis," Olivia said, "with temperature of 103 degrees." She added they were living in a hotel. Hopper's assistant recalled, "After niceties and concern about Benjy, Hedda gets down to business."[15]

"What made you decide to return to the screen in *My Cousin Rachel*?"[16]

"Now, Miss Hopper, let's get one thing straight. I never left the screen. I was deeply attracted by the role . . . I have 22 changes of costume, done by Dorothy Jenkins. It's a wonderful period—just before the hoop skirt. The waists are gathered, the bodice low cut."[17]

"Have you ever been back to Warner since you left?"[18]

"Never."[19]

Hopper asked her to explain why she refused to play Blanche DuBois in Tennessee Williams's *A Streetcar Named Desire*, the best role of the century in the best play of the century. Irene Mayer Selznick's Broadway production had swept the big awards—the Pulitzer, the Critic's Circle—when it opened in 1947 at the Ethel Barrymore Theatre, directed by Elia Kazan and starring Jessica Tandy as Blanche and then-newcomer Marlon Brando as Stanley Kowalski. William Wyler wanted to direct the film at Paramount with Bette Davis as Blanche but backed out, dreading a fight with censors over the play's focus on homosexuality, promiscuity, and rape—taboo subjects in the uptight 1950s. Charles Feldman was trying to acquire movie rights to *Streetcar*, and he spoke with both David and Irene Selznick about partnering with him as producer.[20] David told Irene, now his ex-wife, "I still do not know why you do not produce it yourself,"[21] but Irene, having proved herself on Broadway, which she considered a notch up from the "sharpies," the hard-boiled power players of Hollywood, would remain in the theatre, later scoring successes with *Bell, Book and Candle* and *The Chalk Garden*.[22]

Having finally acquired the rights, Feldman sold Irene's production as a talent package to Warner, but the studio later waffled about using Tandy and Brando, preferring Hollywood stars with name recognition. Brando was initially ruled out in favor of John Garfield, Burt Lancaster, Van Heflin, Edmond O'Brien, John Lund, or Gregory Peck, but Brando's agent Edie van Cleve shrewdly took the matter to Tennessee Williams, who insisted Brando was the perfect Stanley.[23] David saw *Streetcar* as a vehicle for Jennifer Jones and reminded Feldman he'd once said Jennifer was "the girl to play it."[24] Irene wanted Vivien Leigh, who was starring in the London *Streetcar* under the direction of her husband Sir Laurence Olivier.

Olivia was neither Kazan nor Jack Warner's choice for Blanche. Warner wanted Leigh, and Kazan preferred Tandy, feeling that Leigh was under the thumb of Olivier. "Would I like to star in [the movie version]?" asked Tandy, who'd been acclaimed as Blanche in New York and won the

Tony award for best actress of the year. "What do you think? I've heard Olivia de Havilland will probably get the part. She'll be good, darn it. I wish I could say she wouldn't be good, but she will."[25]

Kazan at some point dropped his interest in Tandy and was reported to be "high" on Olivia.[26] The director had a fight on his hands with Warner Brothers because, according to Dorothy Kilgallen, "The Warners are still smarting over the two-year hassle they had with Olivia over her contract—a hassle she won."[27] Eventually Kazan prevailed, and one of the most challenging, beautifully drawn, and sought after parts of all time was Olivia's for the taking.[28]

"You told me once why you turned down the role in *Streetcar,* but I've forgotten," Hedda Hopper said. "What was that again?"

"You know, Charlie Feldman had it in his contract with Warner Brothers that he had the right to ask me to play the part," Olivia replied. "I saw the opening of the play. I didn't like it—well, I won't say I didn't like it, but I was completely confused by the character of the woman. She was required to do things that I thought psychologically unsound. Elia Kazan wanted to see me and discuss it with me. He wrote me a letter but I wouldn't see him . . . I brooded on the part for months."[29] She at last came to understand Blanche while touring with Shaw's play *Candida* in Cleveland. Hopper later recalled, "She went into the psychological discussion of what motivated Blanche."[30]

"It was a shame," Olivia said, "that the picture had already been made and released. But I'm ready to do the remake."[31]

"Have you ever been psychoanalyzed?" Hopper inquired.[32]

"I tried but they failed [Hopper's notes state, 'The psychiatrist was mixed up']."[33]

"You know, you analyze everything too much," Hopper ventured. "You analyze things right out of existence. You're too analytical of yourself."[34]

"Just wait until I do a remake of *Streetcar.* You'll say, 'She was right. It was worth it.'"[35]

Streetcar would be remade twice, first with Ann-Margret in 1984, when Olivia was in her late seventies, and later with Jessica Lange in 1994, when Olivia was in her late eighties. Blanche was thirty.

Another factor in her declining to perform in *Streetcar* was Benjamin. "I had just given birth to my son," she once said. "That was a transforming experience, and when the script was presented to me, I couldn't relate to it."[36]

In 1948 she'd told the AP's Bob Thomas that Hollywood's interest in destructive personalities was "dangerous to civilization . . . a perversion of values."[37] Olivia's online IMDb biography states that she reportedly observed, "'A lady just doesn't say or do those things on the screen.' Olivia de Havilland set the record straight, saying in a 2006 interview that she had recently given birth to her son when offered the part and was unable to relate to the material."[38] According to Louella Parsons, when Kazan offered Olivia the role in a letter, "she said she wanted to see a script first, as the play is censorable. Livvy didn't know how the screen version would turn out . . . She told me that her baby had just taken his first solid food. She was much more interested in discussing young Benjamin's reactions to Pablum than she was in any mere movie."[39]

When Vivien Leigh was offered the role of Blanche, she grabbed it and ran with it, winning her second best-actress Oscar and ensuring a continuing career of substance and distinction for the rest of her life. The movie was a hit with both the public and critics, winning twelve Oscar nominations. *Streetcar*'s historic defiance of the motion picture censors spelled doom for the outmoded Production Code. "*Streetcar* broke the barrier," Geoff Shurlock, the Code's No. 2 man, said. Playing the psychotic Blanche on the London stage and later in the movie may have cost Leigh her sanity, but she'd been unable, artistically, to refuse the part; she had the courage of her convictions and was impervious to the antiquated morality of the time, which was soon to give way to a more liberal and realistic code of ethics.

Olivia was reportedly interested in acquiring from producer Benedict Bogeaus the film rights to Mildred Cram's *The Promise*, a spiritualist novelette advertised as "the story of a woman and a man who plunged beyond death and brought back the answer to the riddle of life."[40]

As Alfred Hitchcock once observed, "Olivia de Havilland was so-so as a glamor girl, but made her real success in plain roles such as *Gone With the Wind* and *Snake Pit*."[41]

———

Olivia went to New York with Goodrich "to try to find herself a good play for Broadway," Sheilah Graham wrote. "It's always been her dream to do a play in New York."[42] Though thirty-five, Olivia played Shakespeare's thirteen-year-old heroine in the 1951 Broadway stage production of *Romeo and Juliet*. Jennifer Jones, whose movie career had fallen apart, was also planning to play Juliet for the Theatre Guild, despite being thirty-two.[43] David and Irene Selznick had divorced because of his affair with Jennifer, and now David spent all his time trying to resuscitate Jennifer's career rather than attending to his own. They finally married in 1949, and he treated Jennifer to every luxury until he went broke. When her career went south, she ran for cover to the Broadway stage, as would other such falling stars as Ginger Rogers, Yvonne De Carlo, Alexis Smith, Debbie Reynolds, Ruby Keeler, Mickey Rooney, Betty Hutton, Joan Fontaine, Glenda Jackson, Marlene Dietrich, Lena Horne, Bette Davis, Van Johnson, Vivian Blaine, Dorothy Lamour, Betty Grable, Franchot Tone, Elizabeth Taylor, and Richard Burton.

On November 12, 1950, Erskine Johnson carried a disturbing item in his Hollywood column stating, "Olivia de Havilland, my New York spies report, showed up at a rehearsal for *Romeo and Juliet* wearing a shiner."[44] Jack Hawkins, who played Mercutio, and who'd later excel in two of the Golden Age's best films, *The Bridge Over the River Kwai* and *Lawrence of*

Arabia, wrote that Goodrich's interference "succeeded in working Olivia into a frightful state of nerves."

Olivia would one day reveal in court that Goodrich assaulted her, made death threats, and endangered their little boy.[45] She wisely kept Benjamin by her side throughout the *Romeo and Juliet* run. AP correspondent Mark Barron wrote, "Olivia de Havilland is a busy star preparing for her Broadway stage debut, making her second major appearance in Shakespeare, touring across the United States and Canada and managing her eight-month-old son. None of these various problems seemed to be bothering Miss de Havilland the other afternoon as she began rehearsals of *Romeo and Juliet*."[46]

The baby already showed signs of keen intelligence. "He's very brilliant," she told Sheilah Graham, and when Sheilah said all mothers say that, Olivia insisted very seriously, "Oh no, he really is. I took care of him even in the hospital. I had a Caesarian and they don't usually let the baby room with you, but I insisted and they were afraid to say no to me."[47]

In mounting the opulent Broadway production—costing $1,400,000 by 2016 standards—no expense was spared, including sets by Oliver Messel, who'd designed the sets and costumes for Vivien Leigh's *Caesar and Cleopatra* in 1945.[48] Peter Glenville was signed to direct. A transplanted Englishman, he'd enjoyed two Broadway successes, *The Browning Version* and *The Innocents*, an adaptation of Henry James's *The Turn of the Screw*. Jack Hawkins commented on "the entire . . . production being focused on her . . . She received all Peter Glenville's attention." For the role of Romeo, Olivia wanted Michael Redgrave, a star at the Old Vic in *Love's Labor Lost* and *As You Like It*, but she had to settle for Douglas Watson, a relative newcomer whose previous appearances in *That Lady* with Katharine Cornell and with Helen Hayes in *The Wisteria Trees* had not saved *That Lady* from being one of Cornell's few disappointments nor *The Wisteria Trees* from being one of Hayes's flops.[49]

Olivia's *Romeo and Juliet* had Broadway all to itself since David decided to cancel Jennifer's New York run and announced he'd tour her *Romeo and Juliet* in England and Italy instead, despite the fact that Ethel Barrymore and Jane Cowl had once played Juliet at the same time, and their competition resulted in box-office receipts.[50] Normally there would have been a great deal of hoopla in the press over a famous movie star coming to Broadway, but Goodrich kept the press away from Olivia.

Romeo and Juliet opened on Broadway on March 10, 1951. The most famous theatre critic of his era, George Jean Nathan, wrote a devastating and unduly cruel review.[51] The anonymous *Time* reviewer was equally punitive, both Nathan and *Time* behaving as if movie stars had no business on Broadway. The *New York Times* delivered the *coup de grace*, but at least Brooks Atkinson, the dean of theatre critics, admitted he fell under the spell of Olivia's "personal enchantment."[52]

Jack Hawkins received a cool brush-off, according to his wife Doreen, who told a journalist, "Jack was awfully hurt . . . He would sit in his hotel room for hours on end, hiding behind the morning papers, not saying a word." Hawkins thought the production was doomed from the start by Goodrich, writing, "To complicate matters, Olivia was at that time married to an author who, for some reason, made it his job to protect Olivia from press publicity. The result of his very efficient endeavors was that when we were ready to open, the American press was just not interested." Leonard Lyons wrote in his column "Broadway Medley," "Miss de Havilland will tour in *Romeo and Juliet* after the Broadway closing. The cumbersome stage set is being re-designed, so that it won't require an extra day to set it up."[53] *Romeo and Juliet* closed on April 21, 1951, after forty-nine performances. Veteran Shakespearean actor Maurice Evans attempted to alleviate the backstage gloom at the Broadhurst, observing, "The mistake you made was in picking a theatre with only one balcony. Shakespeare can only fill the balconies."[54]

The following year, Olivia unveiled her Broadway-bound stage production of George Bernard Shaw's *Candida*, assembling a first-rate production directed by Herman Shumlin, noted for such hits as *Grand Hotel* and *The Little Foxes* and designed by Donald Oenslager, who devised the sets for *The Man Who Came to Dinner*. The show was to tour from the East to the West Coast and back before opening on Broadway.[55] Called the noblest of modern plays by the philosopher/poet G.K. Chesterton, *Candida* explores a romantic triangle—the ineffable Candida, larger than life, her clergyman husband, and a young poet named Marchbanks who wants to liberate her from the dreariness of family life. Kind and nurturing but also mysterious and unfathomable, Candida has the power to make the men who love her realize themselves.

Terry Kilburn, a familiar face in movies since his eleventh year, when he played Tiny Tim in MGM's *A Christmas Carol*, played Marchbanks, and the rugged Australian actor Ron Randell was miscast as Candida's clergyman husband. Opening a pre-Broadway run in San Francisco before launching a national tour, the production did not please San Francisco critics, who gave Olivia such a drubbing the city's Critics' Council declared her Candida "the worst performance of the year."[56] She could chuckle all the way to the bank. The play was grossing about $20,000 per week, the current equivalent of $185,000. She did not take the show to Los Angeles.[57]

An *Oakland Tribune* reviewer wondered, "Why, with nothing at stake, she has chosen to leave the movies and invade a field that is strange to her, I cannot say; but now that she has made that choice, her determination to rise above criticism and carry on is certainly to her credit."[58] When the show reached St. Louis, Missouri, the *Post-Dispatch* reporter Myles Standish interviewed her over dinner, with Goodrich tagging along. She struck Standish as shy and unhappy. "Olivia was nice, keenly intelligent, but very serious, formal and seemingly an introvert."[59] A decade later, following her split from Goodrich, she was back in St. Louis promoting a film, and when Standish took her to lunch at the Park Plaza, she seemed to him a different person, someone who'd overcome her shyness and was "warm, outgoing, witty, and gay."[60]

While Goodrich tinkered with another unpublishable novel in New York, Olivia and Benjamin covered 10,000 miles on the thirty-city tour. One day she came across Benjamin drawing a picture, and he said it was a portrait of God.

"But darling, no one knows what God looks like."

"They will now," the two-and-a-half-year-old prodigy replied.[61]

On weekdays she could leave part of Benjamin's care to a nurse, but one day a week she was a round-the-clock mother. "My one day with Ben was something to look forward to," she said in Baltimore on March 17, 1952. "You have to be careful, of course, taking a baby around the country, but my doctor has recommended a physician in every city."[62]

Before leaving Baltimore, she complained, "It has been several weeks since I've had a whole day with Ben. We felt the performance had run down a bit, and Herman Shumlin joined us for a series of tune-up rehearsals. For the last two weeks we have rehearsed every day during the week and all day Sunday . . . trying to see how much extra sparkle and polish we can give this brilliant play."[63] They worked on one scene per day in the afternoon before curtain time, "waiting eagerly to see its effect in the performance." She found it not unlike making movies, "this going over and over a short scene, then playing it, as best you can, before a camera, or, in this case, audience."[64] When the show was over at 10:45 p.m., she returned to her hotel, drank a cup of hot water, and wrote letters to her father and mother-in-law before retiring.[65]

In Chicago, according to journalist Wood Soanes, the reviewers "were pretty brutal. Only one, Ann Marsters of *The American*, was even remotely kindly."[66] The public flocked to see her, despite the poisonous ire of the

Chicago Tribune's catty critic, Claudia Cassidy,[67] but Olivia got the last laugh. "When my book came out, she asked for an autographed copy through a friend. I got even. I signed the book, 'Magnanimously! Olivia de Havilland.' Claudia was amused by that and even wrote a column about it."[68]

Recalling the Chicago run, Olivia said, "The audiences there paid no attention to the critics. The morning after, there were 50 people at the box office at 9 a.m. And they said that *South Pacific* and *The Moon Is Blue*, in Chicago then, got the overflow from *Candida*. I did two tours with the play and broke seven house records. It's exhausting, but fascinating, and after a while you want to keep moving."[69]

Candida racked up 332 performances during the tour. Winchell wrote that *Candida* "enjoyed a successful treasure hunt on the road."[70]

The show reached Hartford, Connecticut, in early April, performing on the Bushnell Memorial stage,[71] and proceeded to Toronto for a week before the Broadway opening on April 22, 1952. Brooks Atkinson, the *New York Times* critic, wrote, "Miss de Havilland is a beautiful, modest, and sincere lady." George Jean Nathan[72] and Walter Kerr were not impressed.[73] Atkinson wrote that Randell was "intelligent and manly but . . . leaves out the pompousness essential to the part and the play."[74] It's unfortunate that one of the vital and innovative young Method actors looking for work in 1952, among them James Dean and Paul Newman, couldn't have been cast as Marchbanks. In a 1946 production of *Candida*, a young Marlon Brando was Katharine Cornell's choice for the role. In 1952 James Dean was finding work in such TV shows as *Omnibus* and *Robert Montgomery Presents*, but not until a few months after Olivia's *Candida* would he make his Broadway debut in *See the Jaguar*, which opened on December 3 and closed on December 6. Paul Newman in 1951 was studying at the Actor's Studio, and wouldn't work on Broadway until 1953, in *Picnic*.

After only thirty-two performances, *Candida* closed on May 17. The following day, undaunted and resolutely positive in attitude, she was in a corner booth at Sardi's, the favorite watering hole of the theatrical crowd.[75] "You can't be on top all the time," Olivia once said. "It's unnatural."[76] Her work on Broadway was not a failure but a valuable learning experience that cured her of stage fright. "The theatre gives you some old basis of courage that an actress can't get any other way," she declared. It also gave her a chance to see Walter de Havilland, who came down from Victoria, Canada, to visit for a week when the show played Seattle. According to the United Press, she "entertained her 81-year-old father whom she has seen only three times in the last 17 years."[77]

George Cukor was set to direct Daphne du Maurier's enigmatic *My Cousin Rachel* for 20th Century Fox in 1952, and he wanted Vivien Leigh for the title role. The screenwriter Nunnally Johnson, Oscar winner for *The Grapes of Wrath*, thought he had a better idea—wouldn't the heroine, a woman of mystery, be the perfect comeback role for Greta Garbo, long absent from the screen? Cukor was close to the reclusive Swede, having directed her in *Camille* and *Two-Faced Woman*. She agreed to see him in New York, and 20th Century Fox enlisted two of Garbo's closest friends, Gaylord Hauser and George Schlee, to urge her to sign a contract.[78] A German-born nutritionist, Hauser gave diet and health advice to such celebrities as Garbo, Marlene Dietrich, Paulette Goddard, Gloria Swanson, and Ingrid Bergman, and he and his domestic partner Frey Brown often entertained Garbo and her friend, the poet and screenwriter Mercedes de Acosta, in their houses in LA, Palm Springs, and Italy.[79] George Schlee, the husband of fashion designer Valentina, lived in the same Manhattan apartment building, The Campanile, as Garbo, and he and the star became so intimate that Valentina naturally resented Garbo, whose apartment was only a few floors below. The two women never met in the elevator, because the operator was told that when both bells rang, he should answer only one. He would bring one to the lobby before going up for the other.[80]

Nunnally Johnson spoke with Garbo on the telephone and later said, "She went on talking. It was almost as if she were arguing with herself. She began to think of how she looked, in her last pictures, which meant that she was just about as beautiful as a woman can be, and she was disturbed by what the camera would do for her, at her present age."[81] Garbo was forty-seven.

Darryl F. Zanuck, head of Fox, preferred Vivien Leigh, but she had declined before George was hired to direct. Now Leigh told George she would play the role if he'd shoot the picture in England, where she could be with her husband Laurence Olivier. Zanuck said no—this film wasn't worth the added expense of location filming. Zanuck decided to give the role to Olivia. Though George liked her, he didn't see her for the part, and he also objected to Johnson's script so strenuously that he showed it to du Maurier, who agreed it was dull. George dropped out of the film and was replaced by Henry Koster, a run-of-the-mill studio director who'd helmed the sleep-inducing *Bishop's Wife* and would shortly take on the ponderous Biblical epic *The Robe*. Olivia likely accepted the part of Rachel to satisfy her yen to look beautiful again on screen. "She doesn't think the film will add to her Oscar collection, though," a UP correspondent wrote.[82] "It's not that kind of part," Olivia said. "Besides, winning a third Oscar would be pretty difficult. I think I'd have to be a Marie Dressler before I could do that."[83]

The UP correspondent had the impression she'd "nosed out Vivien Leigh, Greta Garbo, and Alida Valli for the role of Rachel."[84] Many were pleased to see Olivia resuming her screen career, Jimmie Fidler writing, "Olivia de Havilland's $175,000 salary [$1,600,000 in today's dollars] for *Cousin Rachel* proves that she's still one of Hollywood's more important purse-onalities, despite her lack of success on the stage."[85]

A maddeningly obfuscatory Gothic period piece, *Rachel* tells the story of Philip Ashley, a young Englishman who falls in love with his older cousin, Rachel Ashley, played by Olivia, the widow of Philip's guardian. Though Philip suspects she killed his guardian, he falls quite inexplicably in love with her and gives her his entire fortune. She promptly seizes control of his house. After he successfully plots her demise, he appears somehow to have discovered that she may very well have been innocent of any crime. The film succeeded in making Olivia look beautiful, but accomplished nothing else, apart from introducing American audiences to Richard Burton, who had not yet had a successful film but created a sensation in the Old Vic's latest *Hamlet*.[86]

Bosley Crowther gave the film an ambivalent notice, deriding its deliberate and perverse inconclusiveness while admiring its high production values—"walnut paneling, old silver, and fabulous jewels"—as well as Burton's performance and to a lesser degree Olivia's. "Olivia de Havilland does a dandy job of playing the soft and gracious Rachel with just a faint suggestion of the viper's tongue," Crowther wrote. "But it is really Richard Burton . . . who gives the most fetching performance . . . His outbursts of ecstasy and torment are in the grand romantic style."[87]

Burton wrote in his diary, "Miss de Havilland would not permit me to have costarring billing with her . . . Miss de Havilland wanted . . . Greg Peck to play my part. I said somewhat testily . . . that I had worked with the greatest living actors and actresses and they hadn't fussed about billing. So I stayed but with a little murder in my heart for Miss de H."[88] Despite these feelings, he placed her in his personal pantheon of the world's great actresses, writing, "I have worked with a great top of ladies. My own E [Dame Elizabeth Taylor] . . . Ava Gardner, Deborah Kerr, Olivia de Havilland, Edith Evans, Claire Bloom, Fay Compton, Rosemary Harris, Rachel Roberts, Jean Simmons, Dorothy McGuire, Helen Hayes, Zena Walker, and my old darling Pamela Brown."[89]

The *Pittsburgh Press* critic wrote, "Perhaps the role of the questionable heroine . . . is not the type ideally suited for Miss de Havilland's long-awaited return to the screen."[90] *Philadelphia Inquirer* reviewer Mildred Martin thought Olivia beautiful but miscast.[91]

My own feeling is that Olivia aced the role, but there wasn't much there to ace.

2 I

Grace under Pressure

The Goodriches had entered a period of estrangement in late 1951. "I was afraid he would become so violent that I might not survive," Olivia said.[1] The formal separation did not occur until May 8, 1952, and on May 18, the INS wire service reported that Olivia would file for divorce "unless differences are reconciled."[2] Hedda Hopper noticed a difference in Olivia, writing on May 30, "She's the same sweet Livey [*sic*], only now more grown up and understanding. Her separation from Marcus Goodrich hasn't left a scar."[3] On June 5, Walter Winchell wrote that Goodrich was going to fight the divorce, citing "'undue influence' by agents and others."[4] Olivia would later state in her memoir *Every French-man Has One*, "I had very regretfully come to realize that a divorce from my first husband was necessary, and in August of 1952 had filed for . . . an interlocutory decree of divorce."[5]

It was while Olivia filmed *Rachel* that the divorce trial took place. "She has asked 20th [Century Fox] for time off to make her court appearance," Dorothy Manners wrote on August 25. The UP headlined: OLIVIA DE HAVILLAND STARS IN PRIVATE DRAMA. "Oscar winner Olivia de Havilland, in one of her most dramatic performances, divorced writer Marcus Goodrich on testimony he beat her in such violent rages she feared for her life," the UP correspondent wrote.[6] "She covered her face and sobbed as she told how Goodrich struck her and threw her onto a bed

217

while she was holding the baby, then four weeks old, in her arms.[7] 'I had to turn my body to shield the baby,' she said."[8]

Under another headline, OLIVIA SOBS CRUELTY STORY FOR DIVORCE, SON'S CUSTODY, the INS reported, "Olivia de Havilland held the courtroom spellbound as she claimed novelist-husband Marcus Goodrich threatened to kill her."[9] Her attorney, Roland Rich Woolley, asked, "Why did you delay filing for your divorce?" After explaining her distaste for divorce and determination to salvage the marriage, she said, "But finally I became afraid for my son, physically and psychologically."[10]

Her testimony lasted for thirty minutes, setting a record in an uncontested divorce, according to the UP.[11] She made it through fifteen minutes before crying, the AP disclosed.[12] "She did not discover until after their marriage," the AP added, "that Goodrich had been married four times previously."[13]

Superior Judge Thurmond Clarke went easy on Olivia, granting her custody of Benjamin, who was almost three. Goodrich was unemployed, and Olivia mercifully waived alimony and said no community property was involved.[14] Sheilah Graham found her "strained when I visited her Beverly Hills Hotel two-room apartment to talk about her future."[15] The columnist had been warned in advance by Olivia's press agent, "Please don't talk about her divorce, because she won't discuss it."[16] Benjamin, wanting his walk, rushed to a chair, upended it, and insisted Olivia keep on tipping the chair up and down. "We all laughed," Graham later wrote. As for the future, Olivia said, "I want to rest and get my strength back. And rent a house and make a home for my son."[17]

She doubted she'd ever again marry, according to a United Press dispatch on August 3, 1952.[18] She intended to devote herself to the rearing of Benjamin and to her work, though she still believed, despite everything, that marriage is the richest of all experiences. Noticing she "looked beautifully sad," the UP correspondent asked what she thought about romance.

"Ah, only my 2-year-old boy," she replied. "I have my son to live for. So I don't think it will be lonely."[19]

She said Benjamin had an awe-inspiring vocabulary and was already using words like "occasionally," and that he spun such imaginative narratives as his recent account of "a picnic where everyone ate pink cellophane sandwiches."[20] In September she decided to wait three months at least before dating, and if she attended a party, she'd ask a married couple to take her.[21]

The bad reviews for *Candida* had done nothing to deter her determination to take an adaptation of Henry James's *The Portrait of a Lady* to Broadway in the fall, but that project was in jeopardy when *My Cousin Rachel* failed to wrap on schedule. Regarding reviews of her stage work, she said, "Whether they're good or bad, they're bound to affect you emotionally. When you are acting on the stage, you're in a very sensitive frame of mind. You must be careful not to let reviews affect your state of mind."[22] *Oakland Tribune* journalist Wood Soanes wrote on July 18, 1952, that *Portrait of a Lady* would probably open in the fall, but without Olivia.[23] By the mid-1950s it was on Broadway with Jennifer Jones, but only for a few performances.

Director William Dieterle, one of her directors in *A Midsummer's Night Dream*, sent her the script for *Elephant Walk*,[24] but in the end cast Vivien Leigh, paying her $150,000—equivalent to $1,400,000 in today's dollars.[25] Leigh fell in love with costar Peter Finch and suffered a nervous breakdown during location work in Ceylon, at one point screaming at Dieterle, "Get out of here quick before I start screaming fire! Fire! Fire! Fire!"—Blanche's ninth scene curtain showstopper in *Streetcar*. Leigh was replaced by twenty-one-year-old Elizabeth Taylor and later underwent electro-convulsive therapy.[26] Afterward, she seemed to her husband Sir Laurence Olivier an altogether different person. Shock therapy had left her "mind totally numbed," Leigh said. "It's worse than before."[27] They were now husband and wife in name only.

John Huston and Olivia resumed their relationship in 1952, though he was also romancing a French actress. "John Huston is back and I think Olivia's got him," said Nunnally Johnson, who'd written and produced *The Dark Mirror*.[28] After Olivia viewed *Moulin Rouge*, John's startlingly beautiful cinematic homage to Toulouse Lautrec, she said, according to Johnson, "At last John has come of age."[29] Nunnally Johnson was with them one evening when John passed out and Olivia tenderly stroked his brow as she attempted to feed him black coffee, "a tender variant of the active Olivia and passive John in their earlier poolside photo of 1942," Johnson said.[30]

After dominating the late 1940s Oscar derby, she wasn't nominated for *My Cousin Rachel*, though the film scored nominations for Burton's supporting role, Joseph LaShelle's cinematography, Lyle Wheeler and John DeCuir's art direction, and Charles LaMaire and Dorothy Jeakins's costumes. None of them won. Apart from three fairly good movies, *Not as a Stranger, The Light in the Piazza, The Proud Rebel,* and the horror potboiler *Hush . . . Hush, Sweet Charlotte*, Olivia did no significant work in films after 1952. The motion-picture industry, hard hit by television, underwent a radical change that year, marking the beginning of the end of Hollywood's Golden Age. Major studios cut contract lists, reduced salaries, decreased film output, and started giving leading roles to new faces, who came cheaper than established stars.[31]

By September 1952 Olivia was thinking of buying a house so she could make a new home for herself and Benjamin. "I'm still living at the hotel," she told Hedda Hopper, "It is very important for Benjamin to have a home. When I was on tour, we traveled 20,000 miles in two years."[32] In December Erskine Johnson reported that Olivia and Joan enjoyed having tea together while visiting their father, but Sheilah Graham wrote that Joan Fontaine was "resisting" a peace offer from Olivia because she resented Olivia's having attracted the lion's share of press coverage during the week Joan married Collier Young. A producer of such B-movies

Olivia (center), born in 1916, and sister Joan Fontaine, born in 1917, with mother Lilian. PHOTOFEST

Left to right: Olivia, Dick Powell, Ross Alexander, and Jean Muir in 1935's *A Midsummer Night's Dream*. PHOTOFEST

It was love at first sight when Olivia first beheld her *Captain Blood* leading man, Errol Flynn. PHOTOFEST

With Joan Fontaine in 1938. Olivia was a full-fledged star and little sister Joan said, "I want to do what you're doing!" PHOTOFEST

Four of the principals responsible for 1939's *Gone With the Wind* (left to right): producer David O. Selznick, Leslie Howard (Ashley Wilkes), Vivien Leigh (Scarlett O'Hara), and Olivia de Havilland (Melanie Hamilton Wilkes). PHOTOFEST

Above: The key to playing Melanie in *Gone With the Wind* was to know that Melanie meant every word she said and never doubted for a minute that Ashley preferred her to Scarlett. PHOTOFEST

In 1939, the United Press reported that a poll of movie industry old-timers elected Olivia the most beautiful woman in Hollywood. PHOTOFEST

After Jimmy Stewart took Olivia to the New York premiere of *Gone With the Wind*, he fell in love with her and ended his affair with Marlene Dietrich. PHOTOFEST

My Love Came Back (1940), one of many forgettable run-of-the-mill movies Warner Bros. imposed on Olivia. Shown with costar Jeffrey Lynn. PHOTOFEST

In the 1940s, at the height of her beauty and talent. PHOTOFEST

Holding hands during a 1942 date with Burgess Meredith, durable star of *Of Mice and Men* and, years later, *Rocky*. Center: Joan Fontaine. PHOTOFEST

With Henry Fonda and Jack Carson in 1942 in *The Male Animal*. PHOTOFEST

Director John Huston loved Olivia, and gave her all the best camera angles in her scenes with Bette Davis in 1942's *In This Our Life*. PHOTOFEST

Olivia and her leading man John Lund, who played both her husband and son in *To Each His Own* (1946). PHOTOFEST

Olivia holds her Oscar for *To Each His Own* at the 1947 Academy Awards ceremony. With her are Jean Hersholt, veteran character actor and Oscar winner for humanitarian service, and Hattie McDaniel, who'd won an Oscar for *Gone With the Wind* in 1939. PHOTOFEST

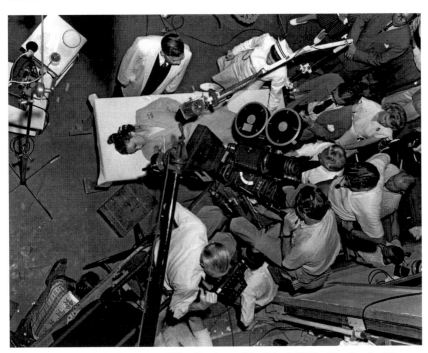

Olivia's long struggle for more difficult roles paid off in 1948's *The Snake Pit*, bringing her another Oscar nomination and the cover of *Time* magazine. PHOTOFEST

Olivia and Montgomery Clift in 1949's *The Heiress*. Thanks to her bold decision to portray a shy wallflower, she won her second best-actress Oscar. PHOTOFEST

Olivia proudly displays her Academy Awards for *The Heiress* (1949) and *To Each His Own* (1946). PHOTOFEST

With *Paris Match* journalist Pierre Galante, Olivia's second husband. PHOTOFEST

Myrna Loy played Olivia's mother in *The Ambassador's Daughter* (1956).
PHOTOFEST

In *Lady in a Cage* (1964), Olivia's costar was a young James Caan. PHOTOFEST

Olivia and Bette Davis costarred in 1964 in *Hush . . . Hush, Sweet Charlotte*.
PHOTOFEST

Facing page top: While making personal appearances before frenetic fans to publicize *Hush . . . Hush, Sweet Charlotte*, Olivia and Bette Davis reminisced about
old times and discussed their children and the current crop of actors. PHOTOFEST

Facing page bottom: Olivia at a Manhattan cocktail party with interior designer
Richard L. Ridge, Abraham Dumas, Joan Fontaine, and Philip van Rensselaer.
RICHARD L. RIDGE COLLECTION

With TCM's Robert Osborne (seated), an admirer who became a close friend in Olivia's senior years. PHOTOFEST

Below: *The Swarm* (1978) was a disaster film short on adequate special effects. Unlike Hitchcock's birds, the bees seemed harmless. PHOTOFEST

as *Outrage* and *The Hitch-Hiker*, Young, the third of Joan's four husbands, fancied himself a peacemaker, according to Louella Parsons, who wrote that he was urging Joan to forgive and forget "any unpleasantness. Olivia is doing her part." Olivia sent Joan a congratulatory wire for her wedding, "which pleased Joan very much," Louella Parsons wrote.[33]

By December 13 Joan was sufficiently over her huff to be quite cordial, according to columnist Harrison Carroll, when she ran into Olivia and three-year-old Benjamin outside Romanoff's and invited them to her house.

"I had a very pleasant afternoon," Olivia told Carroll. "Benjamin played with little Martita, who is a darling child. I got a chance to really meet Mr. Young. I had only seen him a few times to say 'how do you do?'"[34]

"Is the feud between you and Joan over?" Carroll asked.[35]

"Feud is the wrong word," Olivia said,[36] adding that she'd invite Joan and Collier to her home shortly.[37]

Ida Lupino, Young's ex-wife, directed Young's pictures, and had been "best pals for years" with Olivia, Hedda Hopper wrote, until they started "rowing and making up" during their dance routine in the 1943 all-star musical *Thank Your Lucky Stars*. On March 18, 1943, Harrison Carroll reported, "They have made up now."[38]

On December 19, 1952, Olivia left her handprints and signature on Sid Grauman's Forecourt of the Stars on Hollywood Boulevard.[39] At director Vincente Minnelli's 1952 holiday party, Olivia and John Huston arrived together and "they left together," Sheilah Graham wrote, "and were paired the next day at the Santa Anita race track."[40] According to Edith Gwynn, "They were madly in love several years ago, and Olivia's torch burned bright when she strolled the Beverly Hilltops at dawn— alone!"[41] The gossips continued to track her personal life throughout 1953, and after Graham failed to see her for a spell, she wrote, "Olivia de Havilland is living. She got herself a new beau—Hugh Bayne—who took her to lunch at Romanoff's, then to Santa Barbara in his Jaguar, for tea. I lost them for dinner."[42]

The media reported a "new romance between Huston (still married) and Olivia de Havilland . . . [They once] had a hectic love affair—but that was several years ago. And neither is throwing even a bit of rekindling wood on the fire."[43]

In 1953, when Rita Hayworth dropped out of *The Human Beast* to marry Dick Haymes, Olivia assumed the role of a woman who murders her lover. Producer Jerry Wald failed on his promise to sign Marlon Brando, Robert Mitchum, Burt Lancaster, Kirk Douglas, or Montgomery Clift as her leading man.[44] Mitchum was willing, but his boss Howard Hughes wanted him for *The Conqueror*. Columnist Dorothy Kilgallen reported in November that Olivia pulled out of the film "because they couldn't land a top male name to costar her . . . Sounds like a far cry from the Olivia of *The Snake Pit*."[45] Louella Parsons's stand-in Dorothy Manners confirmed that "Olivia didn't get one of the four male stars she insisted on, so she walked."[46] There were some hurt feelings. "Here's why Glen [*sic*] Ford doesn't adore Olivia de Havilland," a reporter wrote. "She turned down Glenn as her leading man. He eventually did the film with Gloria Grahame."[47] A remake of Jean Renoir's *Human Desire*, a precursor to film noir, *The Human Beast* flopped.[48]

Looking for the right part in the right movie—the fate of every free-lancer—is a full-time job. Columnist Harrison Carroll wrote that Olivia told him, "I haven't had time to make any decision. I run my house, I am a mother, I'm a professional woman, and I'm in love. It seems to me I haven't left this telephone all day."[49]

John Huston was filming *Beat the Devil* in Ravello, and Dorothy Kilgallen wrote in February 1953 that he was spending a fortune making long distance calls from Italy to Olivia.[50] John had a good time drinking with script doctor Truman Capote, but Humphrey Bogart, one of the actors on location, disdained the movie, saying only phonies would like it.[51]

Sheilah Graham reported later in February that Olivia was seen at a screening of *The Man in the White Suit* with Alan Campbell.[52]

In March 1953 it cost Olivia $40,000 (adjusted for inflation: $358,000) to settle a lawsuit her former agents Phil Berg and Bert Allenberg had brought against her in 1947. According to the AP, the agency alleged she'd refused to pay 10 percent of her earnings under their contract. She filed a countersuit to nullify the agreement, saying the agency had tried to induce her to appear in *Ivy* without disclosing their financial connection to the picture. A board of arbitration found in the agents' favor, and a settlement was reached.[53]

"There could be a front-page explosion, insiders vow, now that Marcus Goodrich is back in Hollywood," columnist Erskine Johnson wrote on February 23, 1953. "Olivia de Havilland, his almost-ex, hired bodyguards for their son, Benjamin, some months back when there was a tug-of-war with Goodrich over the lad."[54] Goodrich would never succeed in getting Benjamin away from his mother.

She continued her indefatigable search for a suitable starring vehicle, and it appeared for a while that she and Richard Burton might become the next big acting team. Peter Glenville hoped to cast them in *House by the Sea*, the story of a soldier who becomes a WWII deserter and, later, a murderer, but the deal fell through.[55] The ambitious twenty-six-year-old Burton was shopping for a superstar actress he could hitch his wagon to, and he'd find her a few years later in Elizabeth Taylor. They became the most notorious—and richest—acting couple of the movies' Golden Age. Erskine Johnson explained that Olivia and Burton couldn't be teamed again because "there was a big chill between them" by the time they finished filming *My Cousin Rachel*.[56] Graham Greene's novel *The End of the Affair* appealed to Olivia, but the picture bogged down in arguments about whether it should be made in 3-D, a gimmick designed to reclaim the dwindling movie audience from television.[57] Deborah Kerr and Van

Johnson eventually made the film in 1955, and, in a far superior 1999 remake, Julianne Moore was nominated for an Oscar.

In April 1953, Olivia attended the New York premiere of the first 3-D movie, *House of Wax*. She'd appeared with the film's star, Vincent Price, in 1939 in *The Private Lives of Elizabeth and Essex*, Price's third film and her sixteenth. Currently on a personal appearance tour promoting *House of Wax*, Price was staying at the Warwick Hotel in Manhattan, and couldn't have enjoyed reading his reviews, which scorned his acting and ridiculed the movie. Olivia accompanied Price and his wife Mary, Cleveland Amory, author of *The Proper Bostonians*, and Emily Kimbrough, co-author with Cornelia Otis Skinner of *Our Hearts Were Young and Gay*, to "21," ending the evening at the Cub Room of Sherman Billingsley's Stork Club.[58]

Despite the AP's report that Olivia or Gene Tierney would play Eva Peron, Olivia released no films in 1953. According to the NEA wire service, there was no man in her life, and she said, "There may NEVER be again."[59] Erskine Johnson wrote that her "pals are worried about her glum outlook on life and career."[60] They needn't have fretted; romance was just around the corner.

When the sixth Cannes International Film Festival, under the chairmanship of Jean Cocteau, invited her to its April 15–29, 1953, festivities in a letter signed by Pierre Galante, executive editor of *Paris Match* magazine, Olivia wired back that she'd like to attend, but would require accommodations for two.[61] "*Non*," replied Galante, who assumed she was bringing a lover, but it was her son Benjamin she wanted to take, "so I wrote back that I couldn't leave my child," Olivia recalled.[62]

Galante immediately dispatched a second airplane ticket. Hawk-eyed Hedda Hopper took skeptical note of the current trend of social-climbing European journalists "marrying up" by attaching themselves to celebrities.

"The European news clan is doing right well with star marriages these days," she wrote. "Kirk Douglas's wife, Anne Buydens, comes from the fraternity. So does . . . Pierre Galante, and Gregory Peck's best gal, Veronique Passasi, is a news hen, too."[63]

Coco Chanel engaged Galante to write her autobiography, and they worked on it for a while, but the project hit a snag. "The business of writing memoirs is . . . based on anecdote, and the trouble was that Chanel stubbornly refused to relate anecdotes," he said. "She refused to remember . . . To remember would be to evoke a real life when what she really wanted was to forget it in favor of a refined past, an edifying and, most of all, an enlightened life."[64] He gave up and resorted to writing a biography, *Mademoiselle Chanel*, which shows Galante to be a more coherent writer than Marcus Goodrich. His book intermittently evokes high-fashion chic but lapses into repetitiveness and tedious details when it addresses Coco's labyrinthine corporate entanglements.

His pursuit of Olivia he likened to an epic siege, one that would involve, according to Sheilah Graham, "a long period of waiting and testing that might have scared off a less patient wooer."[65] Olivia fell in love with Paris the moment she arrived and with Galante shortly after they met.[66] Arriving at the Paris Orly International Airport she was met by her agent and Galante. For the duration of the Festival, Galante rarely left her side, sitting next to her at the Palais des Festivals et des Congres at every performance and taking the chair next to hers at the huge supper parties that followed screenings. Then at the Austrian gala his sheepish expression changed into a smile, "but he still did not kiss my hand—he held it in the taxi going home," she later wrote.[67]

He was hardly her idea of a Frenchman, whom she'd always thought of as "dapper . . . gay, effervescent."[68] Instead, she found him "handsome but hangdog. Clean-shaven and solemn . . . More intense, though. Sort of hangdog and sheepish."[69] The Festival committee had asked her to bring along one of her Oscars, but "she rejected the proposition as 'undignified and hammy,'" Kilgallen wrote.[70] Errol Flynn was there but evidently not making out as well as Galante. A teenage Barbara Walters, who was a fox in the fifties despite her circular felt skirt with a big felt poodle cutout pasted on it, was on a grand tour of Europe during her junior year at Sarah Lawrence, and later recounted, "In Cannes . . . I got hit on . . . by the notorious playboy actor Errol Flynn, but I paid him no mind. He was way too old."[71]

The U.S. contingent included Olivia, Kirk Douglas, Edward G. Robinson, Anne Baxter, Gary Cooper, Leslie Caron, Charles Boyer, Bing Crosby, Walt Disney, Anatole Litvak, Gregory Peck, Lana Turner, Van Johnson, Mel Ferrer, and William Wyler. Many believed that without American stars there would be no festival, despite the fact that very few U.S.-made films came out winners at Cannes. Nonetheless, one of the top honors, the international prize for best dramatic film, went to the American entry, *Come Back, Little Sheba*, and another U.S. film, *Lili*, won in the best international entertainment category. Shirley Booth took the best-actress prize for *Sheba*. The No. 1 honor, the Palme d'Or, went to Henri Clouzot's *Le Salaire de la Peur* (*Wages of Fear*), and the best-actor prize was won by the star of the same film, Charles Vanel.

Despite America's stellar assemblage, many fans complained the Festival had lost its pizzazz because the celebrities no longer seemed exotic and sexy. "Olivia de Havilland was escorted by her 3-year-old son," one newspaper complained. "Anne Baxter brought her mother. Edward G. Robinson was busy with paperwork. French Riviera old-timers said the 15-day festival looked like the tamest ever."[72] After the Festival, things got more exotic. "Kirk Douglas and Olivia de Havilland are giving the international set plenty to gab about," one journalist wrote. "Acquaintances say they act like they've just discovered each other in a big way. The whole thing started at the Cannes Film Festival and has been carried on through the Riviera and Italy. Which leaves Pier Angeli—once reported in line to become Douglas's bride—out in the cold."[73]

Galante didn't give up his pursuit, trailing Olivia all the way to Los Angeles, where Benjamin accidentally hit him over the head with a potato masher.[74] Within a week or so she announced her engagement to Galante from her quarters in the Shoreham Apartments, and later Galante boarded the *Liberte* to sail for France, alone but full of plans for their future together. Using his clout as a prominent member of the press, he persuaded Air France to send Olivia two tickets to Paris, and in return she agreed to christen the airline's first nonstop Chicago-Paris flight.

22

Marriage French Style

K nown as Capraisiens, the three hundred fifty residents of the languid Loire Valley town of Yvoy-le-Marron awoke on April 2, 1955, with no warning that the day before them would be the most exciting to hit the village since the Hundred Years' War, the 1337–1453 conflict between the Plantagenets and the House of Valois for the throne of France. At first, all they noticed as they began to trickle into the streets after breakfast was that it was a balmy spring morning and "the first green shoots [had] appeared overnight on the trees along the Loire," a United Press correspondent wrote.[1] Then they saw the line of limousines streaming in from Paris and knew something was up in their backwoods hamlet. Soon word went around that someone named Olivia de Havilland from some place called Hollywood was marrying one of their countrymen later in the day.[2] Virtually the entire town showed up for the festivities, dressed in their best clothes.

Among the wedding party were Turkish princess Niloufer, Marcel Pagnol, author of *Marius*, on which Joshua Logan's 1954 Broadway musical and 1961 film *Fanny* were based, and Olivia's matron of honor Fleur Cowles, a *Look* magazine journalist who'd married her boss, Gardner Cowles Jr., and become a director of the company. "I've worked hard, and I've made a fortune," Fleur bragged in *Time* in 1949, "and I did it in a man's world, but always, ruthlessly, and with a kind of cruel insistence, I have tried to keep feminine." Olivia had invited Joan Fontaine and Collier

Young, but they couldn't accept because Joan was "still under treatment for bursitis in my shoulder and, worse than that, Debbie has just come down with mumps. Nobody else in the family—my other daughter, Martita, Collier, or myself—has ever had the disease. We are just waiting to see what happens to us."[3]

Olivia's gray flannel suit was created by Christian Dior, who personally orchestrated all her wedding dress fittings and named the suit "A" because the skirt spread out and had multiple pleats on both sides.[4] Her small white hat had a veil, and her shoes and purse were matching gray flannel. Dior, who'd spearheaded "the New Look Revolution," was present at the wedding.[5] Galante wore a blue suit and was attended by best man Gaston Bonheur, director of *Le Figaro*, the oldest national daily newspaper in France.[6] The thirty-eight-year-old bride and forty-five-year-old groom were fifteen minutes late for the ceremony in the second-floor meeting room of the village council in a red-brick schoolhouse.[7] They finally arrived from the hunting lodge of Mayor Jean Prouvost two miles away. Apart from being a politician and former minister of information for two French governments, Prouvost headed a media empire that included *Paris Match, Marie Claire, Paris-Midi, Paris-Soir, Le Figaro, Tele 7 Jours*—a 3-million-circulation television magazine—and Radio Luxembourg (RTL). As the owner of *Paris Match*, he was Galante's boss.

Five-year-old Benjamin stood behind Olivia during the nuptials.[8] Kilgallen had written earlier, "Benjie is slated to serve as page boy at his mother's wedding . . . His real dad, Marcus Goodrich, is alleged to have given permission for the unusual etiquette bit."[9] After the ceremony, which was conducted by Prouvost, the wedding party went outside to be serenaded by a chorus of schoolchildren singing a French folk tune, "The Song of the Bride," as they waved branches of broom. The entire village was invited to follow the bride and groom on the short drive to neighboring Beaugency, where they enjoyed a glass of white wine with the newlyweds at the seventeenth-century Hotel de L'Abbe, an old monastery that had been restored and now served as a country inn. Overlooking the Loire River, the Hotel de L'Abbe's gardens glowed with hyacinths, crocuses, and jonquils. There was a 120-place luncheon fifteen miles away at a restaurant situated on the banks of the river.

"I hope mother gets married often," Benjamin said. "I just love the rice and the music."[10]

The newlyweds left the following day for Paris and then a ten-day honeymoon on Ischia Island, paradisally positioned overlooking the Bay of Naples, a place of wild beauty with riotous bougainvillea, volcanic thermal beaches, outcroppings of rock that jut into the sea, white-washed houses with brightly painted wooden doors, mountain paths to medieval castles, and glitzy grand hotels with panoramic views of the Mediterranean Sea.

Later, in Rome, journalists again noticed how different Olivia was from her busy days in Hollywood's Golden Age. "Marriage has changed Olivia de Havilland, who used to shrink from publicity," Kilgallen observed.[11] As paparazzi crowded around them, the bride and bridegroom tossed three coins in the Fountain of Trevi. According to legend, if you throw a coin into the Trevi with your back to the fountain, throwing it with your right hand over your left shoulder, it will guarantee a return to Rome; the second coin will bring a new romance; and the third, marriage.

Olivia was scheduled to report to London for a film called *The Quest*.[12] She was also needed in London on April 15 for the premiere of her movie *That Lady*, in which she plays a princess who wears a black patch over her blind right eye, the result of a dueling injury.[13] Terence Young had been so optimistic about *That Lady* he'd predicted Olivia's eyepatch would start a fashion trend, telling a reporter, "Christian Dior indicated he would be inclined to introduce it as a new costume accent. Naturally if Dior gives the idea his sanction it will become widely popular."[14] Alas, the eyepatch became no more popular than the film.

The Galantes wound up their honeymoon in the United States, where Olivia was expected to visit key cities to promote her new film *Not as a Stranger*.[15] When she confronted the ordeal of moving all her belongings to Paris, she experienced some rude awakenings. "Shipping rates are so high Olivia de Havilland postponed her departure for Paris to sell all her furniture at auction," Harrison Carroll wrote.[16] Olivia and Benjamin collected Shadrack, their fourteen-year-old three-legged Airedale terrier, at Orly. A gift from John Huston, the dog had been temporarily detained in America due to illness. All three—Olivia, Ben, and Shadrack—were photographed together and looked very happy to be reunited. Shadrack had lost one of his legs as a puppy but could stand perfectly upright. He was roughly the same size as Benjamin.[17]

The family settled in a little white Paris townhouse, tall and narrow, its intimate rooms small and charming, the first house she'd ever owned. There was a garden in back with a chestnut tree and a fountain frequented by pigeons and sparrows.[18] Benjamin attended a school in the neighborhood and came out well in his first fistfight, also proving his mettle when he extracted his own tooth.[19] According to Leonard Lyons, the fight occurred when "a French boy told him American boys are weaker. Ben proved he's not."[20]

Galante took Olivia shopping, and she splurged at the House of Dior, where she bought three originals. She had a rudimentary knowledge of the French language, but Galante refused to converse with her in his native tongue; early in their marriage he'd talk to her only in English, eager to retain his status as a husband rather than a language coach.[21] The AP wrote six years later, "She . . . judges the progress of her Parisian adjustment to the fact that her husband now converses with her in French."[22]

"I've always adjusted well to my environment," Olivia said. "You have to when you're a naturalized U.S. citizen with a French name born to British parents in Japan."[23]

Benjamin learned French so quickly he won first prize in the French school he attended, and he would spend the rest of his life sounding like Charles Boyer. Shadrack was just as quick to pick up the language, responding appropriately to commands in French. Benjamin wanted some brothers and sisters to play with and gave his mother a book called *A Guide for Newlyweds.*

"Mamma, this will teach you how to care for babies," he advised. Hedda Hopper wrote, "The idea sets well with Olivia, too, who tells me she loves it here [in Paris] and is happy with her husband."[24]

She remained in the French capital partly to avoid a possible lawsuit threatened by Goodrich, who was seeking custody of Benjamin, but Kilgallen suggested another motive, writing that she'd rethought her intention to fly to New York for the premiere of *Not as a Stranger*. "The glamorous, now blond Olivia discovered the trip would be considered a 'break' in the 18 months she is spending abroad to gain a whopping income tax advantage."[25] Olivia would eventually reveal the real reason she moved to Paris was "at the insistence" of Pierre Galante.[26]

In some ways she felt more accepted in France than America. "I don't think American girls are brought up to be self-sufficient," she said. "French women seem more tranquil. They're not so neurotic."[27] Perhaps, she suggested to Sheilah Graham, it was because French husbands spend more time with their spouses. "Businessmen in America don't lunch with their wives. But they do in Paris . . . Pierre and I have decided that we will never be apart for more than two weeks at any time."[28]

Evelyn Keyes, another American expatriate in Paris in the fifties, was John Huston's ex-wife and Olivia's cast-mate in *GWTW*. "The quietest American star in Paris," a journalist wrote, "is Evelyn Keyes, who lives very modestly while studying there between flying trips to America to see Mike Todd."[29] One had to look in the right places to find Keyes—Maxim's, Monseigneur's, Brasserie Lipp, and especially Alexandre's, the mecca of Hollywood-sur-Seine, where she customarily schmoozed, between sips of Dom Perignon, with Robert Capa, the Peter Viertels, John Huston, and the Irwin Shaws.[30]

Sheilah Graham was not surprised when Olivia told her in 1955 she was happy. "She looks it," Graham wrote. "During Olivia's marriage to Marcus Goodrich, she was less friendly, and seemed suspicious of everyone who tried to reach her. But in the two hours we chatted . . . she smiled at everyone who approached her, willingly posed for innumerable candid photographs."[31]

Charles Brackett, who'd once lived abroad, asked Olivia, "In France, in the case of twins, which of the twins is regarded as the senior, having primary rights of heredity?"

"The first to be born," Olivia replied.

"Not at all," Brackett said. "It's the second born. On the theory that the last to get out was the first to get in."[32]

— ⁓ —

In director Stanley Kramer's *Not as a Stranger*, Olivia played Swedish-American Kristina Hedvigson, a self-sacrificing nurse who helps the man she loves, played by Robert Mitchum, get through medical school. A cynical fortune hunter, he rewards her with a wedding ring and heartbreak. Olivia used a singsong Swedish accent, practicing it off-camera as well as on, to make certain she didn't lose the "atmosphere" of the part.[33] She received compliments from both Ingrid Bergman and Greta Garbo for her mastery of Swedish intonation. Her preparation for playing a nurse included witnessing eight major operations as well as extensive coaching by Marjorie LeFevre, an OR nurse who taught her how to handle surgical equipment, master their nomenclature, set up a Mayo stand—an instrument table—thread suture, dress in gown and gloves, go through a scrub-up, and the fine details of surgical technique.[34]

On the set one day Kramer was going for a shot that would establish the first contact between Olivia and Mitchum in a sanitary but dingy-looking hospital cafeteria. Just before they rehearsed, Kramer drew aside new-comer Mara McAfee, who had a small part as one of the nurses. "Mara, stand here and watch Olivia underplay. You might learn something."[35] There was no dialogue and the actors had to perform exclusively with their eyes. As Mitchum approached Olivia, her famously expressive brown orbs showed him she was receptive and would be pleased if he joined her. At the same time, she had to unwrap her napkin, take out the utensils, butter a role, and consume a bite of Swiss steak. Her knife and fork registered too loudly for the sound technicians and Kramer ordered a retake.

"Get me another roll," Olivia said, still in character as a Swede. "What am I saying? All this starch!"[36] Kramer deemed the reshoot acceptable. "If I had done that scene," McAfee told journalist Harrison Carroll, "the food would have stuck in my mouth like cotton and I would have gotten bread crumbs and butter all over my face."[37]

"What would you call that," McAfee asked Olivia, who'd come over to chat with Carroll, "a 200-calorie scene?"[38]

"You are so right," Olivia laughed, still using her accent. "The steak really wasn't so bad but it's not Swedish cooking, I can tell you."[39] She had dyed her hair because the script specified a Nordic blond, and Kramer thought it was a great idea, but Pierre Galante didn't and told her so. "It's not just Pierre, though," she said. "Being a blonde is a real problem for me . . . I've had to have my hair dyed every three days."[40] Galante said it was all right for a while, but insisted she return to her natural "leaf brown" after the film. She wasn't sure she'd comply, possibly mindful of her previous husband's dictatorial ways. "As for my being a blonde, I told Pierre I don't mind reverting in private life to my brunette self, but if I get hundreds of letters telling me I look better as a blond, after the picture is shown . . . then I might just stay blond for my pictures."[41]

She was thirty-eight, and her peroxided tresses in this black-and-white picture created too hard-edged a contrast with her dark eyes and lipstick. Robbed of her natural softness, she no longer seemed like Olivia de Havilland, and Mitchum was too mature for his role. Their love scenes generated no sizzle. They weren't simpatico off-camera either, at least at first.[42] One day he approached her on the set holding a bottle of beer, and she took it from him and delivered a lecture about drinking at work. He liked her boldness and they became good friends[43] At one point, he told Olivia to go boil her girdle, and later, at the wrap party, she gave him an elegantly wrapped gift. "Inside was her girdle—boiled!" an onlooker related.[44]

Bosley Crowther trashed the movie, calling it "burdened with a heavy sense of life [and] the flat performance of Robert Mitchum," but he esteemed Olivia, writing, "Miss de Havilland is warm and appealing . . . but her beaming adoration of the young doctor is . . . not plausibly explained," and he called the picture "a turgid and clumsy affair . . . creeping with ponderous characters." I found it entertaining. Later, in 1955, Olivia was to appear in *Good Morning, Miss Dove*, the story of a spinster school teacher, but ultimately the part was played by Jennifer Jones, who received glowing reviews and immediately went on to film *The Man in the Gray Flannel Suit* opposite Gregory Peck.[45]

23

Grace Kelly and the Jet Set

A mong the film stars invited to the Cannes Film Festival in April 1955 were Olivia, Grace Kelly, Gina Lollobrigida, Esther Williams, Van Johnson, Betsy Blair, Dorothy Dandridge, and Terry Moore. In Paris, Olivia and Galante went to the Gare de Lyon to board *Le Train Bleu*, a luxurious Orient Express-type overnight sleeper connecting the French capital with Cannes. A few moments later Grace Kelly followed them into the train. Kelly was at the zenith of her career as the winner of the Oscar for *The Country Girl*. Though she and Olivia had not met, they had two important things in common besides being movie stars of the first magnitude. "Rupert Allan, once a beau of Olivia de Havilland, is the latest entry in Grace Kelly's date book. He's a writer," Kilgallen reported.[1] The other thing they shared was a deep belief in destiny.

Rupert M. Allan Jr., the West Coast editor of *Look* magazine, had convinced Kelly to attend the Festival. He enjoyed a close relationship with the Cannes committee and served as its unofficial representative in Hollywood, and since he had written three cover stories on Kelly in two years, the Cannes organizers, desperate for big-name stars, asked him to enlist her to lead the American delegation.[2]

Kelly thought mystical powers guided everything in life.[3] She spent a lot of time reading a book called *The Pursuit of Destiny*, which indicated she was cut out for great achievements that would come to her through happenstance.[4] Olivia would be her link to the rest of her life.

Near Cannes was the tiny principality of Monaco, where young Prince Rainier III of the House of Grimaldi, the reigning monarch, wanted to marry a movie star.[5] The publicity stirred up by such a marriage would attract tourists and money to Monaco. Rainier needed funds to fight off Aristotle Onassis, who'd bought up much of Monaco and was the majority stockholder in the Societe des Basins de Mer de Monaco (SBM), which runs the casinos, entertainment, and the three most lavish hotels.[6] "Marilyn [Monroe] was tops on the prince's list of ladies to be auditioned for the role of his bride," Dorothy Kilgallen revealed in the *New York Journal-American* after having been solicited by a friend of Rainier's to introduce him to Monroe.[7] All three—Kilgallen, Rainier's matchmaker, and Monroe—were at the twenty-fifth anniversary ball of Richard and Dorothy Rodgers at the Ambassador Hotel on March 5, 1955. Kilgallen rejected the "dower's commission," telling Rainier's intermediary, "I don't want any commission. Just give me the scoop when it happens."[8] Kilgallen then introduced Rainier's representative to Monroe and her chaperones, Mr. and Mrs. Milton Greene.[9] Feelers were also put out to Monroe by publisher Gardner Cowles regarding the prospect of marrying the prince, and she was interested but was not a Catholic, and therefore ineligible for the position.[10]

Speaking in 2017 of her role in bringing together Grace and Rainier, Olivia said, "I'm tempted to think it was destiny."[11] The Galantes were dining on the train to Cannes when Pierre mentioned the idea of bringing Kelly and Rainier together for a photo spread in *Paris Match*. Gaston Bonheur, editor-in-chief of the magazine, immediately bought the idea. As Grace Kelly was leaving the dining car, Galante and Bonheur urged Olivia to help arrange the meeting, and Olivia spoke to Kelly on the platform between carriages. Kelly agreed to meet Rainier, pending approval by her studio, MGM.[12]

After the train arrived in Cannes, Kelly went to see her lover Jean-Pierre Aumont, Leslie Caron's costar in *Lili*, at the Carlton Hotel.

Jean-Pierre, whom I knew, was the quintessence of Gallic charm and valor. Jean Cocteau had encouraged him at the outset of his career in the 1930s, recognizing that he possessed "the youth, the command, the wildness, the arrogance, the moonstruck quality, the fury" for stardom. As a friend, he was down-to-earth and so thoughtful he insisted, after our dinner at Elaine's restaurant one evening with Ruta Dauphin of the Deauville American Film Festival, on dropping us off at our apartments in his sedan.

Colette, author of *Gigi* and *Cheri*, was also taken with Jean-Pierre, when, as a young man, he called on her in Saint-Tropez. After spending a day digging holes in her garden, he was invited to stay for dinner, and he asked if he could take a shower. Colette told him to get undressed and water her plants. "I had to stand, naked, in the center of her bougainvillea, and let her sprinkle me with her watering can. There was no way to say no to Colette."[13]

When I knew him he was happily married to Marissa Pavan, Oscar-nominated for her part as Anna Magnani's daughter in *The Rose Tattoo*, but he'd never stopped loving his late wife Maria Montez, and called her "the queen of technicolor enchantment . . . spontaneous, direct, and childlike." She "moved easily between the confines of the real and the unreal," Jean-Pierre said. She was "familiar with messages from the beyond, ghosts, and premonitions." Montez died at 39, drowning after fainting from a heart attack while taking a hot bath. She'd never feared dying, telling Jean-Pierre, "Death isn't an end, it's a continuation, an improvement."[14]

When Grace Kelly told Jean-Pierre at Cannes she'd decided to skip the trip to Monaco to meet Rainier, he said, "Grace, you can't possibly do that. He's a reigning prince."[15] She finally decided to go, though she sounded as if she'd prefer to remain with Jean-Pierre.[16] Later, after having talked with the prince in his 235-room palace, she saw Olivia at a Friday afternoon cocktail party in Cannes. "I guessed things had gone wonderfully well by Grace's manner," Olivia recalled. "She was in a state of enchantment."[17]

Still, before Kelly left France, she couldn't resist one last fling with Jean-Pierre.[18]

Later, when Kelly and Rainier's engagement was announced, Olivia said she "was not particularly surprised with [the] news, but I was particularly charmed by it."[19] She was even more charmed by news of the wedding, writing Louella O. Parsons, "All of Monaco seems delighted at the prince's choice and Grace will have a welcome such as she never dreamed of when she arrives. What an exquisite little kingdom she'll reign over."[20] Pregnant with her daughter Gisele, Olivia had to miss the royal wedding.[21]

Kelly had not been happy in Hollywood, and despite immense stardom she was ready to clear out of it. "I hated Hollywood," she said. "It's a town without pity. I know of no other city in the world where so many people suffer from nervous breakdowns . . . I have many acquaintances there, but few friends."[22]

When I saw Princess Grace decades later, she was wandering around Manhattan's Villard Houses, now a hotel, admiring the decor, and seeming so alone. The prince allegedly had dalliances.[23] When a *Playboy* interviewer asked her if she was happy, she replied, "Well, I don't expect to be. I don't look for happiness. So, perhaps I am very content in life, in a way."[24]

—◦—

Hedda Hopper swept into Paris and saw Olivia at a party given by Mrs. Jack Reilly on July 25, 1955. "Olivia de Havilland looked like a dream walking," she wrote.[25] In August Olivia was among the 113 glitterati Elsa Maxwell invited on her 15-day cruise of the Greek islands aboard the 5,500-ton ocean-going yacht *Achilleus*, chartered for $100,000 (inflation adjusted: $900,000) by Greek tycoon Stavros Niarchos. The passengers were part of a new international social group called the Jet Set, rich people who were newly able to move quickly from one exotic locale to another, thanks to BOAC's de Havilland Comet, which introduced passenger jet service in the 1950s. The Jet Set was a turbocharged version of the old café society celebrated by Elsa Maxwell, Cole Porter, Tallulah Bankhead, and Noel Coward.

Though heavyset, unattractive, and a lesbian in a homophobic world, Maxwell had risen in society by organizing imaginative charity balls so diverting they warded off boredom for the rich and famous, who came to depend on her so much they put her up in their mansions for months and sometimes years at a time, picking up all her bills.[26] She was also an unofficial but effective publicist, and the Greek government engaged her to make its serene and sunny isles a tourist destination. Niarchos's yacht was his contribution to Maxwell's ongoing project to promote all things Greek. The media gave the cruise maximum coverage as it plowed the Aegean Sea.

"Sailing out of the Grand Canal with 'Adm.' Elsa Maxwell on the bridge, the good ship *Achilleus* headed for Greece today with a passenger list of bluebloods and bulging bankrolls," an AP correspondent wrote. "Wearing a gold-braided admiral's uniform, Miss Maxwell had a kiss and a bear hug for the social register emissaries accompanying her . . . including France's former premier Paul Reynaud and Olivia de Havilland . . . the Duke and Duchess of Argyll, [and] Metropolitan Opera star Cesare Pepi."[27] The caption for a provocative wirephoto circulated worldwide by International stated, "Gossip in Hollywood undoubtedly will deal with this incident before long. Film star Olivia de Havilland is dancing at Corfu, Greece, with Stavros Niarchos, fabulous financier, who is [the] 'angel' for [the] cruise."[28]

Niarchos, a shipping tycoon operating 80 tankers, was worth $22 billion. In a September 11 UP photo Olivia is shown barefooted, in Capri pants, and smiling as she dances with another ship-owner, Petros Nomikos, at his home on the Greek island of Santorini.[29] On September 19, Sheilah Graham wrote, "No truth to the report of trouble in Olivia de Havilland's paradise with Pierre Galante. The rumors started when Livvy went on the Elsa Maxwell royal cruise . . . without him. Incidentally, I hear there was enough black coffee served on this cruise to sink the boat."[30]

Back in Paris, Olivia found that Benjamin was adapting quickly to growing up abroad. "My son Benjie loves it as much as I do," she told the AP. "He is enrolled in a wonderful French school . . . The French have the equivalent of a college education by the time they are 18 . . . Benjie is a remarkably American boy. Even at five, he is an amazing combination of an intellectual and an athlete. The gentleness of the French culture will do him good. And he'll return to [America] periodically."[31] Benjamin was showing signs of brilliance and high promise, bringing home straight A report cards. He'd soon be a whiz at math. "[Olivia] was literally bursting with pride," wrote Hopper.[32]

Olivia's career revived somewhat in 1956 with the delightfully engaging *Ambassador's Daughter*, a bubbly Parisian romance about a diplomat's offspring and her soldier boyfriend that teamed her with likable John Forsythe. As photographed in the film by cinematographer Michael Kelber, Olivia at forty looked thirty in her Christian Dior clothes and makeup by Boris Karabanoff. "Alexandre, the great French hairdresser, made Olivia look so slick and *soignee*," Hopper noted.[33] Another journalist wrote, "For the first time in [Christian Dior's] career, the fashion czar served as a designer for a film, preparing a $75,000 wardrobe for Miss de Havilland,"[34] but according to the *Los Angeles Times*, the Dior originals cost $100,000 (the 2016 equivalent of $885,000).[35]

For her role as a fashion model, Olivia received advice from Lucky, the then–No. 1 mannequin in Paris.[36] Losing weight was necessary to accommodate the Dior dresses, and Olivia lost ten pounds. Dior invited her to dinner at his home and served an elaborate meal with different wines for each course, one more delicious than the last.

"How could you put such a dinner before me when you know what I went through to take off those 10 pounds?"[37]

"Tonight, my dear," Dior replied, "you are my client. As my client, you can afford to eat all of the extravagances which have been served up to you, and I can enjoy the pleasure of having you as my guest. But tomorrow, you will play my mannequin, and like all my mannequins, you can starve your way back into my gowns." He wouldn't even let her skip dessert.[38]

Played by Forsythe, the soldier in the story eventually marries the ambassador's daughter, and Norman Krasna scoured Paris looking for a church for the wedding scene. Olivia was required to arrive at the Church of St. Etienne du Mont at 5 a.m. in early December 1955 in freezing weather. Over her white satin Dior wedding dress, she wore three bulky overcoats and had a hot-water bottle concealed under her skirt to keep her feet warm in the unheated sanctuary, where she was still waiting at 3 p.m. when a reporter approached her.

"Is there anything you miss in Hollywood?" he asked.[39]

"Sounds corny, but I do miss the weather. Smog and all, the weather in California is not overrated. January in Paris is awful; and it stays awful until the spring. But I wouldn't want to live anywhere else."[40]

At 5 p.m. the assistant director apologized for detaining her all day and said she could go home—they wouldn't be filming that day as planned. She thanked him and asked when to report the following morning, and when he said 5 a.m., she smiled and walked outside to a crowd of cheering fans. Galante was waiting to drive her home.[41]

Gloria Swanson visited the set on assignment from the UP and wrote, "What fun finding old friends and familiar sights . . . Olivia de Havilland I have always admired as a woman. Away from a camera she handles herself with grace and is an asset to our industry"[42]

When the film was released in 1956, Bosley Crowther wrote, "Olivia de Havilland, for all her grace and sweetness, is not exactly a girl . . . There could be more bounce to this picture if it were played by a younger girl."[43] Hard-boiled columnist Sheilah Graham could not have disagreed more, writing, "I must ask Olivia de Havilland for the secret of how she manages to look all of 18 in *The Ambassador's Daughter*. And what clothes!"[44]

Baby Gisele Galante arrived by Caesarian delivery on July 18, 1956, in the American hospital in Paris, weighing 6 lbs. 7 ounces. Three days later a photographer snapped the smiling parents gazing down at their daughter in her mother's arms.[45] Benjamin, who was about to turn seven, was thrilled. "He wanted a sister," Olivia said, "and he's mad about Gisele."[46] She described Benjamin, or Ben, as she called him, as "a strong little boy, and those names have a strong sound. I'm terribly proud of him. He was graduated from the second to the third grade of his school in Paris in June, and this little American boy won four French prizes—in English, reading, arithmetic, and geography. He also got a mention in French, which he speaks beautifully. This pleased him very much."[47] Gisele, too, would prove to be an exceptionally bright child.

Olivia promised Samuel Goldwyn Jr. that she'd be in Hollywood August 15, 1957, to film *The Proud Rebel*, a post-Civil War drama in which Olivia plays a youthful farm spinster who befriends a Southern widower (Alan Ladd) searching for a physician to heal his mute son (ten-year-old David Ladd). While shooting a Utah location scene involving a burning barn, all three stars sustained painful burns when a gust of hot wind blew flames and embers at them. Their injuries, though mild, required treatment by a company doctor.[48] Walter Winchell reported that Olivia "had two miraculous escapes from serious injury [and] still has the shakes from the scares."[49]

Errol Flynn heard there was a party for *The Proud Rebel* at the Beverly Hilton Hotel and decided to attend and surprise Olivia. "As I was walking in, somebody kissed the back of my neck," she recalled. "I whirled around in anger and said, 'Do I know you?'"[50]

"It's Errol," he said.[51]

She hadn't recognized him because he'd changed radically. "His eyes were so sad. I stared into them in enough movies to know his spirit was gone. They used to be full of mischief, with little brown and green glints. They were totally different. I didn't recognize the person behind the eyes."[52] Years of dissipation, during which he'd consumed a fifth of vodka per day and chain-smoked, had finally ruined his health, leaving him with coronary thrombosis (clot in the coronary blood vessels), coronary atherosclerosis (hardening of the arteries), myocardial infarction (blood not reaching the heart), malaria, chronic lung infections, and portal cirrhosis of the liver.[53]

They went to lunch and reminisced about old times, and then she left for Paris and Flynn headed to Africa, where his former fisticuff opponent John Huston directed him in *The Roots of Heaven*. The temperature at the Cameroons location site was 125 degrees and the local men so primitive they went around "with their penises tied to their thighs with leather thongs," Huston wrote. While others in the film crew dropped out right and left, Flynn enjoyed himself, having brought books, potted grouse, French wines, vodka, and drugs, and his drug doctor supplied nightly prostitutes to tide him over until his girlfriend joined him in Bangui.[54] He received top billing and $90,000 for eight weeks, plus $4,000 for living expenses, the equivalent of $785,000 and $35,000, respectively, in today's dollars.[55] Flynn's biographer Jeffrey Meyers found the aging actor "surprisingly effective in his inescapable role as a sad, wasted figure."[56]

When *The Proud Rebel* opened at the Guild Theatre in Manhattan, A. H. Weiler of the *New York Times* called it "an honestly heartwarming drama . . . Olivia de Havilland is the picture of hardy womanhood. Although she is not a couturier's dream, the warmth, affection, and sturdiness needed in the role come across to an observer with telling effect."[57]

Pierre Galante was present one day when Olivia told an interviewer that American men were obsessed with success, failure, sex, and women's breasts. "Perhaps," Galante interjected, "what is wrong with the American male is the American female."[58]

The U.S. Army's 11th Airborne Division in 1958 made Olivia an honorary member, and she appeared in a fatigue shirt with her regulation Army name patch in *Stars and Stripes.*

There were ominous rumblings that year from Goodrich, who threatened, "If I were to write a book about [Olivia], I'd call it *I Married a Woman Who Wanted to Play Juliet*."[59] A few days later, Kilgallen reported Goodrich's book was called *Never Marry an Actress,* and "it can't help but be a thinly-disguised poke at his ex-wife, Olivia de Havilland."[60] On March 6 Kilgallen wrote that Olivia would "serve the legal papers" if her ex-husband published *Never Marry an Actress.*[61]

She started writing a book herself, and got an advance from the toniest of New York publishers, Random House, owned by Bennett Cerf, who loved show business, moonlighted as a TV star, and was married to actress Phyllis Fraser, Ginger Rogers's cousin. "Red faces will be the rage in Hollywood when Olivia de Havilland's tell-all words about life in Movietown reaches these shores in book form," predicted Erskine Johnson on March 17, 1960.[62] Hollywood went slightly crazy as fear spread among actors, producers, and directors who dreaded the prospect of seeing their private and public lives exposed by a two-time Oscar winner. "So firm was the rumor," United Press International reported, "that the book even had a title, *Shelter for Schizophrenics* . . . Olivia's arrival [in LA] was beclouded by the specter of the scandalous book."[63] Speculation about the contents was rife in the press, Earl Wilson writing on May 21, with far more accuracy than either Johnson or the UPI, "Olivia de Havilland finished a book about Paris, won't do an autobiography,"[64] and Kilgallen declared on June 18, "Olivia de Havilland's book is due in November. *Parlez Vous* is a series of vignettes on Paris."[65] According to Hedda Hopper, Olivia told her a literary agent had convinced her to write the book.

"Now you'll be able to tell the truth about your sister Joan," Hopper said.[66]

"But this is a book about jokes," Olivia replied.[67]

Hopper investigated and got the truth, writing, "It's the story of Olivia's life in Paris since she married Pierre Galante."[68]

Errol Flynn, too, would write a memoir, *My Wicked, Wicked Ways*, and, unlike Olivia's book, it would explode with lust, adventure, violence, scandal, and an unprecedented candor that would set a new standard for celebrity memoirs. Olivia came across Flynn one day in Paris, and Sheilah Graham later wrote, "She didn't recognize him . . . Livvy had been secretly in love with him."[69]

Dirk Bogarde was her costar in 1959's *Libel*, the melodramatic story of an aristocratic woman whose happy marriage is threatened when she gets evidence that her husband is an imposter. Bogarde, playing a tweedy and handsome English baronet, is impressive in a multi-layered role, and Olivia is elegant in her Dior clothes, with a photographer, Robert Krasker, who knew how to show a movie star at her best. Hair stylist Joan Johnstone and makeup artist Bill Lodge also understood her beauty and how best to translate it to the big screen in all its perfection, inside and out. After *The Heiress* she wanted to look glamorous on the screen again, and she certainly was. But looks were not enough to impress *New York Times* reviewer Bosley Crowther, who accused her of acting "as if she were balancing Big Ben on her hat."[70] Never mind—she had the things that were important to her at this time in her life. "Olivia," Sheilah Graham wrote, was "currently ensconced in England with husband Pierre Galante, her son, and daughter, for the duration of her *Libel* picture with Dirk Bogarde."[71] They stayed, according to Hedda Hopper, "in a cozy cottage outside London."[72]

When Olivia heard Joan had contracted mononucleosis, she sent weekly letters from Paris and encouraged relatives to do the same. Earlier, in 1954, Olivia had told a reporter, "I saw Joan on Broadway in *Tea and*

Sympathy. She was wonderful." A grateful Joan confided to Louella O. Parsons that she was "carrying around a cable from her sister . . . congratulating her on her notices in *Tea and Sympathy*." Parsons added. "The sisters didn't speak for several years."[73] But Joan insited "their feud was . . . hatched up by Warner Bros."[74]

It had been two years since Olivia left Hollywood, and her trip to LA in April 1960 provided a timely opportunity to assure her friends she had no intention of blasting them in print. Entitled *Every Frenchman Has One*, her collection of essays constituted a droll commentary on Gallic foibles. The *New York Times* reviewer wrote, "This treatise will bring nostalgic, provocative, pince-sans-rire [tongue-in-cheek] pleasure."[75] The *Chicago Tribune*'s John Chapman called it "captivating" and compared her favorably with Jean Kerr and Cornelia Otis Skinner.[76] The *Salt Lake Tribune* reviewer thought it "brisk and hilarious."[77] After publication in 1961, Olivia opened a telegram that read, SUNDAY NEXT YOU MOVE ONTO THE BESTSELLER LIST.[78] According to the *Des Moines Register*'s Olga Curtis, Olivia said her husband, a noted editor, had not helped her at all.

"If you want to know the truth," she said, "Pierre speaks English beautifully but he doesn't write it well. We speak French at home."[79] Her next book would be a novel, she revealed in another 1962 interview, specifying it would be a love story, and since she'd never worked in that genre before, she anticipated difficulties.[80]

On her 1960 trip to LA she also attempted to dispel lingering talk about a feud with Joan. "We are great friends," she said.[81] Later in the 1960s, Joan was willing to help Olivia when "an S.O.S cable arrived . . . [Olivia] was in both financial and marital difficulties and finding her current bills impossible to pay," Joan wrote.[82] Flying to Paris, she went directly to Olivia's house and was met at the door by Gisele and Benjamin, who took her upstairs to Olivia. "I found my sister ill in bed," Joan recalled.[83] "I explained to her that the scarcity of film roles now available to us did not mean the end of our earning capacity . . . There was Broadway, TV, stock, dinner theatre, and the lecture circuit."[84] Joan claimed she referred Olivia to her theatrical agent and lecture bureau. "I then left a sizable check, which she was soon able to repay. She signed with my lecture bureau and eventually had so many bookings that I had to find a new bureau to handle mine."[85] Joan had become a millionaire through investments in oil drilling, citrus groves in Florida, and an apartment building in Beverly Hills, as well as an insurance settlement when her sprawling, many-windowed, shingle-roofed house on Fordyce Road, clinging to a hillside in Brentwood, was destroyed by wildfires high above Los Angeles.[86]

The lecture agent went to work and when bookings for Olivia rolled in, she flew to the United States to begin her tour, lecturing on Hollywood's Golden Age. One of her talks, "From the City of Stars to the City of Lights," was part of the Providence Hospital Auxiliary's Celebrity Lecture Series at the Western Woods Cinema, according to the *Cincinnati Enquirer*.[87] When she called on Joan, she found her in poor health, feverish, unable to eat, sleep, or think clearly, all due, Joan said, to "my toxoplasmosis, or whatever I had."[88] Too much had happened to Joan in too short a time—another marriage gone wrong, two miscarriages in three months, a ruptured affair with *New Yorker* cartoonist Charles Addams, and bitter estrangements from both her daughters.[89] Joan had given up, but then "Sister O'Hara nursed me at Sister's house in Quogue," Joan wrote. "Because of her marital difficulties with her second husband, Pierre Galante, my sister seemed able to understand what I was going through. Olivia undressed me, put me to bed, held me in her arms as she sang a Japanese lullaby from our childhood . . . *Nen, nen, korori, okororiyo*. Still the tears would not stop."[90]

In May 1960 Olivia and Vivien Leigh dined at The Forum of the 12 Caesars in Manhattan. Addressed as Lady Olivier since her husband's knighthood in 1947, Leigh was in New York City to play a cruel, deceitful beauty in Jean Giraudoux's *Duel of Angels*, directed by her friend Robert Helpmann, a dancer known mainly for *The Red Shoes*.[91] Olivier had abandoned Leigh for actress Joan Plowright, and though in the middle of a nervous breakdown Leigh managed to struggle through the opening night of her play and score rave reviews—still the best actress in the world despite rampant manic depression. At Irene Selznick's recommendation she underwent shock treatments, concealing the burn marks from the electrodes with heavy makeup during the play's successful run.[92]

Bette Davis also tried her hand at Broadway in 1960, and Olivia went to see her in *The World of Carl Sandburg*, a concert reading of the poet's work by Davis and a male partner. Though first envisioned as a vehicle for Davis and her husband Gary Merrill, by the time the Sandburg project went into rehearsal their marriage was on the rocks.[93] On stage Davis and Merrill posed as a happy couple but they so detested the sight of each other that they stayed in separate wings of their hotels. Davis finally divorced him and kicked him out of the show, replacing him with Barry Sullivan for the pre-Broadway Florida tour. I caught the show shortly after it opened in New York, by which time Lief Ericson had replaced Sullivan.[94]

Davis reading "the fog comes in on little cat feet" was campy fun, as was her red, white, and blue ball gown. Olivia went backstage and the two old friends enjoyed a chat. For years Davis had begged Joseph L. Mankiewicz to write an *All About Eve* sequel about Margo and Bill's marriage but now she told Mankiewicz to forget it, saying, "Gary and I played it and it didn't work."[95]

In March 1961 MGM invited Olivia to attend the Atlanta re-premiere of *GWTW* in commemoration of the 100th anniversary of the start of the Civil War. Sadly, the real star of the festivities would not be present, Margaret Mitchell having died in 1949 after a drunken off-duty taxicab driver ran over her on Peachtree Street, fracturing her skull, shattering her pelvis, and plunging her into a coma from which she never recovered. The driver, Hugh D. Gravitt, was arrested and charged with drunken driving, speeding, and driving on the wrong side of the street. Police said an "immediate murder indictment" would be sought.[96] Eventually convicted of involuntary manslaughter, he served about ten months in prison. Mitchell was only forty-eight. Her slayer lived until 1994.[97]

Columnist Radie Harris asked Olivia if she remembered the original 1939 Atlanta premiere. "I certainly do," Olivia replied. "I remember most painlessly now how in love I was with John Huston!"[98] Radie was thrilled when Vivien Leigh asked her to accompany her to Atlanta, where they joined Olivia and David O. Selznick at the Georgian Terrace Hotel. Olivia, Leigh, Olivier, Gable, Lombard, Jock Whitney, and the entire *GWTW* contingent had stayed at the Georgian Terrace at the 1939 premiere.[99] Making her entrance at Loew's Grand theatre for the re-premiere, Olivia was a dazzling Hollywood goddess in sleeveless gold lace, fur, and long white gloves. Radie thought "her figure had grown a little matronly,"[100] but if it had, you'd never know it from the newsreel clips, which show Olivia at the top of her movie-star form. The film "brought back such glorious memories," Olivia recalled, "Clark Gable, Leslie Howard, Hattie McDaniel . . . all came alive again on the screen. I felt like it was one big, happy family reunion."[101]

"Olivia de Havilland was most concerned about Selznick," Edward Z. Epstein, Jennifer Jones's biographer, wrote, noting that "he looked terribly old (although only 58), and more disturbingly, his vitality seemed gone."[102] Though David hadn't told Jennifer, he'd recently suffered a heart attack. His spirits revived when the re-premiere audience applauded him and insisted he take the stage. According to Epstein, Olivia "observed that he stood straighter and taller and seemed once again to be the David she'd known."[103] Revitalized, he acquired the stage rights to *GWTW* from the Mitchell estate and auditioned Stephen Sondheim for the job of turning *GWTW* into a musical for the stage. Eventually Harold Rome, composer of the Broadway hits *Wish You Were Here* and *Fanny*, completed a musical spectacular of *GWTW* called *Scarlett*. It became a sensation in Japan, with an all-Japanese cast, but met with less success in London and Los Angeles and never made it to Broadway.

"Why didn't your husband come to Atlanta with you?" Sheilah Graham asked Olivia.

"Well, I'd gone alone to Atlanta in 1939, and I wanted to evaluate the time between then and now by going back alone—it permitted me to remeasure my life."[104]

After the re-premiere, Olivia returned to Paris and took Benjamin, now twelve, to see her movie *The Adventures of Robin Hood*. Her voice was dubbed by a French actress, but Benjamin thought it was his mother's voice and observed that her French had improved considerably since the 1930s.

Maintaining close ties with Bette Davis, Olivia saw her on Broadway in Tennessee Williams's *The Night of the Iguana*, which opened on December 28, 1961, at the Royale Theatre. After the show she went backstage to sign Davis's autograph book, joining Anita Loos, Natalie Schafer, Glenda Farrell, Teresa Wright, Ann Sheridan, Joan Bennett, Fredric March, Joan Crawford, and Tennessee Williams's brother Dakin.[105] Crawford told Davis about a gothic horror novel she'd read, Henry Farrell's *What Ever Happened to Baby Jane?* that had juicy parts for both of them, one a has-been movie star and the other her crazy, abusive sister. Davis was skeptical, suspecting the director, Robert Aldrich, was having an affair with Crawford, which meant he'd favor her. Producer William Frye said he gave a copy of the story to Olivia as well, envisaging her as the invalid sister, a part later played by Crawford.[106]

In *Iguana*, according to Joshua Logan, who'd shortly direct Davis in *Miss Moffat*, a musical version of *The Corn Is Green*, Davis "was svelte, handsome, voluptuous, wicked, wise, raffish, [and] slightly vulgar"[107] as the earthy hotel owner Maxine Faulk, but she left the play because she resented her relatively small role. "When you have been a great film star,"

Williams's agent Audrey Wood wrote, "it must be difficult to sit back-stage in your dressing room for protracted periods in which there is nothing to do but wait for your next entrance."[108]

Released in 1962, *The Light in the Piazza* was Olivia's best movie since *The Heiress*. Rapturously photographed on location in Florence and Rome, it proved to be the major work of her late period, and it is an entertaining film indeed, though still not up to what she could handle as an actress. She was forty-six, her beauty undiminished. The story of a mother's struggle to make sure her mentally challenged twenty-six-year-old daughter, saddled with the mind of a ten-year-old, gets her share of life's normal fulfillments, including love and marriage, it featured the striking but somewhat hard-edged beauty Yvette Mimieux as the daughter. When someone mentioned to Olivia that she'd played Mimieux's mother, Olivia supplied a quick correction.

"I beg your pardon," she said. "Yvette Mimieux played my daughter."[109]

Three years later a reporter asked Mimieux about Olivia. "We met in Paris before she made *Lady in a Cage*," Mimieux said. "Why is it that Bette Davis, Joan Crawford, and Olivia would do those cheap horror films? I can't understand it. They make all women cheap . . . Why not stories about women with strength?"[110] Thirteen years after that smug pronouncement, Mimieux starred in the made-for-TV cheapie *Devil Dog: Hound of Hell*.

When *The Light in the Piazza* opened at the Victoria and Trans-Lux 85th Street theatres in Manhattan, Bosley Crowther was respectful to Olivia but wrong in his assessment of the film. "The satisfaction of seeing Olivia de Havilland once more being a dear is meager compensation for the utter triviality of her new film . . . [which] doesn't work despite the sweet performance of Miss de Havilland."[111]

24

On Broadway with Henry Fonda, on the High Seas with Edward Heath

When Olivia arrived in New York aboard the *Queen Elizabeth* in 1962, Dorothy Kilgallen noticed that she debarked with fifteen pieces of luggage. It would be a busy stay, marking the first time she'd appeared on Broadway since *Romeo and Juliet* and *Candida*. On a brighter note, she'd again be working with Henry Fonda, her *Male Animal* leading man who'd accumulated a Broadway record of solid-gold hits—*Mister Roberts, The Caine Mutiny Court Martial,* and *Two for the Seesaw. A Gift of Time*, the play Olivia and Fonda were taking to Broadway, was the harrowing account of a dying man, Charles Wertenbaker, his gallant wife, Lael, their attempts in his last days to live life fully, and how she finally helps him commit suicide in order to spare him needless suffering.

A Gift of Time was based on Lael Tucker Wertenbaker's book *Death of a Man*, which critics had praised for its unsparing treatment of a subject—death and dying—long considered off-limits. "I love you: Please die"—these were Lael's words to Charles as he slashed his wrists while she pumped painkillers into his arm. It was chilling enough to read in a book; in a live stage performance it would prove to be a difficult endurance test for an audience to witness such torment. Prior to the opening, there were both skepticism and high expectations along the Rialto.

Fonda would be playing Charles Wertenbaker, who, before his terminal cancer, had been *Time* magazine's foreign editor, and Olivia would
play his wife Lael Tucker Wertenbaker, who'd been *Time*'s foreign correspondent in Nazi Berlin. Later both Lael and Charles reported from Paris,
where Hemingway and Irwin Shaw became their friends. The Broadway
adaptation of Lael Wertenbaker's book was prepared by playwright Garson Kanin, who'd had a hit when he directed *The Diary of Anne Frank*.

Olivia attended a party given by Nancy Olson, who'd played William
Holden's girlfriend in *Sunset Boulevard*. Columnist Leonard Lyons later
reported that a friend of John F. Kennedy asked Olivia if she remembered
how a young JFK had asked her for a date during WWII. "As I remember, he was quite persuasive and most persistent," Olivia replied.[1] Though
she'd turned him down, JFK later said, "We'll hear from her yet."[2] Olivia
told JFK's friend, "Tell President Kennedy that my daughter loves him."[3]
The following year, on November 22, 1963, JFK was assassinated in Dallas, Texas.

New York reporters quizzed Olivia about the whereabouts of her husband and young children. "I get through things much better if I'm alone,"
she replied. "I have a tendency to be dependent—to lean on crutches
whenever handy. If the play succeeds, the family will come to New York
for the Easter vacation."[4] Journalist Olga Curtis, who interviewed Olivia
in March 1962, wrote that her family "didn't expect to see her home for
about a year."[5] But Olivia made it clear to the Associated Press that if the
play had a long run, she'd take four weeks off to treat the family to a holiday in Austria. She also intended to bring her family to America during
the spring school vacation and again in the summer.[6]

From Paris, Gisele wrote that her father had assured her that Olivia
had arrived safely in America, adding that she'd achieved second class
on the ski slopes, was sending "1,000 kisses, Mama," and hoped Olivia
was not "too sad" over being away from her.[7] Benjamin, preternaturally
learned for a boy of twelve, wrote about his adventures on the slopes and

the "thrilling power" of flying down a mountainside, where the snow was "formidable."[8] Olivia found his letters "journalistic . . . factual and no romance."[9] He was "the scientific type, fascinated by three-stage rockets . . . [and] engineering."[10] Her son's love, she told reporter Mary Campbell, was "complicated and reserved," whereas Gisele's was "simple and outgoing."[11] When Olivia was working at home, Gisele would write her letters and leave them where Olivia could easily find them.[12]

To one persistent journalist, Olivia said, "I didn't want my family with me while I was coping with opening night . . . My son, Benjamin, is 12 and in boarding school. My daughter, Gisele, is only five and she's home. They run very smoothly without me." As for Pierre Galante, she said that she'd engaged an excellent chef, since French husbands required first-rate food to be contented.[13]

The previous year, she'd mentioned "problems" in connection with a skiing trip she and Galante had taken to Crans sur Sierre in Switzerland. "My first instructor was a big handsome fellow named Georges. My second instructor was a big handsome fellow named Emile. That's when my husband said to me, 'Olivia, we're going back to Paris.'"[14]

Before the New York rehearsals began, Olivia and Fonda researched their roles in Cibourne, on the Spanish border of France, to soak up the atmosphere of the area where Lael and Charles had lived. They took a leisurely walk along the path the Wertenbakers loved in St. Jean-de-Lux, went to a café and ate the kind of fish soup referenced in the play, and visited the radiologists and inspected the room where the X-rays had first been viewed. Olivia searched all over the tiny town, looking for a Basque shirt to give Fonda, but it was off-season and there were none to be found. "I got angry," Olivia later told AP writer Mary Campbell. "I thought, 'This is idiotic that in a Basque town we can't get a Basque shirt.'"[15] In the twelfth shop she visited, she finally found the shirt and presented it to Fonda. They located the Wertenbakers' house and stood in every room. "Everywhere we went," Olivia later recalled, "people knew them and spoke of them beautifully."[16] Fonda added, "As they talked about Wertenbaker their lips were smiling, but their eyes were full of tears. I couldn't take it. I had to get up and leave . . . I thought how are we ever going to get such faces in our cast, but we've done it."[17]

In Philadelphia with Fonda and Kanin before the New York opening, "Olivia de Havilland was the radiant center of a group in the Variety Club," a reporter wrote.[18] "We have no doubt that the play will be well-received," Garson Kanin said. "My stars are equally enthusiastic." He was going to call the play *Last of the Wine* until his wife, actress Ruth Gordon, told him she'd found the perfect title in James Jones's novel *From Here to Eternity*. "Prewitt said life is merely a gift of time," Gordon related.[19] Olivia told Leonard Lyons, "The play fulfills me because I play the indispensable woman."[20]

Each day she arrived at the theatre at 5:30 p.m., and contemplated her performance for three hours.[21] In the final days before the New York premiere, she began to feel the pressure and lose sleep.[22] Fonda gave her orange tea and said it would put her to sleep in ten minutes. "Well, I was asleep in half an hour," she said. He supplied her with capsules containing skull cap, passion flowers, and pulsitilla. "I do like . . . pulsitilla—to help a person who is tense and nervous and has . . . trouble sleeping," she said. One day a stage light overheated and exploded as Olivia and Fonda rehearsed a scene. Both were sprayed and cut by flying glass.[23]

Columnist Earl Wilson wrote that Olivia was good at getting publicity for the show and told him, "It's a shame Hank Fonda's such a nice guy—we could have a ball having a feud."[24] On February 22, 1962, opening night brought respectful but less than smash-hit reviews. Walter Kerr, the most insightful of New York critics, wrote, "Olivia de Havilland . . . is self-contained from the first verdict to the ultimate deliberate violence . . . Her mellow voice helps soften a bravery that could quickly turn to rhetoric."[25] The AP critic thought both Olivia and Fonda "performed with brilliant understanding," but voiced reservations about the play's "insistent emphasis on harrowing clinical details."[26] Reviewer E. B. Radcliff found Fonda "more filled with bravo than bravery; more typical of an actor than an author,"[27] and another critic wrote that Olivia "seldom rises above mere mechanical playing . . . It is an uncalled-for play . . . with cliché observations and a depressing odor of ether."[28]

Both the play and its leading lady had their champions. The *Chicago Tribune*'s John Chapman wrote, "I have ducked almost all her movies. I've seen her on the stage now and again, but not until she appeared in *A Gift of Time* did she really reach me as an actress."[29] Backstage one night, a stranger approached Olivia and handed her a gold double love-knot ring, saying, "I want you to have this," and disappeared.[30] Hedda Hopper called the play "one of the most beautiful, poignant love stories I've ever seen."[31] Fonda's biographer Howard Teichmann would later write, "The sensitive and talented Olivia de Havilland was his leading lady, but that was not enough . . . While the notices were filled with praise, ticket buyers stayed away. 'It's the only show I've ever been in,' Fonda says, 'where they didn't applaud the final curtain. People found the play too painful to accept. Instead they waited outside the stage door to tell me how grateful they were in hushed voices.'"[32]

Although Olivia was known throughout the entertainment world for her professionalism, she went up on her lines one night, according to Leonard Lyons. Someone spread a false report that Pierre Galante was in the audience, and Olivia realized for the first time "how many sexy scenes there were," Lyons wrote. Every time Fonda embraced her passionately that night, the thought of Galante watching them "made Miss de Havilland lose track of her lines," the columnist reported.[33]

The show closed on May 12, 1962. By summer she was in Washington, D.C., where the American Newspaper Women's Club feted her and members of the Company of the Shakespeare Summer Festival at a cognac-and-coffee klatch. When a reporter asked if French males prefer younger women, she said it wasn't true. The reporter insisted that

Frenchmen visiting the United States went after young girls, and Olivia replied, "When away from home, Frenchmen simply adopt the ways of the barbaric people they are visiting."[34] In an August 28 interview she told reporter Ida Jean Kain that French women welcome each stage of growth and come into their own in middle age. The touchstone of growth is experience, she said, "and you cannot have experience without having years."[35] She turned forty-six on July 1.

In Paris, she and Cary Grant were taking in a fashion show at the Crillon Hotel on the Place de la Concorde when an anti-American demonstration broke out across the street. Olivia and Grant ducked out a back door to avoid picketers yelling, "Yankee go home!" as well as the reporters and paparazzi on the scene.[36] France lost the Algerian war in 1962, and historically anti-Americanism intensifies during periods of French uncertainty and military humiliations. The French had nothing in particular against Americans, but by defying the United States, the world's greatest superpower, they kept from feeling emasculated.

When Olivia returned to her townhouse, she found, as *maitresse de maison*, things to be not as they were when she'd left five months ago. A new Spanish maid did not speak either French or English, and also could not cook, which was unfortunate since the regular cook had been hospitalized. Preparing meals was not Olivia's strong point, but if she wore a comfortable pair of tennis shoes the chore was at least bearable.[37]

Fascinated with French educational methods, she visited Gisele's school, where the teacher began her class of five-year-olds by asking, "Are you intelligent?" The kids replied, *"Mais OUI."* Olivia concluded, "She assumes they are. They assume they are. And they are. There you are."[38] Gisele could already read, write, add, subtract, and hold forth on Caesar, Charlemagne, the Druids, and the Christians and the lions. Some French children study Latin and Greek for seven years, and many are fluent in English. Although Gisele spoke only French at this point, she'd pick up English later on. "It's a marvelous system; it's Alsatian," Olivia said. "Girls start at four. They go back and forth with little brief cases. They love it." Olivia rejects the notion that American children are incapable of this kind of education. "I'm the mother of two," she said, "and that is the proof of it." At home, Gisele had a nurse, and the children had their own cook. They lived on the third floor, which included a dining room and kitchenette. Their meals were delivered on a dumbwaiter, and the nurse washed the dishes and sent them back down. It was necessary to keep the nurse and the cook apart, since in France they never seem to get along, and in the few cases where they do, "they gang up on the mistress of the house," Olivia said.[39] It was mandatory and normal in France, Olivia said, to have a certain degree of tension between a nurse and a cook so the mistress could always be in control.[40]

There were unmistakable signs that the Galante marriage was in trouble. Galante would write in his biography, *Mademoiselle Chanel*, "Like actresses, fashion designers generally leave only a fleeting memory."[41] In 1962 they'd separate, though they continued to live in the same residence for the next six years, no doubt in order to provide a normal home life for the children. Galante eventually moved across the street, but he and Olivia remained friends, even after their divorce in 1979. When he was diagnosed with lung cancer, she took care of him until his death in 1988.

Edward Heath, Great Britain's Lord Privy Seal, came into Olivia's life in 1962 during an Atlantic crossing on the *Queen Elizabeth*. He was on his way to a conference in Ottawa. "I studied my script, he memorized his speech," she told a *New York Times* reporter in 1976. Then things got more interesting. They danced all night during a storm at sea. "You know, the only reason I was able to dance with Mr. Heath?" she later asked an interviewer. "I'd been drinking red wine. I made up my mind I was not going to be sick, even though the waves were breaking over the ship like tiger's teeth . . . Anybody could have danced with Mr. Heath at the height of an Atlantic gale if they'd finished off the bottle with their meal."[42] She quite liked him, later recalling, "I saw him persisting in games of squash, with the ship at all sorts of angles. And then I saw what a sensitive man he is. We had an SOS message from a freighter after two men had been badly injured in a boiler-room explosion. They had no doctor onboard. The *Queen* located the ship but was unable to lower a doctor because the seas were too mountainous. The captain had to tell us that it would be a case of losing nine lives in a bid to save two. I remember the shadow that came over Edward's face as he heard that we had to turn away and leave these two injured men to their fates."[43] She and Heath would see each other again. Author Michael McManus, who worked for Heath for five years, wrote that his former employer "was a gay man who had sacrificed his personal life to his political career, exercising iron self-control and living a celibate existence."[44]

<hr />

It seems incredible that Olivia never made a foreign film even though she resided in Paris throughout the mid-twentieth-century European cinematic renaissance that reinvented the art of film in movies such as *La Dolce Vita*, *A Man and a Woman*, *Jules and Jim*, *La Strada*, *Wild Strawberries*, *The Seventh Seal*, *Winter Light*, *Persona*, *Breathless*, *Nights of Cabiria*, *The 400 Blows*, *Hiroshima Mon Amour*, *Last Year at Marienbad*, and *L'Avventura*. At the time Olivia was still a knockout in her late forties, and she would have been perfect as Catherine Deneuve's mother in 1964's *The Umbrellas of Cherbourg*. A reporter asked her in 2011 if she'd ever been offered a movie role in her adopted country. "No, I wasn't," she replied. "And I'll tell you a very droll story. I thought that I had made great progress with my French when a grand dame said to me one day: 'You speak French very well, Olivia, but you have a slight Yugoslav accent.' I suppose there were not parts in French movies for actresses with Yugoslav accents."[45]

The French New Wave brought in a cool, detached style appropriate for a Godless Cold War world that could perish in an instant. The eternal verities no longer seemed to apply. "I never met Goddard," Olivia said. "I never met Truffaut. I never met Brigitte Bardot."[46]

25

Grand Guignol: Having Fun with Bette Davis in *Hush . . . Hush, Sweet Charlotte*

A fter the Academy of Motion Picture Arts and Sciences in 1962 singled out Bette Davis's macabre, overdrawn performance in *What Ever Happened to Baby Jane?* for an Oscar nomination as best actress of the year, Olivia attended the presentation ceremony on April 8, 1963, at the Santa Monica Civic Auditorium, hosted by Frank Sinatra, and sat backstage with Davis in Sinatra's dressing room as they waited to hear if Davis had won. Davis and costar Joan Crawford had fought so viciously on the set that Jack L. Warner sneered, "I wouldn't give you a dime for those two washed up old bitches."[1] Nonetheless they gave him a smash hit and succeeded in inventing a new genre called Grande Dame Guignol, which would create jobs for aging A-list actresses such as Shelley Winters in *Whoever Slew Auntie Roo?*, Geraldine Page and Ruth Gordon in *Whatever Happened to Aunt Alice?*, Agnes Moorehead in *Dear Dead Delilah*, Tallulah Bankhead in *Die! Die! My Darling*, Zsa Zsa Gabor in *Picture Mommy*, and Gloria Swanson in *Killer Bees.*[2] Though these distinguished performers, some of them Oscar winners, were reduced to playing hags and psycho biddies, at least they could find work, and even, in Davis's case, get a crack at the Oscar.

Crawford, who'd won the gold statuette for *Mildred Pierce* years before, was so livid that the Academy snubbed her for *Baby Jane* that she set out to sabotage Davis by "doing everything she possibly could to keep me from winning," Davis said.[3] Anne Bancroft, nominated for *The Miracle Worker*, couldn't attend the presentation ceremony, and Crawford persuaded Bancroft to let her accept the Oscar for her in the event she won.

According to Davis, nominees or their substitutes were assigned backstage dressing rooms with TV monitors that year, but Oscar authorities Mason Wiley and Damien Bona wrote, "Bette was ensconced in Sinatra's dressing room with Olivia de Havilland." Davis felt sure she had the Academy Award in the bag.[4] "When Anne Bancroft's name was announced [as the winner], I am sure I turned white," Davis recalled.[5] Fuming in a thick cloud of cigarette smoke, Davis watched the TV monitor helplessly as Crawford read a prepared speech from Bancroft: "There are three reasons why I won this award, [producer] Fred Coe, [director] Arthur Penn, and [playwright] William Gibson."[6] Davis recalled, "Crawford floated down the hall past my door. I will never forget the look she gave me. It clearly said, 'You didn't win and I am elated!'"[7]

"Let's get out of here," Davis told Olivia, and William Frye took Davis to a party at the Beverly Hilton, where they were joined by "Bobby [Davis's sister], B.D. [Davis's daughter Barbara Davis Sherry Hyman], Robert Aldrich and his wife, and Olivia de Havilland." Davis snatched a fifth of scotch from the table and filled her glass. "This is for La Belle Crawford," she said, and someone told her vodka was Crawford's drink. "I don't care what she drinks," Davis snapped. "This is going in her fucking face. I refuse to be in the same room with her. I don't care how big the room is."[8]

Davis insisted they all repair to her home, where she immediately retired to the kitchen and prepared a meal of scrambled eggs and toast. Frye made the mistake of observing that Crawford had looked elegant, and Davis threatened him with a kitchen knife. "You make me sick," she said, and went back to slicing bread.[9]

After Crawford bowed out of 1964's *Lady in a Cage*, Olivia assumed the leading role.[10] "That old rumor is hot again," Kilgallen wrote on April 28, 1965. "Olivia de Havilland to marry writer Luther Davis. Maybe, but in past seasons Livvy always has wound up back in Paris with Pierre Galante."[11] Yale-educated and a former Air Force major, the virile, attractive Luther Davis wrote the screenplays for *Kismet*, *The Hucksters*, and *B.F.'s Daughter*.[12] Hedda Hopper reported on May 3, "Olivia de Havilland doesn't care who knows that she's madly in love with Luther Davis. They were all over town together."[13] A journalist who interviewed Olivia wrote on May 23, "Her future is not unclouded. Her second marriage is rumored to be in trouble, though, characteristically, she does not discuss it."[14]

On April 29 Sheilah Graham commented, "Everyone is so terribly civilized these days." Pierre Galante, she reported, was coming to the United States to publicize his book *Berlin Wall*, and although he and Olivia had "legally separated for several months," they were on the friendliest of terms. Would he, Graham wondered, her pen dripping irony, serve as "best man if and when Olivia marries Luther Davis." Davis both wrote and produced Olivia's 1964 film *Lady in a Cage*.[15]

The film concerns a woman trapped in her house and terrorized by punk hooligans, including one played by James Caan. Olivia told reporter Myles Standish of the *St. Louis Post-Dispatch* that the picture was "an acid commentary on human nature."[16] Filmographer Tony Thomas wrote, "She believed the film said something valid about the crime situation in large, modern cities . . . She also admitted that she owned a share of the profits."[17] But her interest in the material was genuine. "We think we are civilized," she said, "but underneath there is a core of barbarianism lurking, ready to be let loose by disaster or catastrophe. Luther Davis . . . got the idea from the power failure which tied up Manhattan."[18] Davis knew of a woman who was trapped in an elevator, and when she set off the alarm, it signaled to thieves and rapists that someone inside the building was probably helpless, so they broke in and raped her. As in the 1964 Kitty Genovese murder case, the woman's cries for help were ignored by neighbors and passersby. "Most of us are at fault that way," Olivia said, recalling the time she was driving home from the studio and failed to notify the police that burglar alarms were ringing at two places she passed.[19] Her dedication to what she deemed the film's social significance was such that she "spent almost every working hour of those four weeks [of shooting] in that elevator cage. I was as glad to get out of there as the woman I was playing."[20]

New York Times critic A.H. Weiler called the film "a monster . . . the seemingly grim troupe that fashioned this sordid, if suspenseful, exercise in aimless brutality merely appears to be made up of cynics without a point of view . . . Cause and effect and moral issues are avoided or touched upon. A discerning viewer is just left curious and repelled."[21]

While in St. Louis to promote the film, Olivia had lunch with Myles Standish, who later wrote, "Now 47 years old, she is still beautiful . . . warm, outgoing, witty, and gay . . . a hostess, a gourmet, a cosmopolite . . . and is known as one of the best-dressed women in Paris."[22]

Someone inquired if Olivia was part of the Grand Guignol craze that engulfed Davis and Crawford after *What Ever Happened to Baby Jane?* "I was asked to play the psychiatrist who turns mad in a rather crude shocker, *Shock Treatment*, and turned it down."[23] All that changed when Davis called her in 1964 with an offer too good to refuse.

"Livvy," Davis said, "you simply must take this role," referring to the part of Miriam Deering in *Hush . . . Hush, Sweet Charlotte* that had just been abandoned by Joan Crawford, whose phantom illness concealed her real reason for avoiding the set—she was fed up with being upstaged by Davis the same way she'd been in *Baby Jane*.[24] Olivia was vacationing in Switzerland with Benjamin and Gisele, and she declined the role, but Davis persuaded her to peruse the *Charlotte* script and get back to her. She read the script several more times. Katharine Hepburn, Vivien Leigh, and Loretta Young had already rejected the role. "I can just about stand

to look at Joan Crawford at six in the morning on a southern plantation," Leigh said, "but I couldn't possibly look at Bette Davis."[25] Barbara
Stanwyck also turned it down, saying, "I don't believe in horror stories for
women, and I wouldn't play a part like that if I were starving."[26] Such lofty
standards did not prevent her, in her final film, from screaming her way
through Grand Guignol director William Castle's creepy Gothic horror
tale, *The Night Watcher*."[27]

Robert Aldrich, who'd directed *Baby Jane* and other high-camp
classics such as *Kiss Me Deadly* and *Autumn Leaves* and now was set to
undertake *Sweet Charlotte*, rang Olivia, and they discussed the script,
about which she voiced objections impossible to resolve on the phone.
Determined to sign her, he took three airplanes, a train, and a goat trail
to find her in the Swiss mountains, where they talked for four days.[28]
Aldridge bought her suggestion that the one-dimensional role of Miriam Deering needed more depth and ambivalence, and he offered her
$100,000 (inflation adjusted: $777,000). She would have to rush to the
United States immediately because delays owing to Crawford's illness
had already forced Aldrich to cancel location filming in Louisiana and
build a $200,000 ($1,500,000) replica of Houmas House on Fox's sound
stage 7.[29] "Olivia flew to Hollywood within a week of Miss Davis's call,"
a journalist wrote.[30] Davis received $200,000 ($1,500,000) for *Charlotte*.[31]

The transition from Crawford to de Havilland did not run smoothly.
When Aldrich told Davis he'd convinced Olivia to replace Crawford, he
did so in absolute confidence because he needed two days to handle legal
matters, but Davis immediately leaked to her press agent Rupert Allan,
who passed the scoop on to the media. "I'm glad for Olivia—she needed
the part," Crawford said. "Aldrich made no effort to reach me . . . It stinks
. . . I cried for nine hours."[32]

In Los Angeles Olivia and her children settled in the Beverly Hills
Hotel for a protracted stay. Both Benjamin, fifteen, and Gisele, eight,
loved their vacation in the posh resort. During an interview she said her

family enjoyed living in Paris, but she felt the children should be exposed to American history and "get the feel of this country."[33] She respected the verve, stimulation, and spectacle of the American past and wanted her children to be aware of their rich heritage. Benjamin's namesake, his paternal great-great-grandfather, was a physician and signer of the Texas Declaration of Independence and the Constitution of the Republic of Texas.[34] Born in 1799, Dr. Goodrich served in the Alabama state legislature before settling in Washington, Texas, a small town near the Brazos River in south central Texas, in 1834. As a representative of the town, he attended the Texas Convention of 1836 to sign the historic documents. He died in 1860.[35]

"Ben has American history in his bones," Olivia said, adding that she'd like to buy a house in the United States, but since she owned one in Paris, she'd have to "figure out a way to get very, very rich."[36]

Bette Davis welcomed Olivia to LA by hosting an old-fashioned clambake and lobster fest at her home.[37] "Bette Davis and Olivia de Havilland have become buddy-buddy friends," columnist Harold V. Cohen wrote. "The girls discovered while making *Hush . . . Hush, Sweet Charlotte* that they dig each other."[38] When production resumed on September 9, 1965, Olivia's children visited the set but were bored by the glacial pace of filmmaking, neither of them having inherited their mother's interest in cinema. Gisele's only comment after seeing *GWTW* had been, "*Maman*, you had very bad taste. You liked Scarlett, that terrible woman!"[39] One thing the children did inherit from their mother, both of whose husbands were ordinary looking, was extreme beauty. Gisele was petite and pretty after the fashion of such elegant gamins as Leslie Caron and Audrey Hepburn. At fifteen Ben was darkly attractive, resembling Dean Stockwell, star of *Long Day's Journey Into Night* and *Sons and Lovers*.

Davis and Olivia loved talking about their kids. "It's his last year at home," Davis said, referring to her thirteen-year-old adopted son Michael Merrill, who "passed through a knock-'em-dead-blond-boy phase between the ages of five and sixteen," according to Davis biographer Ed Sikov. Michael had somehow survived growing up with a mother who, he said, "was very volatile and could get angry at a moment's notice."[40] Davis said the movies' current goddesses were Angie Dickinson, Tuesday Weld, Mary Tyler Moore, and Elizabeth Ashley. The gods, she predicted, would be Michael Parks, Michael Landon, Mike Connors, Steve McQueen, Jim Garner, and Robert Redford."[41] She was right about McQueen and Redford. James Dean lookalike Michael Parks would fall short of major stardom, but he certainly held his own with Bette Davis in a 1962–1963 season Perry Mason episode. When Davis, playing his lawyer, visited his jail cell in a mink coat, he read her the riot act and kicked her out. Leaving, she turned and said seductively, "Good night, toughie."

In the ghoulish *Hush . . . Hush, Sweet Charlotte*, Southern belle Charlotte Hollis is jilted by her married lover (Bruce Dern) and apparently takes revenge by beheading him, though it is not entirely clear that she is the murderer, even when his severed head rolls across the floor and comes to rest at her feet. Everyone thinks she's crazy, and she certainly acts it in the late, bug-eyed Bette Davis style. Her poor relation, Miriam, played by Olivia, moves in, scheming to steal Charlotte's money, but when Charlotte discovers Miriam had seen her lover's wife murder him, she pushes a stone urn from the balcony of her plantation manse and mashes Miriam to a bloody pulp. Absurd as it sounds, the film is consistently diverting. In Olivia's frightening scenes with Davis and the equally histrionic Agnes Moorehead, it is Olivia who dominates the screen by capturing her character's ferocious, merciless, and murderous nature.

"I was pleased with it—and my performance," Olivia said.[42]

While making the film in Los Angeles, she decided she enjoyed being in the capital of the movie industry more than she ever had while a resident. She could now view it through her offsprings' delight in its attractions.[43]

When *Sweet Charlotte* opened at the Capitol and other theatres in New York, Bosley Crowther hated it but rather liked Olivia, denouncing the film as "calculated and coldly carpentered . . . grossly contrived, purposely sadistic, and brutally sickening . . . de Havilland [is] far more restrained [than Davis] but nonetheless effective dramatically in her off-beat role."[44] Davis, according to the high-brow critic Kenneth Tynan, yanked a cardboard piece of Grand Guignol "to the level of art," and he called her "a wasted Bernhardt, with her screen-filling eyes and electrifying vocal attack."[45]

The movie was a box-office triumph. A Davis–de Havilland nationwide *Sweet Charlotte* publicity tour, replete with an entourage of ten, was announced, but, according to Kilgallen, "The publicity tour of Bette Davis and Olivia de Havilland on behalf of *Hush . . . Hush, Sweet Charlotte* broke up before it started because of a spat, but it's been renewed to the accompaniment of hugs and kisses, sweetness and light. They plan to start next week."[46] On the first of their three days of personal appearances in New York City movie houses, Olivia and Davis emerged from their hotel, The Plaza, and found a sizable crowd eager to greet two of the last remaining giants of the fast-fading Golden Age.

Olivia told Davis that Joan Crawford had checked into The Plaza, and the fans had probably come to get a look at her.[47] Davis wasn't amused, judging from her thin smile. They proceeded to their engagements via bus, accompanied by ten policemen, and they could have used fifty more. The ten-man squad had to charge hand in hand to drive a wedge through the boisterous mobs. Olivia commented on the extreme youth of their assembled admirers, remarking that their mothers and fathers were only babies when she and Davis made their film debuts.[48] Olivia good-naturedly conversed with the fans, and when one of them called out, asking her age,[49] she said she was forty-eight,[50] and when another wanted to know if she and Joan Fontaine were in touch,[51] she rejoined that at the moment they were separated by 3,000 miles.[52]

Kilgallen reported that over 50,000 people had shown up to cheer Olivia and Davis, that a near-riot broke out at Loew's Metropolitan in Brooklyn, that Davis was shoved over the curbstone by the mob, and that four hysterical fans were saved by patrolmen as a bus bore down on them. "Three of the special officers required treatment for cuts and bruises received in the melee," Kilgallen added, "but it was all in a good cause, because the cash registers are ringing merrily at the box office."[53]

The two stars joined an interviewer from the NEA wire service, Joan Crosby, at a table facing the windows in a corner of The Plaza's stately Edwardian Room, and Olivia said she was a newcomer to publicity tours, but that Davis had traveled extensively for *Whatever Happened to Baby Jane?* and was showing her the ropes.[54] Referring to Olivia as "Livvy," Davis assured her that national touring was easy because the main effort required was getting on and off the bus.[55] Olivia mentioned that Davis's *Baby Jane* tour was the first of its kind ever, and that it had been a phenomenal hit with the public.[56] Davis had been surprised to find ten police officers on her bus for crowd control, fearing that no one would show up at her appearances. Many stars felt that way, she explained, because they didn't want to feel like egotistical morons.[57]

Olivia was wearing a white-and-navy-blue Dior suit, and Davis was dressed in black, with a leopard jacket and leopard chapeau. The conversation turned to the difference between Hollywood's Golden Age and 1965, and Davis bemoaned the lack of opportunity for young actors in television series, in which they're always playing the same character, to grow as artists. When Davis was at Warner, she portrayed everything from a prostitute to a queen. That was how, she pointed out, she and Olivia, assaying a variety of roles, had mastered their craft.[58]

"I don't know how some of these actresses pose in the nude with so little artistry," Olivia said. "We never tried, Bette, but we could do much better."[59]

"Nudity is here to stay," Davis said. "Jean Harlow was somewhat like Marilyn Monroe, but Marilyn was a better actress than Jean."[60]

"I wish I'd seen Harlow in films, Bette."[61]

"Don't. It's tragic. Even Jean herself said she wasn't a good actress."[62]

Journalist Margaret McManus interviewed Olivia in her Plaza suite and liked her "wide, warm smile . . . She was . . . [wearing] a sapphire and diamond pin about the size of a ping-pong ball. At the top, in Hollywood, they do pay well."[63] Though Olivia had often disdained television in the past, she now welcomed the work, hosting "The Bell Telephone Easter Show" on NBC, introducing Dorothy Collins, Richard Tucker, Anita Gillett, and the Mormon Tabernacle Choir. On "The Celebrity Game," she appeared with Roddy McDowell, Jack Palance, Charlie Weaver, Hedda Hopper, Jim Bacchus, Nick Adams, Suzanne Pleshette, and George Jessel, exchanging views on whether women should worry more about remaining single than men do. Olivia and Davis were on ABC's "Hollywood Palace" and various daytime game shows.

"I kind of liked it," Olivia said. "I never dreamed . . . I'd enjoy being on television, but I rather did.[64] In the future, TV would be an increasingly important part of her life, giving her roles in *The Big Valley, Noon Wine, The Love Boat, Murder Is Easy,* and *North and South II.*[65]

Winding up the *Sweet Charlotte* tour, Olivia said she'd had a good time and found Hollywood a different and far better place.[66] She was so popular with the press that when she returned to Paris the NEA correspondent Dick Kleiner wrote that Hollywood seemed somewhat drearier in her absence.[67]

Back at home, Olivia told a journalist that living in Hollywood was necessary for a continuing career in films. Good roles were still available to her there, but she decided to put her children's needs first.[68] It was better for Benjamin and Gisele to live in France, where "the education" and "the discipline" were first-rate.[69] Benjamin, she disclosed, was first in his class, Gisele was already sewing her own frocks, and both were fluent in English and French. "That is indispensable these days."[70] Much less suited to parenting than Olivia, Joan Fontaine simply gave up, packing her adopted daughter Martita back to Peru where she'd found her and sending her full daughter Debbie Dozier back to live with her father in California, explaining, "I could not work and at the same time control a headstrong adolescent."[71]

In 1965, the Cannes Film Festival chose Olivia to be its first woman jury president, a job she found "both exhilarating and intimidating to be the first at/of anything . . . However . . . I did enjoy presiding over a committee composed entirely of men."[72] Explaining the selection process, she said, "There were 20 films to judge. We split them into four groups of five per group, or was it five groups of four? We made the final decision by voting for a single victory among these winners."[73] The jurors awarded the Grand Prix to Richard Lester for *The Knack and How to Get It*, an ephemeral and whimsical relic of London's Swinging Sixties—an odd choice in a year that saw the release of David Lean's *Dr. Zhivago* and John Schlessinger's *Darling*.

On July 8, 1967, Olivia and columnist Radie Harris were lunching on the patio of the Beverly Hills Hotel, where both of them were staying. Eventually Olivia retired to her suite, and around 9 a.m. the following morning she rang Radie and asked in a muffled voice, "Have you had your radio or TV on yet?"

"No, why? Is there any news I've missed?"

"Radie, darling, I don't know how to break this to you. Vivien is dead!"

Olivia rushed down the hall to Radie's room and tried to comfort her as she began to sob. "It can't be true," Radie said. "No one dies of tuberculosis these days."[74] But Leigh was gone, at only fifty-three. Her Hollywood memorial was held at the University of Southern California, where the speakers included George Cukor, Greer Garson, Gladys Cooper, Judith Anderson, Claire Bloom, and Stanley Kramer. Poor George toppled at one point from his chair and landed on the floor. When it was

Garson's turn to introduce a film clip from *Waterloo Bridge*, she was asked if she could make it to the stage without falling over George.

Though Leigh had lived in great luxury, she'd handled her finances exceedingly well, leaving 252,681 pounds, the mid-1980s equivalent of 2.5 million pounds. A memorial bench was erected in Eaton Gardens opposite her apartment with an inscription from *Antony and Cleopatra*: "Now boast thee, Death, in thy possession lies a lass unparallel'd."

26

Benjamin's Illness, Olivia's Faith, Prime Minister Edward Heath, *Airport '77*, and TV

Talking about her French-educated son Benjamin, now sixteen, to Associated Press feature writer Vivian Brown, Olivia said that many people have the mistaken notion that the French are sophisticated, but actually they aren't. "In fact, French boys are terrified of English girls," she said. Boys dispatched to Britain to study were advised beforehand that English girls were "precocious. At 16 my son was telling me how fast the English girls were, and he has been leery even of having his English cousins visit him when I am not around."[1]

Sadly, this bright and promising young man was stricken by a serious illness. "Benjie was diagnosed with Hodgkin's Disease at the age of 19," Olivia told AP correspondent Bob Thomas, who noted, "Her eyes glistened as she recounted long, pain-wracked years of radiation and other treatment. His white blood count fell so low that he was subject to the slightest ailment."[2]

Caregiving is surely life's most challenging job. Olivia sought and received spiritual strength at the American Cathedral in Paris. "She looked after him herself," the Very Reverend Sturgis Riddle, a longtime friend and dean emeritus of the Paris cathedral, said. "She had faith that through love and prayer he would be helped."[3]

Olivia told reporter Vivian Brown in 1973 that Gisele enjoyed cooking, and though Olivia admitted, "I am not a great cook," she could make a mean *osso buco*.[4] French girls are more apt to enjoy the woman's place in the home because it's a prestigious position with a title—*Maitresse de Maison* (mistress of the house)—more appealing than housewife. The *Maitresse de Maison* was regarded as the CEO of a multifarious mini-corporation, the home. Americans should abolish the word "housewife," she said.[5]

In 1976, during a break in filming *Airport '77* at Universal, Olivia placed a "get-well call" to syndicated columnist Earl Wilson, who was suffering from a virus with a 103-degree temperature. The subject of her marriage came up, and Wilson later wrote that Olivia and Galante had resided in the same town house "for 13 years, maybe 14, he in one part, she in another—the closest of friends . . . They were 'separated' most of the time, but 'together.'"

"But this year," she said, "I think we're going to straighten it out. Untangle it."

The columnist asked her if she was getting married again, and she said, "'If I do . . . ,'" and left it at that.

The Galantes divorced in 1979.

If the mighty forces had been quiescent after *The Heiress*, they reappeared once she connected with the church and its inspiring clerics and congregations. "Ten years ago, on Christmas Eve 2001, I heard for the first time Olivia de Havilland read the Scriptures in the Cathedral of the Holy Trinity, Paris," Bishop Pierre Whalon wrote.[6] While acquiring the knack of being an effective church reader, she underwent some "excoriating" critiques from Rev. Frederick Northrup, canon of the Episcopal

American Cathedral in Paris.[7] "He described my initial efforts as 'lamentable,'" Olivia recalled, but she persisted. According to Bishop Whalon, "Blessed with a resonant alto voice as well as her training, she reads with a natural authority."

In the United States, she has read the Bible lesson in Sunday services at Manhattan's St. Bartholomew's Church and, as one of 32 members of the campaign cabinet, raised funds for the $100 million "Venture in Mission" drive to support service projects, making appearances in numerous dioceses such as San Diego, Atlanta, Baton Rouge, and St. Louis. "It's a movement for strength to go forth and do God's will," she said. "It's a thrilling thing in life whenever we can do something to make things better."[8] Invited to take to the pulpit and preach, she declined. "As the mother of a son and daughter," an Associated Press correspondent wrote, "she was indeed accustomed to delivering sermons, but for the sake of an entire congregation, felt she should limit herself to reading the lesson."[9]

When Paris was torn by student riots in the 1970s, she helped settle an anti-Vietnam strike at the American University, which later awarded her an honorary degree in humane letters.[10] Olivia gave serious consideration to ending her expatriate life in Paris and thought of moving to Washington, D.C. "I would like to see if there wasn't some sort of niche I could fill where I would be useful," she told an interviewer. "After all, I chose to be American and I feel I owe the country something."[11] In the coming years such show business figures as Ronald Reagan, John Gavin, Shirley Temple, Al Franken, and Donald Trump would invade Washington. In the end, Olivia did not move to the capital; had she, the U.S. government, which placed Temple and Gavin in diplomatic posts, would have been wise to make Olivia its ambassador to France, where she'd entertained diplomats for years, or Japan, where she'd been born.

Directed by Michael Anderson, Olivia's 1972 film *Pope Joan*, in which she played a nun, traces the life of a girl born in Mainz, Germany, played by Liv Ullman, who becomes a powerful orator after teaching herself to read and write. She takes her vows as a nun, later survives harrowing crises at the hands of Saxon attackers, and travels to Greece and finally Rome. Posturing as a monk, she becomes Pope Leo's secretary. When he dies, she's elected pope, but her body is torn to pieces when it is learned she's a woman. Despite the efforts of a distinguished cast including Maximilian Schell, Trevor Howard, Lesley-Anne Down, Kier Dullea, and Franco Nero, the film failed to attract an American distributor, though it survives as a DVD.

"Learning is the child's profession," Olivia said in connection with her sixteen-year-old daughter Gisele, who attended school six days per week, beginning at 8:10 a.m. and returning home at 5:30 p.m. with heavy homework assignments. Exams were difficult, especially the one at the conclusion of grade 12, which was, Olivia said, "horrendous . . . But . . . children are so well educated, they need no more schooling."[12] She felt Gisele was "too young in spirit" for American schools. "She has never been anywhere, not even a movie, with a boy."[13] Olivia planned to treat her daughter in the summer of 1973 to an educational tour of the United States that would take them from Jamestown, Plymouth Rock, Sturbridge, Washington, D.C., and Philadelphia to the Western states.

A few years later, in 1976, Olivia described Gisele as a "ravishing" *jeune fille* of nineteen.[14] She kept her mother busy, according to BYT News Service's Angela Taylor, handling the many telephone calls and writing down the entreaties of Gisele's numerous suitors.[15]

"It's Rene, or Olivier, or Bruni," Olivia said.[16] When Gisele gave a party, Olivia helped prepare the food. As a mother, she was enjoying a substitute experience of all the youthful joys she missed when, as a girl of eighteen, she took on a demanding full-time job at Warner.[17] Gisele was a University of Paris second-year law student, living in the 16th Arrondissement, where neighbor Valery Giscard d'Estaing's red spaniel despised Gisele's French bulldog. When d'Estaing was elected president of France and moved to the Elysee Palace, the bulldog was relieved.

Olivia declined an opportunity to work when her daughter faced her difficult baccalaureate tests for college. She was offered a film set in a brothel, in which she was to play a woman of ill repute. Mindful of her responsibilities to Gisele, she turned down the part.[18]

Angela Taylor noted that Olivia's elevated diction was occasionally interspersed with hoots of mirth when she reminisced about old beaux she didn't wed, such as Howard Hughes and John Huston, and the men who managed to get her to the altar.[19]

In the late 1970s, Benjamin recovered at twenty-nine, a kind of mir-acle—or just a mother's love, faith in God, prayer, and consistent, tender caregiving. Taylor reported that Benjamin became an American after his French schooling was completed. He lived in Austin, Texas, in a student commune, and Olivia visited him when her lecture tours took her to the United States.[20] Though coping with a serious illness, he persisted in his studies, possibly due to his mother's encouragement and no doubt gener-ous financial support. Majoring in statistical mathematics at the Univer-sity of Texas, he graduated and later successfully carried out his duties as a Lockheed Aircraft scientist.[21]

In the mid-1970s, Sir Edward Heath was back in Olivia's life. He was now England's Prime Minister. "Her phone rang in London and a very British voice announced it was 10 Downing Street calling to extend the Prime Minister's invitation to Chequers," Robert M. Klein wrote in the *New York Times*. Olivia recalled in 1976, "I thought 'Checkers'?' Was it a dog or a game?"[22]

Chequers is the official country retreat of England's incumbent PMs. Olivia commissioned Christian Dior to create a flowing rainbow-hued chiffon dress, and on the appointed day, she left the Dorchester Hotel in

London and made her way through a crowd of admirers to a Rolls Royce with the help of the Dorch's top-hatted doorman. A chauffeur drove her forty miles to Chequers, a sixteenth-century Gothic mansion located in Buckinghamshire at the foot of the Chiltern Hills. Arriving early, she waited in the Rolls outside the grounds of the estate, and when at last she arrived at the mansion, Heath was waiting for her on the lawn, dressed in a white dinner jacket.[23]

"I was beckoning to you to come on," he said. "I spotted your car. But you obviously didn't see me."[24]

Publisher Robert Allan of Allan and Unwin Ltd. and six other guests joined them for a dinner of roast duck. The Prime Minister told Olivia that it must be "adorable" to reside in Paris,[25] and later gave her a tour of Chequers, named after the trees that grow on its 1,500 acres, though some attribute the appellation to the English version of the game checkers. Among the treasures he showed her that evening was a portrait of Oliver Cromwell, who held England together during its bloody civil wars and became head of government in 1653.

Olivia told Heath about her de Havilland ancestors, some of whom supported Cromwell in Charles I's war against Cromwell, calling themselves Roundheads. Heath brought out a Renaissance ruby ring once worn by Queen Elizabeth I, and Olivia mentioned her film *The Private Lives of Elizabeth and Essex*. They discussed music, a subject Heath loved, and she hoped he'd play the piano for his guests. Unlike another pianistic head of state, Harry S. Truman, who played the "Missouri Waltz" as a leggy Lauren Bacall perched provocatively atop his piano, Heath did not perform that night. Olivia said she'd light a candle for him in Notre Dame de Paris, the 1163 cathedral that contains what is purported to be Jesus Christ's Crown of Thorns, a fragment of the True Cross, and one of the Holy Nails.[26]

Later, she remarked to interviewer Lynne Bell, "Poor Mr. Heath. Isn't it terrible the way they try to marry him off to every second woman who dines at Chequers?"[27] Bell later wrote, "And don't they realize—she smiles with huge delight at the joke of it—that she is legally separated from her French husband. If only they knew how difficult it is to get out of that—assuming she wanted to marry again, which she doesn't."[28] Olivia confessed to a "deep admiration" for Heath.[29] They remained friends, but he was a confirmed bachelor, living in rooms in the all-male London club The Albany.

When the Delacorte Press sent me to Paris in 1973 to meet with Olivia and discuss her autobiography, I felt a little like Lambert Strether in Henry James's novel *The Ambassadors*—dispatched abroad to bring home something of value. Strether came to Paris to extricate his fiancée's American son from the clutches of his French mistress, Madame de Vionnet; I was there in hopes of acquiring the memoirs of a legendary actress.

After checking into L'Hotel on the Rue des Beaux-Arts, I called Olivia, who announced in a happy, plummy voice, "This is Olivia de Havilland." The words rolled out majestically, and with all the impact of Strauss's *Thus Spake Zarathustra*, but without a trace of affectation or pomposity. It was the sound of a person pleased to be who she was. We arranged to meet for lunch the following day at L'Hotel.

Arriving precisely on time, fresh-faced and still beautiful at fifty-seven, and appropriately dressed in a navy blue outfit, she was civil but somewhat reserved and wary. I launched immediately into business, suggesting *Gone With the Wind* would be a good place to open her memoir, and then after a few pages, flash back to her childhood. She did not encourage further pursuit of this subject. Eventually she warmed to me and opened up when I stopped asking her questions and started talking about myself, telling her how, as a graduate student at Columbia, I'd written my master's essay on Henry James, author of *Washington Square*, the novel on which *The Heiress* was based. On hearing this she flashed the famous de Havilland smile, and I realized that I'd gained her trust. We spent roughly half the long luncheon talking about her work on *The Heiress*, and we spoke of family. I came away from what amounted to our first editorial conference with the impression that it was the present moment, with all its exigencies, that held more interest for her than the past.

For me, a lifelong cineaste, it had been momentous and pleasurable to spend time with an actress I'd long admired. My friend Jean-Yves LeGavre, a French fashion designer, stopped by our table and joined us for coffee, and he and Olivia had a lively conversation in French, which she seemed to enjoy. As we waited in the lobby for her taxi, I introduced her to my colleague, Eugene Braun-Munk of Editions Stock, Delacorte Press author James Jones's French publisher, who expressed interest in acquiring French rights to Olivia's proposed book. Then along came my next appointment, who also joined us. Suddenly, it was like a small party. Olivia was gracious to all of us, and I decided I liked her very much. I still do.

Her long-awaited memoir has still not appeared. In 1962, she told *Des Moines Register* reporter Olga Curtis: "When I was writing a lot of people got the idea I would discuss my Hollywood years. There's nothing about Hollywood in my book, because nothing amusing happened to me there—I always felt a book should be fun to write as well as to read." She may well have changed, because in recent years she's given many interviews about Hollywood to such reporters as Dotson Rader, Anita Gates of the *New York Times*, and Bill Stadiem of *Vanity Fair.*

———◆———

Returning to Hollywood, Olivia filmed *Airport '77* for an old friend, producer William Frye. The third installment of the enormously successful *Airport* franchise that had started in 1970 and grossed nearly $50 million (adjusted for inflation: $361,000,000), *Airport '77* costarred Jimmy Stewart and Lee Grant. The 1975 best-supporting-actress Oscar winner for

Shampoo, Lee resorted to *Airport '77*, a generic disaster movie, to pay the bills, like many stars in their senior years. "One for the money, two for the show—this one was definitely for the money," Lee confessed.[30]

Olivia plays Emily Livingston, who's traveling with an African-American woman whom she rescues when their plane crashes into the ocean, sinks to the bottom, and is flooded by cascades of seawater. The climactic scene was to be shot on a sound stage where a huge airplane was floating in a tank of water under two massive vats of water suspended above it. These were to be released on the passengers at a signal from Bill Frye. Olivia was always to be found high in the rafters, watching the actors below and chatting with the stagehands.

"All right, who wants to be first," Frye shouted into his bullhorn. "Oh, me, me," called Olivia from an overhead grid. "Me! I want to do it!"[31]

Lee Grant recalled, "My jaw dropped as I watched Olivia, a seventy-ish daredevil heroine, perched eagerly on her seat in the plane while tons of water arched and fell on her, then shake her little head as she bobbed up to the surface, smiling."[32]

Though the film grossed $30 million (adjusted for inflation: $118,500,000), the reviews were abysmal, *Variety* disdaining its "formula banality," but it paid for Lee Grant's new house on the ocean side of the Pacific Coast Highway in the exclusive Malibu Colony. "Saying yes to everything is in an actor's DNA," Lee said. "Second-rate films I've acted in were filled with famous employable actors, whose money advisors told them, 'Take the money and run.'"[33] Jimmy Stewart was philosophical about the critical drubbing, saying, "Well, you know, you never start out to make a bad picture, but it's that kind of business."[34]

In 1977, TV personality Robert Osborne of Turner Classic Movies interviewed Olivia for three hours over several bottles of champagne in LA, and their friendship was cemented for life. "Rarely does a Sunday go by that we don't talk on the phone," he reminisced in 2016. "We travel together and stay in exotic hotels."[35]

When Bette Davis received the American Film Institute's Life Achievement Award, Olivia was on hand at the Beverly-Hilton Hotel to deliver a heartfelt tribute. Ray Stricklyn, who played Davis's son in *The Catered Affair* and later worked as her publicist at John Springer and Associates, was Davis's escort that night, March 1, 1977, and LA director David Galligan, Ray's longtime domestic partner, recalled, "She adored Ray. She was an absolute harridan with me, but she was a pussycat with him."[36] On the following evening, Ray took Davis to Studio One, a West Hollywood gay club where sixty-four-year-old Geraldine Fitzgerald was opening her cabaret act, "Geraldine Fitzgerald Singing Songs of the Street," later shortened to "Streetsongs." According to Davis's biographer Ed Sikov, Olivia, Robert Osborne, and Mr. and Mrs. Paul Heinreid were also in attendance. Between such ditties as "Danny Boy" and "Saturday Night at the Rose and Crown"—delivered, according to the *New York Times*, in a charmingly husky voice capable of alternating between "a lilting shimmer of sound" and "a glorious bray"[37]—Fitzgerald reminisced about her childhood in Ireland, where an uncle told her, "Geraldine, don't worry about doing it well; it's more interesting to be mediocre than to contemplate others' perfection."

"That took a weight off my mind," she said.[38]

I didn't catch Fitzgerald's act, but I did meet her around this time, and was surprised that in her sixties she was was wearing her hair very long, her grey tresses hanging straight down to her waist. She wore a floor-length cotton print skirt, and for all the world could have passed for a pioneer woman heading west in a covered wagon, puffing on a corncob pipe. I admired her for having the nerve to dress any way she liked and yet be comfortable at a sophisticated cocktail party full of women in designer clothes. She was, after all, Lady Lindsay-Hogg.

During and after Fitzgerald's show in Hollywood, Davis was mobbed by a group of gay fans."[39] Davis loved the attention.[40] Now sixty-nine, she said she was ready for a "sissy" spouse with whom she could share art, fine wines, and movies, not to mention the housework, shopping, and cooking. Only gays were smart enough to admire her, she said, adding, "They make the average male look stupid."[41] Her only problem in attracting such a mate was her rudeness, which not even fawning acolytes could tolerate. When David Galligan called her to see if she'd do an interview for a charity for mentally retarded children—Davis's daughter Margot Merrill was in Lochland, a home for the developmentally disabled in Geneva, New York—Davis hissed, "*Why* would you *think* I'd be interested in *that*? Don't *ever call me again!*"[42]

William Morrow and Company issued Joan Fontaine's autobiography *No Bed of Roses* in 1978. I was a senior editor there at the time, editing Shelley Winters and Sammy Davis Jr., but I had nothing to do with Joan's book, and I didn't read it until I started researching the present volume. Morrow was known at the time for such best-selling autobiographies as those of Sophia Loren and Doris Day. According to Joan, "I was assigned three editors, all of whom had conflicting opinions. So I just wrote it the way I had originally conceived, and that's what is being published."[43] The critics liked her style, the *Chicago Tribune*'s Stephen F. Rubin writing, "*No Bed of Roses* is a surprise. It contains yards of material of genuine interest . . . [Fontaine] display[s] a sincere and often successful knack for 'writing' rather than 'dictating' a book, so often the case with star memoirs."[44] The *Los Angeles Times* reviewer Robert Kirsch agreed, writing, "Miss Fontaine's book is better than most of the genre."[45] The *Cincinnati Enquirer*'s Sheila M. Mitchell found Joan "absorbing and literate."[46]

Larry Hughes, Morrow's president, hosted a publication day party for Joan, at which both Andy Warhol and I photographed her as she spoke with the dapper theatrical lawyer L. Arnold Weissberger. When the crowd began to thin out, Joan spoke with the fiction editor of *Good Housekeeping* magazine, Leonhard Dowty. "She wanted to go to dinner and have someone to take her home," Len told me the next day. He declined. "I already had a date that night for after the party," Len said.

"She was very lonely," Leonida Karpik, the Morrow publicist who handled Joan's national book tour, told me in 2016. "No one liked her. She was a little terror. She insisted on 'deep salmon-colored roses' and a very particular brand of water for her book signing at B. Altman's. One day we lunched together and had vodka and blini at the Russian Tea Room that she insisted paying for."

"Don't trust men," Joan admonished Leonida. "'Where is your husband? Men are fools, not to be trusted, ever."

"She did not get along with her sister," Leonida continued as we spoke in 2016. "She was a has-been and thought she could keep reporters waiting for hours. When one savaged her in print, she blamed me and never spoke to me again. I had set up the interview for her with [a Washington, D.C.] reporter. Joan made her wait for an hour and a half. Subsequently the article was pretty nasty with a horrible photo of Joan. Joan was furious." Judy Flander, a *Washington Star* reporter, wrote, "She does not speak conversationally [but] delivers her lines in a theatrically throaty voice, flinging a hand to her heart, tossing her head high. She is in turn imperious, condescending, deceptively gracious, unwittingly revealing. She never for one moment forgets—or lets you forget—who she is or, more accurately, who she was."

Flander was astonished by the grandeur of Joan's palatial condo, occupying the entire fifth floor of an East Side building in Manhattan, and featuring a "drawing room that stretches acres to medieval windows . . . [and a] dark-beamed library" with a fireplace. "This is all mine," she said. "I did it all myself. Not one person helped me. I earned it. I paid for it. I live here. I love it."[47]

Leonida Karpik recalled, "She made many demands at her book signings that were not well attended. Don't remember if the book ever hit the bestseller list. I doubt it." Leonida said our pub party was at the Four

Seasons restaurant, and when I told her I thought it had been held at another, less posh venue, perhaps Seafood of the Aegean, she laughed and said, "Oh, we gave parties all the time in those wonderful days before they took away everyone's expense account."[48] Joan's three-month publicity tour took her around the United States and then to England for three weeks. In LA, Joan left the Beverly Hills Hotel when Olivia checked in and returned when she left.[49]

John Huston's autobiography, *An Open Book*, appeared in 1980. According to Huston's biographer Jeffrey Meyers, Knopf editor Charles Elliott "said that Huston didn't want to reveal himself and that he couldn't make him more forthcoming and outspoken."[50] Huston admitted, "The whole story has not been told, of course. I've refrained from making any dark disclosures regarding my secret life."[51] Olivia's name comes up more than once, and very favorably.[52] Referring to *In This Our Life*, the film they made together, Huston wrote, "It was very flattering for me—a director with only one picture behind him—to be given a picture with Warner's top stars: Bette Davis, Olivia de Havilland, Charles Coburn, George Brent, and Dennis Morgan."[53] In two of the photos in the book, John and Olivia are holding each other closely during a 1941 fishing trip.[54] Upon publication, *An Open Book* received a predictably tepid critical press. *New York Times* critic Michiko Kakutani thought "the almost willful lack of introspection diminished the impact of the memoir," and the Virginia Kirkus trade review called John's deceptively titled *An Open Book* "curiously muted . . . stubbornly impersonal."[55]

Though Olivia was far from the limelight in which she had lived for three decades, she expressed no regrets. "People in Hollywood feel that they must perpetually be on the crest of the wave, not realizing that it is against all the rules of life," she said.[56] Failure, she added, is "a natural and inevitable part of living. When they have their big success they don't realize that they only have a short lease on it. They think they have bought it freehold."[57]

Television kept her in the game. In 1979, in *Roots: The Next Generations*, she appeared as Mrs. Warner, wife of a former Confederate officer played by Henry Fonda. The miniseries was watched by an estimated 110 million viewers.

She became the go-to actress when an imperious presence was needed on TV. She played the Queen Mother in the 1982 telefilm *The Royal Romance of Charles and Diana*, in which she displayed her timeless valentine face and creamy voice to regal advantage. She appeared in a supporting role, the dowager Empress Maria, in the 1986 miniseries *Anastasia: The Mystery of Anna*. Such eminent actresses as Eugenie Leontovich, Helen Hayes, and Angela Lansbury also played the empress over the years. The *New York Times* TV critic praised Olivia's "beatific elegance." She received the Golden Globe for her performance, winning over such estimable nominees in the best supporting actress category as Geraldine Page, Lilli Palmer, and Piper Laurie. At the presentation ceremony in the ballroom of the Beverly Hilton Hotel, hosted by Cheryl Ladd and William Shatner, before a glittering audience that included such Golden Age luminaries as Loretta Young and Anthony Quinn, Olivia said:

"They didn't make a mistake. My name is right there. Back home, I have a Golden Globe just like this one [for best actress in *The Heiress*]. It's vintage 1949. So my Golden Globe back home has been waiting 37 years for a mate. And at last I can take this companion back to keep it company. I would like to express my appreciation to everyone at Telecom and NBC for choosing me to play Her Imperial Highness. And I would also like to thank the members of the Foreign Press Association in each of the languages which they speak as the representatives of a number of countries, but alas they number 45. So I will limit my appreciation to the simple words, thank you very much."

For playing another historical figure, the Duchess of Windsor's Aunt Bessie Merryman in NBC's 1988 movie *The Woman He Loved*, she was nominated for a Primetime Emmy Award for outstanding supporting actress, but Julie Harris took the prize.

Olivia kept working on her book—"a far bigger project than I had realized," and told the *Los Angeles Times*, "It's going to take a long time."[58]

Absent from movies for many years, she told the Associated Press, "I've taken a long vacation, but I wouldn't object to a fascinating part in a first-rate project . . . The offers still come but not what I'm looking for."[59] Hollywood had once done a much better job of keeping its senior-citizen stars busy in supporting roles. One-time first lady of the American theatre Ethel Barrymore made twenty-one movies between 1940, when she was sixty-one, and her death in 1957.

Olivia had never lost her interest in John Huston and once wrote him, "I heard your voice [in the 1966 film *The Bible*]. It was an extraordinary experience, for no one had told me that you had done the soundtrack, and, of course, with the first word I knew it was you speaking. It brought back, with a rush, the year of 1942 and the Aleutians, and the film you made there, that beautiful film, and *I've Got Sixpence*, and your voice on the soundtrack for that picture, and, well, many things. I hope all goes well with you—I always have, I always will."[60]

Responding to her note, John invited her to visit him at his country retreat, a Georgian manor house called St. Clerans in County Galway in Ireland's Western coastal area. "And I went," Olivia told journalist Dotson Rader.[61] John's daughter Angelica Huston described what it was like to approach the imposing Big House. "Some 20 miles in from the coast, the West Country looked as if the sea had recently washed over it—the hawthorn trees on the high embankments turned their shoulders from the wind."[62] Rising majestically above a stone-and-concrete moat was a three-story, seventeen-room 1784 Palladian-style manse, the Big House, with a four-columned gray stone entrance.

Over the years, guests at St. Clarens included Burgess Meredith, Mary Hemingway, and Elaine and John Steinbeck, who were all expected to dress for dinner, women in gowns, men in black ties, and, for members of the hunt, scarlet tailcoats with white silk lapels. An expert hunter and horseman, John was Joint Master of the Hunt for the Galway Blazers. With his horses, children, wives, mistresses, fox hunting, and frequent filmmaking junkets, John was leading a hectic life. He was "wonderful to talk and listen to, most of the time—fascinating company," Olivia said.[63] She'd planned to stay at St. Clerans "for five days [but] I lasted only three. And escaped. So I think, although I didn't have my heart's greatest desire, which was marriage with him . . . I was lucky."[64]

27

Sunset and Evening Star

Olivia outlived all her suitors and husbands, as well as most of her family and friends. Errol Flynn died in 1959, hounded to the grave by problems with women. In his final days he took his teenage mistress Beverly Aadland to Canada to sell his yacht *Zaca* to Mr. and Mrs. George Caldough in order to raise money for a marriage settlement. His health was so shot that extensive travel at this point was a crazy, suicidal idea; only recently Aadland had found him "in a deep stupor . . . He was half in and half out of a big armchair, his arms hanging down limply, his eyes glazed, his glasses slipped away down on his face."[1] Arriving at the Vancouver airport, he told reporters, "The rest of my life will be devoted to women and litigation. I like young women because they give you a feeling of youth . . . I've always been the one to burn the midnight Errol."[2]

After the Caldoughs paid him $100,000 for the *Zaca*, he and Aadland left for their flight to Los Angeles, but he died on the way to the airport.[3] Unexpectedly plunged into deep mourning, Olivia "felt a great sense of grief and loss."[4] Few showed up at his funeral at Forest Lawn Cemetery's Church of the Recessional in Glendale. Mickey Rooney, Raoul Walsh, Jack Oakie, and "Big Boy" Williams served as pallbearers. "Errol was the personification of gallantry, the essence of bravery, the great adventurer," Jack L. Warner said in his eulogy.[5] Dennis Morgan, star of *The Desert Song*, sang Robert Louis Stevenson's "Requiem": "Under the wide and starry sky dig the grave and let me lie: glad did I live and gladly die . . .

Home is the sailor, home from the sea, and the hunter home from the hill."[6] Flynn's dashing son, Sean, turned down a publisher's request for a book to be titled *Life With Father*.[7] As good-looking and athletic as his father, he'd been raised by Lili Damita, who sent him to the best schools. After making *Son of Captain Blood* and other movies, he became a reckless and brilliant photographer of the Vietnam War, selling his pictures to *Paris Match* and a film to CBS-TV before his capture and torture by the Vietcong. He was reportedly injected with Thorazine and buried alive.[8]

David O. Selznick in the mid-1960s was still trying to dream up projects for Jennifer Jones, even though he'd had a heart attack in 1962. He still awoke each morning thinking he'd like to do another film, looked at a script or two, and placed a few phone calls, but by 2 p.m. all he wanted was a nap. "Very few people have mastered the art of enjoying their wealth," he said. "I have mastered that art and therefore I spend my time enjoying myself."[9] I spoke with him around this time in New York. Though sixty-three, he was glowing—all pink skin and wavy silver hair—evidently in excellent health. We kicked around ideas about a book I hoped to commission. I was in my late twenties, in my first job in publishing, and didn't yet know that the first thing you do with celebrities is find them a writer.

Later I sat next to David and Jennifer at a performance of the Actors Studio production of *Strange Interlude*, unable to take my eyes off Jennifer, stupendously chic in haute couture, probably one of Balenciaga's spectacular black taffeta cocktail dresses. David planned to film the O'Neill play with Jennifer as Nina Leeds, the role Geraldine Page played that night. Though he had always longed to be a writer, in these last days of his life it was probably the last thing on his mind. He succumbed to a coronary occlusion on June 22, 1965. Olivia saw Arthur and Bubbles Hornblow at the opening of *Kismet* in New York, and said, "Isn't it awful about David?" The Hornblows went on to a party at the Pierre and were shocked to see

Irene. "I went to the party," Irene said, "because I didn't want to stay at home and blow my brains out."[10]

Pallbearers at the Church of the Recessional in Forest Lawn, which seated two hundred, included William S. Paley, president of CBS, William Wyler, Christopher Isherwood, Alfred Hitchcock, Sam Spiegel, and Samuel Goldwyn. Cary Grant read a tribute written by Paley: "The one word that fits David better than any other is 'extravagance' . . . I cannot help but think our world will never be the same, nor will heaven. And if we are lucky enough to get there too, David will see that all the arrangements are made, and if I know my man, I am sure he will manage to get some of us in who wouldn't make it otherwise—and he will be grinning, and he will be full of joy and laughter, and he will tell us what to do, and he will be David."[11] Joseph Cotten, star of Selznick's *Duel in the Sun, Since You Went Away, The Third Man,*[12] and *Portrait of Jenny,* extolled David's larger-than-life greatness, and George Cukor read a eulogy by Truman Capote praising David's vitality and good taste. Irene recalled David's words to Bubbles Hornblow when, after he collapsed at her dinner party, she tried to help: "It's all right, Bub. It's not much fun anymore."[13] Irene, who did not attend despite Jennifer's pleas, asked Katharine Hepburn to read Rudyard Kipling's *If,* which included the lines, "If you can make one heap of all your winnings and risk it on one turn of the pitch-and-toss . . . yours is the earth and everything that's in it."[14]

Jennifer received a letter from Jock Whitney, who wrote, "I have never loved any man more—nor ever will."[15] After David's debts were paid off, she was left with just under $1 million, a glum fate for a woman who dreamed of having a full-time hairdresser.[16] George Masters, who styled Jennifer's hair but had to attend to other clients as well, said she attempted suicide.[17] She recovered, replaced an ailing Kim Stanley in a bad film, *The Idol,* was scorned in 1966 by Broadway critics in *The Country Girl,* again tried to kill herself, appeared as a former porn star in the film *Angel, Angel, Down We Go,* and married the multimillionaire industrialist

Norton Simon, at last acquiring a live-in hairdresser. "Early in 1974," her biographer Beverly Linet wrote, "after Olivia de Havilland rejected the sympathetic part of a lonely widow wooed by a phony bond salesman in Irwin Allen's spectacular disaster epic *The Towering Inferno*, Jennifer signed for the role."[18] She looked frightening on the new giant screen, too much makeup, too much jet-black hair dye, and too much plastic surgery. Two years later her twenty-one-year-old daughter, after a suicide attempt, abortion, and confinement in a psychiatric ward, jumped from her twenty-two-story Wilshire Boulevard apartment building to her death.[19] Norton Simon named Jennifer chairman of the board of directors of the Norton Simon Museum, and she did an exemplary job of overseeing his $250-million collection of masterpieces. It was the most impressive role she'd played since *Ruby Gentry*, the story of a backwoods girl who rose to the top of the corporate ladder.

David O. Selznick's greatest discovery, the fragile but seemingly indestructible Vivien Leigh, worked steadily and brilliantly until the day she died, never once accepting a role beneath her. Leigh once swapped her Eaton Square flat in London for Joan Fontaine's apartment at 160 East 72nd Street, an arrangement that led to grief for both, Leigh charging burglary and Joan complaining of feline filth and stench. "The hall coat closet contained a box of kitty litter that had not been changed in weeks," Joan related.[20] When she tried to store her car in Leigh's empty parking space in London, Leigh told her, "You are *not* to use my gar-rahge," and hung up.[21]

At the end of Joan's stay in London, she returned to her New York apartment, but Leigh said, "What am I to do, throw my luggage into the street?"[22] It got worse. Leigh finally returned to London only to find that "some precious things were missing from the flat," her lover Jack Merivale said. "Poor V was distracted as some of them belonged to Larry. So the insurance people and the CID have been in and out and made our life rather miserable."[23] The purloined valuables were expensive watches

Olivier had given Leigh, who sicced the F.B.I. on Joan, Lilian, and her maid, but Joan pleaded innocence. "When I arrived at Eaton Square," Joan said, "I had had the housekeeper put away anything of value. I never saw the watches . . . [but] a New York columnist printed that I had stolen the valuable timepieces."[24]

At seventy-seven, Charles Brackett died at his home in Beverly Hills on March 9, 1969. "I wish I could have been there to pay Charlie my last devoted and deeply affectionate respects," Olivia said, "my last time with Charlie who had given so much to my own life."[25]

Radie Harris was still going strong when she and Sheilah Graham stopped to chat at my booth in the Russian Tea Room in the mid-1980s. One of Sheilah's eyes had gone bad, but both girls were spry and happy. Radie wrote her last "Broadway Ballyhoo" column for *The Hollywood Reporter* in 1989 and was forced into retirement, or she'd probably still be writing it. She entered the Actors Fund Nursing Home in Englewood, New Jersey, where she told me old friends like Doug and Mary Lee Fairbanks still visited her. Over Radie's bed to the day she died in February 2001 at the age of ninety-six was a portrait of Vivien Leigh as Scarlett.

Radie had been the last surviving member of the Golden Age's Greek chorus of gossip columnists. Sheilah had died of congestive heart failure at eighty-four in Palm Beach, Florida, in 1986. I recalled something she'd written in *The Rest of the Story*, the book I edited in the early 1960s: "Sitting at my typewriter, banging out the items, I sometimes laugh as I stir my witch's brew, putting in the onions and the herbs to give indigestion to the people I don't like or to those I think have slighted me, the great me. And it's true that I sometimes mistake my typewriter for my teeth, because the more I bite, the more my column will be read."[26]

Louella O. Parsons wrote her last column in 1965 and died at ninety-one in a nursing home in Santa Monica, California, of arteriosclerosis on December 9, 1972. Hedda Hopper succumbed to double pneumonia on February 1, 1966, in Cedars of Lebanon Hospital in Los Angeles at eighty-eight. Jimmie Fidler died at his home in Toluca Lake in the San Fernando Valley in 1988. Fidler had once been slapped in the face by Errol Flynn, who later said, "Fidler told one too many lies about the motion picture business."²⁷ The columnist's wife "jabbed me with a fork," Flynn said.²⁸ The fracas occurred at the Mocambo, and, as usual, Flynn was on the side of the angels. Fidler had been toadying to a Senate committee on another of the government's attempts to bust Hollywood for spreading propaganda.

———

"I was hosting a cocktail party for the April in Paris Ball when Joan Fontaine called and asked if she could bring a guest," interior designer Richard Ridge recalled. "I was prepared to tell her absolutely not; I'd selected the guest list very carefully and even had doormen posted downstairs to make sure no one crashed the party. But when I found out the person she wanted to bring was Olivia de Havilland I called her and said, 'Absolutely bring Olivia.'"²⁹

The sisters arrived "both in cocktail dresses," Ridge recalled. "They had a good time at the party. Photographers were there, and I got a nice shot of Joan, Olivia, Philip van Rensselaer, and several other guests."³⁰ One of the guests, Pat Loud, recalled speaking with both sisters. Pat was the subject of the PBS series *An American Family*, which inspired the 2011 movie *Cinema Verite*, in which Diane Lane portrayed Pat. "Joan was still elegant and beautiful but icy and regal," Pat said in 2016. "Olivia was warm and friendly. The party was in the late 1970s."³¹

Ridge gave me a photo showing him that night with Olivia, Joan, and socialite Philip van Rensselaer. Both Philip and Ridge were longtime friends of mine. Ridge gave some of the best parties in New York (he still does). Philip, scion of an old New York family and author of *That Vanderbilt Woman*, was dropped from the *Social Register* for running around with Barbara Hutton, the Woolworth heiress whose notorious affairs annoyed high society's top 400. Philip was fascinated with Joan Fontaine and wrote that she was involved with playboy Fred Bechman, whose "sexual energy was strong," Philip noted. "Every few days he'd vanish to Mexico City . . . He and Joan Fontaine were having one hell of a time."[32] Philip knew Prince Aly Khan, who counted Joan among his conquests "at the zenith of his allure . . . A woman was never the same after a night with Aly. Goddesses like Joan Fontaine and Gene Tierney had been Aly-infatuated."[33]

When Lilian Fontaine fell victim to terminal cancer in 1974, Joan opted for terminating life support, convinced it was pointless to prolong the "pain and indignity, possibly to die on the operating table. Olivia . . . was now taking charge of the life and death of our 88-year-old mother."[34] As Lilian clung to life, Joan went away to tour in *Cactus Flower*, leaving responsibility for Lilian to Olivia. "I called her the last Empress of China," Olivia said.[35] With Gisele by her side, Olivia groomed her mother daily, made her up, and gave her beauty treatments and pedicures. Lilian looked forward to what she called "the upcoming celestial cocktail party, a reunion with everyone she loved, complete with martinis."[36] Joan constantly moved from place to place on tour, and it must've been impossible for Olivia to keep her posted on their mother's condition. Lilian died in February 1975.[37]

William Dozier, whom Joan divorced in 1951, observed both sisters at Lilian's memorial and later reported, "We went up the hillside near the place where Lilian taught drama to the local young people. Olivia and Joan and [Robert] Balzer [a wine authority and friend of the family] scattered Lilian's ashes in three installments. Olivia gave a . . . deep-chested sigh as she threw the ashes. Joan, very characteristically, just tossed them away."[38] Dozier still harbored resentments over the ugly custody battle for their daughter Debbie that ensued at the time of their divorce almost one quarter of a century earlier. He couldn't have been pleased when, the instant Joan was rid of him, she became a globe-trotting playgirl, enjoying well-publicized liaisons with Aly Khan; the Earl of Warwick; United

Nations Ambassador Adlai Stevenson; and John "Shipwreck" Kelly, the former New York Giants halfback who got his nickname because of the mess he made of opposing defensive lines. He went on to more triumphs as an investment banker, Florida real-estate tycoon, big-game hunter, and golfer who played with President Richard Nixon and the Duke of Windsor. Joan's marriage to Dozier inspired one of her better-known *bons mot*—"marriage, as an institution, is as dead as the dodo bird."[39] She made it clear that parenthood, with its "station wagons and dog's life," was not for her. "I could not allow myself to be inextricably painted into a corner, to be buried in domesticity as my talented mother had been."[40]

Joan led a life jam-packed with derring-do and romance, including a marriage proposal from Joseph Kennedy, who'd once dabbled in movies. "You know, I've had a helluva life," Joan said, "not just the acting part, I've flown in an international balloon race. I've piloted my own plane. I've ridden to the hounds. I've done a lot of exciting things."[41]

Associated Press correspondent Bob Thomas wrote that Olivia was now conversant with the rock 'n' roll scene because "her daughter became engaged to French pop idol Johnny Halliday [*sic*]. 'He is a national sensation,' Miss de Havilland marveled about the singer."[42] Known as "the French Elvis," Hallyday, the stage name of Jean-Phillippe Smet, though virtually unknown in the United States, sold 80 million records worldwide. Gisele eventually married art collector Edward R. Broida.[43]

~

Howard Hughes's physician, Dr. Wilbur Thain, was with him when he died at 1:27 p.m., April 5, 1976, at seventy, while on a private plane from Acapulco to Houston. The cause of his death was kidney failure due to dehydration from prolonged massive doses of aspirin. He left no will, but his relatives received $2.5 billion. The final amount dropped into the millions due to lawyers' fees and the vicissitudes of the market during protracted litigation.[44]

Toward the end of Jack. L. Warner's life, he was so disoriented and enfeebled that he got lost in his office building on the Warner lot, had to retire, and suffered a stroke in 1974 that left him blind, speechless, and unresponsive to family and friends. He died in 1978, leaving most of his $15 million fortune to his widow Ann. Olivia attended his memorial at the University of Southern California, which closed with Mel Blanc's familiar rendition of Porky Pig's farewell, "A-bee-a-bee-a-bee-a-bee-that's all, folks." Ann died at eighty-two of diabetes and a heart condition in 1990.

In 1978, Olivia still looked healthy and vivacious at sixty-two in *The Swarm*, one of the string of disaster movies producer Irwin Allen made after his film version of Paul Gallico's *Poseidon Adventure* invented the genre. She plays a schoolmistress with a Southern accent in a little town under attack by a swarm of African killer bees, and dies in a train wreck while attempting to escape. Though Olivia thought Irwin Allen, who also directed, "shows tremendous insight into personal relationships,"[45] she was not well served by the orange dress and scarf that costumer Paul Zastupnevich gave her to wear nor by hair stylist Ruby Ford. "The local drugstore must do land-office business selling hair spray to the school-mistress, played by Olivia de Havilland," wrote *New York Times* reviewer Janet Maslin, who denounced the movie, save for a few merciful words for Michael Caine, who, she wrote, can "apparently do anything, except give a bad performance."[46] The unconvincing special effects by L.B. Abbott, which made the approaching bees look like "clouds of nutmeg," Maslin wrote, were not nearly as scary as James Basevi's locust hordes in 1937's *The Good Earth*, despite four decades of technological progress. In a 2009 interview with John Lichfield, Olivia referred to *The Swarm* as "that terrible movie about bees. A truly awful movie."[47]

Sir Michael Caine wrote in his memoir, *What's It All About*, that Olivia told him, "'When I was working with Errol [Flynn] they used to call me the Iron Virgin because I would not make love with him. He even had a bet for $100 with some of the crew that he would make it with me before the end of the movie.' Suddenly she halted and pointed to a certain spot in the hills that rise behind the studio. 'That's where Errol won his hundred dollars,' she said naughtily." Olivia denied Caine's assertion, claiming he misquoted her.[48] Certainly, as quoted by Caine, she sounds nothing like the Olivia I knew; that's just not the way she talked in our conversations. "I said that nothing had happened, against everyone's expectations," she told Lichfield, "but I pointed to a hillside and said that I did remember a rather memorable picnic on just such a hill with another man. In the book the words 'with another man' disappear."[49]

She was on hand at the 1978 Oscar show at the Dorothy Chandler Pavillion to present Margaret Booth, whose work spanned from the silent *Orphans of the Storm* to *The Goodbye Girl*, with an honorary Academy Award for exceptional contribution to the art of film editing. Emcee Bob Hope tendered Olivia a fulsome introduction, calling her "the beautiful star of *The Swarm*, which will soon be buzzing into your neighborhood hive. She's a very special lady who I've long worshipped from afar. She insisted on it . . . She will be admired forever."[50] Before handing the Oscar to Booth, Olivia pointed out that in sixty-two years, "[Booth] has run a lot of celluloid through her Moviola. She has been . . . nanny, surgeon, guardian, and court of last resort for many a problem picture."[51]

Aglow in diamonds and rubies in 1988, Olivia was back at the Oscar podium, this time at the Los Angeles Shrine Auditorium, to present the award for best art direction-set decoration. "As an actress," she said, "I have spanned eight centuries on the screen from *Robin Hood* . . . through the Civil War to the present day. All of us who have traveled through history in the movies are especially indebted to the art director . . . the artist who magically invents for us a particular time and place."[52] The Oscar went to Ferdinando Scarfiotti, Bruno Cesari, and Osvaldo Desideri for Bernardo Bertolucci's *The Last Emperor*, which also won best picture, best director, writing, cinematography, costume design, sound, film editing, and music score, but the highlight of the evening was the shocking transparent silk net gown which concealed none of Cher's formidable physical assets when she accepted the best-actress Oscar for *Moonstruck*, thanking her makeup man and her hairdresser. "Oh, I think she's such a rascal," Olivia commented later. "She has the most beautiful figure in the world, and a marvelous face. I must say I thought she was wearing black velvet. Then I realized she was just wearing lace—and nothing else! I let out a gasp, and then I thought, 'Oh, isn't she funny. She put that on just to make people do that.'"[53]

At twenty-one, Olivia's daughter Gisele appeared in a Laurence Olivier movie, *A Little Romance*, directed by George Roy Hill. A press report stated that since she'd studied law, "if a movie career doesn't pan out, she can always head for the courts."[54]

Grace Kelly died at fifty-two, on September 14, 1982, after a car crash in Monaco, from the stroke that had triggered the accident. Princess Diana, Nancy Reagan, and Cary Grant attended her funeral in Monaco, watched by a television audience of 100 million.[55] In Jimmy Stewart's funeral eulogy he said, "Grace brought into my life . . . warm light . . . Every time I saw her was a holiday."[56]

Olivia observed her seventieth birthday in 1986. "That was Olivia de Havilland . . . having lunch at the Red Fox Inn in Middleburg," Chuck Conconi wrote in the *Washington Post*, adding, "She traveled into the Northern Virginia countryside from the Ritz-Carlton Hotel, where she had been staying, to celebrate with her daughter, Gisele Galante."[57]

On August 28, 1987, John Huston expired at ninety-eight of pneumonia and emphysema, in Middletown, Rhode Island, while sleeping, mercifully ending a decade of torture during which he fought for every breath. He had come to Rhode Island to produce, and act in, his final film *Mister North*. "The film moves slowly and doesn't really hold our attention," Roger Ebert wrote. "*Mr. North* glows briefly and then slides out of focus."[58]

By 1991 Benjamin had achieved so much during his long and difficult battle with Hodgkin's lymphoma, but eventually he was unable to go to work, and Olivia brought him to her house in Paris where she watched over him every waking minute. "Eventually the cancer worsened," she said.[59]

Her life was strewn with "great crashing disasters," she'd once said. After surviving a broken home in her childhood, a court fight with a major studio, and two divorces, she'd had to cope for years with her beloved son's terminal cancer.[60] He died on October 1, 1991, at the age of forty-two, from over-radiation during treatment for cancer. One groans in pain and grief when attempting to imagine the unfathomable agony of a mother whose child must suffer and die. All we know is that Olivia somehow survived overwhelming grief, perhaps because of selfless service at the American Cathedral and throughout the Anglophone community, including hosting benefits and fund-raisers at her home for the American Library and the American University in Paris.[61] Once again, she'd been bold, she had sacrificed for her son when he needed her, and mighty forces had rushed in to help her, just as they had when she was an aspiring teenager trying to get into movies. As a member of the Anglican Church, she may have found comfort in the immortal lines of the Anglican poet and preacher John Donne, who wrote, "Death, be not proud . . . One short sleep past, we wake eternally and death shall be no more."

Marcus Goodrich, ninety-three, died three weeks after Benjamin, of heart failure, on October 20, 1991, at the Libby Convalescent Center in Richmond, Virginia.[62] He was buried as an honored serviceman in Arlington National Cemetery.

When a reporter asked Olivia if she were still interested in romance, she replied, "A man in my life? What a divine idea! I am the woman who arrives at parties alone and goes home with a married couple. That is carrying Episcopalian discretion to a very great extreme."[63] She kept busy as the spokesperson for the Episcopal Church's $100 million fund-raising drive, helped raise $7 million by speaking in Texas and Ohio, and taped TV and radio spots to raise money for black colleges.

Jimmy Stewart died in 1997, at eighty-nine, in his Beverly Hills home, of cardiac arrest and a blood clot in his lung. He had seen no point in living after his wife Gloria died. Plunged into depression, he became a recluse. Critic Andrew Saris crowned him "the most complete actor-personality in the American cinema," and *Film Comment*'s Robert Horton called him "America's most beloved man."[64] His funeral was held at the local Presbyterian Church with full military honors, and he was interred at Forest Lawn Memorial Park. When someone had once asked him how he wanted to be remembered, he replied, "I hope people will say things like 'I remember there was this film and Jimmy Stewart was dancing with some girl, and the floor opened up and underneath was a swimming pool, and they fell in'. . . It's a wonderful thing to have been able to give people little pieces of time that they can remember."[65]

Burgess Meredith also died at eighty-nine, also in 1997, of Alzheimer's disease and melanoma in Malibu, California. "Like the seasons of the year, life changes frequently and drastically," Meredith had once written. "You enjoy it or endure it as it comes and goes, as it ebbs and flows."[66] His parting words to actors were, "If you have an emotional scene to do and the temptation is to really act the hell out of it, to be visibly shaken or to cry, even, *don't* . . . Emotions . . . are not seen but felt."[67]

After Olivia's ex-husband Pierre Galante fell ill with lung cancer and was hospitalized, she compassionately moved him into the town house in Paris. He died at eighty-eight on September 20, 1998, in Paris. The magnanimity she displayed in her relationship with Galante in his final years was a gesture worthy of Melanie Hamilton, and it was typical of the savior role she appeared to have adopted at the time we met. Though her achievements as an artist of the first rank were amazing, her service to others was equally impressive.

28

Grand Slam: Legion of Honor, National Medal of Arts, Dame Commander

On the sixtieth anniversary of *Gone With the Wind*, in 1999, the publisher of Paris's *International Herald Tribune* Lee Huebner and his wife Berna gave a large party in honor of Olivia at UNESCO headquarters. "Her toast—'Let us raise a mint julep to our stars on that great veranda in the sky!' was typical of Olivia's unique way with words," Ms. Huebner recalled. "No star is more brilliant."[1]

At the Academy Awards commemorative celebration of Oscar's 75th anniversary, Sunday, March 23, 2003, at the Kodak Theatre on Hollywood and Highland, Olivia swept on stage to the grand Tara theme from *GWTW* in a flowing diaphanous gown of electric blue, her silver hair a glowing nimbus. She received a historic ten-minute standing ovation from a starry audience, waiting it out with poise and obvious pleasure, and then introduced fifty Oscar-winning actors and actresses, all seated on the stage. Her address rolled off her tongue in orotund mellifluousness. "This night is a memorable one and so was [my] night fifty-two years ago. Much has changed in our world since then, but what hasn't changed is our love of the movies and their ability to inspire and help us through troubled times. Tonight we celebrate the seventy-fifth birthday of the Academy Awards and the great artists who have over the years added so much to our lives through their work."[2]

On April 14, 2006, Gisele called Olivia and said her husband had died. Age seventy-two, Edward Broida had expired of cancer. "Do you want me there?" Olivia asked.[3] Despite being an octogenarian well beyond most senior citizens' traveling years, she immediately booked a flight from Paris to the United States, was by Gisele's side in her Malibu home the next day, and was still there in mid-June, when an Associated Press correspondent interviewed her. Seated in the shade of an old bougainvillea tree and dressed in a fashionable black skirt, full white blouse, and comfortable, age-appropriate black low heels, Olivia received the journalist in Gisele's sunny garden. He later wrote that when Pierre Galante had died in 1998, Olivia had "help[ed] Gisele, her daughter with Galante, make it through periods of depression."[4] Gisele would marry Andrew Chulack in 2011. Olivia, unlike former glamour girls who fight the aging process and conceal or lie about their ages, told the reporter that she was eagerly looking forward to her ninetieth birthday on July 1, and she regarded longevity as one of the victories of life. Her attitude reflects a significant change in modern culture. The term "old people" is politically incorrect and has been replaced by "senior citizens." Instead of mourning the loss of youth and middle age, many seniors celebrate the wisdom that comes from experience. Having ascended the throne of age, they see life clearly and find it more intriguing than ever before.[5]

When the interviewer asked Olivia if she missed performing on screen, stage, and television, she said that although the world of make-believe had once served her very well, she no longer wanted to live in a fantasy world. Real life was far more fascinating than the reflection of it in art.[6] *The Snake Pit*, she said, was her favorite role, but she also liked *The Heiress, To Each His Own,* and *The Dark Mirror.* She said nothing about *Gone With the Wind.* The reporter noted that for years Olivia had been mentioning her memoirs but without publishing them. It had proved impossible, she replied, to tell her story without first exploring her origins. This quest had taken her to England, where she learned more about her grandfather and her parents. She engaged a researcher to continue her search for the truth in the land of her forebears.[7] She also hired an assistant in San Francisco and provided a list of her remembrances of having been a two-year-old arriving in California from Japan. At considerable cost, the research assistant verified the accuracy of details pertaining to her early life in the United States. "Now I think I can start writing and see it through."[8]

In 2006 she received three standing ovations on her ninetieth birthday at the Samuel Goldwyn Theatre in Beverly Hills, emceed by the *Hollywood Reporter*'s Robert Osborne, and presented by the Academy of Motion Picture Arts and Sciences, the president of which, Sid Ganis, said she was the longest-serving member of the Academy, having joined in 1941. Dressed in a white suit with a knee-length skirt, scoop-neck collar, and matching pumps, she grinned and said, "The years do pass. The pounds do accumulate. Thank you for recognizing me."[9]

She was at last awarded the National Medal of Arts in 2008. America's highest civilian honor, it was presented by President George W. Bush "for her persuasive and compelling skill as an actress in roles from Shakespeare's Hermia to Margaret Mitchell's Melanie. Her independence and integrity and grace won creative freedom for herself and her fellow film actors."[10] The citation served as a reminder that she'd changed California law for the better when she sued Warner sixty-four years ago.

In July 2009 Olivia gave the *Independent* an interview on the occasion of *GWTW*'s seventy-fifth anniversary and the one-hundredth anniversary of Errol Flynn's birth. "Come and sit on this side of me," she told interviewer John Lichfield, "so that I can hear you better. And I do encourage you to help yourself. Please have at least a sip of champagne."[11] She said she'd made a fresh start on her memoir, twice put aside because of bereavements, and hoped to have a completed manuscript by September. "I feel like a survivor from an age that people no longer understand. I want to try to explain what the 1930s—the Golden Age of Hollywood—was truly like." It didn't sound like much fun as she ticked off her familiar litany of complaints: the slavery imposed by studio contracts, long hours beginning at 6:30 a.m., making five movies in her first year, the intrusiveness of studio publicists.[12] Still a member of the Academy of Motion Picture Arts and Sciences, she received DVDs of all Oscar-nominated movies but didn't exercise her voting privileges since she didn't watch all the movies. "I would watch anything with Meryl Streep in it," she said. *GWTW* came up, and she remarked, "I would say that [Melanie] is the person that I would like to be, but also the person that I may never be."[13]

She still hears from fans and has collected a dozen metal drawers of letters. She intends to answer them all. "One must," she said.[14] One admirer sent an annual letter and flowers each year from Scotland. For nine years, Olivia's been planning to send him a long reply and no doubt will, eventually.

About her life and career, she said, "I feel not happy, not contented, but something else. Just grateful for having lived and having done so many things that I wanted to do and have also had so much meaning for other people."[15] One of those meaningful things was the de Havilland Law, which has helped many entertainers since its enactment in 1944. Johnny Carson, host of *The Tonight* Show, used it to break his contract with NBC. Eventually he stayed with the network, but vastly improved his contract, reducing his workload and getting part ownership of the show.[16] Jared Leto, Oscar winner for his role as a transgender woman in *Dallas Buyers Club*, and his rock band 30 Seconds to Mars were embroiled in 2009 in a nasty $30 million contract dispute with their record company. "Despite having sold millions of records," Leto explained, "not only were we not going to get paid a penny, but we were millions and millions of dollars in debt. So we discovered there was a law in the state of California which is actually called the de Havilland Law."[17] Leto's attorney used Olivia's law to free the band from bondage, and the record company settled and signed the band anew, issuing their album *This Is War* to critical acclaim.

"I was more than surprised," Olivia told *People*'s Peter Mickelbank, "to hear from Jared Leto. I was enchanted!"[18]

"We had a wonderful time together [in 2010]," Leto recalled, "and I thanked her for fighting the studios back then so I could fight them now. It was amazing to meet her."[19]

"He came to my house to thank me for the De Havilland Decision, which he and his band . . . had utilized victoriously in a similar contractual dispute," Olivia said. "It's wonderful knowing the Decision continues to be useful to artists and other professionals these many years later."[20] Its lasting impact was evident in 2016 when rapper Wiz Khalifa sued his manager and record company to void a contract that allegedly violated the de Havilland Law.[21] In another case, according to the book *Hollywood and the Law*, "The de Havilland Law brought 20th Century-Fox TV to the bargaining table when the *Modern Family* sitcom stars Julie Bowen, Ty Burrell, Jesse Taylor Ferguson, Ed O'Neil, Eric Stonestreet, and Sofia Vergara . . . charged their contracts violated California's seven-year limit on personal service contracts."[22] *Variety* called de Havilland vs. Warner Brothers "a landmark case . . . still relevant in the industry today."[23]

When *People* magazine's Peter Mickelbank inquired what advice she'd give her "younger self," she replied, "Take a long leave of absence from the Warner contract and go to Mills College, where the scholarship I had won in 1934 is still waiting for me."[24]

She was appointed a Chevalier (or Knight) of the Legion of Honor, France's highest decoration, awarded at the Elysee Palace on September 12, 2010, when she was ninety-four, by President Nicolas Sarkozy, who said, "You honor France by having chosen us . . . You are a rebel because you are the only one who dared file a suit against the studios to defend the liberty of actors. You won. It's exceptional."[25]

Much of her time and strength went into projects helping other senior citizens. She provided the voiceover in a documentary about life's most tragic cases, people who've lost their memory, which in the end is all that is left to define us and tell us who we are. *I Remember Better When I Paint* deals with art and other creative activities that benefit victims of Alzheimer's disease. Lara Gabrielle Fowler, an admirer, observed Olivia socializing after she introduced the film at a screening at the American Library in Paris in 2011 and later wrote, "Always the social butterfly, she stayed long after the event was over, talking to people, and ignoring the whispers in her ear that her taxi was outside. After three or four ignored whispers, the organizers finally told a reporter from the *Independent* that it really was time to go, and Olivia disappointedly sighed, 'Oh, they're making me leave!'"[26]

A Paris friend of Olivia's, Patricia Wells, the only woman ever to become restaurant critic of *L'Express*, said on March 19, 2011, "A memorable, rollicking, and boisterous lunch today with actress and Parisian Olivia de Havilland (age 94 and loving every moment of life) enjoying champagne, briny oysters from Utah Beach, and a few sips of Pouilly Fumé from the Loire Valley. We talked of present moments, old times, and times to come."[27]

However humble the honor, such as the tiny town of Marshfield, Missouri's Cherry Blossom Festival Hubble Medal of Initiative, Olivia accepted it graciously. Though at ninety-five she didn't attend, she sent, as requested, a few words about *GWTW* to be read at the climactic banquet given in honor of the film's seventy-fifth anniversary: "I know that the joy I feel is shared by the other five surviving members of the cast of *Gone With the Wind*, who have been honored with their own medals, two of whom are with you in the flesh this evening, both of whom play Melanie's sons at different stages as the newborn Beau—Mickey Kuhn and Patrick Curtis. I am certain that Ann Rutherford, Alicia Rhett, and Mary Anderson are also with you on this extraordinary occasion. I think too that other members of the cast are with you in spirit and have assembled on the veranda of the great plantation in the sky. Vivien Leigh, Clark Gable, Leslie Howard, Hattie McDaniel, and Butterfly McQueen are wearing with immense pride their Hubble Medal. God bless my fellow cast members in whatever realm they may be."[28]

By 2004 Olivia had watched *GWTW* 26 times. "Whenever I . . . see it, something absolutely magical happens. Within five minutes, I'm so captivated . . . I want to know what's going to happen next. Quite seriously. The film has that extraordinary power."[29]

As for the men in her life, she said, "I don't think there was anyone I did meet or could have met with whom I could have had a lasting marriage."[30] If she had a regret, it was that so many of her peers had died. "All the artists I had known during the Golden Era [now live] elsewhere, including the after world," she told the AP on her one hundredth birthday.[31]

In her senior years Joan Fontaine was a determinably independent woman living with her dogs in her house, Villa Fontana, located on three acres on Lower Walden, just past Carmel Highlands in north central California. She told *Vanity Fair* that she was contented, that her greatest achievement was peace and tranquility, that she regretted her recklessness, that the greatest love of her life was the English language, that virginity was the most overrated virtue, that du Maurier and the Brontes were among her favorite writers, and that she'd like to die "in bed, alone."[32]

She had dedicated her autobiography to her mother, though she wrote, "To my knowledge Mother saw only one film of mine . . . Never, ever, did Mother acknowledge that she had seen me on the screen during my entire Hollywood career."[33] When asked if she loved her mother, Joan could only say, "Ahhhhhh."[34] Words couldn't express how much she adored Lilian. According to *Vanity Fair*'s William Stadiem, Olivia helped Joan recover a measure of the Christian faith that had been instilled in them during childhood. When Joan fell ill, despite what Olivia calls Joan's "genuine disbelief," Olivia's faith in God proved contagious, and Joan at last emerged from luxurious isolation and joined Saint Thomas Episcopal Church on Fifth Avenue.[35]

On December 15, 2013, Joan died in her sleep in Carmel at the age of ninety-six in Villa Fontana and was cremated. "I was shocked and saddened to learn of the passing of my sister, Joan Fontaine, and my niece, Deborah," Olivia said, "and I appreciate the many kind expressions of sympathy that we have received."[36] A friend of twenty-five years, Noel Beutel, a Sotheby's International Realty broker and executor of Fontaine's estate, had lunched with Joan the previous week, and recalled, "She was an amazing woman, she had such a big heart and she will be missed."[37] Joan left the proceeds from the sale of her house to the Monterey Society for the Prevention of Cruelty to Animals (SPCA), where she'd adopted three of her dogs.[38] "That could be worth between $2 million and $3 million," wrote Tom Leyde in the *Monterey Herald*. Her gift was to be used to improve the SPCA's Animal Care and Adoption Center, which would dedicate a wing of the building to her memory.[39] "She was a wonderful person," Beutel said, "just a wonderful friend . . . [Handling the estate has] been an overwhelming job. I'm honored that she trusted me enough to have me handle it."[40] Valued in excess of $1 million, the contents of Joan's home would be offered by Christie's in four auctions, and the house was listed by Christie's at $2.6 million. Joan's Oscar, expected to fetch $300,000 at auction, was withdrawn when the Academy threatened to sue, stating, "Oscars should be won, not purchased."[41]

"Joan loved her animals and that's where it's all going," Beutel said.[42]

She was not alone in preferring dogs to people; so did Sigmund Freud, who said people were incapable of the unconditional love dogs display, Charles de Gaulle, who observed that the better he got to know people, the more he liked dogs, Robert Louis Stevenson, who thought dogs would get to heaven before homo sapiens, and philosopher Arthur Schopenhaur, who thought dogs were smarter, morally superior, and more amusing than people. Drew Barrymore bequeathed her house to her dog Flossie, and Elton John's English cocker spaniel Arthur Dwight was best man at his wedding to David Furnish. Marilyn Monroe said, "Dogs never bite me. Just humans."[43] Doris Day, Joan's longtime Carmel neighbor, owns a ten-acre hilltop complex of buildings with a spectacular view of Carmel Valley, including a house for her 48 dogs with its own kitchen. She told *Vanity Fair*, "All I ever wanted [was] . . . a baby, a husband who really loved ne, a home, all the happiness that they could bring. I never got that."[44] Becoming an animal welfare activist, she co-founded Actors and Others for Animals, founded the Doris Day Animal Foundation, which funds non-profit causes to help animals and animal-lovers, formed the Doris Day Animal Legacy, which lobbies for animal protection through legislative action, originated the annual Spay Day USA, and established the Horse Rescue Adoption Center in Murchison, Texas. "I love people and animals," she said, "but not necessarily in that order."[45]

Dressed in an embroidered black velvet gown, gold Chanel ballet slippers, and wearing her signature pearl necklace, Olivia declined, during an interview in Paris, to discuss her career, explaining that she'd do it "only in writing," where she could check the facts for accuracy.[46] "I want to be a font of truth," she said.[47] "So how do I feel about older age? Crazy about it! Wouldn't trade it for anything!"[48]

The reporter admired "her elegant swoop of white hair, her sharp mind, witty charm, [and] engaged bright eyes," but noted that her vision and hearing were limited.[49] Olivia didn't complain, because she'd remained bold, and mighty forces were still bearing her along. In 2015, the Cannes Film Festival honored her, along with Jane Fonda and producer Megan Ellison, the thirty-year-old responsible for *Zero Dark Thirty* and *American Hustle*.[50] The French people revere her. When President Nicolas Sarkozy met her, he said he could hardly believe he was seeing the real Melanie at last. One of Gisele's former classmates, Pascal Negre, found Olivia to be still sexy in her senior years. "She told the story of how she rejected John F. Kennedy when he was in Hollywood visiting Robert Stack after his

PT-109 service days," Negre recalled. "She said she was too busy and had to rehearse. Poor JFK!"[51]

William Stadiem's 2015 article in *Vanity Fair* demonstrated that she'd lost nothing of her skill in wooing the press. "As a going-away gift she offered me those *Spellbound* earrings that I had admired, to give to my mother," Stadiem wrote. "She [also] presented me with a magnificent coffee-table book on the vanished glories of the city."[52] In February 2016 Olivia proved a good sport when she won the Oldie of the Year Award conferred by a satirical magazine, the *Oldie*. She couldn't attend the presentation banquet in London but sent word she was "utterly delighted the judges deemed there was sufficient snap in my celery to win the honor."[53] Founded by former *Private Eye* editor Richard Ingrams to take an irreverent stand against ageism, the magazine had conveyed the same honor on the Queen Mother in 2001. "It's deeply gratifying to find myself in the company of the Queen Mother, whose record I have long wanted to match as well as that of so many other distinguished recipients," Olivia said.[54]

Issued in 2016, a centennial commemorative edition of her 1961 memoir *Every Frenchman Has One* included a new essay in which she wrote, "I have the idea that anyone who has ever heard my name has the distinct impression that I was put under the sod years ago just before they buried Lillian Russell. And so, when I wonder if you know that I've lived in France, I'm sure you don't, because I'm certain that you think me peacefully interred, and in good old Native American soil. If that's the case, you're in for a surprise."[55]

On the 107th anniversary of Errol Flynn's birth, Olivia said, "On June 20, I will raise a glass of champagne to Errol, as I always do."[56] When her one-hundredth birthday arrived on July 1, she celebrated by having cocktails and dinner with friends. Speaking of Joan, she told the AP, "'Dragon Lady,' as I eventually decided to call her, was a brilliant, multi-talented person, but with an astigmatism in her perception of people and events which often caused her to react in an unfair and even injurious way. If Dragon Lady were alive today, out of self-protection I would maintain my silence."[57]

Olivia is one of the world's 455,000 centenarians, up from 23,000 in 1955, according to the population division of the United Nations. The Associated Press found Olivia to be "for her years . . . in surprisingly good health," but noted, "age-related macular degeneration has damaged her vision," and her hearing was impaired, but not so much that she failed to hear a too-personal question and call her AP inquisitor a "rascal."[58] "A keen sense of humor," the reporter noted, was among her enduring gifts.[59] She lost her good friend, the always polite and proper Robert Osborne, in 2017, and gave Gisele a message to read at his memorial in Manhattan's Morgan Library. Osborne had once "gently asked if I could call him Robert," Olivia recalled. "I might have slipped and called him 'Bob.' But I never made the ultimate error and called him 'Bobby!'"[60] Liz Smith reported in David Patrick Columbia's *New York Social Diary* that "the *piece de resistance* was Gisele Galante Chulack . . . who spoke touchingly about Osborne as a great and compassionate friend to her mother and to their entire family."[61] Mourners at the Osborne memorial included Michael Feinstein, Robert Wagner, Jill St. John, Diane Baker, Arlene Dahl, and Ben Mankiewicz. Like Olivia, Jane Powell couldn't attend but sent a message.

When Olivia appeared on Queen Elizabeth II's Honor List in 2017 she became a Dame Commander of the Order of the British Empire— Dame Olivia, OBE, a member of the highest Orders of Chivalry. "I am extremely proud," she said. "To receive this honor as my 101st birthday approaches is the most gratifying of my birthday presents."[62] She joined a handful of titled actresses, including Maggie Smith, Judi Dench, Elizabeth Taylor, Julie Andrews, Joan Collins, Angelina Jolie, Angela Lansbury, and Helen Mirren. The origins of Chivalry date back to 1327, when monarchs gathered around them powerful subjects they could trust. Knights bound themselves into various Orders, such as soldiers and monks. The Dame-hood, a relatively recent addition, was the first Knighthood for women.

All Orders of Chivalry are handled by the Central Chancery of the Orders of Knighthood, which is located behind St. James's Palace and issues all decorations and medals, most of which cost around one hundred pounds each. Recipients are invited to an Investiture customarily performed by the Queen in Buckingham Palace, but the Queen does not personally select Knights and Dames.[63] Nominations come from such sectors of the government as the Department of Culture (performing artists), the Foreign Office (diplomats), the Health Department (doctors), the Ministry of Defense (soldiers), and the Royal Household (the Queen's staff). One thousand recommendations come from the Ceremonial Office, which is a part of the Cabinet Office. The public usually submits some 3,500 names on forms provided by the government. Eight screening committees are established, and the heads of each serve on the Main Honors Committee, chaired by the head of the Civil Service and responsible for coming up with the final list of approximately 1,350, which goes to the Prime Minister and finally the Queen.

When Queen Elizabeth II was asked which part of her job she enjoyed most, she replied, "The Investitures."[64]

One by one, the lights of the Golden Age of Hollywood have gone out, except for one—Dame Olivia, the last surviving star of a bygone era when movies were young. "I think of Errol all the time," she reportedly said. "In different ways, almost every day."[65] She still, in 2015, occasionally watched *GWTW* and it didn't make her melancholy but instead glad to see Gable, Leigh, McDaniel, and Howard "vibrantly alive on screen . . . I experience a kind of reunion with them, a joyful one."[66]

She has several circles of friends, including the U.S. community centered around the American Cathedral in Paris—"fascinating and worthwhile people," as she described them to AP correspondent Thomas Adamson in 2016. The secret to her longevity she attributed to exercise and the three L's: "love, laughter, and learning."[67] Happiness she maintains by going to church, seeing her friends, staying in fit shape by climbing the stairs daily in her Paris residence, working the *Times* crossword puzzle, and coping with pain by viewing it as a learning experience rather than a prelude to death.[68] Although she'd moved to France in 1953 to accommodate a spouse's "insistence,"[69] she could say, over half a century later, that the City of Light was "a marvelous development in my life."[70] Of one thing she is sure. "We'll always have Paris," she said.[71]

And, of course, those imperishable movie masterpieces *Gone With the Wind* and *The Heiress*—"they stay inside you," she said, "always with you."[72]

Epilogue

In Paris in 2017, Dame Olivia had been hearing talk about *Feud: Bette and Joan*, an eight-part docudrama exploring the rivalry between Bette Davis and Joan Crawford, scheduled to be broadcast on the cable channel FX. "I was interested to see how it would portray my dear friend Bette Davis," she said. Eventually she learned from friends and family that her identity was being represented in one of the characters on the program. "No one from Fox had contacted me about this to ask for my permission, to request my input, or to see how I felt about it . . . When I then learned that the Olivia de Havilland character called my sister Joan 'a bitch' and gossiped about Bette Davis and Joan Crawford's personal and private relationship, I was deeply offended."[1]

FX producer Ryan Murphy later said that he chose not to consult Dame Olivia because he "didn't want to be disrespectful and ask her, 'Did this happen? Did that happen? What was your take on that?'"[2] Directed by Murphy, the first episode premiered on March 5, 2017, viewed by 3.8 million.[3] Though Olivia had no involvement in the relationship of Davis and Crawford and never commented on it, *Feud* drags her in as the narrator and framing device for the program, and represents her as saying, in the opening scene during a fake interview,[4] "For nearly half a century, they hated each other, and we *loved* them for it."[5] These words are blatantly at odds with Olivia's style and values as I observed them at close range as her editor at the Delacorte Press in the 1970s. She would never have taken pleasure in hatred of any kind, or participated in the elevation of such conduct. Watching *Feud*, I found almost none of the statements made by the de Havilland character, certainly not the negative portrayal of her as another female actor who would gossip and stab friends and

321

relatives in the back, supported by my own research. The theme of *Feud* seems to be that women in Hollywood will do just about anything to one another, no matter how unscrupulous, to get ahead. Whatever basis there may be for suggesting that Davis and Crawford are examples of this kind of behavior, there is no basis for portraying Olivia de Havilland as part of that story line. In fact, as this book details, she refused to respond in kind when insulted publicly by her own sister, Joan Fontaine. She took the high road, and maintained dignified silence, refusing to comment on her sister's negative accusations while Joan was alive.

Dame Olivia immediately filed a lawsuit against FX in Los Angeles Superior Court for unauthorized commercial use of her name and identity and false light defamation. "The FX series puts words in the mouth of Miss de Havilland which are inaccurate and contrary to the reputation she has built over an 80-year professional life, specifically refusing to engage in gossip mongering about other actors to generate media attention for herself," her attorneys Suzelle M. Smith, Don Howarth, and Zoe Tremayne stated, adding that the program showed her in "a false light to sensationalize the series" and increase profit.[6]

"The gist of her claims," Judge Holly E. Kendig wrote, is that FX "knowingly and recklessly published false statements about her, and portrayed her as endorsing *Feud*."[7] FX, she added, did not deny that it intentionally broadcast a fake interview of Dame Olivia speaking about the "feud" between Bette Davis and Joan Crawford, nor did FX deny that it portrayed her as uttering vulgar statements about Joan, which were never made, calling her a "bitch" to other members of the profession while she was alive, and making negative remarks about Frank Sinatra.[8]

FX filed a motion to have Dame Olivia's case tossed out, but Justice Kendig refused, ruling that she "has successfully met her burden in showing that she has a likelihood of prevailing on the merits," and set a date for a jury trial on the merits. FX appealed, and Justice Anne Egerton of the Court of Appeal reversed Justice Kendig's ruling, maintaining that persons portrayed in an "expressive work" do "not own history" and cannot "control, dictate, approve, disapprove, or veto the creator's portrayal of actual people."[9]

Speaking for Dame Olivia, Suzelle Smith stated, "The opinion is breathtaking in its failure to follow established precedent from both the Court of Appeal and the Supreme Court. It ignores the rule of law that the Justices cannot weigh the evidence and must credit all plaintiff's evidence. The Court of Appeal, unlike the trial court, has taken on itself the role of both judge and jury, denying Miss de Havilland her Constitutional rights in her name or to defend her reputation against knowing falsehoods. This is an entirely pro-industry decision, and was clearly written before the hearing less than a week ago." She noted that "the official biography of Justice Egerton, a recent appointee to the Court of Appeal, states that the justice was previously the West Coast General Counsel of the National Broadcasting Company (NBC) and before that was a partner at Munger Tolles & Olson, the firm representing FX in this case."[10]

One of the oddest claims in Justice Egerton's 36-page opinion concerned the "key issue . . . the use twice by De Havilland's character—played in the series by Catherine Zeta-Jones—of the word bitch in reference to Fontaine. De Havilland's lawyer argued that no record exists of de Havilland ever using the word, much less to identify Fontaine. FX's lawyer cited an on-the-record comment that De Havilland has made referring to Fontaine as a 'Dragon Lady.' Justice Halim Dhanidina, one of three judges on the panel, asked de Havilland's attorney, 'Is there a substantial difference between calling someone a bitch and a Dragon Lady?' De Havilland's attorney replied 'Yes, there is, your honor,' adding, 'In my household, if you say the word "bitch," you get your mouth washed out.'"[11]

In Justice Egerton's opinion, had *Feud* made the reference to Joan Fontaine as "dragon lady" rather than "bitch," the "effect on the mind of the reader" would not have been appreciably different.[12] The Court seemed to miss the point that Dame Olivia never commented on her sister during her life, as *Feud* has her doing. Only on her 100th birthday, years after Joan's death, did Olivia finally break her silence, saying her sister, whom she referred to as Dragon Lady, had an "astigmatism" about some people and events.[13] By definition Dragon Lady is a powerful Asian woman like Madame Ngo Dinh Nhu of Vietnam, Devika Rani of India, or Anna May Wong. Smith pointed out that "Olivia did not use the profane word 'bitch' to refer to Joan but a subtle fairly highbrow allusion, which no literate person would think was vulgar. Both Joan and Olivia were born in Japan and so the term had another layer of symbolic cleverness. That someone would equate Dragon Lady and bitch as having even remotely the same meaning is baffling to Olivia and anyone else who fairly investigates the phrase. And again, this was long after Joan's death—in true keeping with Olivia's lifelong preference not to retaliate."[14] In the evidence presented to the Court, Cort Casady, an industry expert, screenplay writer, and producer, testified that "bitch" and "Dragon Lady" did not have the same dictionary meaning or implication and that the portrayal was untrue and harmful to the professional reputation of Dame Olivia.[15] David Ladd, who starred with her in *The Proud Rebel*, and was a former senior executive of MGM, gave similar testimony.[16] Justice Egerton, ignoring the evidence submitted by Dame Olivia, stated that the *Feud* portrayal was "overwhelmingly positive" and, based on FX's declarations, declared that no reasonable juror could find the portrayal "highly offensive" as a matter of law.[17] The Court of Appeal does not explain how a reasonable judge, the Honorable Holly Kendig, could have reached exactly the opposite conclusion. Nor does it explain why judges are now casting themselves as film critics.

Woven throughout this book is the feud Joan tried to create with Dame Olivia, who simply would not go there. As Smith puts it, "She took the high ground and did not defend herself, refusing to descend into a cat fight of the type *Feud* wanted to and did promote as truth. Why isn't it interesting and inspiring to learn that it is really possible to exercise restraint and good manners, even in the face of bad manners and personal, hurtful attacks? Olivia is a role model to so many because she could control any natural instinct to give back as good as she got. She could have done that, with justification, but she chose not to do that. This is the Olivia that *Feud* so disgracefully dishonored. And the California Court of Appeal does not even seem to understand the difference, which is even more sad."[18]

Feud's depiction of Dame Olivia as a gossiping, disloyal friend to Bette Davis and a person who would use profanity about her sister to other actors is inconsistent with my research, as I have set forth in this book. In April 2018 Dame Olivia's attorneys were petitioning the California Supreme Court for review.[19] She has expressed her deep conviction that the principles at stake go far beyond her own mistreatment, stating, "I feel very strongly that I must appeal to the Supreme Court for my sake and for the sake of many others in the future. I, and other individuals in like circumstances, should not be denied our constitutional right to trial by jury."[20]

Acknowledgments

To Dame Olivia de Havilland, who cordially consented to talk and dine with me in Paris in 1973.

To attorney Suzelle M. Smith: My deepest gratitude for helping me steer a true course, and for the gift of your expertise, time, and energy, graciously and generously given. And for the words that have inspired me: "Ellis, we all appreciate your intention to honor Olivia as she richly deserves."

To my friend Paul N. Bibler. "Two people are better off than one, for they can help each other succeed. If one person falls, the other can reach out and help . . . A person standing alone can be attacked and defeated, but two can stand back-to-back and conquer."—Ecclesiastes 4:9–1

To Jeff Schmidt for placing my manuscript.

To Rick Rinehart, my brave editor and publisher at Globe Pequot/ Rowman and Littlefield.

To attorney Thomas L. Edwards, for hours of brilliant advice and good fellowship.

～～

To the journalists, many of whom spoke with Olivia and reported her words: William Stadiem, Dotson Rader, John Lichfield, Bob Thomas, John S. Truesdell, Hedda Hopper, Robert M. Klein, Sheilah Graham, Radie Harris, Earl Wilson, Anita Gates, Lara Gabrielle Fowler, Vivian Brown, Lynne Bell, George Shaffer, Linda Lane, Harrison Carroll, Erskine Johnson, Howard Heffernan, Lucie Newville, Alice L. Tildesley, Peter Haldeman, Rosalind Shaffer, Louis Berg, Sidney Skolsky, Emily Andrews, Dan Thomas, Dee Lowrance, Glenn Kenny, Rick du Brow,

Angela Taylor, Thomas Adamson, Missy Schwartz, Sara Day, Julia Felsenthal, Adrian Gamble, Ida Jean Kain, Andre Sennwald, Robin Coons, Henry McLemore, Wood Soanes, Hubbard Keavy, Louella O. Parsons, Dick Kleiner, Paul Harrison, Clarke Wales, Alice Pardoe West, Thomas Wiseman, Jimmie Fidler, Scott Feinberg, Myles Standish, Ronald Reagan, Michael Thornton, Olga Curtis, Peter Mikelbank, Joan Crosby, Nancy Tartaglione, Judy Flander, Irene Thirer, Leonard Lyons, Walter Winchell, Rosemary Hite, Emily Belser, Nick Thomas, George W. Cornell, Amy Fine Collins, Read Kendall, May Mann, Julia Hilder, Nardine Saad, Inga Arvad, Robert Van Gelder, Robert K. Hutchens, J. Maurice Ruddy, John Chapman, Donald Kirkley, Jack Gaver, Virginia Vale, Aline Bosley, Patricia Clary, Robin Adams Sloan, Vernon Scott, Allen B. Dodd, Sean M. Wright, Patricia Wells, Aline Mosby, Harold V. Cohen, Stephen E. Rubin, Roderick Mann, Marilyn Beck, Mary Campbell, Mary Vespa, Tom Leyde, Dr. Marty Nemko, David Kaufman, Kristin McMurran, Rajeen Syal, Victoria Miller, Nancy Conant Richards, Angela Danovi, and Dorothy Kilgallen.

To authors Judith M. Kass, Robert Matzen, Gail Kinn, Jim Piazza, Joan Fontaine, Ingrid Bergman, Bette Davis, Lillian Gish, J. Randy Taraborrelli, Ginger Rogers, Gavin Lambert, David Thomson, William Frye, Lee Grant, Audrey Wood, Michael Shagow, Errol Flynn, Evelyn Keyes, Tony Thomas, David Niven, Barbara Walters, Angelica Huston, Ray Stricklyn, Mason Wiley, Damien Bono, Gary Fishgall, Jean-Pierre Aumont, Jeffrey Meyers, John Huston, Burgess Meredith, Richard Burton, Brian Aherne, Terry Moore, Florence Aadland, Christopher Andersen, Rudy Behlmer, Katharine Hepburn, Yvonne De Carlo, Victoria Wilson, Kate Summerscale, Michael Caine, Anne Edwards, Sam Staggs, Joe Morella, Edward J. Epstein, Gerald Clarke, Alexander Walker, Paul McDonald, Philip Van Rensselaer, Irene Mayer Selznick, Patrick McGilligan, Gloria Swanson, Beverly Linet, Robert LaGuardia, Patricia Bosworth, Michael Munn, Michelangelo Capua, Jhan

Robbins, Ed Sikov, Marc Eliot, Donald L. Bartlett, James B. Steele, Pierre Galante, Jonathan Coe, Kathleen Brady, James Spada, Donald Spoto, Charles Brackett, Howard Teichmann, Edward Sorel, John Henry Steele, Laurence Leamer, and David King Dunaway.

To my family: Lu Bradbury and Bill and Joyce Amburn, and to the memory of my mother and father, E.D. and Belma Amburn.

To my friends: Gwynn G. Rakeker, Suzanne Ray, Shannon Miller, Ken Houpt, Mike Horton, Billy O'Connor, Wanda Kay Lee, Alissa Old Crow, Zack Zeder, Nimai Larson, Mike Vedder, Tyler Flanagan, Pat Bern, Jason Hodges, Jennifer Donsky—and the late Vanessa "Van" McCarver and Marshall G. Streib.

To Wendy Tucker for sage counsel.

To Ross Claiborne, publisher of James Jones and Irwin Shaw, for invaluable editorial guidance.

To Cathy Griffin for superb research.

To Pat Loud, Richard Ridge, and Leonida Karpik for interviews and photos, and to all who were instrumental over the years in the making of this writer and his books—David O. Selznick, George Cukor, Joshua Logan, Jimmy Stewart, Kim Novak, Shelley Winters, June Allyson, Radie Harris, Sheilah Graham, Rex Reed, Sammy Davis Jr., Richard Howard, Robert Weil, Al Lowman, Patricia Soliman, John J. Geoghegan, Lena Wickman, Joseph McCrindle, Ernie Quick, Sherry Arden, and Diane Reverand.

To Mitch Douglas for steadfast friendship.

To Lynn Zelem for shepherding my manuscript through production, and to Jan Fehler for copyediting.

To Ron Bernstein, vice president of International Creative Management, and to George and Peggy DiCaprio for kind help whenever I'm in Los Angeles.

To Margaret Fries, Linda Thomas, Tom Mosley, Annina Jest, Merna Wimsatt, Andrew Tate, Pam and David Lee, Adelaide Kiszka, Dot

O'Neil, Jane McKenna, Tom and Annie Otto, Peggy Jellema, Fred Beard, Gene Smith, Dorothy Deluca, James Green, and all my neighbors at The Atrium who keep the home fires burning.

To my teachers: Lorraine Sherley, Paul Dinkins, Warren K. Agee, and Karl Snyder at TCU, Lewis Leary at Columbia, and Patricia Edwards, Hattie Frey, and Elsie Cathey at Poly High.

To Frank Vriale for encouraging this enterprise, and to lifelong friend Ronny Dieb for supporting me in all my endeavors.

To my medical team at Shands: Drs. Bill Mendenhall, Ying Lu Nagoshi, Matthew McKillop, Joshua Billingsley, Maithili Shenoy, Brian Charles Weiner, and Alexandra Lucas.

And to my pastor, J. Mark Johns, who said, "When we attempt bold things for God, we can expect bold things from God."

Endnotes

PROLOGUE

1 Vivian Brown (AP): "Olivia de Havilland Likes France for Child Rearing," *Cincinnati Enquirer*, Cincinnati, Ohio, February 11, 1973, p. 133.
2 Lynn Bell: "No, She Isn't the Future Mrs. Heath," *Sydney Morning Herald*, Sydney, New South Wales, Australia, August 26, 1971, p. 16.

1. LAND OF THE RISING SUN

1 Anita Gates: "Joan Fontaine, Who Won An Oscar for Hitchcock's *Suspicion*, Dies at 96," *New York Times*, New York, December 15, 2013.
2 Academy of Achievement online: "The Last Belle of Cinema," American Academy of Achievement oral history interview with Olivia de Havilland, October 5, 2006, Washington, D.C.
3 Ibid.
4 Linda Lane: "Miss de Havilland Wins Coveted Costume Role," *News-Review*, Roseburg, Oregon, November 7, 1936, p. 10.
5 Rosemary Hite: "A Cozy Evening with a Star—Joan Fontaine," *San Bernardino County Sun*, San Bernardino, California, December 4, 1978, p. 13.
6 William Stadiem: "De Havilland's Bumpy Flight," *Vanity Fair*, May 2016, p. 153.
7 Joan Fontaine: *No Bed of Roses*, New York: Berkley, 1978, p. 2.
8 Ibid., p. 4.
9 Ibid., p. 154.
10 Academy of Achievement online: "The Last Belle of Cinema."
11 Ibid.
12 Stadiem: *Vanity Fair*, p. 154.
13 The Rt. Revd Pierre Whalon, D.D.: "Reading the Bible as a Statement of Faith," Anglican online.
14 Academy of Achievement online: "The Last Belle of Cinema."
15 Fontaine: *No Bed of Roses*, p. 19.
16 Ibid., p. 25.
17 Ibid., p. 29.
18 Academy of Achievement online: "The Last Belle of Cinema."
19 Stadiem: *Vanity Fair*, pp. 153–154.
20 Ibid.
21 Erskine Johnson, NEA: "Erskine Johnson in Hollywood," *Courier News*, Blytheville, Arkansas, December 10, 1954, p. 18.
22 Fontaine: *No Bed of Roses*, p. 310.
23 "Golden Girl: The Divine Olivia de Havilland," *London Independent* web page, July 13, 2009.
24 Thomas Adamson (AP): "AP Interview: De Havilland Breaks Silence on Sibling Feud," July 1, 2016, AP web page.

25 Hedda Hopper: Olivia de Havilland interview, raw transcript, September 10, 1952, quoted in Matzen: *Errol and Olivia*, Pittsburgh: GoodKnight Books, 2010, pp. 3, 4.

26 From an article on sisters Pier Angeli and Marisa Pavan, *Denton Record-Chronicle*, Denton, Texas, July 12, 1955, p. 12.

27 Bob Thomas, AP: "Joan Fontaine . . . ," *Bee*, Danville, Virginia, February 28, 1955, p. 21.

28 Fontaine: *No Bed of Roses*, p. 71.

29 Hopper: Olivia de Havilland interview in Matzen: *Errol and Olivia*, Pittsburgh: GoodKnight Books, 2010, p. 2.

30 Stadiem: *Vanity Fair*, p. 157.

31 Ibid., p. 156.

32 NPR online, "100 Years of Olivia de Havilland Handling Sexism, Her Sister, and Scarlett O'Hara," Bob Mondello, Florida's WUFT-FM web page.

33 Bob Thomas: "Acting Sisters on Speaking Terms Again," *Winona Republican-Herald*, Winona, Minnesota, July 24, 1953, p. 13.

34 *St. Louis Post-Dispatch*: June 7, 1935, p. 52.

35 J. Maurice Ruddy: "Fairy Tale of Dreams Come True," *Oakland Tribune*, Oakland, California, August 11, 1935, p. 68.

36 *Chicago Tribune*: "She Rises to Stardom by Taking Mother's Advice," March 14, 1935, p. 73.

37 "The Last Belle of Cinema," quoted in Matzen: *Errol and Olivia*, p. 6.

38 Alice L. Tildesley: "Girls Had Just About as Much Freedom 800 Years Ago as They Have Today," *Oakland Tribune*, Oakland, California, February 13, 1938, p. 63.

39 Louis Berg: "Always a Bridesmaid," *Cincinnati Enquirer*, November 17, 1946, p. 122.

40 Lucie Newville, *San Bernardino County Sun*, San Bernardino, California, March 3, 1940, p. 27.

41 Matzen: *Errol and Olivia*, Pittsburgh: GoodKnight Books, 2010, p. 84.

42 Ibid., p. 7.

43 Ibid., p. 21.

44 Ibid., p. 7.

45 Ibid., p. 8.

46 Ibid., p. 8, quoting Richard Huber: "Olivia—the Bellicose Belle," *Coronet*, July 1958.

47 Alice L. Tildesley, *Palm Beach Post*, West Palm Beach, Florida, February 13, 1938, p. 18.

48 "Academy of Achievement online: "The Last Belle of Cinema," quoted in Matzen: *Errol and Olivia*, p. 8.

49 Matzen: *Errol and Olivia*, p. 7.

50 Fontaine: *No Bed of Roses*, p. 43.

51 Matzen: *Errol and Olivia*, p. 8.

2. MAX REINHARDT, DICK POWELL, MICKEY ROONEY, AND JAMES CAGNEY

1 Matzen: *Errol and Olivia*, p. 8.

2 Ibid.

3 Ibid.
4 Ibid.
5 Ibid.
6 Ibid.
7 Ibid.
8 Ibid.
9 John S. Truesdale: *St. Louis Post-Dispatch*, February 9, 1941, St. Louis, Missouri, p. 55.
10 Academy of Achievement online: "The Last Belle of Cinema."
11 Jack Warner with Dean Jennings: *My First Two Hundred Years in Hollywood*. New York: Random House, 1964.
12 *St. Louis Post-Dispatch*: St. Louis, Missouri, June 7, 1935, p. 52; Judith M. Kass: *Olivia de Havilland*, New York: Pyramid, 1976, p. 19; Lane: *News-Review*.
13 Bob Thomas: "Mrs. Fontaine Says Daughters Not Really Mad," *Times*, San Mateo, California, July 24, 1953, p. 10.
14 Ivan Kahn Collection, 1930s–1940s, "Talent Scout," Margaret Herrick Library of the Academy of Motion Picture Arts and Sciences, Beverly Hills, California.
15 Lane: *News-Review*.
16 "Academy of Achievement online: "The Last Belle of Cinema."
17 Charles Higham: *Sisters*, New York: Dell, 1984, p. 47.
18 Wallis memo, February 15, 1935, quoted in Matzen, p. 12.
19 Wallis memo, March 7, 1935, quoted in Matzen, p. 3.
20 IMDb online: "Ross Alexander," Biography.
21 Olivia de Havilland: "Mickey Rooney: The Eternal Boy Wonder," April 10, 2014, *Time* Entertainment web page.
22 Dee Lowrance: "No Sister Act," *Akron Beacon Journal*, Akron, Ohio, July 27, 1941, p. 82.
23 Ibid.
24 Tony Thomas: *The Films of Olivia de Havilland*, Secaucus, New Jersey: Citadel Press, 1983, p. 57.
25 *Chicago Tribune*: "She Rises to Stardom by Taking Mother's Advice."
26 Missy Schwartz: "Olivia de Havilland: A Life in Pictures, *A Midsummer's Night Dream (1935),*" February 2, 2015, Entertainment web page, Gallery.
27 Stadiem: *Vanity Fair*, p. 157.
28 Ibid.
29 Ibid.
30 Ibid.
31 Fontaine: *No Bed of Roses*, p. 53.
32 Ibid., p. 56.
33 Ibid., p. 57.
34 Ibid.
35 Ibid.
36 Lyle W. Nash: "A Star Remembers," *Pasadena Independent*, Pasadena, California, April 6, 1960, p. 8.
37 Lane: *News-Review*.

38 Ibid.
39 Louis Berg: "Always a Bridesmaid," *The Cincinnati Enquirer*, Cincinnati, Ohio, November 17, 1946, p. 122.
40 Frank S. Nugent: "Joe E. Brown Returns in a Merry Film Version of Ring Lardner's *Alibi Ike*," *New York Times*, New York, July 17, 1935.
41 Judith M. Kass: *Olivia de Havilland*, New York: Pyramid, 1976, p. 24.
42 Tony Thomas: *The Films of Olivia de Havilland*, p. 17.
43 Academy of Achievement online: "The Last Belle of Cinema."
44 Tony Thomas: *The Films of Olivia de Havilland*, p. 17; Matzen: *Errol and Olivia,* p. 13.
45 Tony Thomas: *The Films of Olivia de Havilland*, p. 64.
46 Dan Thomas: "Twinkle, Twinkle Little Star," *Pittsburgh Press*, Pittsburgh, Pennsylvania, May 17, 1935, p. 31.
47 Ibid.
48 Ibid.
49 Bob Thomas: "Mrs. Fontaine Says Daughters Not Really Mad."
50 Stadiem: *Vanity Fair*, p. 157.
51 Fontaine: *No Bed of Roses*, p. 63.
52 Lowrance: "No Sister Act," p. 82.
53 Rosalind Shaffer: "Olivia de Havilland, Mother's Girl," *Chicago Tribune*, Chicago, Illinois, March 14, 1937, p. 73.
54 *her share of the rent: Los Angeles Times*, Los Angeles, California, December 16, 2013, p. 13. *Olivia was paying the rent:* Joan Fontaine: *No Bed of Roses*, p. 71. *no-future little sister: Los Angeles Times*, December 16, 2013.
55 "People," *Chicago Tribune*, Chicago, Illinois, September 24, 1978, p. 32.
56 Fontaine: *No Bed of Roses*, p. 97.

3. ERROL FLYNN

1 Matzen: *Errol and Olivia*, p. 18.
2 Jeffrey Meyers: *Inherited Risk*, New York: Simon & Schuster, 2002, p. 107.
3 Rudy Behlmer, editor: *Inside Warner Bros (1935-1951)*, New York: Viking, 1985, p. 20.
4 Ed Sikov: *Dark Victory*, New York: Holt, 2007, p. 81.
5 Behlmer, editor: *Inside Warner Bros. (1935-1951)*, p. 20.
6 Errol Flynn: *My Wicked, Wicked Ways*, New York: Dell, 1959, p. 229.
7 *The Adventures of Errol Flynn*: Turner Classic Movies DVD Video 67041, Top Hat Productions; Academy of Achievement online: "The Last Belle of Cinema."
8 *The Adventures of Errol Flynn*, TCM.
9 Hal B. Wallis: *Starmaker*, quoted in Matzen: *Errol and Olivia*, p. 18.
10 Flynn: *My Wicked, Wicked Ways*, p. 229.
11 Academy of Achievement online: "The Last Belle of Cinema."
12 Ibid.
13 Ibid.
14 Ibid.
15 *The Adventures of Errol Flynn*, TCM.

16 AP: "Olivia de Havilland Likes Parisian Role," *Asbury Park Press*, Asbury Park, New Jersey, May 28, 1961, p. 30.

17 Matzen: *Errol and Olivia,* p. 21.

18 *He made people feel young and alive*: Matzen: *Errol and Olivia*, p. 18. *If you work with the boy*: Behlmer, editor: *Inside Warner Bros. (1935-1951)*, New York: Viking, 1985, p. 24.

19 Matzen: *Errol and Olivia,* p. 21.

20 Ibid., pp. 20–21, quoting Marjorie Pierce: "Olivia Returns to Saratoga," *San Jose Mercury*, October 18, 1979.

21 Ibid., p. 19, quoting "Nothing Short of a Miracle," *Silver Screen*, March 1937.

22 Ibid., p. 22, quoting James R. Silke: "Here's Looking at You, Kid," Boston: Little, Brown, 1976.

23 Ibid., p. 23, quoting Wallis memo to Curtiz, August 27, 1935.

24 Censor report, December 31, 1935.

25 Julia Felsenthal, online: "50 Years Later, Olivia de Havilland's Memoirs of Life in France Is Charming, Cheeky Fun," June 28, 2016. *Vogue* online. Access by title of article.

26 "Flynn Saves His Leading Woman From Peril," *Kentucky Advocate*, Danville, Kentucky, January 11, 1936, p. 2.

27 Matzen, *Errol and Olivia,* p. 19, quoting "Nothing Short of a Miracle," *Silver Screen*, March 1937.

28 Olivia's estimate in "The Last Belle of Cinema." Matzen, *Errol and Olivia,* p. 31, is $1.462 million.

29 Andre Sennwald: "A Newcomer Named Errol Flynn in a Handsome Film Version of Captain Blood, at the Strand," *New York Times*, December 27, 1935.

30 Robin Coons: *Warren Times Mirror*, Warren, Pennsylvania, August 3, 1937, p. 4.

31 Meyers: *Inherited Risk*, p. 118.

32 Ibid., p. 118.

33 *Detroit Free Press*: "Much Teamed Picture Players Prove Strong Box-office Magnet," Detroit, Michigan, March 7, 1943, p. 48.

34 Flynn: *My Wicked, Wicked Ways,* pp. 237–238.

35 Wikipedia: "Olivia de Havilland": *He never guessed I had a crush on him . . . It never occurred to me that he was smitten with me, too.* Emily Andrews: "Errol Flynn? He Never Had His Way With Me," June 17, 2009, *Daily Mail*, retrieved January 21, 2016.

4. *ANTHONY ADVERSE, THE CHARGE OF THE LIGHT BRIGADE,* AND *CALL IT A DAY*

1 Rudy Behlmer: *Inside Warner Bros. (1935-1951)*, New York: Viking, 1985, pp. 30–31.

2 Flynn: *My Wicked, Wicked Ways*, p. 238.

3 American Film Institute (AFI), "Dialogue on Film: Olivia de Havilland," December 1974, quoted in Matzen: *Errol and Olivia,* p. 34.

4 David King Dunaway: *Huxley in Hollywood*, New York: Harper & Row, 1989, p. 208 *passim.*

5 David Niven: *The Moon's a Balloon*, New York: Dell, 1972, p. 202.

6 Sheilah Graham: "David Niven Gets 'No' From Olivia," *Salt Lake Telegram*, Salt Lake City, Utah, September 1, 1938, p. 16.

7 David Thomson: *Warner Bros*, New Haven: Yale University Press, 2017, p. 15.
8 Charles River Editors: *Legends of Hollywood: The Life of Olivia de Havilland*. Available on Amazon.
9 Matzen: *Errol and Olivia*, p. 41; *The Adventures of Errol Flynn*, TCM.
10 Flynn: *My Wicked, Wicked Ways*, p. 238.
11 Dinah Shore, Olivia de Havilland interview, *Dinah!* 1977.
12 Flynn: *My Wicked, Wicked Ways*, pp. 226, 228.
13 *The Adventures of Errol Flynn*, TCM.
14 Kass: *Olivia de Havilland*, p. 31.
15 *The Adventures of Errol Flynn*, TCM.
16 Charles River Editors: *Legends of Hollywood: The Life of Olivia de Havilland*.
17 Lane: *News-Review*.
18 Ibid.
19 *Chicago Tribune*: "She Rises to Stardom by Taking Mother's Advice."
20 Tony Thomas: *The Films of Olivia de Havilland*, p. 89.
21 George Shaffer: "Errol Flynn's a Big Tease, Olivia de Havilland Tattles," *Detroit Free Press*, Detroit, Michigan, January 30, 1937, p. 9.
22 "Weeping Ladies of the Screen," *Brooklyn Daily Eagle*, Brooklyn, New York, May 9, 1937, p. 57.
23 Tony Thomas: *The Films of Olivia de Havilland*, p. 91.
24 Winston Burdett: "'Call It a Day' Arrives at the Capitol," *Brooklyn Daily Eagle*, May 7, 1937, p. 23.
25 *Variety* staff: *The Great Garrick*, December 31, 1939.
26 Virginia Dale: "Star Dust," *Hood County Tablet*, Granbury, Texas, December 9, 1937, p. 3.
27 Walter Winchell: "Little Things About Big People," *Indianapolis Star*, Indianapolis, Indiana, May 3, 1937, p. 4.
28 "Studio Flashes," *The Age*, Melbourne, Victoria, Australia, November 27, 1937, p. 40.
29 Paul Harrison: "Actors Bewildered," *Charleston Daily*, July 12, 1937, p. 12. "Don't Talk About Joan's Sister," *Oakland Tribune*, May 16, 1937, p. 86.
30 *He never guessed:* Wikipedia: *Chemistry:* Emily Andrews: "Errol Flynn? He Never Had His Wicked Way With Me, Says *Gone With the Wind* Star Olivia de Havilland," *Daily Mail*.com, June 17, 2009. *I said that* and *So nothing*: John Lichfield. "Golden Girl, the Divine Olivia de Havilland," *Independent*, July 14, 2009.
31 Evelyn Keyes: *Scarlett O'Hara's Younger Sister*, New York: Fawcett, 1977, p. 50.
32 Ibid., p. 50.
33 Flynn: *My Wicked, Wicked Ways*, p. 294.
34 Matzen, *Errol and Olivia*, p. 41, quoting David Niven: *Bring on the Empty Horses*, New York: Dell, 1975, p. 117.
35 Flynn: *My Wicked, Wicked Ways*, p. 33.
36 Ibid., pp. 31, 35.
37 Ibid., p. 381.
38 Meyers: *Inherited Risk*, p. 124.

39 *The relationship*: Emily Andrews: "Errol Flynn? He Never Had His Wicked Way With Me, Says *Gone With the Wind* Star Olivia de Havilland," Daily Mail.com, June 17, 2009. *It was just*: Kass: *Olivia de Havilland*, p. 42.

40 Kass: *Olivia de Havilland*, p. 40.

41 Meyers: *Inherited Risk*, p. 122.

42 Ibid.

43 Stadiem: *Vanity Fair*, p. 154.

44 Higham: *Sisters*, p. 74.

45 Ibid., pp. 73–74.

46 Ibid., p. 73.

47 Ibid., p. 74.

48 Wood Soanes: *Oakland Tribune*, January 10, 1937, p. 77.

49 Ibid.; Paul Harrison: "Roamin'," *Evening Standard*, Uniontown, Pennsylvania, May 24, 1937, p. 7.

50 Soanes: *Oakland Tribune*, January 10, 1937, p. 77.

51 Lane: *News-Review*.

52 Soanes: *Oakland Tribune*, January 10, 1937, p. 77.

53 Carlisle Jones: "Paul Muni . . . ," *Harrisburg Telegraph*, Harrisburg, Pennsylvania, January 18, 1937, p. 16. *Pittsburgh Press*, Pittsburgh, Pennsylvania, April 18, 1937, p. 68.

54 *Harrisburg Telegraph*: "Gain Weight!" Harrisburg, Pennsylvania, December 2, 1939, p. 8.

55 Charles Start: "All Tired Out After Boning Up on Glamour," *St. Louis Post-Dispatch*, St. Louis, Missouri, January 7, 1951, p. 62.

56 *Ruston Daily Leader*: "The Hollywood Lowdown by Sid," Ruston, Louisiana, April 28, 1937, p. 3.

57 Ibid.

58 Ibid.

59 "Current Women's Fashions Introduced in Past Times by Robust Sex, 'Tis Said," *Freeport Journal-Standard*, Freeport, Illinois, August 17, 1938, p. 7.

60 Hubbard Keavy: "Screen Life in Hollywood," *Wilmington C.H. Record-Herald*, Washington Court House, Ohio, April 6, 1937, p. 5.

61 Sheilah Graham: *Indianapolis Star*, Indianapolis, Indiana, October 4, 1937, p. 7.

62 Ibid.

63 "Olivia de Havilland Makes a Study of Man," *Morning News*, Wilmington, Delaware, May 6, 1937, p. 20.

5. IT'S LOVE I'M AFTER

1 Louella O. Parsons: *Anderson Daily Bulletin*: Anderson, Indiana, May 12, 1960, p. 17.

2 "The Star They Didn't Forget," *Family Weekly*, May 13, 1965, p. 19, reprinted in *The Pantagraph*, Bloomington, Illinois, May 23, 1965, p. 71, and in the *Asbury Park Press*, Asbury Park, New Jersey, May 23, 1965, p. 78.

3 Paul Harrison, NEA: "Hollywood," *Rhinelander Daily News*, Rhinelander, Wisconsin, May 3, 1937, p. 4.

4 Ibid.

5 Ibid.
6 Ibid.
7 Ibid.
8 Ibid.
9 Ibid.
10 Ibid.
11 Ibid.
12 Ibid.
13 Ibid.
14 Ibid.
15 Ibid.
16 Clarke Wales: "Could You Take It?" *Detroit Free Press*, Detroit, Michigan, May 23, 1937, p. 75.
17 *Time* magazine: November 22, 1937.
18 Harrison: "Standout Glimpses at Filmland," *Cumberland Sunday Times*, September 12, 1937, p. 12.
19 *Democrat and Chronicle*: Rochester, New York, July 8, 1937, p. 10.
20 *Santa Ana Register*: Santa Ana, California, October 23, 1937, p. 13.
21 "Studio Flashes," *The Age*, Melbourne, Victoria, Australia, November 27, 1937, p. 40.
22 Sara Day: "We Go to Some Parties," *Democrat and Chronicle*, Rochester, New York, June 6, 1937, p. 74.
23 Ibid.
24 Louella O. Parsons: "Howard Hughes to Make Film . . . ," *Daily Times*, Davenport, Iowa, July 15, 1938, p. 4.
25 Amy Fine Collins: "The Powerful Rivalry of Hedda Hopper and Louella Parsons," *Vanity Fair*, April 1, 1997.
26 Fidler: "In Hollywood," *Wilkes-Barre Record*, Wilkes-Barre, Pennsylvania, October 2, 1937, p. 4.
27 "Jimmie Fidler: Hollywood's Most Hated Man," September 25, 2014, *Gossip Columnists* online.
28 Amy Fine Collins: "The Powerful Rivalry of Hedda Hopper and Louella Parsons."
29 Fontaine: *No Bed of Roses*, p. 161.

6. JOAN FALLS IN LOVE, OLIVIA MAKES A WESTERN

1 Fontaine: *No Bed of Roses*, p. viii.
2 Ibid., pp. 72–73.
3 Ibid., p. 27.
4 Ibid., p. 39.
5 Ibid., p. 58.
6 Ibid., pp. 75, 76.
7 Ibid., p. 71. Judy Flander: "Famous Movie Queen . . . ," *Washington Star* online.
8 Fontaine: *No Bed of Roses*, p. 71.
9 Judy Flander: "Famous Movie Queen . . . ," *Washington Star* online.
10 Fontaine: *No Bed of Roses*, p. 97–98.

11 Frank S. Nugent: "The Screen: The Music Hall . . . ," *New York Times,* June 25, 1937.
12 Fontaine: *No Bed of Roses*, pp. 75–76.
13 Ibid., pp. *84–85.*
14 Ibid., p. 88.
15 Ibid., p. 72.
16 Ibid., p. 82.
17 Both reviews are quoted by Higham: *Sisters,* p. 67.
18 Higham: *Sisters,* p. 68.
19 Fidler: *The Salt Lake Tribune,* Salt Lake City, Utah, April 7, 1937, p. 9.
20 Higham: *Sisters,* p. 69.
21 Ibid.
22 Kass: *Olivia de Havilland,* pp. 45–46.
23 Byron Haskins: "Gold Is Where You Find It' Mines for Technology," popMATTERS website, November 18, 2014.
24 "Lisa": "Why the Sheridan-Brent Marriage Failed!" on online web page "Remembering Ann Sheridan." *Screenland,* January 1943.
25 Sikov: *Dark Victory,* p. 168.
26 Paul Harrison: "Paul Harrison in Hollywood," *Daily Tribune,* Wisconsin Rapids, Wisconsin, November 16, 1938, p. 9.
27 "Lisa": *Screenland,* January 1943.

7. *THE ADVENTURES OF ROBIN HOOD*

1 Matzen: *Errol and Olivia,* p. 52.
2 Ibid., p. 53.
3 Ibid., p. 55, cites Turner: *The Adventures of Errol Flynn.*
4 Ibid., pp. 55, 198, cites Dotson Rader: "Rewards and Regrets: Olivia de Havilland Talks About Montgomery Clift, Errol Flynn, and Herself," *Parade,* September 7, 1996.
5 Rudy Behlmer: *Behind the Scenes,* Hollywood: Samuel French, 1982, 1989, p. 64.
6 Matzen: *Errol and Olivia,* p. 56.
7 "Castle for New Film, 'Robin Hood'": *Harrisburg Telegraph,* Harrisburg, Pennsylvania, December 1, 1937, p. 9.
8 Behlmer: *Behind the Scenes,* p. 74.
9 Meyers: *Inherited Risk,* p. 123, citing James D'Arc: "Perfect Manners: An Interview with Olivia de Havilland," *American Classic Screen, 3, (January-February 1979), 9.* James Robert Parrish and Don Stanke: *"Errol Flynn," The Swashbucklers,* Carlstadt, New Jersey: Rainbow Books, 1976, p. 285.
10 Matzen: *Errol and Olivia,* citing TCM: *The Adventures of Errol Flynn.*
11 Alice Pardoe West: "Olivia Enjoys Working With Robbin [*sic*] Hood Gang," *Ogden Standard-Examiner,* November 28, 1937, p. 23.
12 Ibid.
13 George Shaffer: "Seeing Hollywood," *Salt Lake Tribune,* May 20, 1936, p. 23.
14 Ibid.
15 Ibid.
16 Louella O. Parsons: *Philadelphia Inquirer,* January 13, 1938, p. 13.

17 *Chicago Tribune:* "She Rises to Stardom by Taking Mother's Advice."

18 Milton Harker: "Film Colony Notes and Gossip," *Quad-City Times*, Davenport, Iowa, March 28, 1938, p. 7.

19 Wikipedia: "Howard Hill."

20 The broadcast is available on YouTube.

21 Wikipedia: An earlier figure, $2 million, is cited by Matzen: p. 75.

22 Nugent: "Robin Hood," May 13, 1938.

23 Wikipedia: "The Adventures of Robin Hood."

24 Roger Ebert: "Great Movie" online, August 17, 2003.

25 American Film Institute online: "Top 100 Movies."

8. BRIAN AHERNE

1 *Morning News*, Wilmington, Delaware, February 22, 1938, p. 10.

2 Stadiem: *Vanity Fair*, p. 154.

3 Matzen: *Errol and Olivia*, p. 84. Higham: p. 79: "She had met Brian Aherne . . . and now that she was back [from England], they dated occasionally."

4 Brian Aherne: *A Proper Job*, Boston: Houghton Mifflin, 1969, p. 266.

5 Ibid., pp. 168–171.

6 Sheilah Graham: "Hollywood Today," *Courier-Journal*, St. Louis, Missouri, June 22, 1952, p. 70.

7 UP: "Lovely Cargo! Glamour Girls Back in U.S.," *Minneapolis Star*, Minneapolis, Minnesota, May 17, 1938, p. 13.

8 *Philadelphia Inquirer:* "Olivia de Havilland Here; 'Not Crazy About Movies,'" Philadelphia, Pennsylvania, May 20, 1938, p. 15.

9 Ibid.

10 Ibid.

11 "Olivia de Havilland Pays Visit Here, Denies Romance," *Pittsburgh Post-Gazette*, Pittsburgh, Pennsylvania, May 21, 1938, p. 11.

12 "Olivia Back in Hollywood," *Pittsburgh Press*, Pittsburgh, Pennsylvania, May 23, p. 14.

13 AP: "Olivia de Havilland Gaining in Health," *Argus-Leader*, August 1, 1938, p. 2.

14 UP: "A Memo to North Carolina: You Were Right About Olivia," *Detroit Free Press*, September 1, 1938, p. 9.

15 Jimmie Fidler: *Santa Ana Register*, Santa Ana, California, June 14, 1937, p. 15.

16 Fontaine: *No Bed of Roses*, p. 88.

17 Ibid., p. 87.

18 Read Kendall: "Around and About in Hollywood," *Los Angeles Times*, Los Angeles, California, September 13, 1938, p. 12.

19 Harrison Carroll: "Behind the Scenes in Hollywood," *Evening Independent*, Massillon, Ohio, November 3, 1938, p. 4.

20 Ed Sullivan: "Hollywood," *Harrisburg Telegraph*, Harrisburg, Pennsylvania, November 15, 1938, p. 6.

21 Ibid.

22 *Chicago Tribune*: "She Rises to Stardom by Taking Mother's Advice."

23 Ed Sullivan: "Hollywood," *Pittsburgh Press*, Pittsburgh, Pennsylvania, December 15, 1938, p. 31.
24 Ed Sullivan: *Harrisburg Telegraph*, Harrisburg, Pennsylvania, December 6, 1938, p. 11.
25 Fontaine: *No Bed of Roses*, p. 88.
26 Ibid., pp. 90–91.
27 Ibid., p. 95.
28 Ibid., p. 96.

9. HOWARD HUGHES

1 Higham: *Sisters*, p. 82.
2 Ibid.
3 Matzen: *Errol and Olivia*, p. 102. Also see "The Last Belle of Cinema."
4 George J. Martin: *Howard Hughes Aviator*, Naval Institute Press, 2004.
5 Stadiem: *Vanity Fair*, p. 156.
6 Christopher Andersen: *An Affair to Remember*, New York: Morrow, 1997, p. 121.
7 Higham: *Sisters*, p. 96.
8 Ginger Rogers: *Ginger: My Story*, New York: HarperCollins, 1991, p. 223.
9 Ibid., p. 224.
10 Ibid., 219–224.
11 Terry Moore: *The Beauty and the Billionaire*, New York: Pocket Books, 1984, p. 65.
12 Ibid., p. 309.
13 Vernon Scott (UPI): "Howard Hughes's 'wife' claims settlement," May 24, 1983, UPI web page.
14 Compiled from my interviews with Yvonne De Carlo, Betty Hutton, Shelley Winters, June Allyson, Peggy Lee, and Stewart Granger and such sources as Barbara Leaming: *Katharine Hepburn*, New York Crown, 1995, pp. 346–347, 355. Laurence Leamer: *As Time Goes By*, New York: Harper & Row, 1980, p. 229. Shelley Winters: *Shelley II*, New York: Simon and Schuster, 1989, p. 151. Internet: "Howard Hughes's Wives, Girlfriends . . . ," Ranker web page. "Howard Hughes": www.spartacus-educational.com.
15 Keyes: *Scarlett O'Hara's Younger Sister*, p. 73.
16 "Howard Hughes the Tortured Aviator": August 2005, Deep Cove Crier website.
17 Leamer: *As Time Goes By*, New York: Harper & Row, p. 131.
18 Sheilah Graham: *The Rest of the Story*, New York: Coward-McCann, 1964, p. 162.
19 Ibid., p. 163.
20 Ibid.
21 Peter Mikelbank: "Olivia de Havilland Opens Up . . . ," *People*, July 7, 2016.
22 Hermione Eyre: "Hollywood's Sweetheart: Olivia de Havilland," *Evening Standard* online, March 18, 2010.
23 Tony Thomas: *The Films of Olivia de Havilland*, p. 132.
24 Kass: *Olivia de Havilland*, p. 77.
25 Matzen: *Errol and Olivia*, p. 95. On p. 94, he calls it "the nervous breakdown she experienced over J.L.'s [Jack L. Warner's] refusal to loan her out for *Gone With the Wind*, combined with the stress of her assignment to *Dodge City*."
26 Ibid.

27 Ibid.

28 *You wear things that cut . . . part if they'd ever let her*: Laury Martin, *Arizona Republic*: Phoenix, Arizona, January 1, 1939, p. 33. *I'm so tired of being . . . kind of parts I'd like*: Harold Heffernan, "'Sweet Girl' Wants to Get 'Vixen' Roles,'" *St. Louis Post Dispatch*, St. Louis, Missouri, October 18, 1939, p. 37.

29 Heffernan: "'Sweet Girl' Wants to Get 'Vixen' Roles."

30 Memo to Wallis, January 6, 1939, quoted in Matzen, p. 107

31 "Howard Hughes," *True*, May 1966, quoted in Matzen, p. 107.

32 Bob Thomas (AP): *Manitowoc Herald-Times*, Manitowoc, Wisconsin, April 17, 2003, p. 22. The accounts differ as to whether the party was given by Jack and Ann Warner or by David O. Selznick.

33 Alice Pardoe West: *Ogden Standard-Examiner*: Ogden, Utah, May 14, 1939, p. 13.

34 Ibid.

35 "Olivia de Havilland: A Life in Pictures," Entertainment web page.

36 Bosley Crowther: "Screen: James Cagney in Nostalgic Comedy of the 1890's, *Strawberry Blonde*, at the Strand," *New York Times*, New York, February 22, 1941.

37 Academy of Achievement online: "The Last Belle of Cinema."

38 Ibid.

39 Ibid.

10. DAVID O. SELZNICK

1 Richard Harwell, editor: *Margaret Mitchell's Gone With the Wind Letters*, New York: Macmillan, 1976, pp. xxxiii–xxxiv.

2 Stadiem: *Vanity Fair*, p. 154.

3 Fontaine: *No Bed of Roses*, p. 112.

4 Ibid., p. 94.

5 Ibid., p. 112.

6 Academy of Achievement online: "The Last Belle of Cinema."

7 Ibid.

8 Matzen: *Errol and Olivia*, p. 95.

9 Ibid.

10 Ibid.

11 Anita Gates: "The Good Girl Gets the Last Word," *New York Times*, November 7, 2004, p. 32.

12 David O. Selznick: *Memo From David O. Selznick*, New York: The Modern Library, 2000, p. 191.

13 David Thomson: *Showman*, New York: Knopf, 1992, p. 286.

14 Higham: *Sisters*, p. 84.

15 Ibid.

16 Ibid., 87.

17 Academy of Achievement online: "The Last Belle of Cinema."

18 Jean-Pierre Aumont: *Sun and Shadow*, New York: Norton, 1977, p. 71.

19 Diana McLellan: *The Girls*, New York: St. Martin's Press, 2000, passim; Kate Summerscale: *The Queen of Whale Cay*, New York: Viking, 1997, pp. 198-201.

20 *scumbag*: David Thomson: *Warner Bros,* New Haven: Yale University Press, 2017, p. 2.
help her get the part: Academy of Achievement online: "The Last Belle of Cinema."
21 Stadiem: *Vanity Fair,* p. 155.
22 Academy of Achievement online: "The Last Belle of Cinema."
23 Harwell, editor: *Margaret Mitchell's Gone With the Wind Letters*, p. 246.
24 Ibid., pp. 246–247.
25 Matzen: *Errol and Olivia*, p. 104.
26 Louella O. Parsons: *Democrat and Chronicle*, Rochester, New York, January 17, 1939, p. 6.
27 Ed Sullivan: *Harrisburg Telegraph*, Harrisburg, Pennsylvania, February 6, 1939, p. 12.
28 Selznick: *Memo From David O. Selznick*, pp. 173–174.
29 Thomson: *Showman*, p. 286. Harwell, editor: *Margaret Mitchell's Gone With the Wind Letters*, p. 246.
30 Gavin Lambert: *GWTW*, Boston: Atlantic Monthly Press, 1973.
31 Michael Sragow: *Victor Fleming*, Lexington, Kentucky: University Press of Kentucky, 2013, p. 332.
32 "*GWTW* actors' salaries, in today's dollars," The Data Lounge online.
33 Harwell, editor: *Margaret Mitchell's Gone With the Wind Letters*, p. 246.
34 "*GWTW* actors' salaries, in today's dollars," "The Data Lounge" online. In Selznick's *Memo From David O. Selznick*, Viking edition, p. 267, Gable's salary was budgeted at $150,000, which comes to $2,650,000 in today's dollars.
35 IMDb online: "*Gone With the Wind,*" Trivia.
36 David O. Selznick: *Memo From David O. Selznick*, p. 153; IMDb online: "*Gone With the Wind,*" Trivia.
37 Harwell, editor: *Margaret Mitchell's Gone With the Wind Letters*, p. 271.
38 Rudy Behlmer: *Inside Warner Bros. (1935-1951)*, New York: Viking, 1985, p. 84.
39 Pride online: "Who the F Is Fabled Lover Mercedes de Acosta." Axel Madsen: *The Sewing Circle*, Secaucus, New Jersey: Carol Publishing Group, 1995.
40 Wikipedia: "Ona Munson."
41 Thomson: *Showman*, p. 272.
42 Selznick: *Memo From David O. Selznick*, p. 153.
43 Valerie J. Nelson: "Ann Rutherford Dies at 94; actress was in 'Gone With the Wind,'" *Los Angeles Times*, June 12, 2012.
44 IMDb online: "*Gone With the Wind,*" Trivia. Wikipedia: "Hattie McDaniel." Seth Abramovitch: "Oscar's First Black Winner Accepted Her Honor in a Segregated 'No Blacks' Hotel in LA." *Hollywood Reporter* online.
45 Butterfly McQueen in the video of a program hosted by Christopher Plummer, online on an Olivia de Havilland fan web page.
46 Butterfly McQueen video, Olivia de Havilland fan web page.
47 David O. Selznick: *Memo From David O. Selznick*, Viking edition, p. 187.
48 Thomson: *Showman*, p. 219.
49 Selznick: *Memo From David O. Selznick*, Modern Library edition, p. 188.
50 Ibid., p. 185.
51 Thomson: *Showman*, p. 271.

52 Ibid., p. 271.
53 Ibid., p. 264.
54 Ibid., p. 281.
55 David O. Selznick: *Memo From David O. Selznick, p. 198.*
56 Anne Edwards: *Vivien Leigh,* New York: Simon and Schuster, 1977, p. 95.
57 Harwell: *Margaret Mitchell's Gone With the Wind Letters,* p. 245.
58 Ibid., pp. 245–246.
59 Ibid., pp. 260–261.
60 Ibid., p. 347.
61 Helen Bower, Free Press Movie Office: *Detroit Free Press,* Detroit, Michigan, July 18, 1954, p. 141.
62 IMDb online: *"Gone With the Wind,"* Trivia.
63 Olivia de Havilland online fan page.
64 *Independent* website: "Golden Girl: The Divine Olivia de Havilland," October 22, 2011.

11. GEORGE CUKOR, F. SCOTT FITZGERALD, VICTOR FLEMING

1 IMDb online: *"Gone With the Wind,"* Trivia.
2 Harrison, NEA: *Palm Beach Post,* West Palm Beach, Florida, July 9, 1939, p. 8.
3 David Thomson: "The Making of a Legend," Disc Three, *Gone With the Wind,* DVD video 65917, Turner Entertainment/Selznick Properties.
4 David O. Selznick: *Memo From David O. Selznick,* p. 78.
5 Thomson: *Showman,* p. 288.
6 Harwell, editor: *Margaret Mitchell's Gone With the Wind Letters,* p. 250.
7 Lambert: *GWTW,* p. 71.
8 Ibid., p. 170.
9 Ibid., p. 72.
10 Ibid.
11 Sragow: *Victor Fleming,* p. 320.
12 Patrick McGilligan: *George Cukor: A Double Life,* New York: St. Martin's Press, p. 147.
13 Thomson: *Showman,* p. 294.
14 Fleming's actual wording, according to his biographer Michael Sragow, was, "Your fucking script is no fucking good." Sragow: p. 322.
15 Lambert: *GWTW,* p. 80.
16 Thomson: *Showman,* p. 290, cites Boze Hadleigh, preface to his interview with Cukor, the director's last published interview.
17 McGilligan: *George Cukor: A Double Life,* p. 150.
18 Ibid.; Sragow: p. 320.
19 McGilligan: *George Cukor: A Double Life,* p. 150.
20 Ibid., p. 150.
21 Thomson: *Showman,* p. 288.
22 Laurie Ulster: *"Gone With the Wind's* 75th Anniversary . . . ," Biography web page, December 15, 2014.

23 Graham: *The Rest of the Story*, p. 10.
24 McGilligan: *George Cukor: A Double Life*, p. 150.
25 Thomson: *Showman*, p. 291.
26 Sragow: *Victor Fleming*, p. 318.
27 Thomson: *Showman*, p. 293-294.
28 Irene Mayer Selznick: *A Private View*, New York, Knopf, 1983, p. 216.
29 Sragow: *Victor Fleming*, p. 318.
30 Ibid., p. 320.
31 Ibid., p. 321.
32 Ibid.
33 Ibid.
34 Ibid.
35 Ibid., p. 333.
36 Matzen: *Errol and Olivia*, p. 116.
37 Sragow: *Victor Fleming*, p. 324.
38 Ibid., p. 5.
39 Ibid., p. 39.
40 Ibid., p. 9.
41 Ibid., p. 9.
42 Ibid., p. 7.
43 Katz: p. 52. Anita Gates: "The Good Girl Gets the Last Word," *New York Times*, November 7, 2004, p. 32.
44 Sragow: *Victor Fleming*, p. 321.
45 Ibid.
46 Kass: *Olivia de Havilland*, p. 52.
47 American Film Institute (AFI), "Dialogue on Film: Olivia de Havilland," December 1974, quoted in Matzen: *Errol and Olivia*, p. 117
48 Ibid.
49 Sragow: *Victor Fleming*, pp. 338-339.
50 Thomson: *Showman*, p. 284. Sragow: p. 339.
51 Thomson: *Showman*, p. 298.
52 Wikipedia: "Sidney Howard."
53 Wikipedia: "Ben Hecht."
54 Ibid.
55 Max Wilk: *Schmucks With Underwoods: Conversations With Hollywood's Classic Screenwriters*, Hal Leonard Corp., Wikipedia.
56 Sragow: *Victor Fleming*, p. 322.
57 Anne Edwards: *Vivien Leigh*, New York: Simon and Schuster, 1977, p. 103. Phatual online: *"Gone With the Wind a Disastrous Success."*
58 Shagow: *Victor Fleming*, p. 340.
59 Thomson: *Showman*, p. 299.
60 Anita Gates: "The Good Girl Gets the Last Word."
61 Edwards: *Vivien Leigh*, p. 102.
62 Harrison: *The Palm Beach Post*, p. 8.

63 Ibid.

64 Academy of Achievement: "Olivia de Havilland."

65 Gates: "The Good Girl Gets the Last Word."

66 Gates: "The Good Girl Gets the Last Word." IWM staff online: "How Alan Turing Cracked the Enigma Code," January 5, 2018. William Stephenson: *A Man Called Intrepid*, The Lyons Press: Guilford, Connecticut, 1976, 2000. Wikipedia. Alan Royle, Historical Movie Info online: "Leslie Howard—Hero or Just Unlucky?"

67 "How We Do Run On: A *Gone With the Wind* Scrapbook" web site quoting Guy Flatley, "Butterfly's Back in Town," *New York Times*, July 21, 1968, p. 18.

68 Online fan web page, from a program hosted by Christopher Plummer.

69 IMDb online: "*Gone With the Wind*," Trivia.

70 Shagow: *Victor Fleming*, p. 341.

71 IMDb online: "*Gone With the Wind*," Trivia.

72 "*GWTW* Actors Salaries in Today's Dollars," The Data Lounge web page.

73 Shagow: *Victor Fleming*, p. 346.

74 Keyes: *Scarlett O'Hara's Younger Sister*, p. 30.

75 "Butterfly McQueen," Browse Biography web page.

76 *Independent* website: "Golden Girl: The Divine Olivia de Havilland," October 22, 2011.

77 Matzen: *Errol and Olivia*, pp. 123-124. Olivia de Havilland: "The Dream That Never Died: *Gone With the Wind*," *Look*, December 12, 1967, quoted in Matzen: *Errol and Olivia*, p. 124.

78 AP: "Olivia de Havilland Likes Parisian Role," *Asbury Park Press*, Asbury Park, New Jersey, May 28, 1961, p. 30.

79 Ibid.

80 Shagow: *Victor Fleming*, pp. 342-343.

81 Ibid., p. 341.

82 Ibid., p. 350.

83 Thomson: *Showman*, p. 301.

84 Ibid., *p.* 302.

85 Keyes: *Scarlett O'Hara's Younger Sister*, pp. 33, 35.

86 Rudy Behlmer: *Inside Warner Bros. (1935-1951)*, New York: Viking, 1985, p. 98.

87 Kass: *Olivia de Havilland*, p. 38. Matzen: *Errol and Olivia*, pp. 124, 127–128. Tony Thomas: *The Films of Olivia de Havilland*, p. 150.

88 American Film Institute (AFI), "Dialogue on Film: Olivia de Havilland," December 1974, quoted in Matzen: p. 122.

89 Sikov: *Dark Victory*, p. 151.

90 Glenn Kenny: "Olivia de Havilland," *Premiere*, October 2004, quoted in Matzen: *Errol and Olivia*, p. 122.

91 Warner unit manager Frank Mattison to studio production manager T.C. Wright, June 12, 1939, quoted in Behlmer: *Inside Warner Bros (1935-1951)*, p. 97.

92 Ibid., pp. 97-99.

93 De Havilland to Warner, July 18, 1939, quoted in Behlmer, *Inside Warner Bros (1935-1951)*, p. 99.

94 Kenny: "Olivia de Havilland," *Premiere*, October 2004, quoted in Matzen: *Errol and Olivia*, p. 124.

95 Sikov: *Dark Victory*, p. 151.

96 Flynn: *My Wicked, Wicked Ways*, p. 301.

97 Ibid.

98 Ibid., p. 302.

99 Ibid., p. 306.

100 Sikov: *Dark Victory*, p. 156.

101 Behlmer: *Inside Warner Bros (1935-1951)*, p. 100.

102 Dick Kleiner: "Broadway 'First Lady': She'll Take Manhattan," *Wausau Daily Herald*, Wausau, Wisconsin, December 28, 1962, p. 8.

103 "The Screen: Errol Flynn Catches a Tudor in Strand's Film of *The Private Lives of Elizabeth and Essex*," *New York Times*, New York, December 2, 1939.

104 *had never asked*: Joan Fontaine: *No Bed of Roses*, p. 95. *to pass inspection*: Ibid., p. 97. "Despite these pious disclaimers, Joan continued dating Howard Hughes, but later revealed that she never fell in love with him, explaining, "I was afraid of him. . . . He had no humor, no gaiety, no sense of joy, no vivacity. . . . Everything seemed to be a 'deal,' a business arrangement, regardless of the picture he had tried to paint of our future together."

105 Ibid., p. 98.

106 Ibid., p. 98-99.

107 "*The sparks flew*: Joan Fontaine: *No Bed of Roses*, p. 99. "*I was afraid*: Judy Flander: "Joan Fontaine: Thorns, Roses," *Washington Star*, reprinted in *St. Louis Post-Dispatch*, St. Louis, Missouri, September 29, 1978, p. 51.

108 Higham: *Sisters*, p. 175.

109 UP: "Stars Marry," *Nevada State Journal*, Reno, Nevada, August 21, 1939, p. 2.

110 Lucie Neville: "Graduates From 'Sister' to Star," *San Bernardino County Sun*, San Bernardino, California, March 3, 1940, p. 27.

111 Neville: "Graduates From 'Sister' to Star."

112 Brian Aherne: *A Proper Job*, Boston: Houghton Mifflin, 1969, p. 86.

113 Fontaine: *No Bed of Roses*, p. 173. King News Syndicate, *Syracuse Post-Standard*, May 8, 1949, p. 24.

114 Aherne: *A Proper Job*, pp. 307, 328.

115 Ibid., p. 315.

12. THE ATLANTA AND NEW YORK PREMIERES OF *GONE WITH THE WIND*

1 Thomson: *Showman*, p. 319.

2 UP: "Hollywood Film Shop," *La Grande Observer*, La Grande, Oregon, November 7, 1939, p. 6.

3 Alexander Walker: *Vivien*, New York: Grove Press, 1987, pp.137-138.

4 David O. Selznick: *Memo From David O. Selznick*, p. 259.

5 Irene Mayer Selznick: *A Private View*, p. 222.

6 Thomson: *Showman*, p. 262.

7 Fred Kaplan: *Gore Vidal*, New York: Doubleday, 1999, p. 61, quoted on Wikipedia.
8 Graham: *Indianapolis Star*, Indianapolis, Indiana, April 25, 1948, p. 68.
9 Walker: *Vivien*, p. 137.
10 Adrian Gamble: "'GWTW' Premiere at Loew's Grand Theater in Atlanta," Skyrise Cities web page.
11 UP: "*GWTW* Set to Observe Anniversary," *Odessa American*, August 8, 1954, p. 17.
12 UP: "*GWTW* Set to Observe Anniversary."
13 Larry Worthy: "Atlanta Premiere of *Gone With the Wind*," About North Georgia web page.
14 UP: "Henry McLemore Comments," *Oakland Tribune*, Oakland, California, December 13, 1939, p. 21.
15 UP: "Henry McLemore Comments."
16 *'supervised' the directors*: Lambert, *GWTW*, p. 150. *me and my poor*: Edwards: *Vivien Leigh*, p. 113.
17 Thomson: *Showman*, p. 324.
18 Ibid.
19 Walker: *Vivien*, p. 138.
20 Ibid.
21 Edwards: *Vivien Leigh*, p. 113.
22 Jhan Robbins: *Everybody's Man: A Biography of Jimmy Stewart*, New York: Putnam, 1985, p. 67, quoted in Marc Eliot: *Jimmy Stewart*, New York: Harmony Books, 2006, p. 178.
23 Marc Eliot: *Jimmy Stewart*, pp. 177–178. Matzen: *Errol and Olivia*, p. 133.
24 Matzen: *Errol and Olivia*, p. 133.
25 Gary Fishgall: *Pieces of Time: The Life of James Stewart*, New York: Scribner, 1997, p. 137.
26 Fishgall: *Pieces of Time: The Life of James Stewart*, p. 130.
27 Joshua Logan: *Josh*, New York: Delacorte, 1976, p. 120.
28 Alice Hughes: *Indianapolis Star*, Indianapolis, Indiana, December 27, 1939, p. 4.
29 *New York Daily News:* "When *Gone With the Wind* Premiered . . . ," December 20, 1939.
30 Parsons: *Courier-Journal*, Louisville, Kentucky, December 22, 1939, p. 19.
31 "When *GWTW* Premiered December 20, 1939," Daily News Entertainment web page.
32 Frank S. Nugent: "David Selznick's *GWTW* Has Its Long-Awaited Premiere at the Astor and Capitol, Recalling Civil War and Plantation Days in the South—Seen as Treating Book With Great Fidelity," *New York Times*, December 20, 1939, p. 31.
33 Kate Cameron: *New York Daily News*, December 20, 1939, quoted in "When *GWTW* Premiered December 20, 1939," Daily News Entertainment web page.
34 Andrew Sarris: "The Moviest of All Movies," *Atlantic Monthly*, March 1973, p. 67.
35 Judith Crist: "Glorious Excesses," *Atlantic Monthly*, March 1973, p. 73.
36 Hughes: *Indianapolis Star*, December 27, 1939, p. 4.
37 Robert Ruark: "It's a Wonderful Life," *Reno Gazette-Journal*, Reno, Nevada, March 28, 1955, p. 4.

38 *Guinness World Book Records*, 2014. Wikipedia: "List of Highest-Grossing Films."

13. JIMMY STEWART

1 Both Stewart and Ford were involved in *How the West Was Won,* a Cinerama triptych with three different directors. Jimmy's cameo was directed by Henry Hathaway.
2 Ken Morgan: "Hollywood Keyhole," *Alton Evening Telegraph*, Alton, Illinois, February 28, 1942, p. 13.
3 Fishgall: *Pieces of Time: The Life of James Stewart*, p. 139.
4 Peter Bogdanovich, IndieWire website: "*Destry Rides Again*," September 28, 2011.
5 Eliot: *Jimmy Stewart,* p. 130.
6 Ian Wood: *Dietrich*, Cornwall, U.K., MPG Books, p. 186, quoted in Eliot: p. 137.
7 Richard Freeman: "Closet Hollywood," *New York Times*, New York, January 7, 2001. Wikipedia: "Marlene Dietrich."
8 Logan: *Josh*, p. 58; Fishgall, p. 87.
9 Lowrance: "No Sister Act"
10 Ibid.
11 Louella O. Parsons: *Louisville Courier-Journal*, Louisville, Kentucky, December 22, 1939, p. 19.
12 Eliot: *Jimmy Stewart,* p. 137.
13 Ibid., p. 130.
14 Ibid., p. 137.
15 John Maroney: "Olivia de Havilland Recalls Her Role in the Cold War," *Wall Street Journal*, September 7, 2006.
16 Behlmer, editor: *Inside Warner Bros (1935–1951)*, p. 139.
17 Higham: *Sisters,* p. 116.
18 Ibid.
19 Eliot: *Jimmy Stewart*, pp. 178–179.
20 Michael Munn: *Jimmy Stewart*, New York: Skyhorse Publishing, 2006, pp. 107–108.
21 Munn: *Jimmy Stewart*, p. 108.
22 Burgess Meredith: *So Far, So Good*, Boston: Little, Brown, 1994, p. 105.
23 Meredith: *So Far, So Good*, p. 105.
24 Mikelbank: "Olivia de Havilland Opens Up . . . ."
25 Eliot: *Jimmy Stewart*, p. 137.
26 Ibid., p. 130.
27 Fishgall, *Pieces of Time*, p. 138, cites in his Notes Roy Pickard: *Jimmy Stewart: A Life in Film.* New York: St. Martin's Press, 1992.
28 Sikov: *Dark Victory*, p. 157. Jeffrey Meyers: *John Huston*, New York: Crown, 2011, p. 39.
29 Meyers: *John Huston*, p. 39.
30 Sikov: *Dark Victory*, p. 158.
31 Ibid., p. 157.
32 Louella O. Parsons: *Philadelphia Inquirer*, Philadelphia, Pennsylvania, July 25, 1942, p. 16.
33 Harry Niemeyer: *St. Louis Post-Dispatch*, St. Louis, Missouri, March 2, 1949, p. 31.

34 Walter Winchell: *Philadelphia Inquirer*, Philadelphia, Pennsylvania, September 7, 1942, p. 12.

35 Hedda Hopper: *Los Angeles Times*, Los Angeles, California, January 16, 1942, p. 13.

36 Dorothy Kilgallen: "Wedding Bells Soon Ringing Out for Glamour Girl," *Detroit Free Press*, Detroit, Michigan, August 8, 1941, p. 13.

37 Erskine Johnson: *Akron Beacon Journal*, Akron, Ohio, August 23, 1944, p. 7.

38 Dorothy Kilgallen: *News-Journal*, Mansfield, Ohio, September 14, 1942, p. 2.

39 "*Olivia de Havilland is looking*": Hedda Hopper: *Times*, Shreveport, Louisiana, August 24, 1943, p. 2. "*Olivia de Havilland, paged*": Louella O. Parsons: *Fresno Bee*, Fresno, California, September 24, 1942, p. 17.

40 Vanessa Thorpe: "The 'Only Son' of Orson Welles to Take DNA Test," *The Guardian* online, January 30, 2010.

41 Wikipedia.

42 Ibid.

43 Munn: *Jimmy Stewart*, pp. 82–83.

44 Eliot: *Jimmy Stewart*, p. 116.

45 Paul Vitello: "Judy Lewis, Secret Daughter of Hollywood, Dies at 76," *New York Times*, November 30, 2011.

46 Eliot: *Jimmy Stewart*, p. 130.

47 Peter Bogdanovich, IndieWire website: "*Destry Rides Again*," September 28, 2011.

48 Matzen: *Errol and Olivia*, p. 135.

49 Matzen: *Errol and Olivia*, p. 135. Academy of Achievement: "Olivia de Havilland."

50 Stadiem: *Vanity Fair*, p. 156.

51 Irene Mayer Selznick: *A Private View*, p. 222.

52 The photo is online on an Olivia de Havilland fan web page.

53 Eliot: *Jimmy Stewart*, p. 139.

54 Thomson: *Showman*, p. 127.

55 Ibid., p. 327.

56 Ibid., pp. 326–328.

57 Fidler: *Post-Crescent*, Appleton, Wisconsin, December 20, 1939, p. 21.

58 Hermione Eyre: "Hollywood's Sweetheart: Olivia de Havilland," *Evening Standard* online, March 18, 2010

59 Gates: *New York Times*, November 7, 2004.

60 Academy of Achievement: "Olivia de Havilland Interview, Legendary Leading Lady," October 5, 2006, Washington, D.C.

61 Stadiem: *Vanity Fair*, p. 156.

14. VYING WITH VIVIEN LEIGH AND JOAN FONTAINE FOR *REBECCA*

1 Betty Burroughs: "Actress Shuns . . . ," *Morning News*, Wilmington, Delaware, April 14, 1965, p. 13.

2 David O. Selznick: *Memo From David O. Selznick*, Viking edition, pp. 267–268.

3 David O. Selznick: *Memo From David O. Selznick*, Modern Library edition (the memo does not appear in the Viking edition), p. 300.

4 Ibid.
5 David O. Selznick: *Memo From David O. Selznick*, Viking edition, p. 272.
6 Ibid., p. 273.
7 Ibid., p. 272.
8 Ibid., p. 274.
9 Thomson: *Showman*, p. 305.
10 David O. Selznick: *Memo From David O. Selznick*, p. 277.
11 Thomson: *Showman*, p. 309.
12 Fontaine: *No Bed of Roses*, p. 94.
13 Thomson: *Showman*, p. 309.
14 Ibid., p. 279.
15 Ibid., p. 157.
16 Ibid.
17 Ibid.
18 Charles Rivers Editors: *Academy Award Winning Sisters*, unpaged, no publisher or copyright included.
19 Stadiem: *Vanity Fair*, p. 157.
20 Fontaine: *No Bed of Roses*, p. 11.
21 Higham: *Sisters*, p. 118.
22 Kate Cameron: *New York Daily News*, March 29, 1940, Daily News Entertainment web page: "Hitchcock's *Rebecca* Is a Masterpiece: 1940 Review."
23 Rogers: *Ginger, My Story*, p. 224.
24 Ibid., p. 234.
25 Ibid., p. 233.
26 Fontaine: *No Bed of Roses* p. 132.
27 Ibid., p. viii.
28 Judy Flander: "Famous Movie Queen . . . ," *Washington Star* online.
29 Maureen O'Hara and John Nicoletti: *'Tis Herself*, London: Pocket Books, 2004.
30 Mikelbank: "Olivia de Havilland Opens Up . . . ."
31 Ronald Reagan: "'Dutch' Makes His First Scene, He's Scared—but Thrilled! He's an ACTOR—at Last," *Des Moines Register*, Des Moines, Iowa, June 27, 1937, p. 6.
32 Ibid.
33 Ibid.
34 Matzen: *Errol and Olivia*, p. 165.
35 Ibid., p. 139.
36 John Lichfield: "Golden Girl: The Divine Olivia de Havilland," *Independent* web page, July 13, 2009.
37 Matzen: *Errol and Olivia*, p. 137.
38 Irene Zarat: "I Feel Like a Heel About Errol," *Photoplay*, January 1942, quoted in Matzen: *Errol and Olivia*, p. 140.
39 Ibid.
40 Ibid.
41 Matzen: *Errol and Olivia*, p. 140.
42 Ibid., p. 141.

43 Lichfield: "Golden Girl: The Divine Olivia de Havilland."

44 Zarat quoted by Matzen: *Errol and Olivia*, p. 143.

45 Ibid.

46 Matzen: *Errol and Olivia*, p. 139.

47 Ibid., pp. 148–152.

48 Ibid.

49 Ibid.

50 Ibid, pp. 150–151.

51 Ibid.

52 Matzen: *Errol and Olivia*, p. 152.

53 Eliot: *Jimmy Stewart*, p. 158. "In August 1940 . . . killed 40,000." Duncan Anderson: *The World at War 1939–45*, Pleasantville, New York: Reader's Digest, 1999, p. 26.

54 Fishgall: *Pieces of Time*, p. 148.

15. WITH INGRID BERGMAN, BURGESS MEREDITH, JOHN HUSTON, BETTE DAVIS, AND GEORGE BRENT

1 Ingrid Bergman and Alan Burgess: *Ingrid Bergman: My Story*, New York: Delacorte, 1972: pp. 87–88.

2 *"wholly alive and lightens"*: Laurence Leamer: *As Time Goes By*, New York: Harper & Row, 1986, p. 61. *"His swagger is genuine"*: Mel Gussow: "Burgess Meredith, 89, Who Was at Ease Playing Good Guys and Villains, Dies," *New York Times*, September 11, 1997.

3 Warner Bros. memo from Steve Trilling to Hal Wallis, April 14, 1942, quoted in Behlmer, ed.: *Inside Warner Bros.*, p. 201. Edward E. Gloss: *Akron Beacon Journal*, Akron, Ohio, April 29, 1942, p. 19. Laurence Leamer: *As Time Goes By*, New York: New American Library, 1986, p. 116. Ben Cosgrove: *Time*: "The Best Movie of All Time . . . Michael Curtiz's Pop Culture Miracle," November 23, 2012, *Time* web page.

4 Author's interviews with Petter Lindstrom. Also see Laurence Leamer, New American Library Edition, p. 102.

5 Leamer: *As Time Goes By*, New American Library, p. 426.

6 Ibid., p. 104.

7 Ibid.

8 Bergman and Burgess: *Ingrid Bergman: My Story*, p. 332.

9 Tony Thomas: *The Films of Olivia de Havilland*, p. 31.

10 Kass: *Olivia de Havilland*, p. 83.

11 Logan: *Josh*, p. 58. Henry Fonda and Howard Teichmann: *Fonda*, New York: New American Library, 1981, p. 70.

12 Eliot: *Jimmy Stewart*, p. 163.

13 WDW web page: "Who's Dating Who?"

14 Victoria Wilson: *A Life of Barbara Stanwyck*, New York: Simon & Schuster, 2013, p. 801.

15 Ibid., p. 814.

16 Nancy Tartaglione: "Cannes: Oscar Winner Olivia de Havilland Reflects on Experience as Festival's First Female Jury President in 1965," Deadline Hollywood web page May 17, 2017.

17 Crowther: *Hold Back the Dawn,* a Poignant Romance, at the Paramount," *New York Times,* October 2, 1941.

18 Charles Brackett: *It's the Pictures That Got Small,* edited by Anthony Slide, New York: Columbia University Press, 2015, p. 8.

19 Matzen: *Errol and Olivia,* p. 156.

20 Ibid.

21 Ibid.

22 Ibid.

23 Ibid.

24 Tony Thomas: *The Films of Olivia de Havilland,* p. 185.

25 Matzen: *Errol and Olivia,* p. 164.

26 Lichfield: "Golden Girl: The Divine Olivia de Havilland."

27 Ibid.

28 Stadiem: *Vanity Fair,* p. 153.

29 "Ten Eloquent Words": *Detroit Free Press,* Detroit, Michigan, December 1, 1941, p. 6.

30 AP: "Olivia de Havilland Granted Citizenship," *Arizona Republic,* Phoenix, Arizona, November 29, 1941, p. 8.

31 UP: "Olivia de Havilland Becomes U.S. Citizen," *Nevada State Journal,* Reno, Nevada, July 8, 1939, p. 1.

32 Harrison Carroll: "Behind the Scenes in Hollywood," *Jackson Sun,* Jackson, Tennessee, November 5, 1941, p. 4.

33 Walter Winchell: *The San Saba News and Star,* San Saba, Texas, November 13, 1941, p. 4.

34 Anne Hagedorn Auerbach: *Wild Ride,* New York: Holt, 1994, p. 64, quoted by Wikipedia.

35 John S. Truesdell: "Last of the Old-Fashioned Girls, But Olivia de Havilland, Once Demure, Is Changing Into a Sophisticated Lady," *St. Louis Post-Dispatch,* St. Louis, Missouri, February 9, 1941, p. 55.

36 Truesdell: "Around Hollywood With Film Stars," *St. Louis Post-Dispatch,* St. Louis, Missouri, November 2, 1941, p. 55.

37 *Bouncing With Bob,* subhead in article headlined "Franchot's the One . . . ," *Des Moines Register,* Des Moines, Iowa, November 9, 1941, p. 11. *dating Roger Pryor:* Harrison Carroll: "Behind the Scenes in Hollywood," *Jackson Sun,* Jackson, Tennessee, November 9, 1941, p. 4.

38 Steffi Roberts: "From Hollywood Come These Frivolous and Feminine Frills," *Courier-Journal,* St. Louis, Missouri, November 16, 1941, p. 22.

39 Ken Morgan: "Hollywood Key Hole," *Big Spring Daily Herald,* Big Spring, Texas, November 20, 1941, page 5.

40 Jimmie Fidler: *Battle Creek Enquirer,* Battle Creek, Michigan, December 7, 1941, p. 22.

41 Truesdell: "In Hollywood," *Miami News,* Miami, Florida, December 16, 1941, p. 21.

42 "Soldier-Knitter": *St. Louis Post-Dispatch*, St. Louis, Missouri, November 22, 1941, p. 11.

43 Harrison: *Pampa Daily News*, Pampa, Texas, January 13, 1942, p. 4.

44 Steffi Roberts: *St. Louis Post-Dispatch*, St. Louis, Missouri, February 4, 1942, p. 28.

45 Dorothy Kilgallen: *Wilkes-Barre Record*, Wilkes-Barre, Pennsylvania, February 13, 1942, p. 25.

46 Lowrance: "No Sister Act," p. 82.

47 Ibid.

48 Ibid.

49 Jimmie Fidler: *The Times*, Shreveport, Louisiana, November 2, 1941, p. 10.

50 Jimmy [*sic*] Fidler: "Hollywood Roundup," *Evening Standard*, Uniontown, Pennsylvania, November 8, 1941, p. 7.

51 Jimmy [*sic*] Fidler: "Hollywood Roundup."

52 "Olivia Tested in 'Saratoga Trunk'": *Miami News*, Miami, Florida, December 12, 1941, p. 49.

53 Louella O. Parsons: "Gary Cooper to Play Lead Role in 'Bell,'" *Philadelphia Inquirer*, Philadelphia, Pennsylvania, December 4, 1941, p. 15.

54 Leamer: *As Time Goes By*, Harper & Row, p. 100.

55 Academy of Achievement: "Olivia de Havilland Interview, Legendary Leading Lady," October 5, 2006, Washington, D.C.

56 AP: "Could Title . . . ," *Salt Lake Telegram*, Salt Lake City, Utah, December 6, 1941, p. 8.

57 "Virginia's Cries Make Laughs," *Brooklyn Daily Eagle*, Brooklyn, New York, February 1, 1942, p. 38.

58 Bosley Crowther: "The Male Animal," *New York Times*, New York, March 28, 1942.

59 "Her 100th Kiss!": *Gaffney Ledger*, Gaffney, South Carolina, November 4, 1941, p. 2.

60 Keyes: *Scarlett O'Hara's Younger Sister*, pp. 77–78.

61 Mann: "Star's Good Girl Gone Bad, Tires of Sissy-Pants Role," *Ogden Standard-Examiner*, Ogden, Utah, April 26, 1942, p. 29.

62 Sikov: *Dark Victory*, p. 190.

63 Laurence J. Quirk: *Fasten Your Seat Belts*, cited on Toronto Film Society web page "*In This Our Life* (1942)" in notes compiled by Caren Feldman.

64 Sikov: *Dark Victory*, p. 190.

65 Meyers: *John Huston,* p. 88. Sikov: *Dark Victory*, p. 190.

66 Sikov: *Dark Victory*, p. 188.

67 "The Star They Didn't Forget," *Family Weekly*, May 13, 1965, p. 19, reprinted in *The Pantagraph*, Bloomington, Illinois, May 23, 1965, p. 71, and in the *Asbury Park Press*, Asbury Park, New Jersey, May 23, 1965, p. 78.

68 Stadiem: *Vanity Fair*, p. 156.

69 Ibid.

70 "The Star They Didn't Forget," *Asbury Park Press*, Asbury Park, New Jersey, May 23, 1965, p. 78.

71 Ibid.

72 Ibid.

73 Harrison Carroll: *Wilkes-Barre Record*, Wilkes-Barre, Pennsylvania, January 1, 1942, p. 10.
74 Bette Davis: "Foreword," *The Films of Olivia de Havilland* by Tony Thomas, p. 9.

16. OLIVIA AND JOAN COMPETE FOR THE BEST-ACTRESS OSCAR

1 Edwin Schallert: "Academy Dinner Unprecedented," *Los Angeles Times*, Los Angeles, California, February 27, 1942, p. 9.
2 Louella O. Parsons: "Glamour Dimmed . . . ," *Lansing State Journal*, Lansing, Michigan, March 12, 1956, p. 4.
3 Ibid.
4 Schallert: "Academy Dinner . . . ," p. 9.
5 Sidney Skolsky: "The Academy Banquet," *Cincinnati Enquirer*, Cincinnati, Ohio, March 6, 1942, p. 17.
6 Skolsky: "The Academy Banquet."
7 Schallert: "Academy Dinner . . . ," p. 9.
8 Eliot: *Jimmy Stewart*, p. 179.
9 Jimmie Fidler: *Monroe News-Star*, Monroe, Louisiana, February 27, 1942, p. 4.
10 Tony Thomas: *The Films of Olivia de Havilland*, p. 31.
11 Stadiem: *Vanity Fair*, p. 150.
12 Rosalind Shaffer, AP: *Cincinnati Enquirer*, Cincinnati, Ohio, February 27, 1944, p. 49.
13 Ibid.
14 Parsons: "Glamour Dimmed . . . ," *Lansing State Journal*, Lansing, Michigan, March 12, 1956, p. 4.
15 Kass: *Olivia de Havilland*, p. 69.
16 Kinn and Piazza: *The Academy Awards*, p. 60.
17 Skolsky: "The Academy Banquet."
18 Kass: *Olivia de Havilland*, p. 69.
19 Feinberg: *Hollywood Reporter*, December 17, 2013.
20 Jimmie Fidler: "In Hollywood," *St. Louis Star and Times*, St. Louis, Missouri, April 20, 1942, p. 8.
21 *St. Louis Post-Dispatch*, St. Louis, Missouri, May 4, 142, p. 20.
22 Bergman and Burgess: *Ingrid Bergman: My Story*, p. 100.
23 Louella O. Parsons: "Pasternak to Film Tarkington Story," *Philadelphia Inquirer*, Philadelphia, Pennsylvania, January 8, 1942, p. 15.
24 Meredith Woerner: "All the Hollywood Secrets Hidden in the Handprints . . . ," *Los Angeles Times*, Los Angeles, California, May 18, 2017.
25 Kevin Crust: "Who Is Sid Grauman Anyway?" *Los Angeles Times*, Los Angeles, California, May 18, 2017.
26 Joseph Henry Steele: *Ingrid Bergman*, New York: Popular Library, 1959, p. 42.
27 "Conscientious," *Los Angeles Times*, February 10, 1943, p. 42.
28 May Mann: *Ogden Standard-Examiner*, Ogden, Utah, February 28, 1943, p. 7.
29 Julia Hider: "The Hollywood Canteen Where Movie Stars Were at Your Service," November 25, 2016, Messy Nessy web page.

30 Ibid.

31 Nat Dallinger photograph: *Des Moines Register*, Des Moines, Iowa, January 30, 1944, p. 43.

32 "Olivia Entertains Cousin," *Long Beach Independent*, Long Beach, California: January 10, 1943, p. 31. E.V. Durling: "On the Side," King Features Syndicate, *Medford Mail Tribune*, Medford, Oregon, June 4, 1953, p. 19.

33 Fontaine: *No Bed of Roses*, p. 154.

34 Ibid.

35 Wikipedia: "De Havilland Aircraft Company."

36 Matzen: *Errol and Olivia*, pp. 174–175, quoting Grobel: *The Hustons*.

37 Harrison Carroll: *Times*, San Mateo, California, February 27, 1942, p. 6.

38 Mann: "Going Hollywood," *Ogden Standard-Examiner*, Ogden, Utah, April 9, 1942, p. 15.

39 Meyers: *John Huston*, p. 51.

40 *Fresno Bee The Republican:* Fresno, California, July 28, 1942, p. 6.

41 Hopper: *Los Angeles Times*, Los Angeles, California, August 1, 1942, p. 7.

42 Meyers: *John Huston*, p. 86.

43 John Huston: *An Open Book*, New York: Knopf, 1980, p. 15.

44 Meyers: *John Huston*, p. 87.

45 Ibid., p. 40.

46 Huston: *An Open Book*, pp. 61, 63.

47 Meyers: *John Huston*, pp. 49–50.

48 Ibid., pp. 85, 106, 107, 472.

49 Matzen: *Errol and Olivia*, p. 174.

50 Meyers: *John Huston*, p. 104.

51 Ibid., p. 86.

52 Ibid.

53 Ibid., p. 87.

54 Ibid.

55 Ibid.

56 Louella O. Parsons: *Philadelphia Inquirer*, Philadelphia, Pennsylvania, July 25, 1942, p. 16.

57 Meyers: *John Huston*, p. 87.

58 Wikipedia: "John Huston," quoting Lawrence Grobel, *The Art of the Interview*, New York: Random House, 2014.

59 Meyers: *John Huston*, pp. 19-24.

60 Ibid., p. 105.

61 Matzen: *Errol and Olivia*, p. 175, quoting Grobel: *The Hustons*, New York: Scribner's, 1989.

62 Meyers: *John Huston*, p. 87, quoting Grobel: *The Hustons*, p. 225. William Nolan, *King Rebel*, Los Angeles: Sherbourne, 1965, p. 18 and quoted in Grobel: *The Hustons*, p. 224.

17. THE DE HAVILLAND RULE

1 Behlmer, ed.: *Inside Warner Bros.*, p. 234.

2 Academy of Achievement online: "The Last Belle of Cinema."

3 Ibid.

4 *Independent* website: "Golden Girl": The Divine Olivia de Havilland," October 22, 2011.

5 Victoria Amado: "What a Cool Liar You Are, Mellie," *eye* magazine, winter 2015, p. 26.

6 Kass: *Olivia de Havilland,* p. 77.

7 American Film Institute (AFI): "Dialogue on Film: Olivia de Havilland," December 1974, quoted in Matzen: p. 181.

8 Sheilah Graham: "Hollywood Today," *Courier-Journal,* Louisville, Kentucky, June 22, 1952, p. 70.

9 Ibid.

10 *Philadelphia Inquirer,* Philadelphia, Pennsylvania, December 30, 1946, p. 21.

11 Sheilah Graham: *Des Moines Register,* January 5, 1945, p. 7.

12 Sheilah Graham: *Asbury Park Press,* Asbury Park, New Jersey, February 9, 1946, p. 4.

13 Inga Arvad: "Hollywood Today," *Wilkes-Barre Record,* Wilkes-Barre, Pennsylvania, January 9, 1945, p. 5.

14 Harrison Carroll: *Wilkes-Barre Record,* Wilkes-Barre, Pennsylvania, January 12, 1945, p. 9.

15 *St. Louis Post-Dispatch,* St. Louis, Missouri, February 18, 1945, p. 72.

16 Ibid.

17 Jimmie Fidler: *Joplin Globe,* Joplin, Missouri, April 7, 1945, p. 6.

18 Bob Thomas (AP): "Film's No.1 Bachelor Girl Is Willing to Relinquish Title," *Des Moines Register,* Des Moines, Iowa, April 9, 1945, p. 6.

19 Louella O. Parsons: *Philadelphia Inquirer,* Philadelphia, Pennsylvania, April 10, 1945, p. 19.

20 Dorothy Kilgallen: *Pottstown Mercury,* Pottstown, Pennsylvania, April 21, 1945, p. 4.

21 Louella O. Parsons: *Philadelphia Inquirer,* Philadelphia, Pennsylvania, April 23, 1945, p. 15.

22 Harrison Carroll: *Evening Independent,* Massillon, Ohio, April 23, 1945, p. 4.

23 Irene Thirer: "Career Girl de Havilland Talks Films, Romance," *New York Post,* May 3, 1946, University of Southern California (USC) Film Archive.

24 Irene Thirer: "Career Girl de Havilland Talks Films, Romance."

25 Matzen: *Errol and Olivia,* p. 183.

26 Thirer: "Career Girl de Havilland Talks Films, Romance."

27 Louella O. Parsons: *Philadelphia Inquirer,* Philadelphia, Pennsylvania, December 18, 1945, p. 23.

28 Louella O. Parsons: "Hollywood," *Philadelphia Inquirer,* Philadelphia, Pennsylvania, December 28, 1945, p. 25.

29 Sheilah Graham: "Hollywood Today," *Honolulu Star-Bulletin,* Honolulu, Hawaii, March 25, 1946, p. 7.

30 Ibid.

31 Hedda Hopper: "Mom Steps Out," *Angus-Leader,* Sioux Falls, South Dakota, August 30, 1946, p. 8.

32 *Great Falls Tribune,* Great Falls, Montana, January 21, 1946, p. 1.
33 Sheilah Graham: "Hollywood Today," *Kingsport News,* Kingsport, Tennessee, July 24, 1946.
34 United Press: "'Bachelor' de Havilland Is Making Eyes at Major," *Star Tribune,* Minneapolis, Minnesota, March 23, 1946, p. 8.
35 Jimmie Fidler: "In Hollywood," *Pottstown Mercury,* Pottstown, Pennsylvania, April 1, 1946, p. 4.
36 "Lovely Star and Lie Detector," *The Age,* Melbourne, Australia, April 3, 1946, p. 8.
37 Walter Winchell: "On Broadway," Chillicothe, Ohio, May 22, 1946, p. 4.
38 Bette Davis: "Foreword" in Tony Thomas's *The Films of Olivia de Havilland,* p. 9.
39 Hedda Hopper: *Harrisburg Telegraph,* Harrisburg, Pennsylvania, February 16, 1945, p. 15.
40 Academy of Achievement: "Olivia de Havilland," October 5, 2006. *Independent* website: "Golden Girl: The Divine Olivia de Havilland," October 22, 2011.
41 Bette Davis: "Foreword" in Tony Thomas's *The Films of Olivia de Havilland,* p. 9.
42 Kathleen Brady: *Lucille,* New York: Hyperion, 1994, p. 149.
43 Ibid., pp. 149, 151.
44 Matzen: *Errol and Olivia,* p. 184.
45 Huston: *An Open Book,* pp. 96–97.
46 Ibid.
47 Ibid., p. 97.
48 Ibid.
49 Ibid.
50 Ibid., p. 89.
51 "1946 Top Box Office Movies," Ultimate Movie Rankings web page. "*The Jolson Story,*" TCM Film Article web page.
52 Keyes: *Scarlett O'Hara's Younger Sister,* p. 78.
53 Matzen: *Errol and Olivia,* pp.177–178. Meyers: *Inherited Risk,* pp. 59, 178–179, 188.
54 The Phrase Finder web page.
55 Graham: "Marriage Seems to Be Working Out Well for 'Old Maid' Olivia de Havilland," *Courier-Journal,* Louisville, Kentucky, December 1, 1946, p. 60.
56 David Madden, editor: *Rediscoveries,* New York: Crown, 1971, includes Niven Busch's comments on Marcus Goodrich and *Delilah.*
57 Hedda Hopper: "Olivia de Havilland Enjoys Bride's Role," *Los Angeles Times,* Los Angeles, California, December 1, 1946, p. 49.
58 Sidney Skolsky: *St. Louis Post-Dispatch,* St. Louis, Missouri, November 9, 1946, p. 11.
59 Sheilah Graham: "Hollywood Today," *Courier-Journal,* St. Louis, Missouri, December 1, 1946, p. 60.
60 Robert Van Gelder: "Interview With the Author of *Delilah,*" *New York Times,* February 16, 1941.
61 The Editors of *Time*: "Editor's Preface," *Delilah* by Marcus Goodrich, New York: Time Life Books, 1941, p. vii. Van Gelder: "Interview With the Author of *Delilah.*"
62 The Editors of *Time*: "Editor's Preface," *Delilah* by Marcus Goodrich, p. vii.
63 Van Gelder: "Interview With the Author of *Delilah.*"

64 Ibid.
65 Robert K. Hutchens: "People Who Read and Write," *New York Times Book Review*. No date on clipping. Likely the article was written sometime after the 1941 publication of Goodrich's novel *Delilah*.
66 *New York Times*: July 26, 1935.
67 Van Gelder: "Interview With the Author of *Delilah*."
68 "Hollywood Czars Seek 'Agreement' in Mary Astor Suit," *Philadelphia Inquirer*, Philadelphia, Pennsylvania, August 9, 1936, p. 25.
69 Ibid.
70 "Astor Case," *Longview News-Journal*, Longview, Texas, August 12, 1936, p. 3.
71 Edward Sorel: *Mary Astor's Purple Diary*, New York: Liveright, 2016, p. 119.
72 AP: "Mary Astor Gets Ovation," *Ogden Standard-Examiner*, Ogden, Utah, September 16, 1936, p. 1. Most sources list Marylyn's age as four, though one wrote that she was three.
73 "New Celebrities in Mary Astor's Diary," *Evening News*, Wilkes-Barre, Pennsylvania, August 11, 1936, p. 1. Others in Astor's diary: John Barrymore, John Eldredge, Count Alfredo Carpegna, Daniel Silverberg, Dr. Mortimer Rodgers, Carlo Paraga, Evelyn Laye, and George Oppenheimer.
74 Sheilah Graham: "In Hollywood," *Winnipeg Tribune*, Winnipeg, Manitoba, Canada, September 14, 1936, p. 12.
75 "Mystery Woman to Jar Thorpe in Mary Astor Suit," *Chicago Tribune*, Chicago, Illinois, August 10, 1936, p. 8.
76 "Hollywood Czars Seek 'Agreement' in Mary Astor Suit," *Philadelphia Inquirer*, Philadelphia, Pennsylvania, August 9, 1936, p. 25.
77 UP: "Settlement Basis Found in Astor Suit," *Courier-Journal*, Louisville, Kentucky, August 12, 1938, p. 1.
78 Walter Winchell: "On Broadway," *Akron Beacon Journal*, Akron, Ohio, September 15, 1936, p. 25.
79 Sheilah Graham: "Garbo May Not Return to '*Camille*'," *Hartford Courant*, Hartford, Connecticut, September 22, 1936, p. 6.
80 Marcus Goodrich: *Delilah*, New York: Time Life Books, 1941 p. 39.
81 The Editors of *Time*: "Editor's Preface," *Delilah*, p. xiii.
82 Robert K. Hutchens: "People Who Read and Write," *New York Times Book Review*, undated clipping.
83 Ibid.
84 Christopher Andersen: *Jack and Jackie*, New York: Morrow, 1996, p. 81. Andersen interviewed Spalding.
85 Theodore C. Sorensen: *Kennedy*, New York: Harper & Row, 1965, p. 36.
86 Charles Spalding: Recorded interview by John F. Stewart, March 14, 1968, John F. Kennedy Library Oral History Program.
87 Aaron Couch, Erik Hayden: "'I Want You to Meet This Fella, Jack Kennedy': Hollywood Remembers JFK," *Hollywood Reporter*, November 22, 2013.
88 Andersen: *Jack and Jackie*, p. 81.

89 Hermione Eyre: "Hollywood's Sweetheart: Olivia de Havilland," *Evening Standard* online, March 18, 2010.

90 Andersen: *Jack and Jackie*, p. 81.

91 Eyre: "Hollywood's Sweetheart: Olivia de Havilland," *Evening Standard* online.

92 Ibid.

93 Ibid.

94 Andersen: *Jack and Jackie*, p. 81.

95 Jeane MacIntosh: "JFK's Love Affair With New York City," *New York Post*, November 18, 2013.

96 Wikipedia.

97 Christina Cassini: "Preface," *Gene Tierney* by Michael Vogel, Jefferson, North Carolina, 2005, p. ix.

98 Ralph Raffio: "25 Things You May Not Know About JFK," Purple Clover newsletter online.

99 Cassini: "Preface," *Gene Tierney*, p. ix.

100 Wikipedia.

101 Madden, editor: *Rediscoveries*.

102 Sheilah Graham: "Marriage Seems to Be Working Out Well for 'Old Maid' Olivia de Havilland," *Courier-Journal*, Louisville, Kentucky, December 1, 1946, p. 60.

103 Ibid.

104 Ibid.

105 Ibid.

106 Ibid.

107 Ibid.

108 Ibid.

109 Ibid.

110 Ibid.

111 Ibid.

112 Higham: *Sisters*, p. 176.

113 AP: "Actress Olivia de Havilland Ends Marriage on Anniversary," *La Crosse Tribune*, La Crosse, Wisconsin, August 27, 1952, p. 21.

114 Higham: *Sisters*, p. 176.

115 Ibid., pp. 176–177.

116 AP: "Olivia de Havilland Insists on Word 'Obey.'" *Anniston Star*, Anniston, Alabama, August 26, 1946, p. 1.

117 Graham: "Marriage seems . . . ," *Courier-Journal*.

118 Bob Thomas (AP): *Indiana Gazette*, Indiana, Pennsylvania, September 24, 1946, p. 6.

119 *Philadelphia Inquirer*, October 19, 1946, p. 13.

120 Ibid.

121 Madden, editor: *Rediscoveries*.

122 Fontaine: *No Bed of Roses*, p. 185.

123 Dorothy Kilgallen: *Pottstown Mercury*, Pottstown, Pennsylvania, September 13, 1946, p. 4.

124 Walter Winchell: *Akron Beacon Journal*, Akron, Ohio, April 14, 1953, p. 26.

125 *Los Angeles Times*: "Miss de Havilland Wins Divorce From Novelist," August 27, 1952, p. 33.
126 UP: "Olivia de Havilland Stars in Private Drama," *Detroit Free Press*, Detroit, Michigan, August 27, 1952. *Los Angeles Times*: "Miss de Havilland Wins Divorce From Novelist."
127 Bob Thomas (AP): "Olivia de Havilland Is Happily Married," *Lubbock Morning Avalanche*, November 5, 1946, p. 14.
128 Skolsky: *St. Louis Post-Dispatch*, November 9, 1946, p. 11.
129 Ibid.
130 Sheilah Graham: "Marriage Seems to Be Working Out Well for 'Old Maid' Olivia de Havilland."
131 Ibid.
132 Ibid.
133 Ibid.
134 Ibid.
135 "Olivia Admits Husband Is Boss," *Harrisburg Telegraph*, Harrisburg, Pennsylvania, March 25, 1947, p. 13.
136 Ibid.
137 Ibid.
138 Ibid.
139 Ibid.
140 Ibid.
141 Ibid.
142 Ibid.
143 Ibid.
144 AP: "Actress Olivia de Havilland Ends Marriage on Anniversary."
145 Leonard Lyons: "The Lyons Den," *Long Beach Independent*, Long Beach, California, April 18, 1953.
146 Hedda Hopper: "Olivia de Havilland Enjoys Bride's Role."
147 Ibid.
148 Virginia Vale: "Stardust," *Shiner Gazette*, Shiner, Texas, January 9, 1947, p. 7.
149 Ibid.
150 *Dixon Evening Telegraph*: Dixon, Illinois, September 6, 1949, p. 2.
151 Jack Lait Jr.: *Brooklyn Daily Eagle*, Brooklyn, New York, Dec. 17, 1946, p. 6.
152 AP: "Husbands of Oscar-Winning Olivia de Havilland and Joan Fontaine Jump Into Sisters' Old Feud," *San Bernardino County Sun*, San Bernardino, California, March 16, 1947, p. 1.
153 Ibid.
154 Ibid.
155 Louis Berg: "Joan Catches Up," *Indianapolis Star, Indianapolis, Indiana*, June 22, 1947, p. 99.
156 Ibid.
157 Ibid.

158 AP: "Olivia de Havilland Is Going to College," *Iowa City Press-Citizen,* August 1, 1947, p. 1.
159 *Evening Independent,* Massillon, Ohio, September 18, 1947, p. 4.
160 Fidler: *Joplin Globe,* Joplin, Missouri, September 3, 1947, p. 7.
161 *Lead Daily Call:* Lead, South Dakota, September 30, 1947, p. 4.

18. *TO EACH HIS OWN,* THE WITCH HUNT, *THE SNAKE PIT,* AND THE COVER OF *TIME*

1 Fishgall: *Jimmy Stewart,* p. 116.
2 Eliot: *Jimmy Stewart,* p. 203. Wikipedia: "Philip Van Doren Stern."
3 Eliot: *Jimmy Stewart,* p. 203.
4 Mikelbank: "Olivia de Havilland Opens Up . . . ."
5 Leamer: *As Time Goes By,* Harper & Row, p. 104.
6 Brackett: *It's the Pictures That Got Small,* p. 233.
7 Ibid., pp. 232, 246.
8 Ibid., p. 246.
9 Ibid., pp. 245–247.
10 Rogers: *Ginger, My Story,* p. 246.
11 Brackett: *It's the Pictures That Got Small,* p. 249.
12 Ibid., p. 248.
13 American Film Institute (AFI): "Dialogue on Film: Olivia de Havilland," December 1974.
14 Brackett: *It's the Pictures That Got Small,* p. 262.
15 Tony Thomas: *The Films of Olivia de Havilland,* p. 209.
16 Thirer: "Career Girl de Havilland Talks Films, Romance."
17 Johnson, NEA: *Pampa Daily News,* Pampa, Texas, March 18, 1947, p. 2.
18 Brackett: *It's the Pictures That Got Small,* pp. 264–265, 268–272, 213. *Jane Wyman's mother: Daily Notes,* Cannonsburg, Pennsylvania, December 11, 1944, p. 4.
19 *Variety:* December 31, 1945.
20 Brackett: *It's the Pictures That Got Small,* p. 297.
21 Emily Belser, INS: "Oscar Takes Spotlight for Better or Worse," *Cincinnati Enquirer,* Cincinnati, Ohio, March 30, 1955, p. 23. Academy Awards Acceptance Speech Database website. Kinn and Piazza, p. 81.
22 AP: *Des Moines Register,* March 15, 1947, p. 6. AP: "Frederic [*sic*] March, Olivia de Havilland Win . . . ," *Poughkeepsie Journal,* Poughkeepsie, New York, March 14, 1947, p. 8.
23 Parsons: "Olivia de Havilland to Make 'Snake Pit,'" *Morning News,* Wilmington, Delaware, March 17, 1947, p. 13.
24 Wikipedia: "De Havilland Aircraft Company."
25 Fontaine: *No Bed of Roses,* p. 154.
26 Bosley Crowther: "The Screen: *Dark Mirror,* New Mystery, at the Criterion," *New York Times,* October 19, 1946.
27 *Indianapolis Star:* Indianapolis, Indiana, February 24, 1947, p. 18.
28 Higham: *Sisters,* pp. 178–179.

Endnotes

29 *San Bernardino County Sun:* "Actress Sues Agents," San Bernardino, California, September 11, 1947, p. 1.

30 Edith Gwynn: *Pottstown Mercury*, Pottstown, Pennsylvania, August 26, 1953, p. 4.

31 John Meroney: "Olivia de Havilland Recalls Her Role in the Cold War," *Wall Street Journal*, September 7, 2006. Google: Macrohistory & World Timeline, "Ronald Reagan in Hollywood."

32 "Olivia Sprinting," *Daily Times-News*, Burlington, North Carolina, December 27, 1947, p. 10.

33 Thirer: "Career Girl de Havilland Talks of Films, Romance."

34 Bergman and Burgess: *Ingrid Bergman: My Story*, p. 332.

35 Rogers: *Ginger,* pp. 246–247.

36 Harry Niemeyer: *St. Louis Post-Dispatch*, p. 31.

37 Parsons: *Cumberland Sunday Times*, Cumberland, Maryland, August 15, 1948, p. 38.

38 Carroll: "In Hollywood," *Evening Independent*, Massillon, Ohio, September 10, 1947, p. 4.

39 Ibid.

40 Parsons: *Cumberland Sunday Times*, Cumberland, Maryland, August 15, 1948, p. 38.

41 *Time:* "Cinema: Shocker," December 20, 1948, p. 1 (online transcript).

42 Ibid.

43 Ibid.

44 AP: "Actress Olivia de Havilland Ends Marriage on Anniversary."

45 INS: "Olivia Sobs Cruelty Story for Divorce, Son's Custody," *Tennessean*, Nashville, Tennessee, August 27, 1952, p. 7.

46 Bosley Crowther: "'*Snake Pit,*' Study of Mental Ills Based on Mary Jane Ward's Novel, Opens at Rivoli," *New York Times*, New York, November 11, 1948.

47 AP: "Olivia de Havilland Seriously Sick," *Abilene Reporter-News*, Abilene, Texas, April 4, 1949, p. 1.

48 Johnson, NEA: "Hollywood Scene," *La Crosse Tribune*, La Crosse, Wisconsin, August 27, 1952, p. 20.

49 *Morning News:* "Olivia de Havilland Has Another Relapse," Wilmington, Delaware, April 5, 1949, p. 14. *Decatur Daily Review*, Decatur, Illinois, April 5, 1949, p. 6.

50 *Pottstown Mercury:* Pottstown, Pennsylvania, April 8, 1949, p. 4.

51 AP: "Olivia de Havilland of Films Is Improving," *Macon Chronicle-Herald*, Macon, Missouri, April 20, 1949, p. 1.

52 AP: "Olivia de Havilland Becomes Mother," *Winona Republican-Herald*, Winona, Minnesota, September 28, 1949, p. 1.

53 UP: "Olivia de Havilland Gives Birth to Son," *News-Herald*, Franklin, Pennsylvania, September 28, 1949, p. 1.

54 AP: "Actress Olivia de Havilland Ends Marriage on Anniversary." Higham: *Sisters*, p. 196.

55 Ibid.

56 Ibid.

57 *Independent Record*, Helena, Montana, December 24, 1948, p. 4.

58 Parsons: *Cumberland Sunday Times*, Cumberland, Maryland, August 15, 1948, p. 38.

59 Munn: *Jimmy Stewart*, p. 180.
60 Ibid.

19: WORKING WITH MONTGOMERY CLIFT, RALPH RICHARDSON, AND WILLIAM WYLER IN *THE HEIRESS*

1 *The Latter Films of William Wyler, Sequence*, No. 13 (1951), p. 22. Michael A. Anderegg, *William Wyler*, Boston: Twayne Publishers, 1979, p. 12.
2 Olivia de Havilland video interview, Olivia de Havilland fan club page.
3 Ibid.
4 Patricia Bosworth: *Montgomery Clift*, New York: Harcourt Brace Jovanovich, 1978, p. 138.
5 Robert LaGuardia: *Monty*, New York: Primus, 1977, p. 71.
6 Matzen: *Errol and Olivia*, p. 68, quoting Olivia de Havilland in *From a Life of Adventure* by Tony Thomas.
7 Bergman and Burgess: *Ingrid Bergman: My Story*, p. 102.
8 Academy of Achievement: "The Last Belle of Cinema."
9 *supreme symbol*: John Bainbridge: *Garbo*, New York: Dell, 1955, p. 9. *just get up there*: Academy of Achievement online: "The Last Belle of Cinema."
10 Academy of Achievement online: "The Last Belle of Cinema."
11 Hopper papers, September 2, 1952, Margaret Herrick Library, Academy of Motion Picture Arts and Sciences.
12 Gloria Swanson: *Swanson on Swanson*, New York: Random House, 1980, pp. 480–481, 485.
13 Graham: *Indianapolis Star*, May 8, 1948.
14 Turner Classic Movies web page: TCM Film Archive, "The Heiress."
15 Patricia Clary, United Press Hollywood Correspondent: "Hollywood," *Santa Cruz Sentinel*, Santa Cruz, California, July 5, 1948, p. 6.
16 Ibid.
17 Heffernan, NEA: *Akron Beacon Journal*, July 5, 1947, p. 6.
18 Harrison Carroll: *Evening Independent*, Massillon, Ohio, August 30, 1948, p. 4.
19 Bob Thomas (AP): "Ann Sheridan Continues to Live Alone and Likes It," *San Bernardino Sun-Telegram*, April 2, 1950, p. 4.
20 Louella O. Parsons: *Cumberland News*, Cumberland, Maryland, March 8, 1950, p. 17. "Olivia de Havilland in Guest Appearance on Parsons Program," *Jackson Sun*, Jackson, Tennessee, March 5, 1950.
21 Louella O. Parsons (INS): "Lana Turner and Ricardo Montalban," *Albuquerque Journal*, Albuquerque, New Mexico, May 8, 1950, p. 8.
22 Crowther: "'*The Heiress*,' With Olivia de Havilland in Leading Role, Arrives at Music Hall," *New York Times*, New York, October 7, 1949.
23 Hopper papers, September 2, 1952, Margaret Herrick Library, Academy of Motion Picture Arts and Sciences.
24 Ibid.
25 Ibid.
26 Hopper: *Detroit Free Press*, Detroit, Michigan, December 20, 1948, p. 28.

27 Graham: *Indianapolis Star*, Indianapolis, Indiana, November 13, 1948, p. 14.
28 Bosley Crowther: "The Screen in Review: Moving Story of War Against Japan, '*Three Came Home*,' Is Shown at the Astor," *New York Times*, New York, February 21, 1950.
29 Johnson: *Miami Daily News-Record*, Miami, Oklahoma, March 1, 1950, p. 3.
30 AP: "Predict Winners," *Beatrice Daily Sun*, Beatrice, Nebraska, March 22, p. 5.
31 AP: "'Iron Curtain' Between Joan and Olivia Remains Down," *Cumberland News*, Cumberland, Maryland, March 25, 1950, p. 1.
32 Ibid.
33 Earl Wilson: *Detroit Free Press*, Michigan, February 5, 1950, p. 19.
34 Ibid.
35 Ibid.
36 Ibid.
37 Ibid.
38 "First Academy Awards Telecast on NBC," This Day in History [March 19] *Daily Mail* web page.
39 Kinn and Piazza: *The Academy Awards*, pp. 11–12, 98.
40 YouTube video.
41 Ibid.
42 Ibid.
43 Missy Schwartz: "The Last Star: An Evening With Olivia de Havilland," *Entertainment* website, January 29, 2015.
44 YouTube video.
45 IMDb online: "Olivia de Havilland," Biography.
46 Bob Thomas (AP): "Olivia de Havilland and Broderick Crawford . . .," *Ithaca Journal*, Ithaca, New York, March 24, 1950, p. 1.
47 Thomas (AP): "Olivia de Havilland and Broderick Crawford . . . ."
48 Kass: *Olivia de Havilland*, p. 103.
49 Ibid.
50 "Olivia de Havilland Wins Coveted Movie Award for Acting," *Delta Democrat-Times*, Greenville, Mississippi, March 24, 1950, p. 1.
51 UP: "Olivia de Havilland Anxious to Resume Work in Filmland," *Shamokin News-Dispatch*, Shamokin, Pennsylvania, March 27, 1950, p. 11.
52 Ibid.
53 Ibid.
54 Ibid.
55 Ibid.
56 Ibid. "Miss de Havilland Wins Divorce From Novelist."
57 AP: "Actress Olivia de Havilland Ends Marriage on Anniversary."
58 *Los Angeles Times:* "Miss de Havilland Wins Divorce From Novelist."

20. *A STREETCAR NAMED DESIRE*

1 Johnson: "Erskine Johnson in Hollywood," *Shamokin News-Dispatch*, Shamokin, Pennsylvania, April 19, 1950, p. 6.

2 Erskine Johnson: "In Hollywood," *Pampa Daily News*, Pampa, Texas, December 21, 1949, p. 2.

3 AP: "Actress Olivia de Havilland Ends Marriage on Anniversary."

4 Graham: *The Des Moines Register*, Des Moines, Iowa, June 3, 1948, p. 16.

5 Parsons: *The Democrat and Chronicle*, Rochester, New York, September 3, 1947.

6 Matzen: *Errol and Olivia*, p. 185.

7 Hopper papers, September 2, 1952, Margaret Herrick Library, Academy of Motion Picture Arts and Sciences.

8 Mason Wiley and Damien Bono: *Inside Oscar*, New York: Ballentine, 1993.

9 Sheilah Graham: *Indianapolis Star*, Indianapolis, Indiana, December 29, 1952, p. 14.

10 UP: "De Havilland Effects a Reconciliation With Miss Fontaine on His Birthday": *Brooklyn Daily Eagle*, September 1, 1950, p. 1.

11 Jimmie Fidler: *Nevada State Journal*, Reno, Nevada, September 12, 1950, p. 4.

12 "Uncooperative Actors of 1950 Are Named": *Deadwood Pioneer Times*, Deadwood, North Dakota, November 26, 1950, p. 5.

13 UP: "It's Golden Apples for Loretta, Alan," *Berkshire Eagle*, Berkshire, Massachusetts, December 14, 1950, p. 34.

14 Hopper papers, September 2, 1952, Margaret Herrick Library, Academy of Motion Picture Arts and Sciences.

15 Ibid.

16 Ibid.

17 Ibid.

18 Ibid.

19 Ibid.

20 Thomson: *Showman*, p. 552.

21 Ibid.

22 Ibid., p. 502.

23 Scott McKee: "Behind the Camera on *Streetcar*," TCM Film Article, August 5, 2016.

24 Thomson: *Showman*, p. 553.

25 Aline Bosley: "Star of 'Streetcar' Returns As Supporting Film Actress," *Courier-Journal*, Louisville, Kentucky, November 30, 1949, p. 19.

26 Walker: *Vivien*: p. 199.

27 Dorothy Kilgallen: *Times Herald*, Olean, New York, January 23, 1950, p. 8.

28 *Times Herald*: Olean, New York, January 23, 1950, p. 6.

29 Hopper papers, September 2, 1952, Margaret Herrick Library, Academy of Motion Picture Arts and Sciences.

30 Ibid.

31 Ibid.

32 Ibid.

33 Ibid.

34 Ibid.

35 Ibid.

36 Maroney: "Olivia de Havilland Is Setting the Record Straight," *Wall Street Journal*, September 7, 2006.

37 Bob Thomas, AP: "Hollywood News, Views," *Green Bay Press-Gazette*, Green Bay, Wisconsin, August 7, 1948, p. 15.

38 IMDb online: "Olivia de Havilland," Biography.

39 Parsons: *Arizona Republic*, Phoenix, Arizona, December 23, 1949, p. 25.

40 Erskine Johnson: *Pampa Daily News,* Pampa, Texas, February 15, 1950, p. 8.

41 Bob Thomas: "Film Director Says Actors Are Really Children," *Ottawa Journal*, Ottawa, Canada, March 23, 1950, p. 29.

42 Graham: *Indianapolis Star*, Indianapolis, Indiana, July 23, 1947, p. 14.

43 Thomson: *Showman*, p. 514.

44 Johnson: *Akron Beacon Journal*, Akron, Ohio, November 12, 1950, p. 30.

45 Jack Hawkins: Tony Thomas in *The Films of Olivia de Havilland*, p. 40, cites Hawkins's autobiography *Anything for a Quiet Life* (Stein and Day, New York, 1974). *Olivia would one day reveal in court*: AP: "Actress Olivia de Havilland Ends Marriage on Anniversary."

46 Mark Barron (AP): *Courier-Journal*, Louisville, Kentucky, November 26, 1950, p. 81.

47 Sheilah Graham: "Hollywood Today," *Courier-Journal*, Louisville, Kentucky, June 22, 1952, p. 70.

48 Simon Brambles: "'Love's Better Than Ever' Due With Liz' Divorce," *Salt Lake Tribune*, Salt Lake City, Utah, June 6, 1951, p. 25.

49 Jack Gaver, UP: "Up and Down Broadway," *Terre Haute Tribune*, Terre Haute, Indiana, January 4, 1951, p. 4. *Jack Hawkins commented . . . Glenville's attention*: Tony Thomas: *The Films of Olivia de Havilland*, p. 40.

50 *Cincinnati Inquirer*: Cincinnati, Ohio, November 7, 1950, p. 16.

51 "*Goodrich kept the press away*": Jack Hawkins: Tony Thomas in *The Films of Olivia de Havilland* cites Hawkins's autobiography *Anything for a Quiet Life* (Stein and Day, New York, 1974). George Jean Nathan: Higham, *Sisters*, p. 206.

52 Kass: *Olivia de Havilland*, p. 124.

53 *Jack was awfully . . . saying a word*: "Jack's the Big Boy in England Now," *Truth Sunday Magazine* (3342), New South Wales, Australia, February 14, 1954, p. 19 (see footnotes in Wikipedia: "Jack Hawkins"). *To complicate matters . . . just not interested*: Tony Thomas: *The Films of Olivia de Havilland* cites Hawkins's autobiography *Anything for a Quiet Life*. *Miss de Havilland will . . . to set it up*: Leonard Lyons: "Broadway Medley," *The Times*, San Mateo, California, April 20, 1951, p. 16.

54 Lyons: "Broadway Medley."

55 "De Havilland Here Today at Bushnell in Shaw Comedy," *Hartford Courant*, Hartford, Connecticut, April 5, 1952, p. 10.

56 Wood Soanes: "Olivia Shakes off Critics, Plunges on With *Candida*," *Oakland Tribune*, Oakland, California, January 29, 1952, p. 17.

57 Ibid.

58 Ibid.

59 Myles Standish: "A Warmer, Gayer Olivia de Havilland, " *St. Louis Post-Dispatch*, May 31, 1964, p. 86.

60 Ibid.

61 "The Jester," *Oakland Tribune*, Oakland, California, July 31, 1953, p. 48.

62 Donald Kirkley: "Benjamin Briggs Goodrich Is Pal of Olivia de Havilland," *Baltimore Sun*, Baltimore, Maryland, March 17, 1952, p. 9.

63 Ibid.

64 Ibid.

65 Ibid.

66 Wood Soanes: "Olivia Shakes off Critics, Plunges on With *Candida*."

67 Standish: "A Warmer, Gayer Olivia de Havilland."

68 Ibid.

69 Sheilah Graham: "Hollywood Today," *Courier-Journal*, Louisville, Kentucky, June 22, 1952, p. 70.

70 *322 performances*: Soanes: "Olivia Shakes off Critics." *treasure hunt*: Walter Winchell: "New Arrivals," *Salt Lake Telegram*, May 3, 1952, p. 3.

71 "De Havilland Here Today at Bushnell in Shaw Comedy," *Hartford Courant*, Hartford, Connecticut, April 5, 1952, p. 10.

72 *Miss de Havilland is a beautiful*: Walter Winchell quoting Atkinson: *Salt Lake Telegram*, Salt Lake City, Utah, May 3, 1952, p. 3. George Jean Nathan: Higham, *Sisters*, pp. 206–207.

73 Kass: *Olivia de Havilland*, p. 124.

74 Wikipedia: "Ron Randell."

75 *Bashful Olivia de Havilland*: Walter Winchell: *St. Louis Post-Dispatch*, St. Louis, Missouri, May 18, 1952, p. 71. *The most insulting*: Winchell: *Salt Lake Telegram*, Salt Lake City, Utah, May 3, 1952, p. 3.

76 Kass: *Olivia de Havilland*, p. 140.

77 Erskine Johnson: *Portsmouth Herald*, Portsmouth, New Hampshire, August 28, 1952, p. 13.

78 Erskine Johnson (NEA): "In Hollywood," *Independent Record*, Helena, Montana, August 27, 1952, p. 7.

79 Stephen Barrett and William T. Jarvis: *The Health Robbers*, Prometheus Books, p. 349, listed on Wikipedia as the source for Garbo and Acosta's visits with Hauser and Frey.

80 Joshua Logan: *Movie Stars, Real People, and Me*, New York: Delacorte Press, 1978, p. 92. Wikipedia: "Valentina, fashion designer."

81 McGilligan: *George Cukor: A Double Life*, p. 232.

82 UP: "Olivia de Havilland Doubts She'll Try Marriage Again," *Great Falls Tribune*, Great Falls, Montana, August 3, 1952, p. 27.

83 Ibid.

84 Ibid.

85 Jimmie Fidler: *News Press*, Fort Meyers, Florida, June 28, 1952, p. 4.

86 Tony Thomas: *The Films of Olivia de Havilland*, p. 222.

87 Bosley Crowther: "'*My Cousin Rachel*' Presented at the Rivoli," *New York Times*, New York, December 26, 1952.

88 Richard Burton: *The Richard Burton Diaries*, New Haven: Yale University Press, 2012, p. 283.

89 Ibid.

90 *Pittsburgh Press:* "Olivia Returns to Screen," Pittsburgh, Pennsylvania, January 2, 1953, p. 17.
91 Mildred Martin: "*My Cousin Rachel* Opens at Boyd," *Philadelphia Inquirer*, Philadelphia, Pennsylvania, December 26, 1952, p. 32.

21. GRACE UNDER PRESSURE

1 *Los Angeles Times:* "Miss de Havilland Wins Divorce from Novelist."
2 INS: *Star Tribune*, Minneapolis, Minnesota, May 18, 1952, p. 7.
3 Hedda Hopper: "Olivia de Havilland to Star in *Cousin Rachel*," *Los Angeles Times*, May 30, 1952, p. 48.
4 Walter Winchell: *St. Louis Post-Dispatch*, St. Louis, Missouri, June 5, 1952, p. 56.
5 Olivia de Havilland: *Every Frenchman Has One*, New York: Crown, 1961, 1962, 2016, p. 12.
6 UP: "Olivia de Havilland Stars in Private Drama," *Detroit Free Press*, Detroit, Michigan, August 27, 1952, p. 5.
7 Ibid.
8 Ibid.
9 INS: "Olivia Sobs Cruelty Story for Divorce, Son's Custody."
10 *Los Angeles Times*: "Miss de Havilland Wins Divorce From Novelist."
11 UP: "Olivia de Havilland Stars in Private Drama."
12 AP: "Actress Olivia de Havilland Ends Marriage on Anniversary."
13 Ibid.
14 UP: "Olivia de Havilland Stars in Private Drama."
15 Sheilah Graham: "Hollywood Today," *Courier-Journal*, Louisville, Kentucky, June 22, 1952, p. 70.
16 Ibid.
17 Ibid.
18 UP: "Olivia de Havilland Doubts She'll Try Marriage Again," *Great Falls Tribune*, Great Falls, Montana, August 3, 1952, p. 27.
19 Ibid.
20 Ibid.
21 Harrison Carroll: "Behind the Scenes in Hollywood, *Lancaster Eagle-Gazette*, Lancaster, Ohio, September 20, 1952, p. 6.
22 UP: "Olivia de Havilland Doubts She'll Try Marriage Again."
23 Wood Soanes: "Olivia Finds Broadway Stage a Poor Outlet for Her Talents," *Oakland Tribune*, July 18, 1952, p. 20.
24 Louella O. Parsons (INS): *Lubbock Avalanche-Journal*, Lubbock, Texas, October 26, 1952, p. 38.
25 Edwards: *Vivien Leigh*, p. 193
26 Ibid., pp. 195, 199.
27 Alexander Walker: *Vivien*, New York: Grove Press, 1987, p. 214.
28 Meyers: *John Huston*, p. 90.
29 Ibid.
30 Ibid.

31 Erskine Johnson (NEA): "In Hollywood," *Jacksonville Journal*, Jacksonville, Florida, December 25, 1952.

32 Hopper papers, September 2, 1952, Margaret Herrick Library, Academy of Motion Picture Arts and Sciences.

33 *Over a cup of tea*: Erskine Johnson: "Hollywood," *Panama City Herald News*, Panama City, Florida, December 23, 1952, p. 4. *"resisting" a peace offer*: Sheilah Graham: "Hollywood Today," *Arizona Daily Star*, Tucson, Arizona, December 4, 1952, p. 19. *forget "any unpleasantness . . . which pleased Joan very much"*: Louella Parsons: *Courier-Post*, Camden, New Jersey, December 1, 1952, p. 26.

34 Harrison Carroll: "Hollywood," *Evening Independent*, Massillon, Ohio, December 13, 1952, p. 4.

35 Ibid.

36 Ibid.

37 Ibid.

38 *they have made up now*: Harrison Carroll: *Call-Leader*, Elwood, Indiana, March 18, 1943, p. 7. *best pals for years*: Jimmie Fidler: *Times*, Shreveport, Louisiana, February 23, 1943, p. 18. *rowing and making up*: Hedda Hopper: *Los Angeles Times*, Los Angeles, California, March 10, 1943, p. 23. Also see Sidney Skolsky: *Cincinnati Enquirer*, Cincinnati, Ohio, March 7, 1943, p. 57.

39 "Actress Olivia de Havilland Cements Fame": *Los Angeles Times*, Los Angeles, California, December 19, 1952.

40 Graham: "Hollywood," *Pittsburgh Post-Gazette*, Pittsburgh, Pennsylvania, January 3, 1953, p. 5.

41 Ibid., p. 11.

42 Graham: "Hollywood," *Pittsburgh Post-Gazette*, Pittsburgh, Pennsylvania, January 9, 1953, p. 10.

43 Gwynn: "Hollywood," *Pottstown Mercury*, Pottstown, Pennsylvania, January 24, 1953, p. 12.

44 Carroll: "Behind the Scenes in Hollywood," *Lethbridge Herald*, Lethbridge, Alberta, Canada, November 12, 1953, p. 1.

45 *Mitchum was willing*: Sheilah Graham: *Indianapolis Star*, Indianapolis, Indiana, October 24, 1953, p. 10. *because they couldn't land*: Dorothy Kilgallen: *Arizona Republic*, Phoenix, Arizona, November 28, 1953, p. 19.

46 Manners: *Arizona Republic*, Phoenix, Arizona, November 9, 1953, p. 17.

47 *Rhinelander Daily News:* Rhinelander, Wisconsin, April 10, 1954, p. 4.

48 On August 7, 1954, *New York Times* critic Bosley Crowther called *Human Desire* "flat."

49 Carroll: "Behind the Scenes in Hollywood," *Lethbridge Herald*, Lethbridge, Alberta, Canada November 12, 1953, p. 1.

50 Kilgallen: "The Voice of Broadway," *St. Louis Post-Dispatch*, St. Louis, Missouri, February 9, 1953, p. 28.

51 Gerald Clarke: *Capote*, New York: Simon and Schuster, 1988, p. 240. John Huston: *An Open Book*, p. 247.

52 Graham: "News Flashes," *Pittsburgh Post-Gazette*, Pittsburgh, Pennsylvania, February 25, 1953, p. 6.
53 AP: "Olivia de Havilland, Agency Settle Suit," *Lubbock Evening Journal*, Lubbock, Texas, March 4, 1953, p. 5.
54 Erskine Johnson: "Howard Duff to Costar in Film With Wife Ida Lupino," *San Bernardino County Sun*, San Bernardino, California, February 23, 1953, p. 4.
55 Hedda Hopper: *Tucson Daily Citizen*, Tucson, Arizona, December 24, 1952, p. 11.
56 Erskine Johnson (NEA): *Panama City News-Herald*, Panama City, Florida, November 11, 1952, p. 4.
57 Hopper: "Film Version of Graham Greene's *The End of the Affair* Bogs Down," *Pittsburgh Press*: Pittsburgh, Pennsylvania, April 5, 1953, p. 71.
58 Frances Conant Richards: "Early Spring," *St. Louis Post-Dispatch*, April 20, 1953, p. 38.
59 "Peron Film Slated," *Lubbock Morning Avalanche*, Lubbock, Texas, August 22, 1952, p. 36. *There may* NEVER: NEA, *Lubbock Avalanche-Journal*, Lubbock, Texas, August 17, 1952, p. 53.
60 Johnson: "Erskine Johnson in Hollywood," *Courier News*, Blytheville, Arkansas, March 3, 1953, p. 18.
61 Graham: "Olivia de Havilland Seems Happy With Life in Paris," *Courier-Journal*, Louisville, Kentucky, December 11, 1955, p. 58.
62 De Havilland: *Every Frenchman Has One*, New York: Popular Library, 1961, 1962, p. 10.
63 Hopper: "De Carlo . . . ," *Los Angeles Times*, Los Angeles, California, June 11, 1955, p. 18.
64 Pierre Galante: *Chanel*, Chicago: Henry Regnery, 1973, pp. 6–7.
65 Graham: *Courier-Journal*, December 11, 1955, p. 58.
66 Ibid.
67 De Havilland: *Every Frenchman Has One*, Crown, p. 16.
68 Ibid., p. 14.
69 Ibid., p. 16.
70 Kilgallen: "Voice of Broadway," *News-Herald, Franklin*, Pennsylvania, April 13, 1953, p. 4.
71 Barbara Walters: *Audition*, New York: Random House, 2008, p. 109.
72 "Names in the News: Ingrid Lets Rossellini Race": *Ogden Standard-Examiner*, Ogden, Utah, April 17, 1953, p. 1.
73 *Akron Beacon Journal*: Akron, Ohio, September 10, 1953, p. 33.
74 De Havilland: *Every Frenchman Has One*, Crown, p. 16.

22. MARRIAGE FRENCH STYLE

1 UP: "Olivia de Havilland Weds French Writer in Town's Biggest Event," *San Bernardino County Sun*, San Bernardino, California, April 3, 1955, p. 5.
2 UP: "De Havilland Rites Rouse Tiny Village," *Corvallis Gazette-Times*, Corvallis, Oregon, April 2, 1955, p. 1. *Bristol Daily Courier*, Bristol, Pennsylvania, October 1, 1954, p. 4.

3 Carroll: "Hollywood," *Evening Independent*, Massillon, Ohio, March 18, 1955, p. 4.
4 Parsons, INS: "Katy Jurado . . . ," *Marysville Journal-Tribune*, Marysville, Ohio, March 17, 1955, p. 11.
5 UP: "Olivia de Havilland Weds French Writer in Town's Biggest Event."
6 UP: "Olivia de Havilland's Wedding Date Set," *Albany Democrat-Herald,* Albany, Oregon, March 4, 1955, p. 1.
7 AP: "Olivia de Havilland Wed in France," *Ottawa Journal*, Ottawa, Ontario, Canada, April 2, 1955, p. 1. Some newspapers reported the wedding took place in the Town Hall.
8 UP: "Olivia de Havilland Weds French Writer in Town's Biggest Event."
9 Dorothy Kilgallen: "The Voice of Broadway," *Des Moines Register*, Des Moines, Iowa, January 15, 1955, p. 2.
10 *Sydney Morning Herald*: Sydney, New South Wales, Australia, February 26, 1956, p. 71.
11 Kilgallen: *Cincinnati Inquirer*, Cincinnati, Ohio, May 1, 1955, p. 162.
12 UP: "De Havilland Rites Rouse Tiny Village," *Corvallis Gazette-Times*, Corvallis, Oregon, April 2, 1955, p. 1. "Olivia de Havilland Weds French Writer; Whole Village Turns Out for Nuptials," *Delaware County Daily Times*, Chester, Pennsylvania, April 2, 1955, p. 1.
13 Ed Sullivan: "Look for Changes . . . ," *Detroit Free Press*, March 15, 1955, p. 32.
14 *Los Angeles Times*: "New Triumph Seen for Olivia de Havilland," January 23, 1955, p. 104.
15 Earl Wilson: "It Happened Last Night," *Winona Daily News*, Winona, Minnesota, May 11, 1955, p. 4. *Pittsburgh Post-Gazette*, May 13, 1955, p. 4.
16 Carroll: "Behind the Scenes in Hollywood," *Lethbridge Herald*, Lethbridge, Alberta, Canada, January 19, 1955, p. 3.
17 "Shadrack Arrives": *Des Moines Register*, Des Moines, Iowa, February 11, 1955, p. 6. *A gift from John Huston*: Matzen: *Errol and Olivia*, p. 184.
18 *Courier-Journal*: "TV's Money May Hook Her Yet"," Louisville, Kentucky, April 11, 1965, p. 162.
19 Allen B. Dodd (INS): "Olivia de Havilland Plans to Live in Paris," *Kingsport Times*, Kingsport, Tennessee, March 17, 1955, p. 5.
20 Leonard Lyons: *Long Beach Independent*, Long Beach, California, March 22, 1955, p. 14.
21 AP: "Olivia de Havilland Likes Parisian Role," *Asbury Park Press*, Asbury Park, New Jersey, May 28, 1961, p. 30.
22 AP: "Olivia de Havilland Likes Parisian Role."
23 Ibid.
24 Hopper: *Los Angeles Times*, Los Angeles, California, July 4, 1955, p. 29.
25 Kilgallen: *Arizona Republic*, Phoenix, Arizona, June 30, 1955, p. 25.
26 AP, *Daily Mail*: "Timelessly Elegant at 100: *Gone With the Wind*'s Olivia de Havilland celebrates milestone today and finally breaks silence on Golden Age of Hollywood's most infamous sibling rivalry," July 1, 2016.
27 Aline Mosby, UP: "This Star Insists . . . ," *Brooklyn Daily Eagle*, Brooklyn, New York, October 31, 1954, p. 29.

28 Graham: "Olivia de Havilland Seems Happy With Life in Paris," *Courier-Journal*, Louisville, Kentucky, December 11, 1955, p. 58.
29 *Indianapolis Star*, Indianapolis, Indiana: April 9, 1956, p. 17.
30 Keyes: *Scarlett O'Hara's Younger Sister*, p. 169.
31 Graham: "Olivia de Havilland Seems Happy With Life in Paris." *Cincinnati Enquirer*, Cincinnati, Ohio, March 13, 1958, p. 62.
32 De Havilland: *Every Frenchman Has One*, Crown, p. 19.
33 UP: "Olivia Becomes Platinum Blonde": *Racine Journal Times Sunday Bulletin*, Racine, Wisconsin, December 12, 1954, p. 50.
34 *Brooklyn Daily Eagle*: Brooklyn, New York, January 11, 1955, p. 7.
35 Carroll: "Hollywood," *Evening Independent*, Massillon, Ohio, October 21, 1954, p. 4.
36 Ibid.
37 Ibid.
38 Ibid.
39 Ibid.
40 UP: "Olivia Becomes Platinum Blonde."
41 Ibid.
42 Mosby, UP: "Drinking on Set Angers Star de Havilland," *El Paso Herald-Post*, December 21, 1954, p. 23.
43 Ibid.
44 *Mt. Vernon Register-News*: Mt. Vernon, Illinois, February 16, 1955, p. 21.
45 Bosley Crowther: "Screen: *Not as a Stranger* at Capitol," *New York Times*, New York, June 29, 1955.

23. GRACE KELLY AND THE JET SET

1 Kilgallen: *Des Moines Register*, Des Moines, Iowa, September 28, 1955, p. 2.
2 J. Randy Taraborrelli: *Once Upon a Time*, New York: Warner Books, 2003, pp. 31–38.
3 Taraborrelli: *Once Upon a Time*, p. 50.
4 Ibid., p. 87.
5 James Spada: *Grace*, New York: Doubleday, 1987, pp. 167–168, 236.
6 "Mad for Monaco" web site: "Onassis vs. Grimaldi," December 16, 2010.
7 "The Esoteric Curiosa Knowledge Is Power" web page includes the Kilgallen article as it appeared in the January 10, 1956, edition of the *Lakeland Ledger*. On the web page the heading is "H.R.H. Princess Marilyn of Monaco," subheadings: "Prince Rainier and the Belles" and "Dorothy Kilgallen Reports on Broadway."
8 Ibid.
9 Ibid.
10 Spada: *Grace*, p. 236.
11 Peter Mikelbank: "The Incredible Story of How Olivia de Havilland Introduced Grace Kelly to Prince Rainier of Monaco," *People*, May 16, 2017, available online.
12 Ibid.
13 Jean-Pierre Aumont: *Sun and* Shadow, New York: W.W. Norton, 1977, pp. 44-45.
14 Ibid., p. 142.
15 *People*: "When Princess . . . ," February 12, 1996.

16 The official summary of Kelly's life approved by her son in 2006, cited by Spoto: *High Society*, New York: Harmony Books, 2009, p. 205, quoting Yann-Brice Dherbier and Pierre Henri Verlhac: *Grace Kelly—A Life in Pictures*, London: Pavilion, 2006, p. 12. Also see Jean-Pierre Aumont: *Sun and Shadow*, New York: W.W. Norton, 1977, p. 169.

17 Mikelbank: "The Incredible Story of How Olivia de Havilland Introduced Grace Kelly to Prince Rainier of Monaco."

18 Ibid.

19 Mikelbank: "The Incredible Story of How Olivia de Havilland Introduced Grace Kelly to Prince Rainier of Monaco."

20 Parsons: "In Hollywood," *Daily Times*, New Philadelphia, Ohio, February 9, 1956, p. 4.

21 Mikelbank: "The Incredible Story of How Olivia de Havilland Introduced Grace Kelly to Prince Rainier of Monaco."

22 IMDb online: "Grace Kelly," Biography.

23 Taraborrelli: *Once Upon a Time*, pp. 368–369.

24 Ibid., p. 296.

25 Hopper: *Valley Morning Star*, Harlingen, Texas, July 25, 1955, p. 8.

26 Sam Staggs: *Inventing Elsa Maxwell*, New York: St. Martin's Press, 2012, pp. 60–61.

27 AP: "Elsa 'Throws' Cruise Party," *Bridgeport Telegram*, Bridgeport, Connecticut, August 28, 1955, p. 7.

28 International: *Medford Mail Tribune*, Medford, Oregon, September 6, 1955, p. 14.

29 UP: *St. Louis Post-Dispatch*, St. Louis, Missouri, September 11, 1955, p. 29.

30 Graham: *Indianapolis Star*, Indianapolis, Indiana, September 19, 1955, p. 10.

31 Bob Thomas, AP: "Olivia de Havilland Stars in Film *Not as a Stranger*," *Herald and News*, Klamath Falls, Oregon, September 20, 1954, p. 2.

32 Hopper: *Los Angeles Times*, Los Angeles, California, July 4, 1955, p. 29.

33 Hopper: "Grace Kelly to Keep New York Apartment," *Los Angeles Times*, Los Angeles, California, February 29, 1956, p. 69.

34 *Post-Standard*, Syracuse, New York: "Fashion by Dior," September 14, 1956, p. 17.

35 *Los Angeles Times*, Los Angeles, California: "Lavish Wardrobe Worn by Actress in New Feature," August 6, 1956, p. 38.

36 "Expert Coaching": *Des Moines Register*, Des Moines, Iowa, November 24, 1955, p. 17.

37 *Ames Daily Tribune*: Ames, Iowa, January 28, 1956, p. 8.

38 Ibid.

39 *Courier-Journal*, Louisville, Kentucky, December 11, 1955, p. 58.

40 Ibid.

41 Ibid.

42 Gloria Swanson, UP: "Former Actress Finds Movie Making in Paris Real Fun," *Corvallis Gazette-Times*, Corvallis, Oregon, October 14, 1955, p. 3.

43 Crowther: "Screen: *The Ambassador's Daughter* Arrives," *New York Times*, August 30, 1956.

44 Graham: "In Hollywood," *St. Louis Post-Dispatch*, St. Louis, Missouri, April 5, 1956, p. 69.

45 Heritage Images web page, July 21, 1956.

46 Bower: "A Happy Voice Speaks From Italy," *Detroit Free Press*, Detroit, Michigan, September 2, 1956, p. 8.

47 Ibid.

48 UP: "Film Stars Suffer Mild Burns in Cedar City Fire," *Ogden Standard-Examiner, Ogden, Utah,* September 25, 1957, p. 8.

49 Winchell: "On Broadway," *Courier-Post*, Camden, New Jersey, October 14, 1957, p. 20.

50 Matzen: *Errol and Olivia*, p. 190, cites Pierce: "Olivia de Havilland Returns to Saratoga."

51 Ibid.

52 Matzen: *Errol and Olivia*, p. 190, cites Erskine Johnson: "Olivia Recalls 2 Private Wars," *Los Angeles Mirror*, June 26, 1961.

53 Meyers: *Inherited Risk,* p. 295.

54 John Huston: *An Open Book*, pp. 275–279.

55 Meyers: *Inherited Risk*, p. 268. Wikipedia: "Errol Flynn."

56 Meyers: *Inherited Risk*, p. 275.

57 *New York Times*: "Moving Sentiment," July 2, 1958.

58 Thomas Wiseman: "I'll Tell You What's Wrong in Hollywood," *Detroit Free Press*, Detroit, Michigan, November 29, 1959, p. 36.

59 Leonard Lyons: "Bum Officers, Good in Movies," *Times*, San Mateo, California, January 8, 1958, p. 28.

60 Dorothy Kilgallen: "Voice of Broadway," *Shamokin News-Dispatch*, Shamokin, Pennsylvania, January 22, 1958, p. 4.

61 Dorothy Kilgallen: *Shamokin News-Dispatch*, Shamokin, Pennsylvania, March 6, 1958, p. 6.

62 Johnson: *Corpus Christi Caller-Times*, Corpus Christi, Texas, March 17, 1960, p. 29.

63 Vernon Scott: "Olivia de Havilland Back in Hollywood," *Odessa American*, Odessa, Texas, April 7, 1960, p. 33.

64 Wilson: *Times Recorder*, Zanesville, Ohio, May 21, 1960, p. 5.

65 Kilgallen: *Des Moines Register*, Des Moines, Iowa, June 16, 1960, p. 15.

66 Hedda Hopper: *Detroit Free Press*, Detroit, Michigan, February 26, 1965, p. 15.

67 Ibid.

68 Ibid.

69 Graham: "Hollywood Gossip," *St. Louis Post-Dispatch*, St. Louis, Missouri, June 7, 1960, p. 41.

70 Bosley Crowther: "Screen: Drama in Court . . . at Roxy," *New York Times*, New York, October 24, 1959.

71 Sheilah Graham: *Honolulu Star-Advertiser*, Honolulu, Hawaii, March 23, 1959, p. 1.

72 Hedda Hopper: *Chicago Tribune*, Chicago, Illinois, March 14, 1959, p. 69.

73 *When Olivia*: Rick du Brow (UP): "Actress Joan . . .," *Odessa American*, June 1, 1959, *I saw*: *Abilene Reporter News*, November 10, 1954. *carrying around*: Louella O. Parsons: *Lubbock Morning Avalanche*, July 3, 1954.

74 *their feud*: Rick du Brow: "Actress Joan . . .".

75 Julia Felsenthal, online: "50 Years Later, Olivia de Havilland's Memoirs of Life in France Is Charming, Cheeky Fun," June 28, 2016.
76 John Chapman: *Chicago Tribune*, Chicago, Illinois, May 13, 1962, p. 163.
77 *Salt Lake Tribune*: "Olivia Plans Fiction Piece to Follow Top Seller," July 29, 1962, p. 45.
78 Ibid.
79 Olga Curtis: "Olivia Takes Advice; Now She's an Author," *Des Moines Register*, Des Moines, Iowa, May 17, 1962, p. 7.
80 *Salt Lake Tribune:* "Olivia Plans Fiction Piece to Follow Top Seller."
81 UPI: "Olivia Is Writing Book on France," *Logansport Pharos-Tribune*, Logansport, Indiana, April 6, 1960, p. 16.
82 Fontaine: *No Bed of Roses*, p. 286.
83 Ibid.
84 Ibid.
85 Ibid.
86 Ibid., pp. 262–264.
87 *Cincinnati Enquirer*, Cincinnati, Ohio, April 1, 1979, p. 175.
88 Fontaine: *No Bed of Roses*, p. 275.
89 Ibid., pp. 271–279.
90 Ibid., p. 301.
91 Winchell: *Terre Haute Tribune*, Terre Haute, Indiana, May 26, 1960, p. 4.
92 Edwards: *Vivien Leigh*, p. 230.
93 Sikov: *Dark Victory*, p. 244.
94 Ibid., p. 326.
95 Ibid., p. 327.
96 "Margaret Mitchell Dead of Injuries," *New York Times*, New York, August 17, 1949.
97 "Hugh Gravitt, Driver Whose Car Killed Margaret Mitchell," *Los Angeles Times*, April 25, 1994.
98 Radie Harris: *Radie's World*, New York: Putnam, 1975, p. 246.
99 Edwards: *Vivien Leigh*, p. 244.
100 Harris: *Radie's World*, p. 246.
101 "Olivia de Havilland Likes Parisian Role": *Asbury Park Press*, Asbury Park, New Jersey, May 28, 1961, p. 30.
102 Edward Z. Epstein: *Jennifer*, New York: Simon & Schuster, p. 367.
103 Ibid.
104 Sheilah Graham: "Olivia Is an Author," *Miami News*, Miami, Florida, May 28, 1961, p. 70.
105 Sikov: *Dark Victory*, p. 335.
106 Ibid., p. 340.
107 Joshua Logan: *Movie Stars, Real People, and Me*, New York, Delacorte, 1978, p. 289.
108 Audrey Wood and Max Wilk: *Represented by Audrey Wood*, Garden City, New York: Doubleday, 1981, p. 183.
109 Standish: "A Warmer, Gayer Olivia de Havilland." Erskine Johnson: "German Prison Took . . . ," *Bristol Daily Courier*, Bristol, Pennsylvania, July 18, 1961, p. 7.

110 *Detroit Free Press:* Detroit, Michigan, May 9, 1965, p. 22.
111 Bosley Crowther: "Screen: *Light in the Piazza,*" *New York Times,* New York, February 8, 1962.

24. ON BROADWAY WITH HENRY FONDA, ON THE HIGH SEAS WITH EDWARD HEATH

1 Leonard Lyons: *Philadelphia Inquirer,* Philadelphia, Pennsylvania, April 4, 1962, p. 28.
2 Ibid.
3 Ibid.
4 Jerry Gaghan: "Hildegarde . . . ," *Philadelphia Daily News,* Philadelphia Pennsylvania, February 1, 1962, p. 39.
5 Olga Curtis: "Olivia Takes Advice; Now She's an Author," *Des Moines Register,* Des Moines, Iowa, March 17, 1962, p. 7.
6 Mary Campbell (AP): "Tea Is Prescribed for Leading Lady," *Corpus Christie Caller-Times,* March 16, 1962, p. 39.
7 Ibid.
8 Ibid.
9 Ibid.
10 Ibid.
11 Ibid.
12 Ibid.
13 Olga Curtis: "Olivia Takes Advice; Now She's an Author."
14 Erskine Johnson: "German Prison Took . . . ," *Bristol Daily,* Bristol, Pennsylvania, July 18, 1961, p. 7.
15 Campbell (AP): "Tea Is Prescribed for Leading Lady."
16 Ibid.
17 Charles Witbeck: "Henry Fonda to Host Special on Family," *Pittsburgh Post-Gazette,* January 18, 1962, p. 37.
18 Jerry Gaghan: "Hildegarde . . . ,"
19 Adolph J. Stern: *Courier-Post,* Camden, New Jersey, February 3, 1962, p. 20.
20 Leonard Lyons: *Minneapolis Star,* Minneapolis, Minnesota, March 27, 1962, p. 20.
21 Ibid.
22 Campbell (AP): "Tea Is Prescribed for Leading Lady."
23 Fred H. Russell: "Gossip of the Rialto," *Bridgeport Post,* Bridgeport, Connecticut, January 28, 1962, p. 49.
24 Earl Wilson: *Philadelphia Daily News,* Philadelphia, Pennsylvania, April 2, 1962, p. 43.
25 Walter Kerr: "An Analysis of *A Gift of Time,*" *Philadelphia Inquirer,* March 4, 1962, p. 69.
26 William Glover (AP): "Find Play Harrowing," *Lansing State Journal,* Lansing, Michigan, February 23, 1962, p. 25.
27 E.B. Radcliff: "Theatre Conversation Piece," *Cincinnati Enquirer,* Cincinnati, Ohio, May 1, 1962, p. 10.
28 "T.H.P": *Hartford Courant,* Hartford, Connecticut, January 30, 1962, p. 13.

29 John Chapman: *Chicago Tribune*, Chicago, Illinois, May 13, 1962, p. 163.
30 Leonard Lyons: *Minneapolis Star*, Minneapolis, Minnesota, March 27, 1962, p. 20.
31 Hedda Hopper: *Times*, Shreveport, Louisiana, May 11, 1962, p. 32.
32 Henry Fonda as told to Howard Teichmann: *Fonda*, New York: New American Library, 1981, p. 279.
33 Leonard Lyons: *Minneapolis Star*, Minneapolis, Minnesota, March 27, 1962, p. 20.
34 Washington Staff: "Rusk Longs to Return to Classroom," *Indiana Gazette*, June 2, 1962, p. 6.
35 Ida Jean Kain: *Oneonta Star*, Oneonta, New York, August 28, 1962, p. 8.
36 Dorothy Kilgallen: *Star-Gazette*, Elmira, New York, December 11, 1962, p. 13.
37 "Olivia Plans Fiction Piece to Follow Top Seller," *Salt Lake Tribune*, July 29, 1962, p. 45.
38 Campbell (AP): "Tea Is Prescribed for Leading Lady."
39 Ibid.
40 Ibid.
41 Pierre Galante: *Mademoiselle Chanel*, New York: Henry Regnery, 1973, p. 52.
42 "*I studied my script*,": Angela Taylor, "For Olivia de Havilland, a New Real-Life Mother Role," *New York Times*, July 1, 1976. "*You, know, the only reason . . . with their meal.*": Lynn Dell, "No, She Isn't the Future Mrs. Heath," *Sydney Morning Herald*, Sydney, New South Wales, Australia, August 26, 1971, p. 16."
43 Higham: *Sisters*, p. 239.
44 Rajeev Syal: "Whiff of Scandal Still Surrounds Enigmatic Leader," *The Guardian* online, October 5, 2017.
45 *Independent* website: "Golden Girl: The Divine Olivia de Havilland," October 22, 2011.
46 Stadiem: *Vanity Fair*, p. 153.

25. GRAND GUIGNOL: HAVING FUN WITH BETTE DAVIS IN *HUSH . . . HUSH, SWEET CHARLOTTE*

1 Michael Thornton: "Hollywood's Most Venomous Feud," *Daily Mail*, March 4, 2007, pressreader web page.
2 "Taste of Cinema" online, Stacey Davies: "16 Crazy Grande Dame Guignol Horror Films to Freak You Out," January 10, 2015.
3 Sikov: *Dark Victory*, p. 347.
4 Kinn and Piazz: *The Academy Awards*, p. 148; Mason Wiley and Damien Bona: *Inside Oscar*, New York: Ballantine Books, 1993.
5 Sikov: *Dark Victory*, p. 348.
6 Kinn and Piazza: *The Academy Awards*, p. 149.
7 Sikov: *Dark Victory*, p. 348.
8 Ibid.
9 William Frye: "The Devil and Miss Davis," *Vanity Fair*, April 2001, pp. 222–236, 257. Sikov: *Dark Victory*, p. 348.
10 IMDb online: "*Hush . . . Hush, Sweet Charlotte*," Trivia.

11 Kilgallen: "About People: Ross Hunter, . . . ," *Cincinnati Enquirer*, Cincinnati, Ohio, April 28, 1965, p. 12.
12 Wikipedia: "Luther Davis."
13 Hopper: "The McQueens . . . ," *Los Angeles Times*, Los Angeles, California, May 3, 1965, p. 56.
14 *The Pantagraph*: Bloomington, Illinois, May 23, 1965, p. 71.
15 Graham, NANA: *Phoenix Gazette*, Phoenix, California, May 29, 1965, p. 7.
16 Standish: "A Warmer, Gayer Olivia de Havilland."
17 Tony Thomas: *The Films of Olivia de Havilland*, p. 237.
18 Standish: "A Warmer, Gayer Olivia de Havilland."
19 Ibid.
20 Ibid.
21 A.H. Weiler: "Aimless Brutality," *New York Times*, New York, June 11, 1964.
22 Ibid.
23 Ibid.
24 *The Pantagraph*: Bloomington, Illinois, May 23, 1965, p. 71. Crawford's "phantom illness": Sikov: *Dark Victory*, p. 352.
25 "Vivien Leigh," notstarring web page.
26 IMDb online: "*Hush . . . Hush, Sweet Charlotte,*" Trivia.
27 IMDb online: "*The Night Walker.*"
28 IMDb online: "*Hush . . . Hush, Sweet Charlotte,*" Trivia.
29 Ibid.
30 *The Pantagraph*, Bloomington, Illinois, May 23, 1965, p. 71.
31 Sikov: *Dark Victory*, p. 352.
32 Sikov: p. 353. IMDb online: "*Hush . . . Hush, Sweet Charlotte,*" Trivia.
33 *Courier-Journal*: "TV's Money May Hook Her Yet."
34 Declaration of Independence of the Republic of Texas: Texas State Historical Association's web page. Constitution of the Republic of Texas: the University of Texas's "Constitution, Texas Law, Tarlton Law Library" web page.
35 TSHA (Texas State Historical Association) web page: "Goodrich, Benjamin Briggs." Born in 1799, died 1860.
36 *Courier-Journal:* "TV's Money May Hook Her Yet."
37 *Simpson's Leader-Times*: Kittanning, Pennsylvania, September 16, 1965, p. 17.
38 Harold V. Cohen: "At Random: The Monday Wash," *Pittsburgh Post-Gazette*, Pittsburgh, Pennsylvania, February 8, 1965, p. 12.
39 Higham: *Sisters*, p. 224.
40 Sikov: *Dark Victory*, pp. 322, 305.
41 Ibid.
42 Dick Kleiner, NEA: "Show Beat," *Courier-News*, Blytheville, Arkansas, January 2, 1965, p. 4.
43 *Courier-Journal:* "TV's Money May Hook Her Yet."
44 Bosley Crowther: "New Movie at the Capitol Echoes 'Baby Jane,'" *New York Times*, New York, March 4, 1965.
45 Sikov: *Dark Victory*, p. 354.

46 Kilgallen: *Asbury Park Press*, Asbury Park, New Jersey, February 26, 1965, p. 15.
47 Joan Crosby: "Two Movie Greats Talk About Children, Nudity, New Stars," *Cumberland News*, Cumberland, Maryland, March 20, 1965, p. 11.
48 *The Pantagraph*: Bloomington, Illinois, May 23, 1965, p. 71.
49 Ibid.
50 Ibid.
51 Ibid.
52 Ibid.
53 Kilgallen: *The Ottawa Journal*, Ottawa, Ontario, Canada, March 12, 1965, p. 46.
54 Crosby: "Two Movie Greats Talk About Children, Nudity, New Stars."
55 Ibid.
56 Ibid.
57 Ibid.
58 Ibid.
59 Ibid.
60 Ibid.
61 Ibid.
62 Ibid.
63 Margaret McManus: "TV Captures Olivia, Partly," *The Courier-Journal*, Louisville, Kentucky, April 11, 1965, p. 160.
64 McManus: "TV Captures Olivia, Partly."
65 Charles Rivers Editors: *Academy Award Winning Sisters*, chapter 13.
66 Kleiner, NEA: "Show Beat."
67 Ibid.
68 *Asbury Park Press*: "Paris Is Home—Family Is Cause," Asbury Park, New Jersey, May 9, 1965, p. 32.
69 Ibid.
70 Ibid.
71 Fontaine: *No Bed of Roses*, pp. 242, 277–278.
72 Tartaglione: "Cannes: Oscar Winner . . . ," Deadline Hollywood web page.
73 Ibid.
74 Radie Harris: *Radie's World*, pp. 217-218.

26. BENJAMIN'S ILLNESS, OLIVIA'S FAITH, PRIME MINISTER EDWARD HEATH, *AIRPORT '77*, AND TV

1 Vivian Brown (AP): "Olivia de Havilland Likes France for Child Rearing," *Cincinnati Enquirer*, Cincinnati, Ohio, February 11, 1962, p. 133.
2 Bob Thomas (AP): "Olivia de Havilland Recalls Hollywood's Golden Age," *Asbury Park Press*, Asbury Park, New Jersey, June 4, 1997, p. 42.
3 Geni web page: "Benjamin Briggs Goodrich (July 18, 1949–October 1991)."
4 "Olivia Plans Fiction Piece to Follow Top Seller," *Salt Lake Tribune*, July 29, 1962, p. 45.
5 Brown (AP): "Olivia de Havilland Likes France for Child Rearing," p. 133.

6 *get well call . . . if I do*: Earl Wilson: "Olivia de Havilland . . . ," *The Times*, Munster, Indiana, August 23, 1976, p. 26. "*Ten years ago*: Anglicans online: "Reading the Bible as a statement of faith," the Rt Revd Pierre W. Whalon, D.D.

7 George W. Cornell (AP): "Olivia de Havilland Takes to the Pulpit," *Journal News*, White Plains, New York, February 3, 1979, p. 6.

8 *Blessed with a resonant*: Bishop Pierre Whalon, copyright 2012, Anglican online. *It's a movement*: George W. Cornell (AP): "Olivia de Havilland Takes to the Pulpit."

9 George W. Cornell (AP): "Olivia de Havilland Takes to the Pulpit."

10 Stadiem: *Vanity Fair*, p. 158.

11 Bell: "No, She Isn't the Future Mrs. Heath."

12 Brown (AP): "Olivia de Havilland Likes France for Child Rearing," p. 133.

13 Ibid.

14 Angela Taylor (BYT): *Courier News*, Blytheville, Arkansas, July 14, 1976, p. 28.

15 Ibid.

16 Ibid.

17 Ibid.

18 Ibid.

19 Ibid.

20 Ibid.

21 Bob Thomas (AP): "Olivia de Havilland Recalls Hollywood's Golden Age."

22 Robert M. Klein: "For Olivia de Havilland, a Real-Life Movie Role," *New York Times*, July 1, 1976, p. 42. TimesMachine.

23 Higham: *Sisters*, p. 260.

24 Ibid.

25 Ibid.

26 Higham: *Sisters*, pp. 260–261. Tom Heneghan: "Crown of Thorns Relic Paraded From Notre-Dame to Sainte Chapelle in Paris," Faithworld web page. "Crown of Thorns Viewing Hours & Procedures," tripadvisor web page.

27 Lynne Bell: "From Lynne Belle in London," *Sydney Morning Herald*, Sydney, New South Wales, Australia, August 26, 1971, p. 16.

28 Ibid.

29 Ibid.

30 Lee Grant: *I Said Yes to Everything*, New York: Plume, 2014, p. 120.

31 Ibid., p. 313.

32 Ibid., p. 313.

33 Ibid., p. 315.

34 Fishgall: *Jimmy Stewart*, p. 341.

35 Robert Osborne: TCM short subject commemorating Olivia's 100th birthday, July 2016.

36 Sikov: *Dark Victory*, p. 405.

37 John S. Wilson: "Distinctive Voices Display the Vigor of Cabarets," *New York Times*, December 11, 1983.

38 Kristin McMurran: "Geraldine Fitzgerald Is as Irish as Guinness, but She Doesn't Go Flat With Age," *People*, February 6, 1978.

39 Ibid., p. 406.
40 Ray Stricklyn: *Angels and Demons*, Los Angeles: Belle, 1999, p. 198.
41 Sikov: *Dark Victory*, p. 406.
42 Ibid.
43 Bob Thomas (AP): "Joan Fontaine Writes Autobiography," *Asbury Park Press*, Asbury Park, New Jersey, April 21, 1978, p. 28.
44 Stephen E. Rubin: "The Tales Actresses Tell: From Classy Lady and a Brutal 'Savage,'" *Chicago Tribune* Chicago, Illinois, October 7, 1978, p. 163.
45 Robert Kirsch: "Memoirs of Joan Fontaine," *Los Angeles Times*, Los Angeles, California, September 8, 1978, p. 82.
46 Sheila M. Mitchell: "Joan Fontaine's Story," *Cincinnati Enquirer*, December 24, 1978, p. 5.
47 *She was very lonely . . . Joan was furious*: author interview with Leonida Karpik. *She does not speak . . . I love it*: Judy Flander: "Joan Fontaine: Thorns, Roses," *Washington Star*, reprinted in *the St. Louis Post-Dispatch*, St. Louis, Missouri, September 29, 1978, p. 51.
48 Author interview with Leonida Karpik.
49 Marilyn Beck: *San Bernardino County Sun*, San Bernardino, California, September 18, 1978, p. 19.
50 Meyers: *John Huston*, p. 375.
51 Ibid.
52 John Huston: *An Open Book*, "I count those names," p. 5; "It was very flattering," p. 81.
53 Ibid.
54 John Huston: *An Open Book*, photo signature following p. 88.
55 Michiko Kakutani: "A Hollywood Legend's Passions and Peccadillos," *New York Times*, October 27, 1989. Kirkus: September 25, 1980.
56 Kass: *Olivia de Havilland*, p. 140.
57 Thomas Wiseman: "'I'll Tell You What's Wrong in Hollywood," *Detroit Free Press*, Detroit, Michigan, November 29, 1959, p. 36.
58 Roderick Mann: "Olivia Keeps Publisher Waiting," *Los Angeles Times*, December 30, 1980.
59 Bob Thomas (AP): "Olivia de Havilland Recalls Hollywood's Golden Age," *Asbury Park Press*, Asbury Park, New Jersey, June 4, 1997, p. 42.
60 John Huston collection, Academy of Motion Picture Arts and Sciences, quoted in Matzen: *Errol and Olivia*, p. 195.
61 Matzen: *Errol and Olivia*, p. 195, quoting de Havilland in Dotson Rader's "Rewards and Regrets."
62 Anjelica Huston: *A Story Lately Told*, New York: Scribner, 2013, pp. 31–32.
63 Mikelbank: "Olivia de Havilland Opens Up . . . ."
64 Dotson Rader quoting de Havilland in Matzen: *Errol and Olivia*, p. 195.

27. SUNSET AND EVENING STAR

1 Florence Aadland with Tedd Thomey: *The Big Love*, New York: Warner Books, p. 134.
2 Aadland with Thomey: *The Big Love*, pp. 146–147.
3 Ibid., pp. 156–157.

4 Matzen: *Errol and Olivia*, p. 191.

5 Meyers: *Inherited Risk*, p. 297.

6 Ibid., p. 299.

7 Earl Wilson: *Philadelphia Daily News*, Philadelphia, Pennsylvania, April 2, 1962, p. 43.

8 Meyers: *Inherited Risk*, p. 323.

9 "David O. Selznick, 63, Producer of *Gone With the Wind*, Dies": *New York Times*, June 22, 1965.

10 Thomson: *Showman*, p. 692.

11 Beverly Linet: *Star-Crossed*, New York: Putnam, 1986, p. 301. Thomson: *Showman*, p. 700.

12 Selznick was not credited as the producer.

13 Thomson: *Showman*, p. 690.

14 Beverly Linet: *Star-Crossed*, p. 301.

15 Thomson: *Showman*, p. 695.

16 Ibid., p. 696.

17 Epstein: *Jennifer*, p. 385.

18 Ibid., p. 309.

19 Thomson: *Showman*, p. 696.

20 Fontaine: *No Bed of Roses*, p. 282.

21 Ibid., p. 283.

22 Ibid., pp. 283–284.

23 Edwards: *Vivien Leigh*, p. 280.

24 Fontaine: *No Bed of Roses*, p. 285.

25 Brackett: *It's the Pictures That Got Small*, p. 8.

26 Graham: *The Rest of the Story*, p. 153.

27 "Flynn, Fidler Fight in Night Club," *Daily Mirror* web page.

28 Ibid.

29 Author interview with Richard Ridge.

30 Ibid.

31 Author interview with Pat Loud.

32 Philip Van Rensselaer: *Rich Was Better*, New York: Wynwood Press, 1990, p. 88.

33 Ibid.

34 Fontaine: *No Bed of Roses*, p. 304.

35 Stadiem: *Vanity Fair*, p. 158.

36 Ibid.

37 Ibid.

38 Higham: *Sisters*, p. 264 (Dell edition).

39 "Joan Fontaine," BrainyQuote web page.

40 Peter Haldeman: "Look Inside Joan Fontaine's Shingle-Roofed Home in California," *Architectural Digest*, March 2006, reprinted in *AD* online, September 7, 2006.

41 AP: "Joan Fontaine, Oscar Winner for *Suspicion*, Dies at Age 96," *Longview News*, Longview, Texas, December 17, 2013, p. B4.

42 Bob Thomas (AP): "Olivia de Havilland believes in being prepared," *Courier-Post*, Camden, New Jersey, May 1, 1988, p. 79.

43 Olivia de Havilland fan webpage.

44 Donald L. Bartlett and James B. Steele: *Howard Hughes*, New York: Norton, 1979, pp. 619–625. Wikipedia: "Howard Hughes."

45 Tony Thomas: *The Films of Olivia de Havilland*, p. 255.

46 Janet Maslin: "'The Swarm,' by Allen, Flies Onto Screen," *New York Times*, New York, July 15, 1978.

47 John Lichfield: "Golden Girl: The Divine Olivia de Havilland."

48 Michael Caine, *What's It All About*, 1992, p. 395. Also see Meyers: *Inherited Risk*, p. 124.

49 Lichfield: "Golden Girl: The Divine Olivia de Havilland."

50 YouTube: "Margaret Booth Receives an Honorary Award: 1978 Oscars."

51 Ibid.

52 "*The Last Emperor* Wins Art Direction": 1988 Oscars, YouTube.

53 Bob Thomas (AP): "Olivia de Havilland believes in being prepared," *Courier-Post*, Camden, New Jersey, May 1, 1988, p. 79.

54 Robin Adams Sloan: *Garden City Telegram*, Garden City, Kansas, January 3, 1979, p. 16.

55 J. Randy Taraborrelli: *Once Upon a Time*, New York: Warner Books, p. 421.

56 John Walsh: "Amazing Grace: Why We'll Always Adore the Divine Grace Kelly," *Independent* web page.

57 Chuck Conconi: "Personalities," July 2, 1986, *Washington Post* web page.

58 Roger Ebert.com, August 19, 1988.

59 Bob Thomas (AP): "Olivia de Havilland Recalls Hollywood's Golden Age."

60 Bell: "No, She Isn't the Future Mrs. Heath."

61 "Olivia de Havilland: Lady of the Classic Cinema," website.

62 William H. Honan: Goodrich obituary, *New York Times*, October 22, 1991.

63 Mary Vespa: "Amid Divorce . . . ," *People Archive online*, March 5, 1979.

64 Jonathan Coe: *James Stewart*, New York: Arcade, 1994, p. 9.

65 Munn: *Jimmy Stewart*, p. 291.

66 Meredith: *So Far, So Good*, p. 269.

67 Ibid., pp. 263–264.

28. GRAND SLAM: LEGION OF HONOR, NATIONAL MEDAL OF ARTS, DAME COMMANDER

1 Stadiem: *Vanity* Fair, p. 158.

2 YouTube.

3 Today: "De Havilland returns to Hollywood for tribute," Associated Press, June 13, 2006. https://www.today.con/popculture/de-havilland-returns-hollywood-t...

4 Ibid.

5 Ibid.

6 Ibid.

7 Ibid.

8 Ibid.

9 General oneFile: "Belle of the AMPAS Ball: "De Havilland Honored on 90th Birthday, online.

10 Sean M. Wright: "Olivia de Havilland: A Century of Gracious Excellence," July 1, 2016, Angelus online.

11 Lichfield: "Golden Girl: The Divine Olivia de Havilland."

12 Ibid.

13 Ibid.

14 Ibid.

15 Ibid.

16 Wikipedia.

17 Victoria Miller: "Jared Leto on How 100-year-old Olivia de Havilland Saved 30 Seconds to Mars," Inquisitr web page, July 2, 2016.

18 Peter Mickelbank: "*Gone With the Wind* Star Olivia de Havilland on Turning 100—and how Jared Leto 'Enchanted' Her," July 1, 2016, People Movies web page.

19 Victoria Miller: "Jared Leto on How 100-year-old Olivia de Havilland Saved 30 Seconds to Mars," Inquisitr web page, July 2, 2016.

20 Mickelbank: "*Gone With the Wind* Star Olivia de Havilland on Turning 100—and how Jared Leto 'Enchanted' Her."

21 Lorelei Laird: Entertainment and Sports Law online: "Rapper Wiz . . . ," June 3, 2016.

22 Paul McDonald, Emily Carman, Eric Hoyt, Philip Drake: *Hollywood and the Law*, London: British Film Institute Palgrave, 2015, pp. 225–226.

23 Ibid.

24 Mickelbank: "*Gone With the Wind* Star Olivia de Havilland on Turning 100—and how Jared Leto 'Enchanted' Her."

25 Angela Danovi: "Olivia de Havilland Is Awarded the Legion of Honor," Our Blog About Olivia, September 12, 2010.

26 Lara Gabrielle Fowler: "Happy Birthday, Olivia de Havilland," Backlot web page, July 1, 2013.

27 Patricia Wells: "Oysters With Olivia," At Home With Patricia Wells blog, March 19, 2011.

28 Olivia can be seen reciting her message online at Angela Danovi: "Olivia de Havilland Message to 2014 Marshfield Cherry Blossom Festival," April 30, 2014.

29 Gates: *New York Times*, November 7, 2004.

30 Matzen: *Errol and Olivia*, p. 195.

31 AP, *Daily Mail*: "Timelessly Elegant at 100: *Gone With the Wind*'s Olivia de Havilland celebrates milestone today and finally breaks silence on Golden Age of Hollywood's most infamous sibling rivalry," July 1, 2016.

32 "Joan Fontaine," *Vanity Fair* HIVE online.

33 Fontaine: *No Bed of Roses*, pp. 112–113.

34 Judy Flander: "Famous Movie Queen . . . ," *Washington Star* online.

35 Stadiem: *Vanity Fair*, p. 158.

36 Scott Feinberg: "New Details About the Joan Fontaine-Olivia de Havilland Feud Revealed," *Hollywood Reporter*, December 17, 2013.

37 "Joan Fontaine Death," *Independent* web page, December 16, 2013.
38 Tom Leyde: *Monterey County Herald,* October 19, 2014. Ginny: "Old Movie Nostalgia," online, November 8, 2011.
39 Ginny: "Old Movie Nostalgia."
40 Feinberg: *Hollywood Reporter,* December 17, 2013.
41 "Joan Fontaine's Oscar Will Not Be Sold at Animal Rights Auction . . . ," DailyMail .com.
42 Tom Leyde: *Monterey County Herald,* October 1, 2014.
43 Dr. Marty Nemko: "People Who Prefer Dogs to Humans," *Psychology Today* online, May 23, 2011.
44 David Kaufman: "Doris Day's Vanishing Act," *Vanity Fair,* May 1, 2008.
45 Ibid.
46 Missy Schwartz: "The Last Star: An Evening With Olivia de Havilland."
47 Ibid.
48 Ibid.
49 Ibid.
50 Stadiem: *Vanity Fair,* p. 153.
51 Ibid., p. 138.
52 Ibid., p. 158.
53 BBC News website: "Olivia de Havilland Wins Oldie Accolade."
54 "Olivia de Havilland Wins Oldie Award," BB News online, February 2, 2016.
55 Olivia de Havilland: *Every Frenchman Has One,* Crown, p. 12.
56 Nick Thomas: "Centenarian de Havilland Recalls Flynn," *Daily Press,* Newport News, Virginia, July 10, 2016, p. G12.
57 Adamson (AP): "AP Interview: De Havilland Breaks Silence on Sibling Feud."
58 "Olivia de Havilland Talks About Her Sister," USNews on line, July 1, 2016.
59 Ibid.
60 Liz Smith: "Celebrating the Life of Robert Osborne," *New York Social Diary* web page, May 6, 2017.
61 Ibid.
62 Giles Sheldrick: "Queen Honors: Olivia de Havilland 'extremely proud' to be made a Dame," Express online, June 16, 2017.
63 Robert Hardman: *A Year With the Queen,* New York: Touchstone, 2007, p. 52.
64 Penny Junor: *The Firm,* New York: St. Martin's Press, 2005, p. 229.
65 "Olivia de Havilland," Geni web page.
66 Schwartz: "The Last Star: An Evening With Olivia de Havilland."
67 Thomas Adamson (AP): "AP Interview: De Havilland Breaks Silence on Sibling Feud."
68 Stadiem: *Vanity Fair,* p. 158.
69 Adamson (AP): "AP Interview: De Havilland Breaks Silence on Sibling Feud."
70 AP, *Daily Mail:* "Timelessly Elegant at 100: *Gone With the Wind*'s Olivia de Havilland celebrates milestone today and finally breaks silence on Golden Age of Hollywood's most infamous sibling rivalry," July 1, 2016.
71 Stadiem: *Vanity Fair,* p. 158.

72 Eyre: "Hollywood's Sweetheart: Olivia de Havilland," *Evening Standard* online, March 18, 2010.

EPILOGUE

1 Paul Brownfield: "*Feud* Fight," The Independent Online, March 7, 2018.
2 Wikipedia.
3 Littleton: "*Feud* Grabs FX's Highest Series Debut Ratings Since '*People v. O.J. Simpson*,'" *Variety*.com, March 10, 2017.
4 California Court of Appeal, Second Appellate District, Division 3, FX NETWORKS, LLC AND PACIFIC 2.1 ENTERTAINMENT GROUP, INC., Defendants -Appellants, v. OLIVIA DE HAVILLAND, DBE, Plaintiff-Respondent. On Appeal From Los Angeles County Superior Court Case No. BC667011, the Honorable Holly E. Kendig, Dept. 42, Respondent's Brief in Opposition.
5 Paul Brownfield: "*Feud* Fight: Why a Hollywood Legend Is Heading to Court at the Age of 101," The Independent Online, March 7, 2018.
6 Laura Bradley: "Why Olivia de Havilland Is Suing FX Over *Feud: Bette and Joan*, HWD online, June 30, 2017.
7 California Court of Appeal: Respondent's Brief in Opposition.
8 Ibid.
9 Gene Maddaus: "*Feud* Suit Tossed by Appeals Court," *Variety*, March 26, 2018.
10 Press release, Howarth & Smith.
11 Daniel Holloway: "Olivia de Havilland, FX Argue Over the Word 'Bitch' in *Feud* Hearing," *Variety*, March 20, 2018.
12 Ibid.
13 Thomas Adamson: "AP Interview: De Havilland breaks silence on sibling feud," The Associated Press Online, July 1, 2016.
14 Suzelle M. Smith email to author.
15 Declaration and Supplemental Declaration of Cort Casady in Support of Plaintiff's Opposition to Defendants' Motion to Strike Plaintiff's Complaint in the matter of *Olivia de Havilland v. FX Networks, LLC and Pacific 2.1 Entertainment Group, Inc.* , Case Number BC667011.
16 Declaration of David Ladd in Support of Plaintiff's Opposition to Defendants' Motion to Strike Plaintiff's Complaint in the matter of *Olivia de Havilland v. FX Networks, LLC and Pacific 2.1 Entertainment Group, Inc.*, Case Number BC667011.
17 California Court of Appeal, Second Appellate District, Division 3 Opinion, *FX Networks, LLC and Pacific 2.1 Entertainment Group, Inc. v. Olivia de Havilland*.
18 Ibid.
19 Press release, Howarth & Smith.
20 Sam Blewett: "Dame Olivia de Havilland, 101, vows to continue docudrama legal fight," *Independent*.ie, April 5, 2018.

Index

Keyes, Evelyn, 63, 75, 91, 93, 140,
    157, 233
Khan, Aly (Prince), 299
Kilburn, Terry, 210
Kilgallen, Dorothy, 115, 138, 153,
    164, 205, 222, 226, 267;
    on Goodrich book, 246;
    marriage observation of, 231
Kimbrough, Emily, 224
Kind Lady (play), 44
King, Martin Luther, Jr., 101
Kitty Genovese murder case, 268
Klein, Robert, 281
The Knack and How to Get It
    (film), 275
Koch, Howard, 147
Koster, Henry, 214
Kramer, Stanley, 234–35

Ladd, Adam, 244
Ladd, David, 324
Lady in a Cage (film), 267
Lait, Jack, Jr., 168
Lamarr, Hedy, 42
Lamore, James, 138
Lange, Jessica, 206
Langer, Lawrence, 164
Lasky, Jesse, 45
The Last Emperor (film), 302
Latham, Harold, 69
Laughton, Phyllis, 163, 164
lawsuit, 223
Lazar, Irving, "Swifty," 140
LeFevre, Marjorie, 234
LeGavre, Jean-Yves, 284

Leigh, Rowland, 27
Leigh, Vivien, 81, 91, 213, 214;
    Academy Award, 117–19;
    Atlanta premiere of *GWTW*
    and, 99–101, 103–4, 119;
    Atlanta trip, 251; Cukor and,
    80, 83, 88; death of, 275–76;
    dinner with, 249; Fleming
    and, 83–85, 87; Fontaine, J.,
    flat swap with, 296–97; Gable
    and, 88–89; *GWTW* casting
    and, 76–78; *GWTW* wrap
    party and, 92; on looking
    at Davis, B., 269; nervous
    breakdown of, 219; New York
    premiere of *GWTW* and, 105,
    107; Olivier abandoning,
    250; Olivier and, 77, 88,
    117–18, 204; *Rebecca* and,
    123–24; shock therapy, 219;
    A Streetcar Named Desire and,
    204, 206
Leisen, Mitchell, 134, 175
Le Roy, Mervyn, 44
Lester, Richard, 275
Leto, Jared, 310–11
Lewis, Judy, 116
Lewis, Sinclair, 159–60
Leyde, Tom, 314
Libel (film), 247
Liberty Films, 173
Lichfield, John, 301–2, 309
Life Achievement Award, 286
The Light in the Piazza (film),
    220, 253

About the Author

Ellis Amburn graduated from Texas Christian University in 1954, moved to New York City, and studied literature at Columbia University with Mark Van Doren, Lionel Trilling, F.W. Dupee, Gilbert Highet, and Eric Bentley. After the Army and a stint at *Newsweek*, he worked at G.P. Putnam's Sons in 1960 as first reader for Lois Dwight Cole, the editor who discovered *Gone With the Wind*. Eventually he became vice president and executive editor of the Putnam imprint, Coward-McCann. In 1970 he moved to the Delacorte Press as its editor in chief, then to William Morrow in 1978, and was called back to Putnam in 1980 to become the company's editorial director.

His authors included Jack Kerouac, William Golding, Dame Muriel Spark, John le Carre, Allison Lurie, Jean Cocteau, Rex Reed, Rona Jaffe, John Braine, Elizabeth Goudge, David Storey, Gail Sheehy, Brooks Atkinson, Frank G. Slaughter, Joyce Haber, Frances Parkinson Keyes, Belva Plain, Paul Gallico, Howard Taubman, Marisa Berenson, Neil Sedaka, Dr. Carl Rogers, Sir Francis Chichester, Rogers Hornsby, Jean Anouilh, Edgar Cayce, Ruth Montgomery, Milton Berle, Shelley Winters, Sammy Davis Jr., Ann Todd, Stewart Granger, June Allyson, and Priscilla Presley.

Leaving his career as an editor in 1986, he collaborated on their autobiographies with such stars as Kim Novak, Shelley Winters, Peggy Lee, and Zsa Zsa Gabor. Michael Korda of Simon & Schuster engaged him to co-author volume two of Shelley's memoir.

His first biography, *Dark Star: The Roy Orbison Story*, appeared in 1990, followed by biographies of Janis Joplin, Buddy Holly, Kerouac, Elizabeth Taylor, Warren Beatty, and Jack Nicholson.

Amburn lives in Gainesville, a town in North Central Florida near the Suwannee River.